WORKSHOP MANUAL

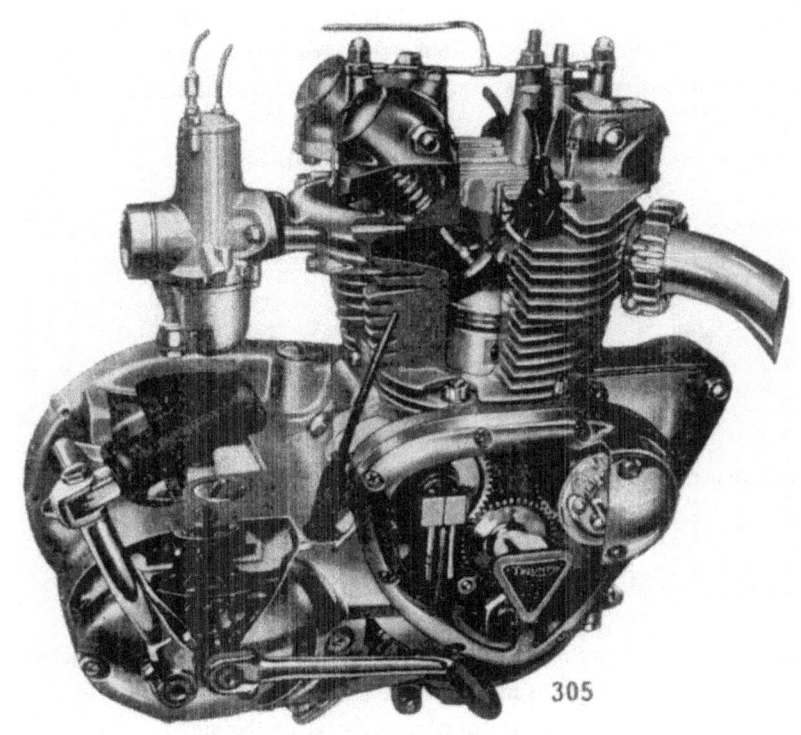

UNIT CONSTRUCTION 350 c.c. and 500 c.c. TWINS

T100 • T90 • 5TA • 3TA INCLUDING FROM ENGINE No. H29733

TRIUMPH ENGINEERING CO LTD
MERIDEN WORKS · ALLESLEY · COVENTRY · ENGLAND
TELEPHONE MERIDEN 331   TELEGRAMS "TRUSTY" COVENTRY

IMPORTANT

PRIOR TO UNDERTAKING ANY MAINTENANCE OR REPAIR TASKS THE READER IS INSTRUCTED TO REVIEW THE INFORMATION REGARDING ENGINE NUMBERS ON THE REAR COVER OF THIS MANUAL.

PUBLISHER'S INTRODUCTION

Welcome to the world of digital publishing ~ the book you now hold in your hand was printed using the latest state of the art digital technology. The advent of print-on-demand has forever changed the publishing process, never has information been so accessible and it is our hope that this book serves your informational needs for years to come. If this is your first exposure to digital publishing, we hope that you are pleased with the results. Many more titles of interest to the classic automobile and motorcycle enthusiast, collector and restorer are available via our website at www.VelocePress.com. We hope that you find this title as interesting as we do.

NOTE FROM THE PUBLISHER

The information presented is true and complete to the best of our knowledge. All recommendations are made without any guarantees on the part of the author or the publisher, who also disclaim all liability incurred with the use of this information.

TRADEMARKS

We recognize that some words, model names and designations, for example, mentioned herein are the property of the trademark holder. We use them for identification purposes only. This is not an official publication.

INFORMATION ON THE USE OF THIS PUBLICATION

This manual is an invaluable resource for those interested in performing their own maintenance. However, in today's information age we are constantly subject to changes in common practice, new technology, availability of improved materials and increased awareness of chemical toxicity. As such, it is advised that the user consult with an experienced professional prior to undertaking any procedure described herein. While every care has been taken to ensure correctness of information, it is obviously not possible to guarantee complete freedom from errors or omissions or to accept liability arising from such errors or omissions. Therefore, any individual that uses the information contained within, or elects to perform or participate in do-it-yourself repairs or modifications acknowledges that there is a risk factor involved and that the publisher or its associates cannot be held responsible for personal injury or property damage resulting from the use of the information or the outcome of such procedures.

WARNING!

One final word of advice, this publication is intended to be used as a reference guide, and when in doubt the reader should consult with a qualified technician.

INTRODUCTION

THIS manual has been compiled and prepared to provide the necessary service information for workshop, fitter, technical staff and individual owner, wishing to carry out basic maintenance and repair work on the TRIUMPH 350 c.c. and 500 c.c. series of unit construction twin cylinder models, subsequent to engine No. H49833. However, most of what is written and illustrated here applies equally to earlier models in this range.

GENERAL DATA for all models within the above range is provided in ready reference form, and a separate section covering Service Tools is fully illustrated at the end of this manual.

The manual is divided into sections dealing with major assemblies, throughout the machine, each section sub-divided into sequence order corresponding to normal operations of strip down, examination and rebuilding procedure.

ENGINE AND FRAME NUMBERS

NOTE: The engine number is located on the left hand side of the engine immediately below the cylinder barrel to crankcase flange. The engine type is incorporated as a prefix to the engine number.

The frame number of the machine is stamped on the left side of the machine, on the frame headlug, beneath the top fork lug, and forward of the fuel tank.

Both the engine and frame numbers should be given IN FULL in any correspondence relating to the machine either with the main Distributor or the Triumph Service Department.

Eastern U.S.A. Distributors:
The Triumph Corporation,
P.O. Box 6790,
Towson, Baltimore 4.
Maryland 21204.
Cables: Triumph, Baltimore.

Western U.S.A. Distributors:
Johnson Motors Inc.,
P.O. Box 2765,
East Huntington Drive,
Duarte, California.
91010.

UNIT CONSTRUCTION 350 & 500cc ENGINE/FRAME NUMBERS

1963   H29733 - H32464

1964   H32465 - H35986

1965   H35987 - H40527

1966   H40528 - H49832

1967   H49833 - H57082

1968   H57083 - H65572

1969   H65573 - H67331

1969 ONWARDS ALPHA NUMERIC ENGINE/FRAME NUMBERS

In 1969 Triumph introduced a new system of numbering engines and frames. There are two letters, a five digit number, and a model designation. The first letter represents the month, the second the model year, and a number which began at 00100 for each model year. Each model year usually started in August and ran until July of the next year. The year of manufacture is the model year. For example: ECXXXXX would be a 1969 model manufactured in May of 1969, and NCXXXXX would be a 1970 model manufactured in October of 1969. The letter "V" after the model designates a 5 speed gearbox.

MONTH	YEAR
A = JANUARY	C = 1969
B = FEBRUARY	D = 1970
C = MARCH	E = 1971
D = APRIL	G = 1972
E = MAY	H = 1973
G = JUNE	J = 1974
H = JULY	K = 1975
J = AUGUST	N = 1976
K = SEPTEMBER	P = 1977
N = OCTOBER	X = 1978
P = NOVEMBER	A = 1979
X = DECEMBER	B = 1980

CONTENTS

	SECTION
GENERAL DATA	
LUBRICATION SYSTEM	A
ENGINE	B
TRANSMISSION	C
GEARBOX	D
FRAME & ATTACHMENT DETAILS	E
WHEELS, BRAKES & TYRES	F
TELESCOPIC FORK	G
ELECTRICAL SYSTEM	H
SERVICE TOOLS	J

FACTORY SERVICE ARRANGEMENTS IN THE UNITED KINGDOM

CORRESPONDENCE

Technical Advice, Guarantee Claims and Repairs

Communications dealing with any of these subjects should be addressed to the **SERVICE DEPARTMENT.**

> In all communications the full engine number complete with all prefix letters and figures should be stated. This number will be found on the L.H. side of the crankcase just below the cylinder flange.

TECHNICAL ADVICE

It will be appreciated how very difficult it is to diagnose trouble by correspondence and this is made impossible in many cases because the information sent to us is so scanty. Every possible point which may have some bearing on the matter should be stated so that we can send a useful and detailed reply.

REPLACEMENT PARTS

Replacement parts are no longer supplied direct from the factory to the individual owner. They should be obtained from the nearest local Triumph dealer.

There is a nation-wide network of stockists, a list of which is available from the factory on request.

REPAIRS

Before a motorcycle is sent to our Works an appointment must be made. This can be done by letter or telephone. When an owner wishes to return his machine for guarantee repairs, he should first consult his Dealer as we do not normally accept machines in our Repair Shop until the Dealer has inspected them. Frequently the Dealer can overcome the trouble without the delay and expense of sending the machine to the Works. This avoids the machine being out of use for some days when it could be on the road. Where parts such as cylinders, petrol tanks, etc., are forwarded for repair, they should be packed securely so as to avoid damage in transit. The owner's name and address should be enclosed together with full instructions. In the case of complete motorcycles, a label showing the owner's name and address should always be attached and all accessories such as tools, inflator, handlebar mirrors and other parts removed.

SERVICE EXCHANGE RECONDITIONED UNITS

A range of service exchange reconditioned units is available from the Factory Service Department. This list includes petrol tanks, front forks, front and rear frames, clutch plates, brake shoes, etc., which are supplied after the return of the original equipment for inspection and acceptance. Operation of this scheme is maintained solely through the Dealer network.

WORKSHOP MANUAL SUPPLEMENT

TWIN CYLINDER MACHINES 500 c.c. (30 ins.)
T100S, T100T, T100 C, T100R
from Engine Number H65573
(updating Workshop Manual 99-0843 to 1973 condition)

TRIUMPH ENGINEERING CO LTD
MERIDEN WORKS · ALLESLEY · COVENTRY · ENGLAND

TELEPHONE MERIDEN 331
COVENTRY 20221

TELEGRAMS "TRUSTY" COVENTRY
TELEX "TRUSTY" 31305

REF. 99-0950

INTRODUCTION

This Supplement has been prepared in order that the latest Workshop Manual, Ref. WSM5 may be updated to include machines produced during the 1969 season, that is machines after engine number H65573.

These pages should be inserted at the end of the Manual, and where a section is headed with two prefix letters, that section should be read in conjunction with the corresponding section in the main part of the manual.

ENGINE AND FRAME NUMBERS

NOTE: The engine number is located on the left side of the engine, immediately below the cylinder barrel flange. The number is stamped onto a raised pad, over a series of Triumph motifs. This makes any alteration by an unauthorised person clearly visible.

After engine number H67330, the system of numbering is changed, and a prefix is added indicating the month and year of manufacture.

The first letter indicates the month of manufacture as follows:—

A	January
B	February
C	March
D	April
E	May
G	June
H	July
J	August
K	September
N	October
P	November
X	December

The second letter indicates the season year of manufacture as follows:—

C	1969
D	1970
E	1971
G	1972
H	1973
J	1974
K	1975
N	1976
P	1977
X	1978
A	1979
B	1980

The third Section is a numerical block of five figures which commence with engine number 00100. The fourth Section indicates the model.

Example

	Month	Year	Number	Model
	N	C	00100	T100R

The frame number is stamped on the left side of the frame headlug, beneath the top fork lug, and forward of the fuel tank. Both the engine and frame numbers should coincide.

WORKSHOP MANUAL SUPPLEMENT

CONTENTS

from Engine Number H65573

	SECTION
GENERAL DATA	
LUBRICATION SYSTEM	AA
ENGINE	BB
TRANSMISSION	CC
GEARBOX	DD
FRAME & ATTACHMENT DETAILS	EE
WHEELS, BRAKES & TYRES	FF
TELESCOPIC FORK	GG
ELECTRICAL SYSTEM	HH
SERVICE TOOLS	JJ

TRIUMPH GUARANTEE

For the latest terms of guarantee please consult your nearest dealer or distributor.

PROPRIETARY FITTINGS

Ancillary equipment which is fitted to our motorcycles is of the highest quality and is guaranteed by the manufacturers and not by ourselves. Any repairs or claims should be sent to the actual maker, or one of their accredited agents who will always give owners every possible assistance. The following are the addresses of the various manufacturers.

Carburetters	Amal Ltd., Holdford Road, Witton, Birmingham, 6.	**Sparking Plugs**	Champion Sparking Plugs Co. Ltd. Feltham Middlesex.
Chains	Renold Chains Ltd., Wythenshawe, Manchester.	**Speedometers**	Smith's Industries Ltd., Cricklewood Works, London, N.W.2.
Electrical Equipment	J. Lucas Ltd., Great Hampton Street, Birmingham, 18.	**Tyres**	Dunlop Rubber Company Ltd., Fort Dunlop, Birmingham, 24.
Rear Suspension	Girling Ltd., Birmingham Road, West Bromwich, Staffordshire.		The Avon India Rubber Co. Ltd., Melksham, Wilts.

500 c.c. (30 cu. in.) TRIUMPH TIGER DAYTONA SPORTS (T100R)

500 c.c. (30 cu. in.) TRIUMPH TIGER 100 (T100S)

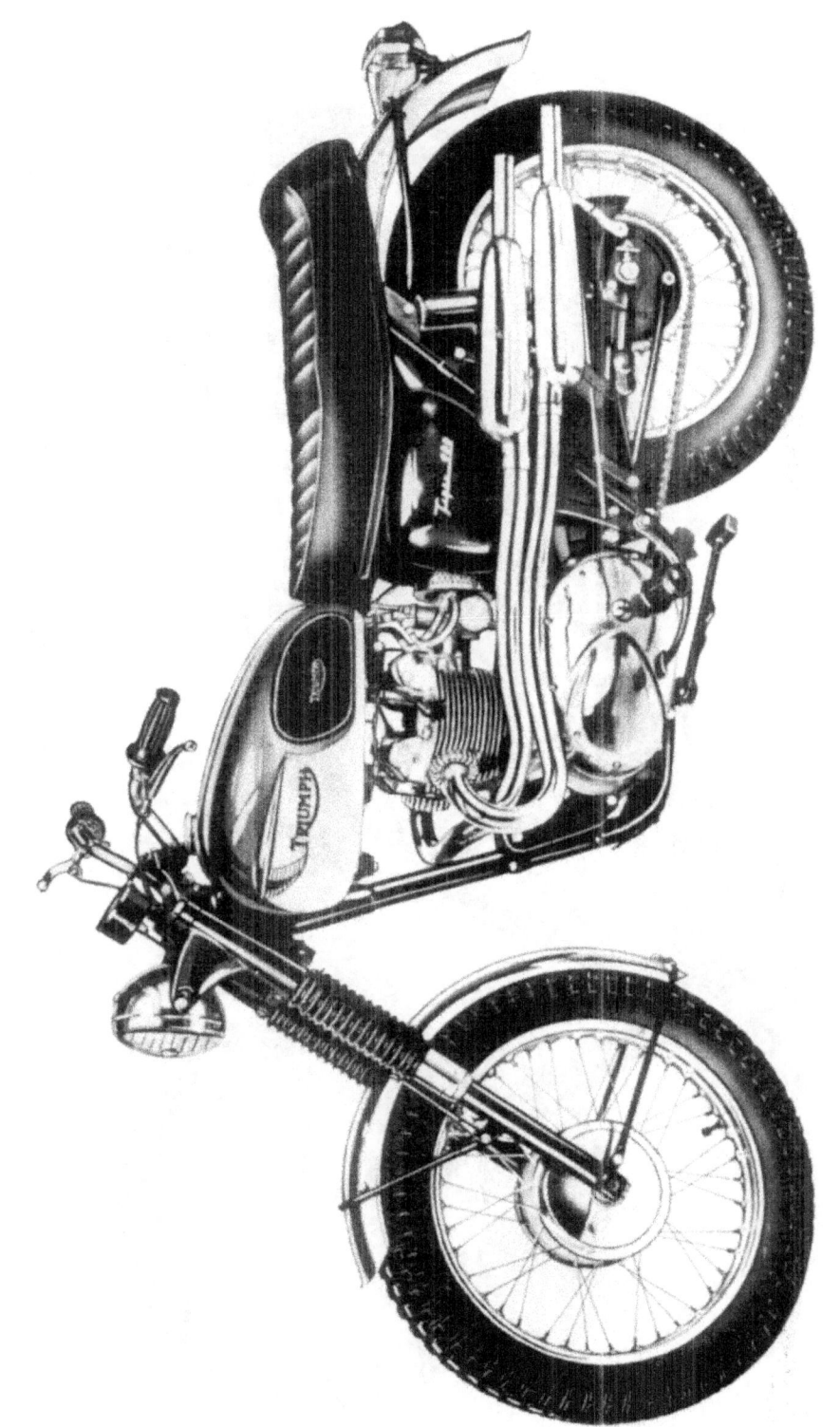

500 c.c. (30 cu. in.) TRIUMPH TIGER 100 (T100C)

500 c.c. (30 cu. in.) TRIUMPH TIGER DAYTONA SPORTS (T100T)

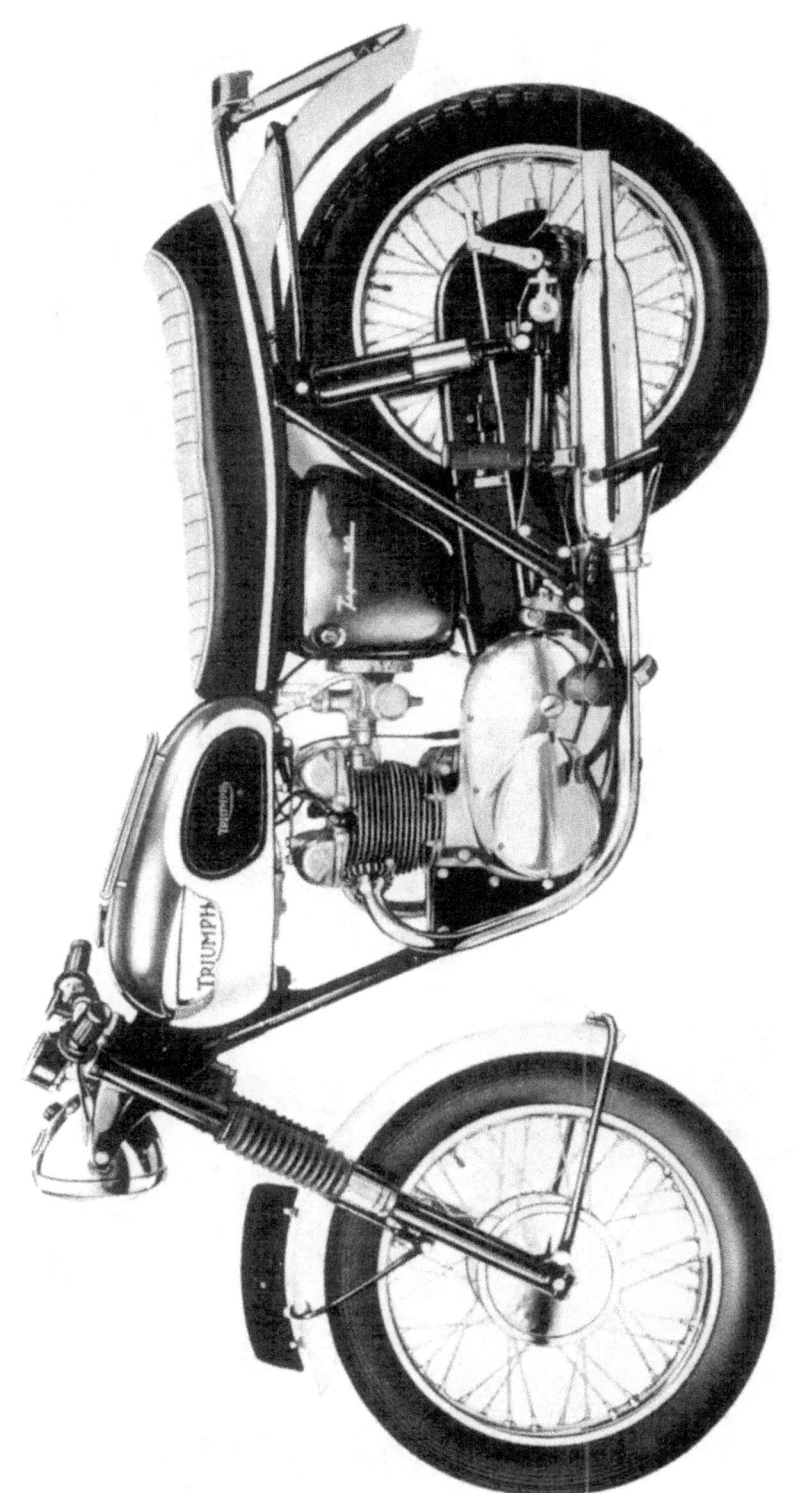

350 c.c. (21 cu. in.) TRIUMPH TIGER 90 (T90)

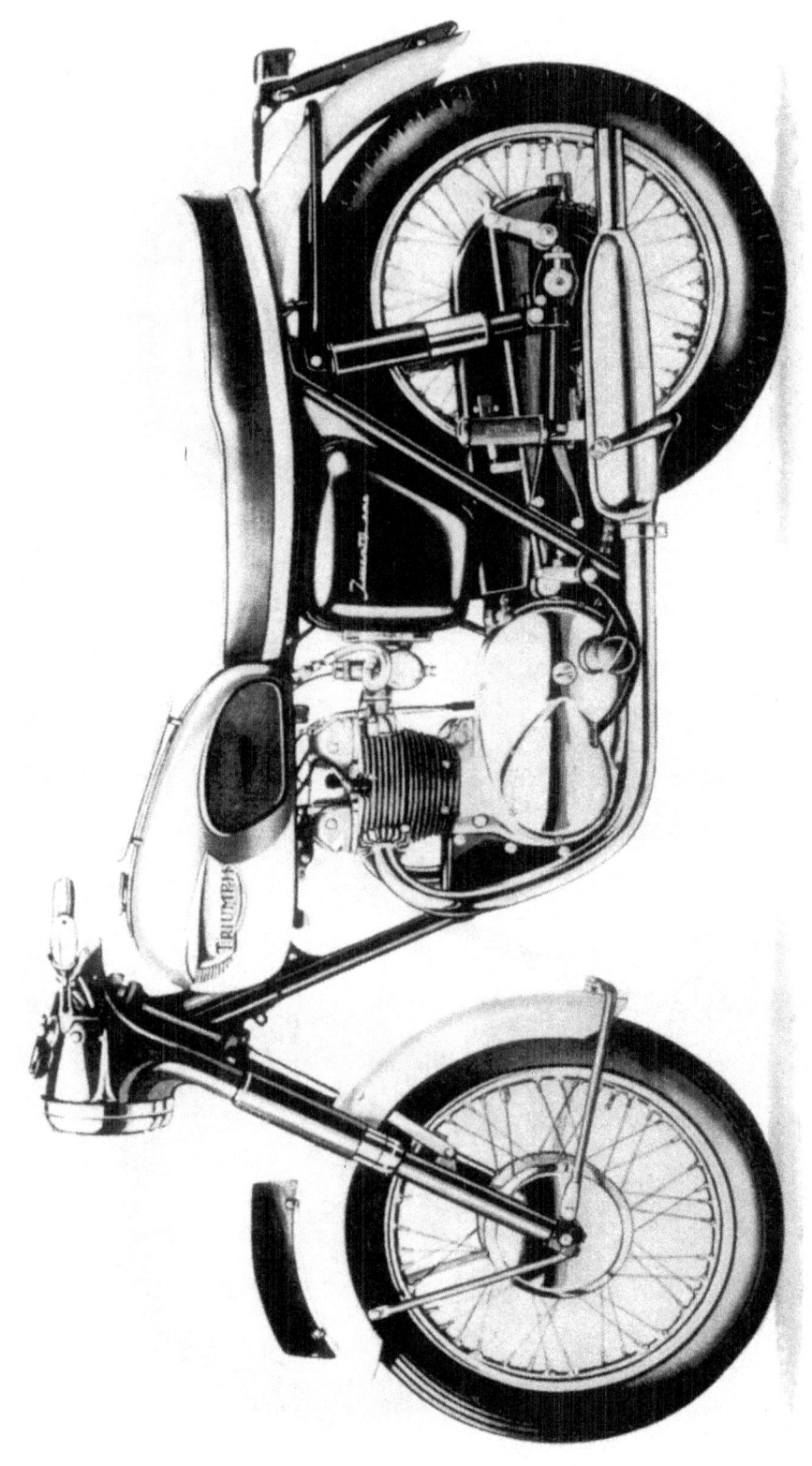

350 c.c. (21 cu. in.) TRIUMPH TWENTY-ONE (3TA)

5TA SIMILAR EXCEPT FOR COLOUR AND ENGINE CAPACITY
BOTH DISCONTINUED AT ENGINE NUMBER H.49832

GENERAL DATA

T100SS—TIGER 100
T100T—DAYTONA TIGER 100
T90—TIGER 90
5TA—SPEED TWIN
3TA—MODEL TWENTY-ONE

Also Alternative Fitments for T100 Sports Models

Note:—Throughout this Section, read **All** Models as for T100SS Model unless otherwise detailed under the particular Model

GENERAL DATA
MODEL T100S—TIGER 100
LUBRICATION SYSTEM

OIL PUMP
- Body material … Brass
- Bore diameter: Feed … ·3748/·3753 in.
-   Scavenge … ·4372/·4377 in.
-   Scavenge (Before H.49833) … ·4877/·4872 in.
- Plunger diameter: Feed … ·3744/·3747 in.
-   Scavenge … ·4369/·4372 in.
-   Scavenge (Before H.49833) … ·4872/·4869 in.
- Valve spring length … $\frac{1}{2}$ in.
- Ball diameter … $\frac{7}{32}$ in.
- Aluminium crosshead width … ·497/·498 in.
- Working clearance in plunger heads … ·0015/·0045 in.

OIL PRESSURE RELEASE VALVE
- Piston diameter … ·5605/·5610 in.
- Working clearance … ·001/·002 in.
- Pressure release operates … 60 lb./sq. in. (4·22 kg./sq. cm.)
- Spring length (Free) … $1\frac{3}{8}$ in.
- Load at $1\frac{3}{16}$ in … 8 lbs.
- Rate … 42·3 lbs.

OIL PRESSURE
- Normal running … 60 lb./sq. in.
- Idling … 20/25 lb./sq. in.

ENGINE

BASIC DETAILS
- Bore and stroke … 69 × 65·5 mm.
- Bore and stroke … 2·7165 × 2·58 in.
- Cubic capacity … 490 c.c. (30 cu. ins)
- Compression ratio … 9·0:1
- Capacity of combustion chamber … 27 c.c. (1·66 cu. in.)
- Power output (B.H.P. @ R.P.M.) … 34 @ 7,000

CRANKSHAFT
- Type … Forged two throw crank with bolt-on flywheel
- Left main bearing, size and type … 72 × 30 × 19 mm. Ball Journal
- Right crankshaft main bearing journal dia. … 1·4375/1·4380 in.
- Right main bearing bore, size and type … 1·4390/1·4385 in. Steel backed copper lead lined bush. Under sizes available: —0·010 in., —0·020 in., —0·030 in.
- Left main bearing housing dia. … 2·8321/2·8336 in.
- Right main bearing housing dia … 1·8135/1·8140 in.
- Big end journal dia. … 1·4375/1·4380 in.
- Min. regrind dia. … 1·4075/1·4080 in.
- Crankshaft end float … ·008/·017 in.

CONNECTING RODS
- Material … Alloy 'H' Section RR.56
- Length (centres) … 5·311/5·313 in.
- Big end bearings type … Steel backed white metal
-   Bearing side clearance … ·013/·017 in.
-   Bearing diametral clearance … ·0005/·0020 in. minimum.

GUDGEON PIN
- Material … High tensile steel
- Fit in small end bush … ·0005/·0012 in.
- Diameter … ·6882/·6885 in.
- Length … 2·151/2·156 in.

SMALL END BUSH
- Material … Phosphor Bronze
- Outer dia. … ·782/·783 in.
- Length … ·890/·910 in.
- Finished bore dia. … ·6905/·6910 in.

GENERAL DATA

T100S MODEL—(cont)

PISTONS

	From H.49833	Before H.49833
Material	Aluminium Alloy die casting	
Clearance: Top of skirt	·0050/·0072 in.	·0075/·0085 in.
Bottom of skirt	·0030/·0045 in.	·002/·003 in.
Gudgeon pin hole dia.	·6882/·6886 in.	·6882/·6886 in.

PISTON RINGS

Material ... Cast iron
Compression rings (taper faced):
  Width ... ·0615/·0625 in.
  Thickness ... ·092/·100 in.
  Fitted gap ... ·010/·014 in.
  Clearance in groove ... ·001/·003 in.
Oil control ring:
  Width ... ·124/·125 in.
  Thickness ... ·092/·100 in.
  Fitted gap ... ·010/·014 in.
  Clearance in groove ... ·0005/·0025 in.

VALVES

Seat angle (included) ... 90°
Head diameter: Inlet ... 1$\frac{7}{32}$ in.
    Inlet (Before H.49833) ... 1$\frac{7}{16}$ in.
    Exhaust ... 1$\frac{5}{16}$ in.
Stem diameter: Inlet ... ·3095/·3100 in.
    Exhaust ... ·3090/·3095 in.

VALVE GUIDES

Material ... Hidural
Bore diameter (Inlet and exhaust) ... ·312/·313 in.
Outside diameter (Inlet and exhaust) ... ·5005/·5010 in.
Length: Inlet ... 1$\frac{3}{4}$ in.
    Exhaust ... 1$\frac{3}{4}$ in.

VALVE SPRINGS (Inner—Yellow, Outer—L/Blue Spot)

	Outer	Inner
Free length	1$\frac{1}{2}$ in.	1$\frac{19}{32}$ in.
Total number of coils	6	8$\frac{1}{4}$

Total fitted load:
  Valve open ... 136 lbs.
  Valve closed ... 63 lbs.

VALVE TIMING

Set all tappet clearances @ ·020 in. (·5 mm.) for checking
- Inlet opens 34° before top centre
- Inlet closes 55° after bottom centre
- Exhaust opens 48° before bottom centre
- Exhaust closes 27° after top centre

ROCKERS

Material ... High tensile steel forging
Bore dia. ... ·4375/·4380 in.
Rocker spindle diameter ... ·4355/·4360 in.
Tappet clearance (cold): Inlet ... ·002 in. (·05 mm.)
    Exhaust ... ·004 in. (·10 mm.)

TAPPETS

Material ... High tensile steel forging—Stellite Tip
Tip radius ... $\frac{7}{8}$ in.
Tappet diameter ... ·3110/·3115 in.
Clearance in guide block ... ·0005/·0015 in.

GD GENERAL DATA

T100S MODEL—(cont)

TAPPET GUIDE BLOCK
Diameter of bores	·3120/·3125 in.
Outside diameter	1·000/·9995 in.
Interference fit in cylinder block	·0005/·0015 in.

CAMSHAFTS
Journal diameter: Left	·8100/·8105 in.
Diametral clearance: Left	·0010/·0025 in.
End float	·005/·008 in.
Cam lift: Inlet	·314 in.
Exhaust	·296 in.
Base circle diameter: Inlet and exhaust	·812 in.

CAMSHAFT BEARING BUSHES
Material	Steel backed bronze
Bore diameter (fitted): Left	·8125/·8135 in.
Outside diameter: Left	·906/·907 in.
Length: Left inlet	1·114/1·094 in.
Left exhaust	·922/·942 in.
Interference fit in crankcase: Left	·002/·003 in.

TIMING GEARS
Inlet and exhaust camshaft pinions:	
No. of teeth	50
Interference fit on camshaft	·000/·001
Intermediate timing gear	
No. of teeth	42
Bore diameter	·5618/·5625
Intermediate timing gear bush:	
Material	Phosphor bronze
Outside diameter	·5635/·5640 in.
Bore diameter	·4990/·4995 in.
Length	·6775/·6825 in.
Working clearance on spindle	·0005/·0015 in.
Intermediate wheel spindle	
Diameter	·4980/·4985 in.
Interference fit in crankcase	·0005/·0015 in.
Crankcase pinion:	
No. of teeth	25
Fit on crankcase	+·0003 in.
	−·0005 in.

IGNITION TIMING

	From Eng. No. H.49833	Before Eng. No. H.49833
Crankshaft position: (B.T.D.C.)		
Static timing	13°	16°
Fully advanced	37°	40°
Piston position: (B.T.D.C.)		
Static timing	$\frac{3}{64}$ in.	·060 in. (1·52 mm.)
Fully advanced	$\frac{5}{16}$ in.	·360 in. (9·144 mm.)
Advance range:		
Contact breaker	12°	12°
Crankshaft	24°	24°

CONTACT BREAKER
Gap setting	·014–·016 in. (·35–·40 mm.)
Advance range	12° (24° crankshaft)
Fully advanced at	2,000 r.p.m.

GENERAL DATA

T100 MODEL—(cont)

CYLINDER BLOCK
Material	Cast iron
Bore size	2·7160/2·7165 in.
Maximum oversize	2·7360/2·7365 in.
Tappet guide block housing diameter	·9985/·9990 in.

CYLINDER HEAD
Material	DTD 424 Aluminium Alloy
Inlet port size	1 in. dia.
Exhaust port size	1¼ in. dia.
Valve seatings:	
Type	Cast-in
Material	Cast iron

FUEL SYSTEM
Carburetter:	
Amal type	376/273
Main jet size	190
Pilot jet size	25
Needle jet size	·106
Needle type	C
Needle position	3
Throttle valve:	
Type	376/3½
Return spring free length	2½ in.
Carburetter nominal bore size	1 in.
Air cleaner type	Felt or paper element

TRANSMISSION

CLUTCH DETAILS
Type	Multiplate with integral shock absorber
No. of plates: Driving (bonded)	6
Driven (plain)	6
Pressure springs:	
Number	3
Free length	1 $\frac{31}{32}$ in.
No. of working coils	9½
Spring rate	58½ lbs./in.
Approximate fitted load	42 lbs.
Bearing rollers:	
Number	20
Diameter	·2495/·2500 in.
Length	·231/·236 in.
Clutch hub bearing diameter	1·3733/1·3743 in.
Clutch sprocket bore diameter	1·0745/1·0755 in.
Thrust washer thickness	·052/·054 in.
Engine sprocket teeth	26
Clutch sprocket teeth	58
Chain details	Duplex endless—⅜ in. pitch × 78 links

CLUTCH OPERATING MECHANISM
Conical spring:	
Number of working coils	2
Free length	1 $\frac{3}{32}$ in.
Diameter of balls	⅜ in. dia.
Clutch operating rod:	
Diameter of rod	3/16 in. dia.
Length of rod	9·562/9·567 in.

GENERAL DATA

GEARBOX

T100 MODEL—(cont)

RATIOS

Internal ratios (Std.) 4th (Top)	1·00:1
3rd	1·22:1
2nd	1·61:1
1st (Bottom)	2·47:1
Overall ratios: 4th (Top)	5·70
3rd	6·95
2nd	9·18
1st (Bottom)	14·09
Engine R.P.M. @ 10 M.P.H. in 4th (Top) gear	763
Gearbox sprocket teeth	18

GEAR DETAILS

Mainshaft high gear:
- Bore diameter (bush fitted) ... ·7520/·7530 in.
- Working clearance on shaft ... ·0020/·0035 in.
- Bush length ... $2\frac{5}{8}$ in.
- Bush protrusion length ... $\frac{3}{8}$ in.

Layshaft low gear:
- Bore diameter (bush fitted) ... ·689/·690 in.
- Working clearance on shaft ... ·0015/·003 in.

GEARBOX SHAFTS

Mainshaft:
- Left end diameter ... ·7495/·7500 in.
- Right end diameter ... ·6685/·6689 in.
- Length ... $9\frac{1}{64}$ in.
- Length (before H.49833) ... $8\frac{51}{64}$ in.

Layshaft:
- Left end diameter ... ·6845/·6850 in.
- Right end diameter ... ·6870/·6875 in.
- Length ... $5\frac{3}{8}$ in.

Camplate plunger spring:
- Free length ... $2\frac{1}{2}$
- No. of working coils ... 22
- Spring rate ... 5–6 lbs./in.

BEARINGS

High gear bearing	30 × 62 × 16 mm. Ball journal
Mainshaft bearing	17 × 47 × 14 mm. Ball journal
Layshaft bearing (left)	$1\frac{1}{16} \times \frac{7}{8} \times \frac{3}{4}$ in. Needle roller
Layshaft bearing (right)	$\frac{5}{8} \times \frac{13}{16} \times \frac{3}{4}$ in. Needle roller

KICKSTART OPERATING MECHANISM

Ratchet spring free length ... $\frac{1}{2}$ in.

GEARCHANGE MECHANISM

Plungers:
- Outer diameter ... ·3402/·3412 in.
- Working clearance in bore ... ·0015/·0035 in.

Plunger springs:
- No. of working coils ... 16
- Free length ... $1\frac{1}{16}$ in.

Outer bush bore diameter ... ·623/·624 in.
- Clearance on shaft ... ·001/·003 in.

Quadrant return springs:
- No. of working coils ... 18
- Free length ... $1\frac{7}{8}$ in.

FRAME AND ATTACHMENT DETAILS

T100 MODEL—(cont)

HEAD RACES
- No. of balls: Top ... 24
- Bottom ... 24
- Ball diameter ... $\frac{3}{16}$ in.

SWINGING FORK
- Bush type ... Phosphor bronze strip
- Bush bore diameter ... ·8745/·8750 in
- Spindle diameter ... ·8735/·8740 in.
- Distance between fork ends ... $7\frac{7}{16}$ in.

REAR SUSPENSION
- Type ... Swinging fork controlled by combined spring/hydraulic damper units. (Bolted up after H.49833).
- Spring details:
  - Fitted length ... 8 in.
  - Free length ... $8\frac{3}{16}$ in.
  - Mean coil diameter ... $1\frac{3}{4}$ dia.
  - Spring rate ... 145 lbs./ins.
  - Colour code ... Blue/Yellow
  - Load at fitted length ... 38 lbs.

WHEELS, BRAKES AND TYRES

WHEELS
- Rim size: Front and rear ... WM2-18
- Type: Front ... Spoke—single cross lacing.
- Rear ... Spoke—double cross lacing.
- Spoke details: Front ... 40 off 8/10 SWG butted $5\frac{17}{32}$ in. U.H. Straight
- Rear: Left side ... 20 off 8/10 SWG butted $7\frac{9}{16}$ in. U.H. 90°
- Right side ... 20 off 8/10 SWG butted $7\frac{7}{8}$ in. U.H. 90°

WHEEL BEARINGS
- Front and rear, dimensions and type ... 20 × 47 × 14 mm. Ball journal
- Front spindle diameter (at bearing journals) ... ·7868/·7873 in.
- Rear spindle diameter (at bearing journals) ... ·7862/·7867 in.

Q.D. REAR WHEEL
- Bearing type ... $\frac{3}{4} \times 1\frac{7}{8} \times \frac{9}{16}$ in. Ball journal
- Bearing sleeve: journal diameter ... ·7490/·7495 in.
- Brake drum bearing ... $\frac{7}{8} \times 2 \times \frac{9}{16}$ in.
- Bearing sleeve: journal diameter ... ·8740/·8745 in.
- Bearing housing: internal diameter ... 1·9980/1·9990 in.

REAR WHEEL DRIVE
- Gearbox sprocket ... See "Gearbox"
- Rear wheel sprocket teeth ... 46
- Chain details:
  - No. of links: Solo ... 102
  - Pitch ... $\frac{5}{8}$ in.
  - Width ... $\frac{3}{8}$ in.
- Speedometer gearbox drive ratio ... 19:10

BRAKES
- Type ... Internal Expanding
- Drum diameter: Front ... 7 in. } ± ·002 in.
- Rear ... 7 in.
- Lining thickness: Front and rear ... ·187/·197 in.
- Lining area: Front and rear ... 14·6 sq. in.

GD GENERAL DATA

T100 MODEL—(cont)

TYRES

Size: Front	3·25 × 18 in. Dunlop ribbed
Rear	3·50 × 18 in. Dunlop K70
Tyre pressure: Front	24 lb./sq. in. (1·7 kg./sq. cm.)
Rear	24 lb./sq. in. (1·7 kg./sq. cm.)

FRONT FORKS

TELESCOPIC FORK

Type	Telescopic with oil damping
Spring details:	
Free length	9¾ in.
No. of working coils	12½
Spring rate	26½ lbs./in.
Colour code	Yellow/blue

Bush details: Material	Top bush	Bottom bush
Length	1 in.	·870/·875 in.
Outer diameter	1·498/1·499 in.	1·4935/1·4945 in.
Inner diameter	1·3065/1·3075 in.	1·2485/1·2495 in.

Stanchion diameter	1·3025/1·3030 in.
Working clearance in top bush	·0035/·0050 in.
Fork leg bore diameter	1·498/1·500 in.
Working clearance of bottom bush	·0035/·0065 in.

12 VOLT ELECTRICAL SYSTEM

Battery	1 Lucas 12 volt battery PUZ5A or earlier 2 Lucas 6 volt batteries connected in series (MKZ9E)
Rectifier type	Lucas 2DS506
Alternator type	Lucas RM19
Horn	Lucas 8H 12 volt

Bulbs:	No.	Type
Headlight	Lucas 414	50/40 watts pre-focus
Parking light	Lucas 989	6 watts MCC
Stop and tail light	Lucas 380	6/21 watts offset pins
Speedometer light	Lucas 987	2 watts MES
Main beam indicator light (where fitted)	Lucas 281	2 watt (BA7S)
Ignition warning light	Lucas 281	2 watt (BA7S)

Zener diode type	ZD 715
Coil type	Lucas MA12 (12v.) 2 off
Contact breaker type	Lucas 4CA (12° range)
Fuse rating	35 amp.

SPARKING PLUGS

Type	Champion N4
Plug gap settings	·020 in. (·5 mm.)
Thread size	14 mm. × ¾ in. reach

GENERAL

CAPACITIES

Fuel tank	3 gall (3·6 U.S. galls, 13·5 litres)
Oil tank	6 pint (7·2 U.S. pints, 3·5 litres)
Gearbox	⅔ pint (375 c.c.)
Primary chaincase	½ pint (300 c.c.)
Telescopic fork legs (each leg)	⅓ pint (190 c.c.)

T100 MODEL—(cont)

BASIC DIMENSIONS
Wheel base	53½ in. (136 cm.)
Overall length	83¼ in. (211·5 cm.)
Overall width	26½ in. (67·3 cm.)
Overall height	38 in. (96·5 cm.)
Ground clearance	7½ in. (19 cm.)

WEIGHTS
Unladen weight	337 lbs. (153 kgm.)
Engine unit (dry)	106 lbs. (48 kgm.)

TORQUE WRENCH SETTINGS (DRY)
Flywheel bolts	33 lb./ft.
Conn. rod bolts	27 lb./ft.
Crankcase junction bolts	15 lb./ft.
Crankcase junction studs	20 lb./ft.
Cylinder block nuts	35 lb./ft.
Cylinder head bolts (⅜ in. dia.)	25 lb./ft.
Rocker box nuts	5 lb./ft.
Rocker box bolts	5 lb./ft.
Rocker spindle domed nuts	25 lb./ft.
Oil pump nuts	6 lb./ft.
Kickstart ratchet pinion nut	40 lb./ft.
Clutch centre nut	50 lb./ft.
Rotor fixing nut	30 lb./ft.
Stator fixing nuts	20 lb./ft.
Headlamp pivot bolts	10 lb./ft.
Headrace sleeve nut pinch bolt	15 lb./ft.
Stanchion pinch bolts	25 lb./ft.
Front wheel spindle cap bolts	25 lb./ft.
Brake cam spindle nuts	20 lb./ft.
Zener diode fixing nut	1½ lb./ft.
Twin carburetter manifold socket screws	10 lb./ft.

GENERAL DATA

MODEL T100T—"DAYTONA"

FOR DATA NOT GIVEN HERE REFER TO GENERAL DATA—MODEL T100S

ENGINE

BASIC DETAILS
- Compression ratio ... 9·7:1
- Power output (B.H.P. @ R.P.M.) ... 39 @ 7400

VALVES
- Head diameter inlet ... $1\frac{17}{32}$ in.
- Head diameter exhaust ... $1\frac{5}{16}$ in.

PISTONS
- Clearance: Top of skirt ... ·0050/·0072 in.
- Bottom of skirt ... ·0030/·0045 in.

VALVE TIMING
Set all tappet clearances @ ·020 in. (·5 mm.) for checking ...
- Inlet opens 40° before top centre
- Inlet closes 52° after bottom centre
- Exhaust opens 61° before bottom centre
- Exhaust closes 31° after top centre

TAPPETS
- Tip radius ... $1\frac{1}{8}$ in.

CAMSHAFTS
- Cam lift: Inlet ... ·314 in.
- Exhaust ... ·314 in.

TIMING GEARS
- Inlet and Exhaust camwheels ... 3 Keyway

CYLINDER HEAD
- Inlet port size ... $1\frac{1}{16}$ in.

FUEL SYSTEM
- Carburetters (two)
  - Amal type ... 376/324 and 325
  - Main jet size ... 200
  - Pilot jet size ... 25
  - Needle jet size ... ·106
  - Needle type ... C
  - Needle position ... 3
  - Throttle valve:
    - Type ... 376/3½
    - Nominal bore size ... $1\frac{1}{16}$ in.
  - Air cleaner type ... Coarse felt

WHEELS AND BRAKES

- Drum diameter: Front ... 8 in.
- Lining thickness: Front ... ·183 in.
- Lining area: Front ... 23·4 sq. in.

REAR WHEEL DRIVE
- Rear chain: No. of links ... 102

GENERAL

BASIC DIMENSIONS
- Weight ... 341 lb. (154·7 kg.)

GENERAL DATA

MODEL 5TA—SPEED TWIN

(DISCONTINUED AFTER ENGINE NUMBER H.49833)

FOR DATA NOT GIVEN HERE REFER TO GENERAL DATA—MODEL T100

ENGINE

BASIC DETAILS
- Bore and stroke ... 69 × 65·5 m.m.
- Bore and stroke ... 2·7165 × 2·58 in.
- Cubic capacity ... 490 c.c. (30 cu. in.)
- Compression ratio ... 7:1
- Capacity of combustion chamber ... 35 c.c. (2·14 cu. in.)
- Power output (B.H.P. @ R.P.M.) ... 27 @ 6,500

PISTONS
- Material ... Aluminium Alloy die casting
- Clearance: Top of skirt ... ·0065/·0075 in.
-     Bottom of skirt ... ·001/·002 in.
- Gudgeon pin hole diameter ... ·6882/·6886 in.

VALVE TIMING
- Set all tappet clearances @ ·020 in. (·50 mm.) for checking
  - Inlet opens 34° before top centre
  - Inlet closes 55° after bottom centre
  - Exhaust opens 48° before bottom centre
  - Exhaust closes 27° after top centre

VALVES
- Seat angle (included) ... 90°
- Head diameter: Inlet ... 1 7/16 in.
-     Exhaust ... 1 5/16 in.
- Stem diameter Inlet: ... ·3095/·3100 in.
-     Exhaust ... ·3090/·3095 in.

VALVE GUIDES
- Material ... Cast iron
- Bore diameter (Inlet and exhaust) ... ·3130/·3120 in.
- Outside diameter (Inlet and exhaust) ... ·5005/·5010 in.
- Length Inlet: ... 1 3/4 in.
-     Exhaust ... 1 3/4 in.

ROCKERS
- Material ... High tensile steel forgings
- Bore diameter ... ·4375/·4380 in.
- Rocker spindle diameter ... ·4355/·4360 in.
- Tappet clearance (Cold): Inlet ... ·002 in. (0·05 mm.)
-     Exhaust ... ·004 in. (0·10 mm.)

IGNITION TIMING
- Crankshaft position (B.T.D.C.)
  - Static timing ... 12°
  - Fully advanced ... 36°
- Piston position (B.T.D.C.)
  - Static timing ... 0·035 in. (0·90 mm.)
  - Fully advanced ... 0·310 in. (7·93 mm.)
- Advance range:
  - Contact breaker ... 12°
  - Crankshaft ... 24°

5TA MODEL—(cont)

FUEL SYSTEM
Carburetter
    Amal type ... 376/273
    Main jet size ... 190
    Pilot jet size ... 25
    Needle jet size ... ·106
    Needle type ... C
    Needle position ... 3
    Throttle valve:
        Type ... 376/3½
        Return spring free length ... 2½ in.
        Carburetter nominal bore size ... 1 in.
Air cleaner type ... Felt or paper element

GEARBOX

RATIOS
Internal ratios: 4th (Top) ... 1·00:1
        3rd ... 1·22:1
        2nd ... 1·61:1
        1st (Bottom) ... 2·47:1
Overall ratios:
    4th (Top) ... 5·40
    3rd ... 6·59
    2nd ... 8·69
    1st (Bottom) ... 13·34
Engine R.P.M. @ 10 M.P.H. in 4th (Top) gear ... 720
Gearbox sprocket teeth ... 20
Layshaft bushes, material ... Bronze
    Bore size L/H ... ·6865/·6885 in.
    Bore size R/H ... ·690/·689 in.
    Interference fit in casing R/H ... ·0005/·0015 in.
    Interference fit in Kickstart assembly L/H ... ·0005/·0015 in.

FRAME AND ATTACHMENT DETAILS

REAR SUSPENSION
Spring details:
    Fitted length ... 8 in.
    Free length ... 8 3/16 in.
    Mean coil diameter ... 1¾ in.
    Spring rate ... 145 lb./in.
    Colour code ... Blue/yellow
    Load at fitted length ... 38 lb.

WHEELS, BRAKES AND TYRES

WHEELS
Rim size: Front ... WM2–18
Spoke details: Front ... 40 off 8/10 SWG butted 5 17/32 in. U.H. Straight
Rim size: Rear ... WM2–18

REAR WHEEL DRIVE
Gearbox sprocket teeth ... See "Gearbox"
Rear wheel sprocket teeth ... 46
Chain details:
    No. of links ... 103
    Pitch ... 5/8 in.
    Width ... 3/8 in.
Speedometer gearbox drive ratio ... 2:1

TYRES
Size: Front ... 3·25 × 18 in. Avon Speedmaster
    Rear ... 3·50 × 18 in. Avon Speedmaster
Tyre pressures: Front ... 24 lb./sq. in. (1·7 kg./sq. cm.)
        Rear ... 24 lb./sq. in. (1·7 kg./sq. cm.)

5TA MODEL—(cont)

FRONT FORKS

Spring details:
- Free length ... 9¾ in.
- No. of working coils ... 12½
- Spring rate ... 26½ lbs./in.
- Colour code ... Yellow/blue

ELECTRICAL SYSTEM

ELECTRICAL EQUIPMENT

Battery type ... Lucas 12 volt (type PUZ5A) or alternatively two Lucas 6 volt (type MKZ9E) connected in series

Rectifier type ... Lucas 2DS506
Alternator type ... Lucas RM19
Horn ... Lucas 8H (12 volt)

Bulbs: (6 volt)

	No.	Type
Headlight	Lucas 414	50/40 watts pre-focus
Parking light	Lucas 989	6 watts MCC
Stop and tail light	Lucas 380	6/21 watts offset pins
Speedometer light	Lucas 987	2 watts MES

Coil type ... Lucas MA12 (12 volt)
Contact breaker type ... Lucas 4CA
Fuse rating ... 35 amp.
Sparking plugs:
- Type ... Champion N4
- Plug gap setting ... ·020 in. (·5 mm.)
- Thread size ... 14 mm.

GENERAL

BASIC DIMENSIONS

- Wheel base ... 53½ in. (136 cm.)
- Overall length ... 83¼ in. (211·5 cm.)
- Overall width ... 26½ in. (67·3 cm.)
- Overall height ... 38 in. (96·5 cm.)
- Ground clearance ... 7½ in. (19 cm.)

WEIGHTS

- Unladen weight ... 340 lbs. (155 kgm.)
- Engine unit (Dry) ... 106 lbs. (48 kgm.)

GENERAL DATA

MODEL T90—TIGER 90

FOR DATA NOT GIVEN HERE REFER TO GENERAL DATA MODEL—T100S

ENGINE

BASIC DETAILS

Bore and stroke	58·25 × 65·5 mm.
Bore and stroke	2·2928 × 2·58 in.
Cubic capacity	349 c.c. (21 cu. in.)
Compression ratio	9:1
Capacity of combustion chamber	19·5 c.c. (1·19 cu. in.)
Power output (B.H.P. — R.P.M.)	27 @ 7,500

PISTONS

Material ... Aluminium Alloy die casting

	From H.49833	Before H.49833
Clearance: Top of skirt	·0049/·0070 in.	·0058/·0068 in.
Bottom of skirt	·0034/·0049 in.	·0043/·0048 in.
Gudgeon pin hole diameter	·5618/·5621 in.	·5618/·5621 in.

VALVES

Seat angle (Inlet and exhaust)	90° included angle
Head diameter: Inlet	$1\frac{7}{16}$ in.
Exhaust	$1\frac{3}{16}$ in.
Stem diameter: Inlet	·3095/·3100 in.
Exhaust	·3090/·3095 in.

VALVE GUIDES

Material	Hidural
Bore diameter (Inlet and exhaust)	·312/·313 in.
Outside diameter (Inlet and exhaust)	·5005/·5010 in.
Length (Inlet and exhaust)	$1\frac{3}{4}$ in.

VALVE TIMING

Set all tappet clearances @ ·020 in. (·5 mm.) for checking

- Inlet opens 34° before top centre
- Inlet closes 55° after bottom centre
- Exhaust opens 48° before bottom centre
- Exhaust closes 27° after top centre

ROCKERS

Material	High tensile steel forging
Bore diameter	·4375/·4380
Rocker spindle diameter	·4355/·4360
Tappet clearance (cold): Inlet	·002 in. (·05 mm.)
Exhaust	·004 in. (·10 mm.)

IGNITION TIMING

Crankshaft position (B.T.D.C.)	
Static timing	16°
Fully advanced	40°
Piston position (B.T.D.C.)	
Static timing	·060 in. (1·52 mm.)
Fully advanced	·360 in. (9·144 mm.)
Advance range:	
Contact breaker	12°
Crankshaft	24°

CYLINDER HEAD

Material	DTD 424 Aluminium Alloy
Inlet port size	1 in. dia.
Exhaust port size	$1\frac{1}{4}$ in. dia.
Valve seatings:	
Type	Cast-in
Material	Cast iron

CONNECTING RODS

Material	'H' Section RR.56 alloy
Material (Before H.49833)	EN 18 steel stamping

GD

GENERAL DATA

TIGER 90—(cont)

FUEL SYSTEM

Carburetter:
- Amal type ... 376/300
- Main jet size ... 180
- Pilot jet size ... 20
- Needle jet size ... ·106
- Needle type ... C
- Needle position ... 3

Throttle:
- Type ... 376/3
- Return spring free length ... 2½ in.
- Carburetter nominal bore size ... 1⅙ in.

Air cleaner type ... Felt or paper element

GEARBOX

RATIOS

Internal ratios:
- 4th (Top) ... 1·00:1
- 3rd ... 1·22:1
- 2nd ... 1·61:1
- 1st (Bottom) ... 2·47:1

Overall ratios:
- 4th (Top) ... 6·03:1
- 3rd ... 7·36:1
- 2nd ... 9·71:1
- 1st (Bottom) ... 14·90:1

Engine R.P.M. @ 10 M.P.H. in 4th gear ... 805
Gearbox sprocket teeth ... 17

FRAME AND ATTACHMENT DETAILS

REAR SUSPENSION

Spring details:
- Fitted length ... 8 in.
- Free length ... 8 3/16 in.
- Mean coil diameter ... 1¾ in.
- Spring rate ... 145 lb./in.
- Colour code ... Blue/Yellow
- Load at fitted length ... 38 lbs.

WHEELS, BRAKES AND TYRES

WHEELS

- Rim size: Front ... WM2-18
- Spoke details: Front ... 40 off 8/10 SWG butted 5 7/32 in. U.H. straight
- Rim size: Rear ... WM2-18

REAR WHEEL DRIVE

- Gearbox sprocket teeth ... See "Gearbox"
- Rear wheel sprocket teeth ... 46

Chain details:
- No. of links ... 102
- Pitch ... ⅝ in.
- Width ... ⅜ in.

Speedometer gearbox drive ratio ... 19 : 10

TYRES

- Size: Front ... 3·25 × 18 in.
- Rear ... 3·50 × 18 in.
- Tyre pressures: Front ... 24 lb./sq. in. (1·7 kg/sq. cm.)
- Rear ... 24 lb./sq. in. (1·7 kg/sq. cm.)

TIGER 90—(cont)

FRONT FORKS

Spring details:
- Free length ... 9¾ in.
- No. of working coils ... 12½
- Spring rate ... 26½ lb./in.
- Colour code ... Yellow/Blue

ELECTRICAL SYSTEM

ELECTRICAL EQUIPMENT

- Battery type ... 1 Lucas 12 volt battery (PUZ5A) or alternatively 2 Lucas 6 volt batteries connected in series (MKZ9E)
- Rectifier type ... Lucas 2DS506
- Alternator type ... Lucas RM19
- Horn ... Lucas 8H (12 volt)

Bulbs:

	No.	Type
Headlight	Lucas 414	50/40 watts pre-focus
Parking light	Lucas 989	6 watts MCC
Stop and tail light	Lucas 380	6/21 watts offset pins
Speedometer light	Lucas 987	2 watts MES
Main beam indicator light (where fitted)	Lucas 281	2 watt (BA7S)
Ignition warning light	Lucas 281	2 watt (BA7S)

- Coil type ... Lucas MA12 (2 off)
- Contact breaker type ... Lucas 4CA
- Fuse rating ... 35 amp.

Sparking plugs:
- Type ... Champion N4
- Plug gap settings ... ·020 in. (·5 mm.)
- Thread size ... 14 mm. × ¾ in. reach

GENERAL

BASIC DIMENSIONS

- Wheelbase ... 53½ in. (136 cm.)
- Overall length ... 83¼ in. (211·5 cm.)
- Overall width ... 26½ in. (67·3 cm.)
- Overall height ... 38 in. (96·5 cm.)
- Ground clearance ... 7½ in. (19 cm.)

WEIGHTS

- Unladen weight ... 336 lbs. (153 kgm.)
- Engine unit (dry) ... 104 lbs. (47·2 kgm.)

GENERAL DATA
3TA—TWENTY-ONE

(DISCONTINUED AFTER ENGINE NUMBER H.49833)

FOR DATA NOT GIVEN HERE REFER TO GENERAL DATA—MODEL 5TA

ENGINE

BASIC DETAILS
- Bore and stroke ... 58·25 × 65·5 mm.
- Bore and stroke ... 2·2928 × 2·58 in.
- Cubic capacity ... 349 c.c. (21 cu. in.)
- Compression ratio ... 7·5 : 1
- Capacity of combustion chamber ... 23·4 c.c. (1·42 cu. in.)
- Power output (B.H.P. @ R.P.M.) ... 18·5 @ 6,500

CYLINDER HEAD
- Material ... D.T.D. 424 Aluminium Alloy
- Inlet port size ... $\frac{7}{8}$ in.
- Exhaust port size ... $1\frac{3}{16}$ in.
- Valve seatings:
  - Type ... Cast-in
  - Material ... Cast iron

PISTONS
- Material ... Aluminium Alloy die casting
- Clearance: Top of skirt ... ·0048/·0058 in.
- Bottom of skirt ... ·0033/·0043 in.
- Gudgeon pin hole diameter ... ·5618/·5621 in.

VALVES
- Seat angle (Inlet and exhaust) ... 90° included angle
- Head diameter: Inlet ... $1\frac{5}{16}$ in. dia.
- Exhaust ... $1\frac{3}{16}$ in. dia.
- Stem diameter: Inlet ... ·3095/·3100 in.
- Exhaust ... ·3090/·3095 in.

VALVE GUIDES
- Material ... Cast iron
- Bore diameter (Inlet and exhaust) ... ·3120/·3130 in.
- Outside diameter (Inlet and exhaust) ... ·5005/·5010 in.
- Length: Inlet and exhaust ... $1\frac{3}{4}$ in.

VALVE TIMING
- Set all tappet clearances @ ·020 in. (·5 mm.) for checking
  - Inlet opens 26½° before top centre
  - Inlet closes 69½° after bottom centre
  - Exhaust opens 61½° before bottom centre
  - Exhaust closes 35½° after top centre

IGNITION TIMING
- Crankshaft position (B.T.D.C.)
  - Static timing ... 6°
  - Fully advanced ... 30°
- Piston position (B.T.D.C.)
  - Static timing ... 0·010 in. (0·25 mm.)
  - Fully advanced ... 0·210 in.
- Advance range:
  - Contact breaker ... 12°
  - Crankshaft ... 24°

ROCKERS
- Material ... High tensile steel forging
- Bore diameter ... ·4375/·4390 in.
- Rocker spindle diameter ... ·4355/·4360 in.
- Tappet clearance (cold): Inlet ... ·002 in. (·05 mm.)
- Exhaust ... ·004 in. (·10 mm.)

CAMSHAFTS
- Journal diameter: Left ... ·8100/·8105 in.
- Diametral clearance: Left ... ·0010/·0025 in.
- End float ... ·005/·008 in.
- Cam lift: Inlet ... ·281 in.
- Exhaust ... ·281 in.
- Base circle diameter ... ·812 in.

CLUTCH DETAILS
- No. of plates: Driving (bonded) ... 5
- Driven (plain) ... 5
- Length of clutch operating rod ... 9·432/9·442 in.

3TA—(cont)

WHEELS, BRAKES AND TYRES

WHEELS
- Rim size: Front ... WM2–18
- Spoke details: Front ... 40 off 8/10 SWG butted $5\frac{17}{32}$ in. U.H. straight
- Rim size: Rear ... WM2–18

REAR WHEEL DRIVE
- Gearbox sprocket teeth ... 17
- Rear wheel sprocket teeth ... 46
- Chain details:
  - No. of links ... 102
  - Pitch ... $\frac{5}{8}$ in.
  - Width ... $\frac{3}{8}$ in.
- Speedometer gearbox drive ratio ... 2 : 1

TYRES
- Size: Front ... 3·25 × 18 in.
- Rear ... 3·50 × 18 in.
- Tyre pressures: Front ... 24 lb./sq. in. (1·7 kg./sq. cm.)
- Rear ... 24 lb./sq. in. (1·7 kg./sq. cm.)

FRONT FORKS

- Spring details:
  - Free length ... $9\frac{3}{4}$ in.
  - No. of working coils ... $12\frac{1}{2}$ in.
  - Spring rate ... $26\frac{1}{2}$ lb./in.
  - Colour code ... Yellow/Blue

FUEL SYSTEM

CARBURETTER
- Carburetter
  - Type ... 375/62
  - Main jet ... 100
  - Pilot jet ... 25
  - Needle jet ... ·106
  - Needle position ... 3
  - Needle type ... B
  - Throttle valve ... 375/3$\frac{1}{2}$
  - Return spring length ... $2\frac{1}{4}$ in.
  - Nominal bore ... $\frac{25}{32}$ in.
- Air cleaner ... Felt or paper element

ELECTRICAL SYSTEM

ELECTRICAL EQUIPMENT
- Battery type ... 1 Lucas 12 volt battery (PUZ5A) or alternatively 2 Lucas 6 volt batteries connected in series (MKZ9E)
- Rectifier type ... 2DS 506
- Alternator type ... RM19
- Horn ... Lucas 8H (12 volt)

- Bulbs:

	No.	Type
Headlight	Lucas 414	50/40 watt pre-focus
Parking light	Lucas 989	6 watts MCC
Stop and tail light	Lucas 380	6/21 watts offset pins
Speedometer light	Lucas 987	2 watts MES

- Coil type ... Lucas MA12 (2 off)
- Contact breaker type ... Lucas 4CA
- Fuse rating ... 35 amp.
- Sparking plugs:
  - Type ... Champion N4
  - Plug gap settings ... ·020 in. (·50 mm.)
  - Thread size ... 14 mm. × $\frac{3}{4}$ in. reach

GENERAL

BASIC DIMENSIONS
- Wheelbase ... $53\frac{1}{2}$ in. (136 cm.)
- Overall length ... $83\frac{1}{4}$ in. (211·5 cm.)
- Overall width ... $26\frac{1}{4}$ in. (67·3 cm.)
- Overall height ... 36 in. (96·5 cm.)
- Ground clearance ... $7\frac{1}{2}$ in. (19 cm.)

WEIGHTS
- Unladen weight ... 340 lbs. (155 kgm.)
- Engine unit (dry) ... 104 lbs. (47·2 kgm.)

GENERAL DATA

ALTERNATIVE DATA FOR SPORTS MODELS FITTED WITH A.C. MAGNETO (E.T.) IGNITION EQUIPMENT

IGNITION TIMING A.C. Magneto (E.T.) Ignition equipment

- Crankshaft position (B.T.D.C.)
  - Static timing ... 27°
  - Fully advanced ... 37°
- Piston position (B.T.D.C.)
  - Static timing ... ·173 in.
  - Fully advanced ... ·320 in.
- Advance range:
  - Contact breaker ... 5°
  - Crankshaft ... 10°

CONTACT BREAKER A.C. Magneto (E.T.) Ignition equipment

- Gap setting ... ·014–·016 in. (·35–·40 mm.)
- Advance range ... 5°
- Fully advanced at ... 2,000 R.P.M.

ELECTRICAL SYSTEM

ELECTRICAL EQUIPMENT A.C. Magneto (E.T.) Ignition equipment

- Alternator type ... RM19 E.T.
- Horn, type ... Clearhooter A585 (6 volt)
- Coil type ... 3 E.T.
- Condensers (Capacitors) ... Lucas 54441582
- Contact breaker type ... Lucas 4CA
- Lighting system:

	No.	Type
Bulbs (6 volt):		
Headlight	Lucas 312	30/24 watts pre-focus
Stop and tail light	Lucas 384	6/18 watts offset pins

- Sparking plugs:
  - Type ... Champion N4
  - Plug gap setting ... ·020 in. (·5 mm.)
  - Thread size ... 14 mm. × ¾ in. reach

WHEELS

FRONT WHEEL

- Rim size ... WM2–19
- Type ... Spoke—single cross lacing
- Spoke details ... 40 off 8/10 SWG butted 6 in. U.H. straight

GEARBOX

RATIOS

- Internal ratios (close):
  - 4th (Top) ... 1·00:1
  - 3rd ... 1·12:1
  - 2nd ... 1·35:1
  - 1st (Bottom) ... 1·99:1
- Internal ratios (wide):
  - 4th (Top) ... 1·00:1
  - 3rd ... 1·37:1
  - 2nd ... 1·97:1
  - 1st (Bottom) ... 3·18:1
- Gearbox sprocket ... 17, 18, 19 and 20 teeth

NOTES

GENERAL DATA

T100S—TIGER 100
T100T—DAYTONA SUPER SPORTS
T100C—TROPHY 500
T100R—DAYTONA

Note:—Throughout this Section, read **All** models as for T100SS Model unless detailed under the particular Model.

GENERAL DATA

MODEL T100S

ENGINE

CRANKSHAFT
Type ... Forged two throw crank with bolt on flywheel
Left main bearing:
   Size and type ... 72 x 30 x 19 m.m. Roller bearing
Left crankshaft main bearing journal dia. ... 1·1805-1·1808 in.
Left bearing housing dia. ... 2·8336-2·8321 in.
Right main bearing:
   Size and type ... 72 x 35 x 17 mm. Ball bearing
Right crankshaft main bearing journal dia. ... 1·3774-1·3777 in.
Right bearing housing dia. ... 2·8336-2·8321 in.
Big-end journal dia. ... 1·4375-1·4380 in.
Minimum regrind dia. ... 1·4075-1·4080 in.
Crankshaft end float ... 0·008-0·017 in.

SMALL END (No Bush)
Diameter ... 0·689-0·6894 in.

GUDGEON PIN (Wrist Pin)
Length ... 2·151-2·156 in.
Diameter ... 0·6883-0·6885 in.
Fit in small end ... 0·0005-0·0011 in.

VALVE GUIDES
Material ... Hidural
Bore dia. (inlet and exhaust) ... 0·3122-0·3129 in.
Outside dia. (inlet and exhaust) ... 0·5005-0·5010 in.
Length (inlet and exhaust) ... 1·760-1·770 in.

FUEL SYSTEM

CARBURETTER
Main jet size ... 190
Throttle valve ... 3½

WHEEL, BRAKES AND TYRES

BRAKES
Type: front ... Internal expanding, twin leading shoe
   rear ... Internal expanding
Diameter front and rear ... 7 in.
Lining thickness ... ·179/·190 in.

ELECTRICAL SYSTEM

Ignition coil type ... Lucas 17M12 (12V. 2 off)

GENERAL DATA

MODEL T100T AND T100R "DAYTONA"
FOR DATA NOT GIVEN BELOW REFER TO T100S

FUEL SYSTEM
Carburetters (two)
- Main jet size ... 180
- Throttle valve ... 3½

WHEELS AND BRAKES

BRAKES
- Type front ... Internal expanding twin leading shoe
- Diameter: front ... 8 in.
- Lining thickness: front ... ·181/·188 in.
- Lining area front ... 23·4 sq. in.

WHEELS
- Rim size: front ... WM2 19 in.

TYRES
- T100T—size: front ... 3·25 x 19 in.
- Type: front ... Avon ribbed
- T100R—size: front ... 3·25 x 19 in.
- Type ... Dunlop K70

FRAME AND ATTACHMENT DETAILS

REAR SUSPENSION
T100R—Spring details
- Fitted length ... 8·4 in.
- Colour code ... Green-green
- Load at fitted length ... 28 lbs.

T100C
FOR DATA NOT GIVEN BELOW REFER TO T100S
ENGINE

VALVE GUIDES
- Material ... Cast iron

WHEELS, BRAKES AND TYRES

WHEELS
- Rim size: front ... WM2 19 in.

BRAKES
- Type: front ... Internal expanding twin leading shoe
- Drum diameter: front ... 7 in.

TYRES
- Size: front ... 3·25 x 19 in.
- Type: front ... Either Dunlop K70 or Dunlop Trials Universal

REAR SUSPENSION
Spring details:
- Fitted length ... 8·4 in.
- Spring rate ... 100 lbs.
- Colour code ... Green-Green
- Load at fitted length ... 28 lbs.

NOTES

SECTION A

LUBRICATION SYSTEM

	Section
ROUTINE MAINTENANCE	A1
TABLE OF RECOMMENDED LUBRICANTS	A2
ENGINE LUBRICATION SYSTEM	A3
CHANGING THE ENGINE OIL AND CLEANING THE OIL FILTERS	A4
OIL PRESSURE	A5
STRIPPING AND REASSEMBLING THE OIL PRESSURE RELEASE VALVE	A6
STRIPPING AND REASSEMBLING THE OIL PUMP	A7
REMOVING AND REPLACING THE OIL PIPE JUNCTION BLOCK	A8
REMOVING AND REPLACING THE ROCKER OIL FEED PIPE	A9
CONTACT BREAKER LUBRICATION	A10
GEARBOX LUBRICATION	A11
PRIMARY CHAINCASE LUBRICATION	A12
REAR CHAIN LUBRICATION AND MAINTENANCE	A13
GREASING THE STEERING HEAD RACES	A14
WHEEL BEARING LUBRICATION	A15
TELESCOPIC FORK LUBRICATION	A16
LUBRICATION NIPPLES	A17
LUBRICATING THE CONTROL CABLES	A18
SPEEDOMETER CABLE LUBRICATION	A19
REAR BRAKE SPINDLE LUBRICATION	A20

LUBRICATION SYSTEM

SECTION A1
ROUTINE MAINTENANCE

	Section
Every 250 miles (400 Kms.)	
Check level in oil tank	A4
Check level in primary chaincase	A12
Every 1,000 miles (1,600 Kms.)	
Change oil in primary chaincase	A12
Lubricate control cables	A18
Grease swinging fork pivot	A17
Remove rear chain for cleaning and greasing	A13
Every 1,500 miles (2,400 Kms.)	
Change engine oil	A4
Every 3,000 miles (4,800 Kms.)	
Check gearbox oil level	A11
Check front forks for external oil leakage	A16
Grease brake pedal spindle	A12
Every 6,000 miles (9,600 Kms.)	
Change oil in gearbox	A11
Change oil in front forks	A16
Every 12,000 miles (19,200 Kms.)	
Grease wheel bearings	A15
Grease steering head bearings	A14

LUBRICATION SYSTEM

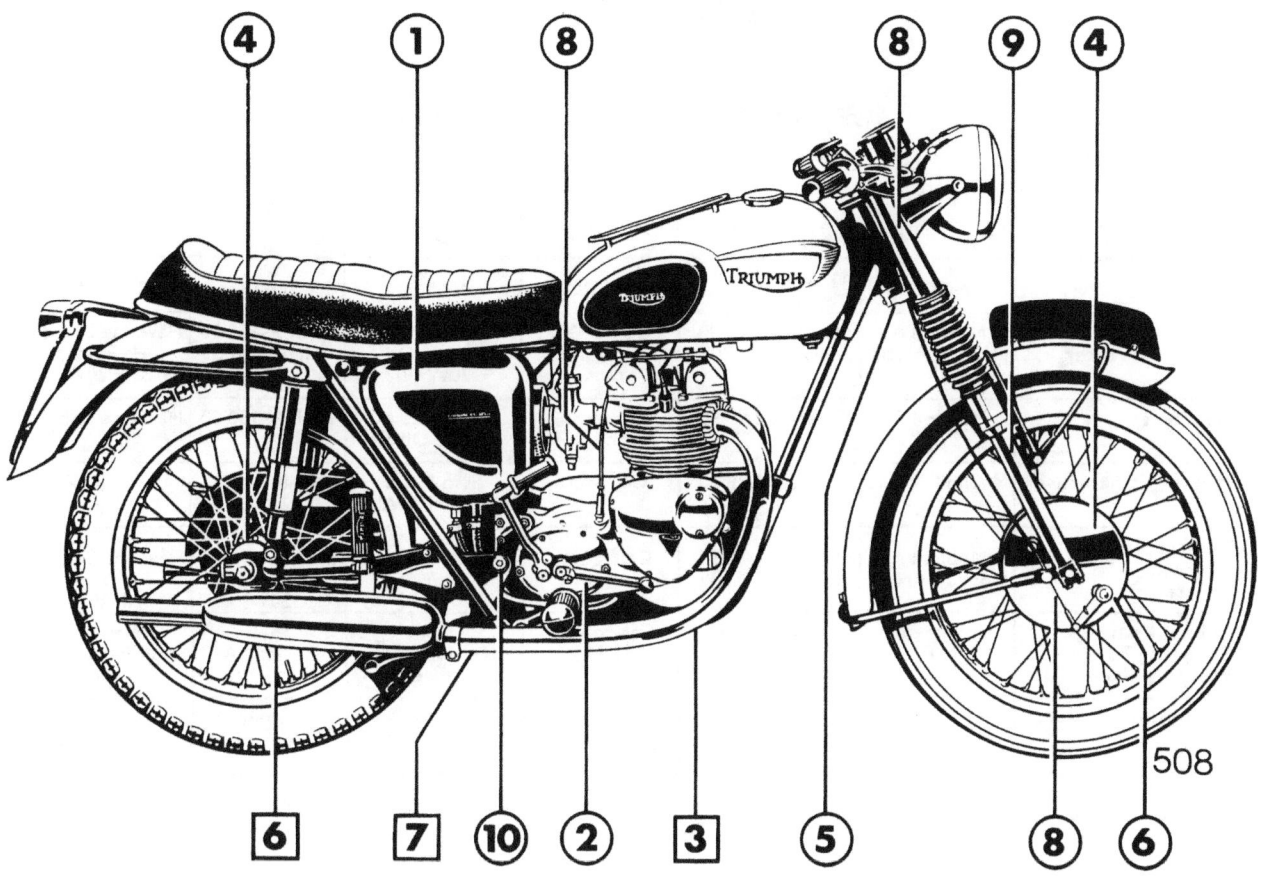

Fig. A1. LUBRICATION CHART
Numbers in circles refer to right side of machine
Numbers in squares refer to left side of machine

GUIDE TO LUBRICATION POINTS

Illustration No.	Description	SAE Oil grade
1	Engine oil tank	20 or 30
2	Gearbox	30
3	Primary chaincase	20
4	Wheel hubs	Grease
5	Steering head	Grease
6	Brake cam spindle	Grease
7	Brake pedal spindle	Grease
8	Exposed cables	20
9	Telescopic fork	20 or 30
10	Swinging fork pivot	Grease
—	All brake rod joints and pins	20

SECTION A2

RECOMMENDED LUBRICANTS

UNITED KINGDOM

UNIT	MOBIL	B.P.	CASTROL	ESSO	SHELL	REGENT
Engine—Summer —Winter	Mobiloil A Mobiloil Arctic	Energol SAE 30 Energol SAE 20W	Castrol XL Castrolite	Esso Extra Motor Oil 20W/30	Shell X-100 30 Shell X-100 20W	Havoline SAE 30 Havoline SAE 20W
Gearbox	Mobiloil D	Energol SAE 50	Castrol Grand Prix	Esso Extra Motor Oil 50	Shell X-100 50	Havoline SAE 50
Primary Chaincase	Mobiloil Arctic	Energol SAE 20	Castrolite	Esso Extra Motor Oil 20W/30	Shell X-100 20W	Havoline SAE 20W
Telescopic Fork Summer Winter	Mobiloil A Mobiloil Arctic	Energol SAE 30 Energol SAE 20W	Castrol XL Castrolite	Esso Extra Motor Oil 20W/30	Shell X-100 30 Shell X-100 20W	Havoline SAE 30 Havoline SAE 20W
Wheel Bearings Swinging Fork Steering Races	Mobilgrease M.P.	Energrease L2	Castrolease L.M.	Esso Multipurpose Grease H	Shell Retinax A	Marfak Multipurpose 2
Easing Rusted Parts	Mobil Spring Oil	Energol Penetrating Oil	Castrol Penetrating Oil	Esso Penetrating Oil	Shell Donax P	Graphited Penetrating Oil

OVERSEAS

UNIT	MOBIL	B.P.	CASTROL	ESSO	SHELL	CALTEX
Engine—Above 90°F. 32°—90°F. Below 32°F.	Mobiloil AF Mobiloil A Mobiloil Arctic	Energol SAE 40 Energol SAE 30 Energol SAE 20W	Castrol XXL Castrol XL Castrolite	Esso Extra Motor Oil 20W/40 10W/30	Shell X-100 40 Shell X-100 30 Shell X-100 20W	Caltex SAE 40 Caltex SAE 30 Caltex SAE 20W
Gearbox	Mobiloil D	Energol SAE 50	Castrol Grand Prix	Esso Extra Motor Oil 50	Shell X-100 50	Caltex SAE 50
Primary Chaincase	Mobiloil Arctic	Energol SAE 20W	Castrolite	Esso Extra Motor Oil 20W/40	Shell X-100 20W	Caltex SAE 20W
Telescopic Fork Above 90°F. 60°—90°F. Below 60°F.	Mobiloil D Mobiloil A Mobiloil Arctic	Energol SAE 50 Energol SAE 30 Energol SAE 20W	Castrol Grand Prix Castrol XL Castrolite	Esso Extra Motor Oil 20W/40	Shell X-100 50 Shell X-100 30 Shell X-100 20W	Caltex SAE 50 Caltex SAE 30 Caltex SAE 20W
Wheel Bearings, Swinging Fork, Steering Races	Mobilgrease M.P.	Energrease L.2	Castrolease L.M.	Esso Multipurpose Grease H	Shell Retinax A	Marfak Multipurpose 2
Easing Rusted Parts	Mobil Spring Oil	Energol Penetrating Oil	Castrol Penetrating Oil	Esso Penetrating Oil	Shell Donax P	Caltex Penetrating Oil

LUBRICATION SYSTEM

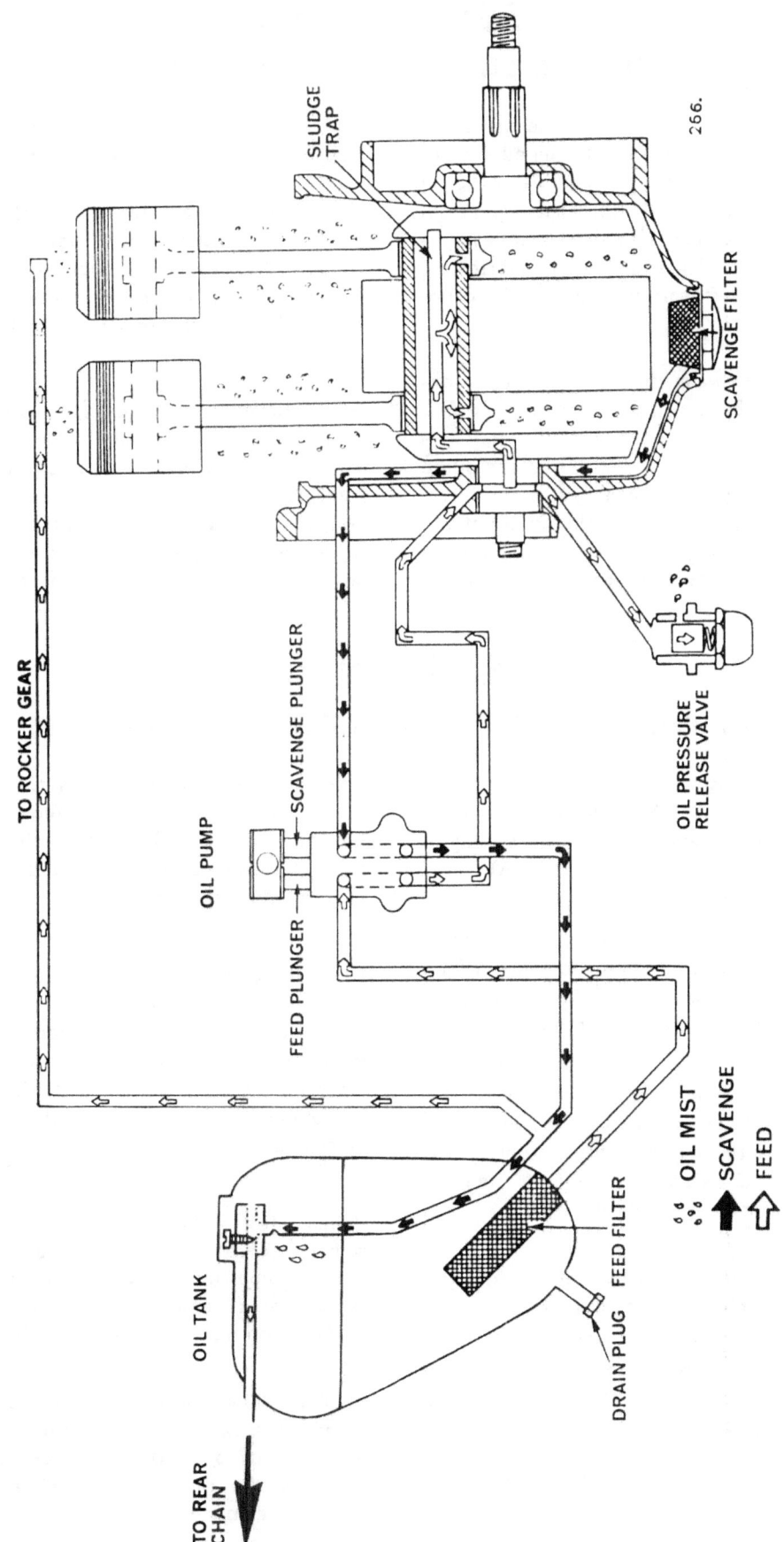

Fig. A2. Engine lubrication diagram

SECTION A3
ENGINE LUBRICATION SYSTEM

The engine lubrication system is of the dry sump type. The oil is fed by gravity from the oil tank to the oil pump; the oil under pressure from the oil pump, is forced through drillings in the right main bearing into the crankshaft whence it escapes through holes to the big end journals, lubricating the cylinder walls, left main bearing and the other internal engine parts.

The oil pressure between the oil pump and crankshaft is controlled by the oil pressure release valve.

After lubricating the engine, oil falls to the sump where it is scavenged through the sump filter, and returned to the oil tank by the action of the oil pump scavenge plunger. The oil pump has been so designed that the scavenge plunger has a greater capacity than the feed plunger; thus ensuring that the sump does not become flooded.

Oil is fed to the valve operating mechanism by means of the rocker oil feed pipe which is connected to the scavenge return pipe at the oil tank. A metering jet in the neck of the oil tank is fully adjustable, and controls the supply of oil to the rear chain.

After travelling through the rocker spindles, the oil is fed into the rocker boxes passing through drillings in the rocker arms onto the push rod end caps, after which it falls by gravity down the push rod cover tubes. The oil then passes through holes drilled in the tappet guide blocks into the sump, where it is subsequently scavenged.

SECTION A4
CHANGING THE ENGINE OIL AND CLEANING THE OIL FILTERS

The oil in new and reconditioned engines should be changed at 250, 500 and 1,000 miles intervals (400, 800 and 1,500 kilometers), during the running-in period and thereafter as stated in Section A1.

It is advisable to drain the oil when the engine is warm when the oil will flow more readily. When changing the oil it is essential that the oil filters are thoroughly cleaned in paraffin (kerosene).

The hexagon headed sump drain plug, which also houses the sump filter, is situated underneath the engine adjacent to the engine bottom mounting lug, as shown in Fig. A3, reference number 4. Remove the plug and allow the oil to drain.

Clean the filter in paraffin (kerosene) and refit the plug but do not forget the joint washer.

The oil tank filter is screwed into the bottom of the oil tank, the oil feed pipe is connected to it by means of a union nut.

Remove the oil tank filler cap, place a drip tray underneath the oil tank and remove the drain plug, or alternatively unscrew the union nut and disconnect the oil feed pipe. Allow the oil to drain for approximately 10 minutes. Unscrew the large hexagon headed oil tank filter and thoroughly clean it in paraffin (kerosene).

It is advisable to flush out the oil tank with a flushing oil (obtainable from most garages), or, if this is not available, paraffin (kerosene). However, if paraffin (kerosene) is used, ensure that all traces are removed from the inside of the oil tank prior to refilling with oil. (For the correct grade of oil see Section A2).

When refitting the oil tank filter do not forget to refit the fibre washer; and when connecting the oil feed pipe union nut, care should be taken to avoid overtightening as this may result in failure of the union nut. Replace the drain plug.

NOTE: The level in the oil tank should be $1\frac{1}{2}$ in. (4 cm.) below the filler cap. Further addition of oil will cause excessive venting through the oil tank breather pipe due to lack of air space.

LUBRICATION SYSTEM

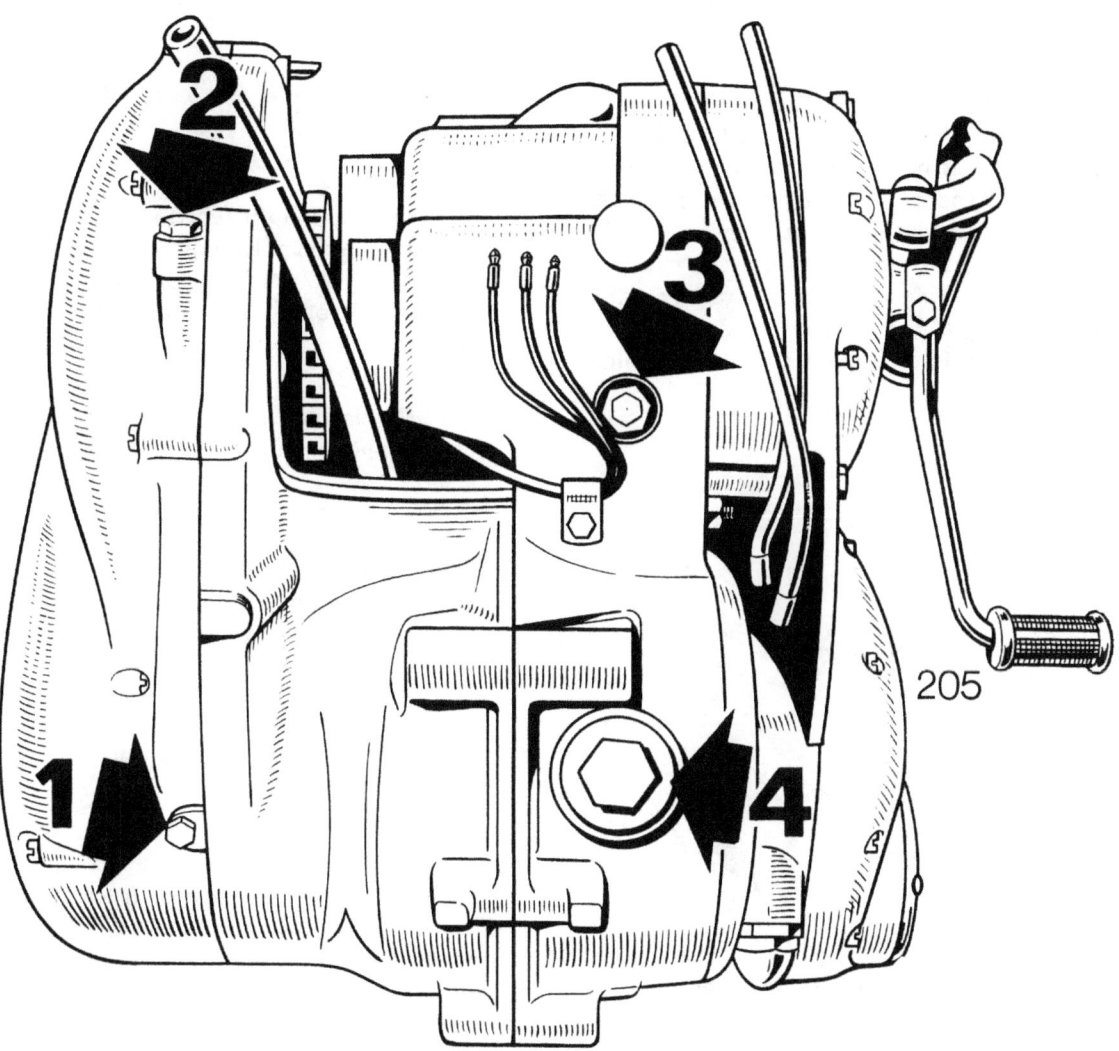

Fig. A3. Underside view of engine/gearbox unit indicating location of drain and level plugs

No. 1 Primary chaincase level plug
    2 Primary chaincase drain plug and chain tensioner adjustment
    3 Gearbox drain and level plug
    4 Sump drain and filter plug

SECTION A5

OIL PRESSURE

The oil pressure is controlled by means of the release valve situated at the front of the engine at the right hand side adjacent to the timing cover.

When the engine is stationary there will be nil oil pressure. When the engine is started from cold, pressure may be as high as 80 lb. sq./in. reducing when hot to a normal running figure of 65/80 lb./sq. in. At a fast idle when hot, pressure should be 20/25 lb./sq. in. Pressure can only be checked with an oil gauge connected to an adaptor replacing the blanking plug at the front of the timing cover (see Fig. A4). This feature appears only after engine number H.49833.

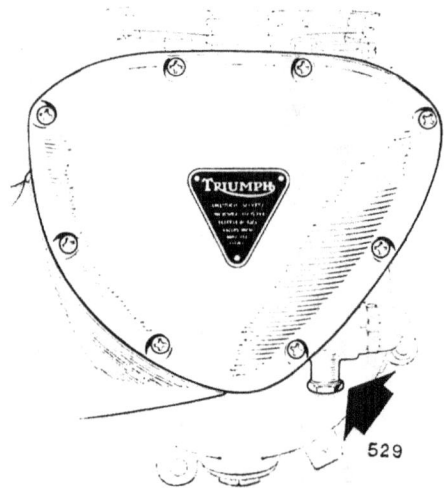

Fig. A4. Showing pressure check point

If satisfactory readings are not obtained check the following:—

(1) That the oil pressure release valve is clean and that the piston has the correct working clearance in the valve body (see GENERAL DATA).

(2) That the oil tank level is not below minimum and that oil is being returned to the tank.

(3) That the sump filter and oil tank filter are clean and not blocked.

(4) That the oil pump is functioning properly and that there is a supply of oil to the pump. Refer to Sections A7 and A8 for checking the oil pump and oil pipes with junction block respectively.

(5) That the drillings in the crankcase connecting the oil pipe junction block to the oil pump are clear.

(6) That the timing side journal of the crankshaft and the plain timing side main bearing are not badly worn resulting in the escape of oil and a drop in pressure.

(7) That the big ends are not badly worn (see GENERAL DATA).

Excessive periods of slow running (such as in heavy traffic), or unneccessary use of the air slide during sold starting can cause dilution in the oil tank, and an overall drop in lubricating pressure due to the lower viscosity of the diluted oil.

Most lubrication and oil pressure troubles can be avoided by regular attention to the recommended oil changes.

LUBRICATION SYSTEM

SECTION A6

STRIPPING AND REASSEMBLING THE OIL PRESSURE RELEASE VALVE

The oil pressure is controlled by means of the release valve situated at the front of the engine at the right side adjacent to the timing cover; it is very reliable and should require no maintenance other than cleaning.

The oil pressure is governed by the spring which is situated within the release valve body.

When dismantling or reassembling the oil pressure release valve do not hold the valve body in a vice as this may cause distortion and result in serious damage.

To remove the complete oil pressure release valve unit from the crankcase, unscrew the hexagonal nut adjacent to the crankcase surface. When removed, the cap can then be unscrewed from the body thus releasing the spring and piston.

Reassembly is carried out in exactly the reverse manner described above, not forgetting to use two new fibre washers.

Thoroughly wash the parts in paraffin (kerosene) and inspect for wear. The piston should be checked for possible scoring and the valve body filter for possible blockage or damage. Check to see that the spring length compares with the figure given in GENERAL DATA.

Fig. A5. Oil pressure release valve

SECTION A7

STRIPPING AND REASSEMBLING THE OIL PUMP

The oil pump is situated inside the timing cover and is driven by an eccentric peg on the nut fitted to the end of the inlet camshaft. The only part likely to show wear after considerable mileage is the oil pump drive block slider, which should be replaced to maintain full pumping efficiency. The plungers and pump body being constantly immersed in oil, wear is negligible.

For removal of the timing cover see Section B26.

The oil pump is held in its position by two conical-nuts and lock washers. When these are removed the oil pump can then be withdrawn from the mounting studs. The scavenge and feed plungers should be removed and the two square caps on the end of the oil pump unscrewed. This will release the springs and balls.

All parts should be thoroughly cleaned in paraffin (kerosene).

LUBRICATION SYSTEM

The plungers should be inspected for scoring, and for wear by measuring their diameters and comparing them with those given in GENERAL DATA.

The springs should be checked for compressive strength by measuring their lengths. Compare the actual lengths with those given in GENERAL DATA.

When reassembling the oil pump all parts should be well lubricated and the oil pump finally checked for efficiency by the following means:—

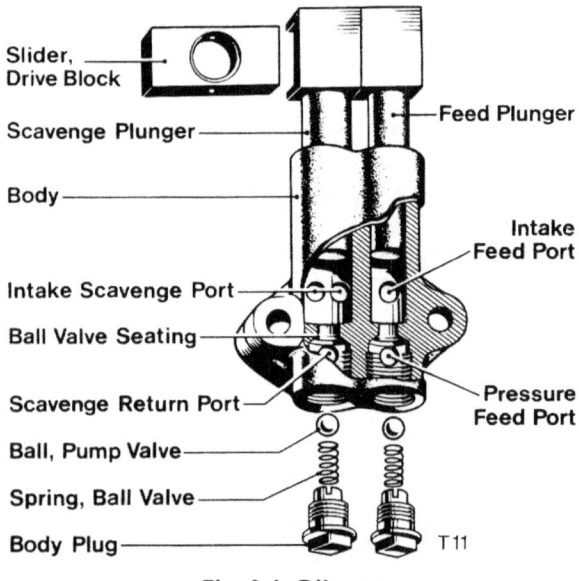

Fig. A.6 Oil pump

The balls themselves should be inspected for pitting and any other irregularities.

Place a small amount of oil in both bores (approximately 1 c.c.) and press the plungers until oil is forced through both outlet ports (these are the two holes nearest the square caps) (see Fig. A6). Place the thumb over the intake ports (the holes nearest the plunger top) and withdraw the plungers slightly. If the oil level falls in either outlet port then the ball valve is not seating properly and the square caps should be removed and the cleaning process repeated. On machines fitted with brass body oil pumps the ball valves can be tapped lightly, but sharply into their seating to ensure an efficient and adequate seal.

The aluminium drive block slider which fits on the eccentric peg on the inlet camshaft nut should be checked for wear on both the bore and in the plunger cross head.

When refitting the oil pump a new gasket should be used and always remember that the cones of the conical nut and washers fit into the countersunk holes in the oil pump body.

When replacing the timing cover care should be taken that the junction surfaces are clean prior to application of the fresh coat of jointing compound.

SECTION A8

REMOVING AND REPLACING THE OIL PIPE JUNCTION BLOCK

Drain the oil from the gearbox by removing the oil drain plug situated underneath the gearbox as shown in Fig. A3 reference No. 3.

Remove the right footrest, disconnect the clutch cable and withdraw the gearbox outer cover as shown in Section D1.

Place a drip tray underneath the oil tank and remove the drain plug, or alternatively, remove the nut securing the oil pipe junction block to the crankcase and allow the oil tank to drain for approximately 10 minutes.

Disconnect the clips and rubber pipes from the oil tank, remove the junction block and thoroughly clean it in paraffin (kerosene).

Check the pipes for cuts and abrasions and that the rubber connections are a good tight fit on the junction block pipes. If there is any doubt about the reliability of the rubber connectors, they should be renewed. Do not forget to retighten the oil pipe clips.

Reassembly is the reversal of the above instructions but remember to fit a new gasket between the junction block and the crankcase. Care should be taken when reassembling the gasket and junction block over the crankcase dowel.

When replacing the rubber connection tubes, care must be exercised to prevent chafing the inside of the rubber connections. Failure to observe this may result in fragments of rubber entering the oil system and causing blockage. Finally reassemble the outer gearbox cover, refit the oil tank drain plug and refill with the recommended grade of oil (see Section A2).

LUBRICATION SYSTEM

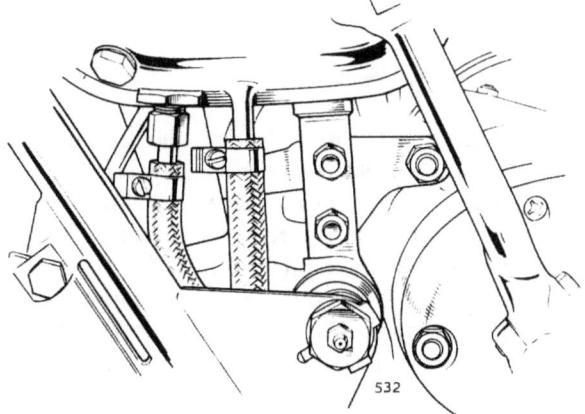

Fig. A7. Oil pipe securing clips

Replace the screwed clips and firmly clamp them in position.

SECTION A9

REMOVING AND REPLACING THE ROCKER OIL FEED PIPE

To disconnect the rocker oil feed pipe for removal, the two domed nuts on top of the inlet and exhaust rocker boxes should be removed from the oil feed bolts, and the banjos withdrawn.

Disconnect the rocker oil feed pipe from the oil tank. To free the rocker oil feed pipe from the frame it may be necessary to disconnect several frame clips from underneath the fuel tank. Care should be taken that the pipe is not bent excessively as this might ultimately result in a fracture. When removed, the rocker oil feed pipe should be thoroughly cleaned in paraffin (kerosene) and checked for blockage by sealing the first banjo with the thumb and the first finger, whilst blowing through the other. Repeat this procedure for the other banjo.

When refitting the rocker oil feed pipe it is advisable to use new copper washers, but if the old ones are annealed they should give an effective oil seal. Annealing is achieved by heating to cherry red heat and plunging in water. Any scale that is formed on the washers should be removed prior to refitting them.

SECTION A10

CONTACT BREAKER LUBRICATION

The contact breaker is situated in the timing cover and it is imperative that no oil from the engine lubrication system gets into the contact breaker chamber. For this purpose there is an oil seal at the back of the contact breaker unit pressed into the timing cover. However, slight lubrication of the cam and also advance unit spindles is necessary. The cam is lubricated by means of an oil soaked wick which should be fed with a few drops of oil (SAE 20 or SAE 30) every 5,000 miles (8,000 kms).

LUBRICATION SYSTEM

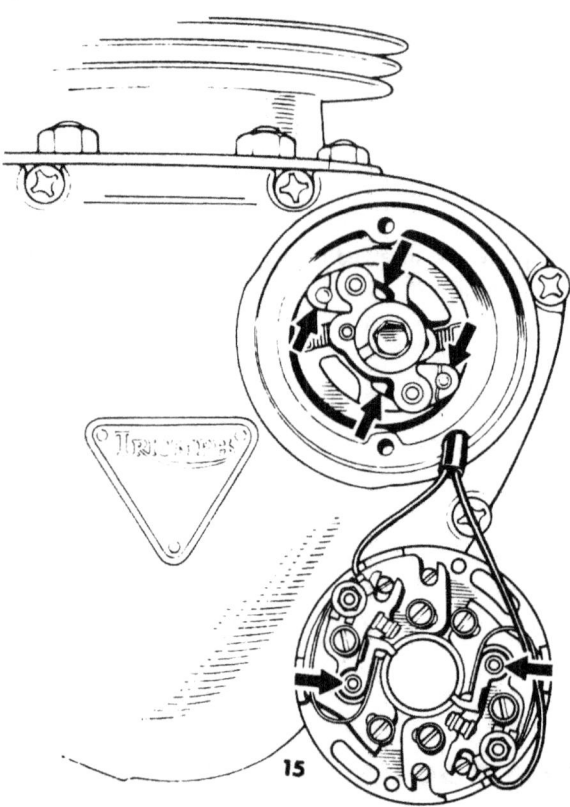

Fig. A8. Contact breaker mechanism lubrication points

To lubricate the auto advance mechanism it is necessary to withdraw the mounting plate. Mark the C.B. plate and housing so that it can be subsequently replaced in exactly the same location, then unscrew the two hexagonal pillar bolts. When the mounting plate is removed, the mechanism should be slightly oiled (see arrows shown in Fig. A8) at the same interval that is given above for the cam wick.

Finally, replace the mounting plate and reset the ignition timing. If the setting has been disturbed, the correct procedure for accurate ignition timing is given Sections B31 and B32.

SECTION A11

GEARBOX LUBRICATION

The gearbox is lubricated by means of an oil bath. Oil is splash fed to all gearbox components including the enclosed gearchange and kickstart mechanisms. The oil in the gearbox should be drained and the gearbox flushed out after the initial 500 mile (800 kms) running-in period. Theafter, the oil should be changed as stated in Section A1.

The oil can be drained from the gearbox by means of the oil drain plug located underneath the gearbox (see Fig. A3 reference No. 3). It is best to drain the oil whilst the engine is warm as the oil will flow more readily.

The gearbox oil filler plug is situated on top of the gearbox adjacent to the clutch cable abutment. When replenishing the oil, the oil drain plug should be replaced omitting the smaller oil level plug which screws into it. Oil should be poured into the gearbox until it is seen to drip out through the oil level plug hole (see Fig. A9), see Section A2 for recommended oil.

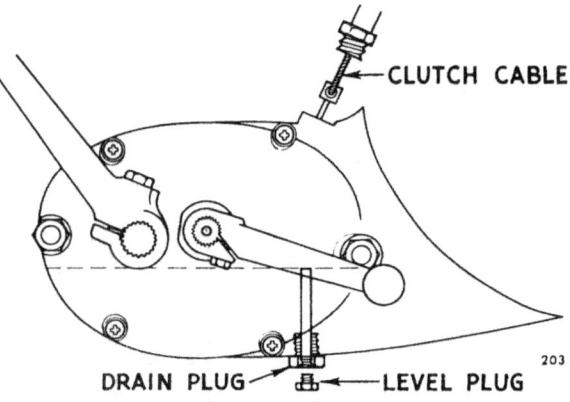

Fig. A9. Gearbox drain and level plugs

LUBRICATION SYSTEM

SECTION A12

PRIMARY CHAINCASE LUBRICATION

The primary chaincase is lubricated by means of an oil bath. To drain the oil first remove the oil drain plug from the bottom of the chaincase adjacent to the left footrest. (See Fig. A3 reference No. 2). This plug also gives access to the chain tensioner. To remove the plug on the earlier models it may be necessary to loosen the left footrest. This can be done by slackening off the footrest mounting bolt and giving the footrest a sharp tap in a downwards direction to release it from its locking taper. When the plug is removed allow the oil to drain for approximately 10 minutes and replace the plug, with the fibre washer.

So that the correct amount of oil can be put into the primary chaincase there is an oil level plug situated at the front underside of the chaincase. (See Fig. A3, reference No. 1). Alternatively, the correct level can be achieved by using a measure of ½ pint (300 cc.) capacity. Use SAE 20 Oil.

Fresh oil should be added through the plug adjacent to the left hand rear of the cylinder barrel base.

The oil in the primary chaincase should be changed as stated in Section A1.

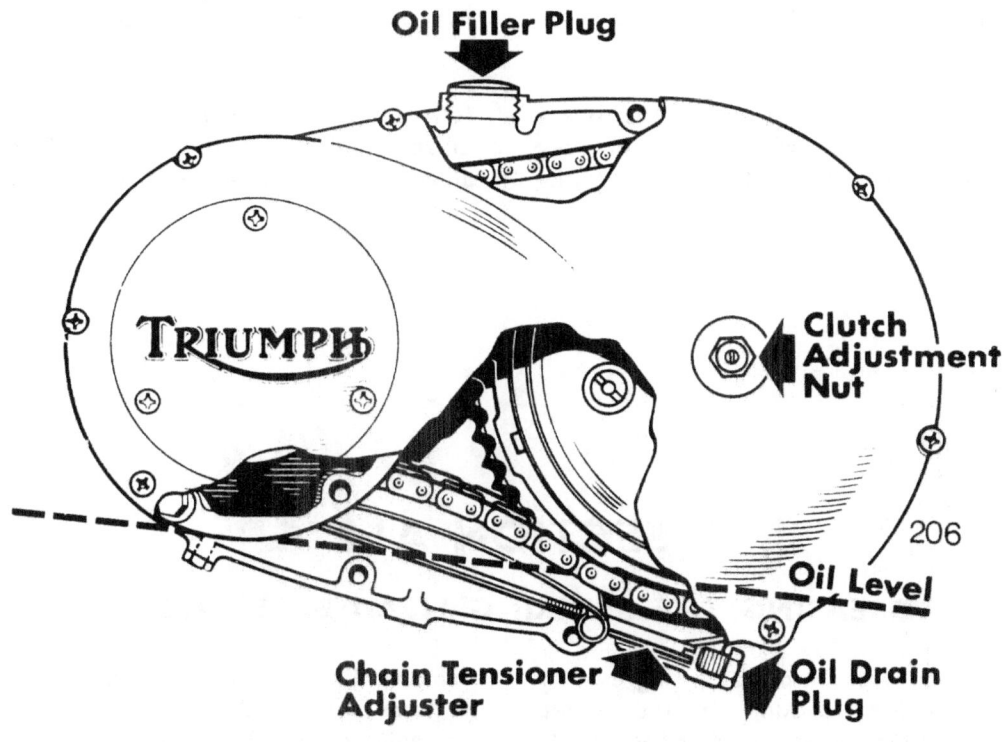

Fig. A10. Section through the primary chaincase

SECTION A13

REAR CHAIN LUBRICATION AND MAINTENANCE

The rear chain is automatically lubricated by means of an adjustable metering jet feed from the engine return oil line, the required feed being obtained by adjustment of the metering screw in the oil tank filler cap neck.

In addition the chain should be treated in the following way every 1,000 miles (1,500 kms):—

Disconnect the connecting link and remove the chain. If available, connect an old chain to the end of the chain being removed and draw it onto the gearbox sprocket until the chain to be cleaned is clear of the machine and can be disconnected.

Replace by connecting to the old chain, which is then used to pull the cleaned and lubricated original over the gearbox sprocket.

Remove all deposits of road dust etc., by means of a wire brush. Clean thoroughly in paraffin (kerosene) and allow to drain.

Inspect the chain for excessive wear of the rollers and pivot pins and check that the elongation does not exceed $1\frac{1}{2}\%$. To do this, first scribe two marks on a flat table exactly 12 ins. (30·5) apart, place the chain opposite the two marks. When the chain is compressed to its minimum free length the marks should coincide with two pivot pins 20 links apart. When the chain is stretched to its maximum free length, the extension should not exceed $\frac{1}{4}$ in. (6.25 mms). If it is required to remove a faulty link, or shorten the chain, reference should be made to Section C11.

To lubricate the chain, immerse it in melted grease (melt over a low flame, or, more safely over a pan of boiling water) and allow it to remain in the grease for approximately 15 minutes, moving the chain occasionally to ensure penetration of the grease into the chain bearings. Allow the grease to cool, remove the chain from the bath and wipe off the surplus grease.

The chain is now ready for refitting to the machine.

NOTE: the connecting link retaining clip must be fitted with the nose end facing in the direction of the motion of the chain.

SECTION A14

GREASING THE STEERING HEAD BALL RACES

The steering head races are packed with grease on assembly and require repacking with the correct grade of grease at the intervals stated in Section A1.

Removal and replacement of the ball bearings is comprehensively covered in the Front Fork Section.

When the balls are removed they should be cleaned in paraffin (kerosene), also, the cups fitted to the frame head lug and the cones fitted to the middle lug stem should be cleaned thoroughly by means of a paraffin (kerosene) soaked rag, then inspected for wear, cracking or pitting.

The fresh supply of grease should be utilised to hold the balls in position in the cups whilst the fork is assembled.

LUBRICATION SYSTEM

SECTION A15

WHEEL BEARING LUBRICATION

The wheel bearings are packed with grease on assembly but require repacking with the correct grade of grease at the intervals stated in Section A1.

The bearings on both the front and rear wheels should be removed, cleaned in paraffin (kerosene) and assembled with the hubs well packed with the correct grade of grease. For details concerning the grade of grease to be used (which is the same for both wheels) see Section A2.

Removing and replacing the bearings for the front and rear wheels is comprehensively covered in Section F8.

SECTION A16

TELESCOPIC FORK LUBRICATION

The oil contained in the front fork has the dual purpose of lubricating the stanchion bearing bushes and also acting as the suspension damping medium. Therefore it is imperative that the fork legs have an equal amount of oil in them.

Oil leakage at the junction between the stanchion and bottom fork leg is prevented by means of an oil seal and an 'O' ring. If there is excessive oil leakage at this junction it may be necessary to renew the oil seal (see Section G7), but before undertaking this work, the forks should be checked to ensure that there is the correct amount of oil in each of the fork legs. The correct amount of oil for each fork leg is ½ pint (190 cc.).

The oil seal holders should be checked to ensure that they are screwed sufficiently tightly on to the bottom members to compress the 'O' rings otherwise oil leakage may occur.

Particular attention should be given to the oil change periods. The forks should be drained and refilled with the correct summer or winter grade of oil every spring and autumn if the mileage covered is less than the distance in Section A1.

To drain the oil from the fork legs remove the two small hexagonal drain plugs adjacent to the left and right ends of the front wheel spindle.

Oil can be expelled at a greater rate by compressing the fork two or three times.

To refill the fork legs on machines fitted with Sports headlamp, the fork hexagonal cap nuts must be unscrewed and withdrawn, and the correct amount of oil poured into each fork leg.

Access to the cap nuts can be gained by removing the nacelle top cover (if fitted) and handlebar as described in Section G1 and G2 respectively. Then, by means of spanner D220, the hexagonal cap nuts (1½ ins. across the flats) can be unscrewed and withdrawn. The correct amount of oil should then be poured into each fork leg.

To refill the fork legs on earlier machines incorporating nacelle equipment first replace the drain plugs complete with fibre washers then slacken the headlamp securing screw adjacent to the speedometer and withdraw the headlamp and rim assembly.

Remove the two small hexagonal filler plugs from the stanchions (these are located approximately 3 ins. from the top lug and should be facing forward towards the headlamp aperture) and pump the advised amount of oil into each fork leg by means of a pressure can or gun. For the recommended grade of oil see Section A2.

When refitting the filler plugs do not forget the fibre washers.

If a pressure can or gun is not available the method recommended for filling the fork legs with oil is similar to that of the sports models with separate headlamp, i.e. removing the cap nuts.

SECTION A17

LUBRICATION NIPPLES

Both the brake operating cams and the swinging fork pivot bearings should be lubricated by means of the lubrication nipples.

The brake cams have integral lubrication nipples. Care should be taken that the surface of the nipple is not damaged. Slight distortion may be removed with a fine grade file.

The front and rear wheel brake cam and spindle bearing surfaces should be sparingly lubricated with the correct grade of grease (Section A2). This can be done by giving the lubrication nipples on the ends of the cams one stroke each from a grease gun. However, if the grease does not penetrate, the brake cams should be removed and cleaned thoroughly in paraffin (kerosene). Cam bearing surfaces should then be greased on reassembly.

SWINGING FORK PIVOT

The greasing nipple is situated at the right hand end of the swinging fork spindle and should be given several strokes with a high pressure grease gun until the grease is extruded through each of the pivot bearings.

If the grease does not penetrate then the pivot must be removed to ensure adequate lubrication. Removal of the swinging fork is detailed in Sections E10 and E11. Prior to engine number H.49833 the swinging fork grease nipple is located underneath the right hand side swinging fork lug.

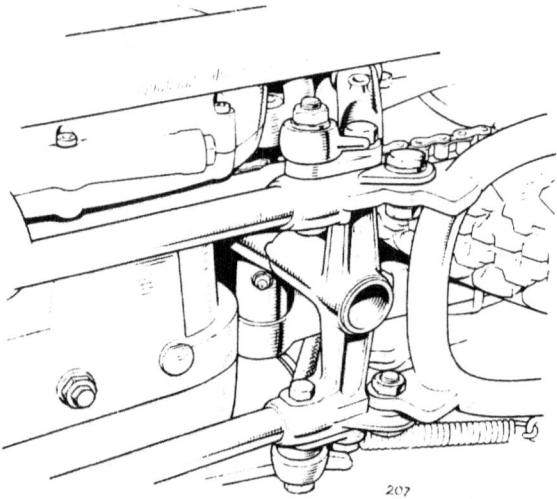

Fig. A11. Swinging fork pivot lubrication nipple before H.49833 (underside view of frame)

SECTION A18

LUBRICATING THE CONTROL CABLES

The control cables can be periodically lubricated at the exposed joint with a thin grade of oil (see Section A2).

A more thorough method of lubrication is that of feeding oil into one end of the cable by means of a reservoir. For this, the cable can be either disconnected at the handlebar end only, or completely removed.

The disconnected end of the cable should be threaded through a thin rubber stopper and the stopper pressed into a suitable narrow neck can with a hole in its base. If the can is then inverted and the lubricating oil poured into it through the hole, the oil will trickle down between the outer and inner cables. It is best to leave the cable in this position overnight to ensure adequate lubrication.

LUBRICATION SYSTEM

SECTION A19

SPEEDOMETER CABLE LUBRICATION

The speedometer cable should be lubricated by means of grease (see Section A2 for correct grade).

It is not necessary to completely remove the cable, but only to disconnect it from the speedometer and withdraw the inner cable. To do this on nacelle models first remove the headlamp unit by slackening the securing screw adjacent to the speedometer on the nacelle. Unscrew the union nut at the base of the speedometer, withdraw the inner cable and clean it in paraffin (kerosene). Smear the surface with grease, except for 6 ins. (15 cm.) nearest to the speedometer head.

SECTION A20

BRAKE PEDAL SPINDLE LUBRICATION

The brake pedal spindle is bolted to a lug on the downtube of the sub frame. The spindle should be covered with a fresh supply of grease occasionally otherwise corrosion and inefficient operation may result.

To gain access to the spindle, slacken off the rear brake rod adjustment, unscrew the brake pedal retaining nut and withdraw the pedal.

Remove any rust from the spindle with fine emery. Clean the bore of the pedal and smear the spindle with grease (see Section A2) prior to refitting.

Do not forget to replace the spring and plain washer between the retaining nut and brake pedal.

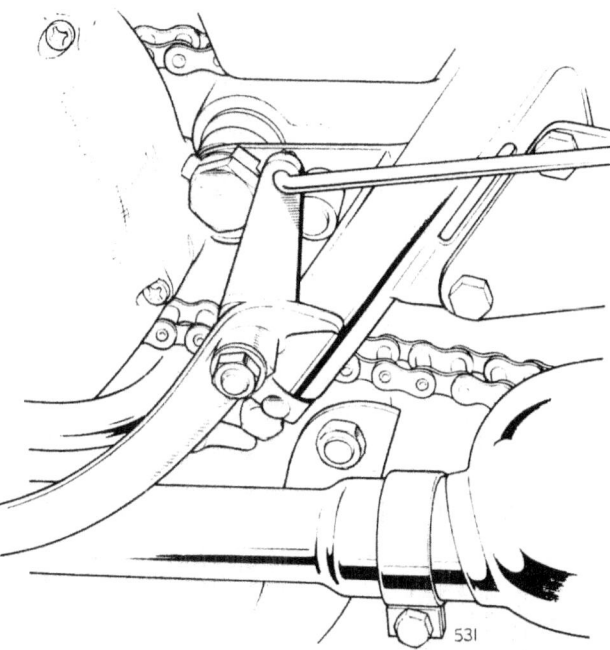

Fig. A12. Brake pedal spindle lubrication

NOTES

SECTION AA

LUBRICATION SYSTEM

	Section
RECOMMENDED LUBRICANTS	AA2
CHANGING THE OIL AND CLEANING THE FILTERS	AA4
OIL PRESSURE	AA5
CONTACT BREAKER LUBRICATION	AA10B
LUBRICATING CONTROL CABLES	AA18

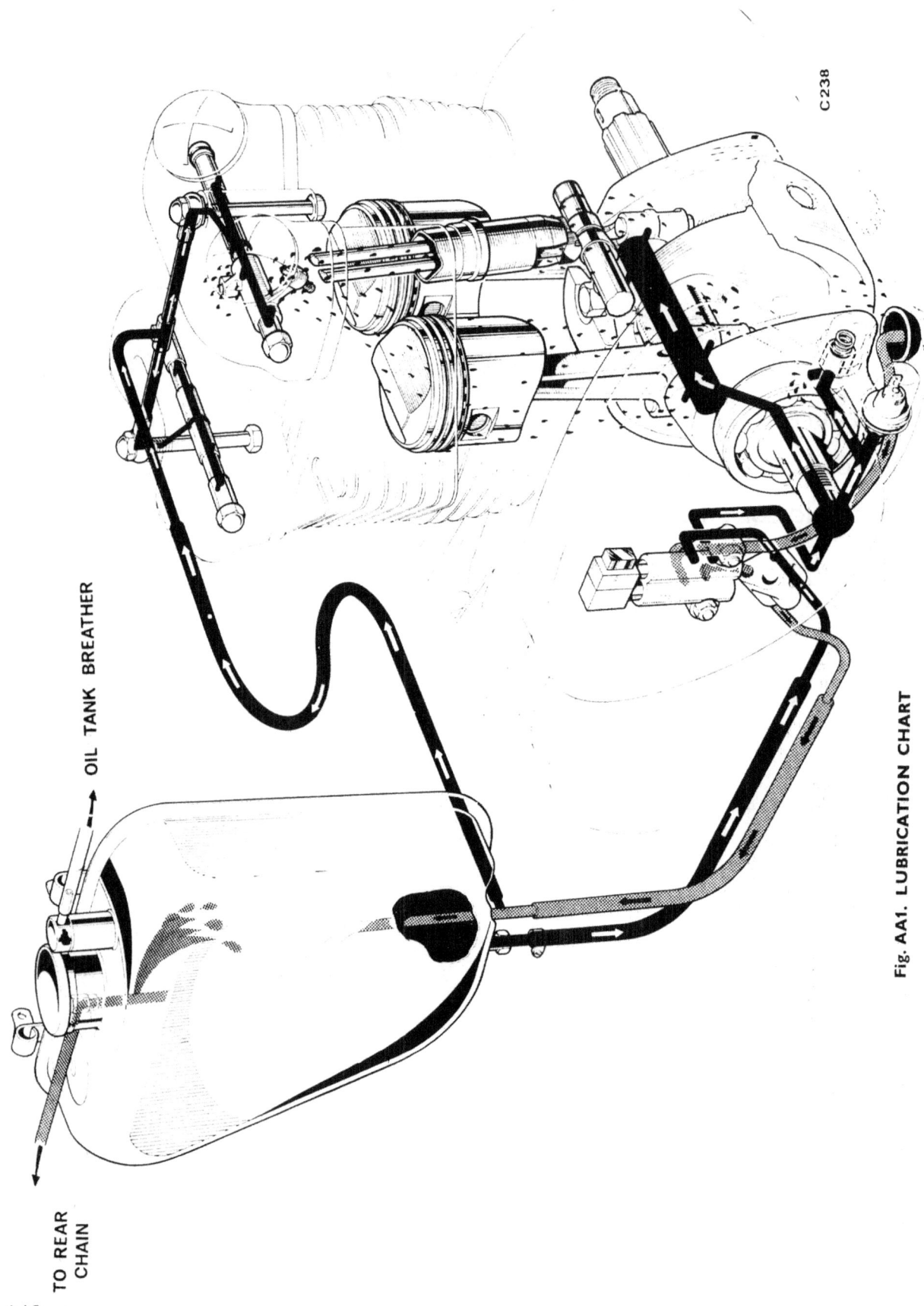

Fig. AA1. LUBRICATION CHART

ENGINE LUBRICATION SYSTEM

The engine lubrication system is of the dry sump type. The oil is fed by gravity from the oil tank to the oil pump, and the oil under pressure from the pump is forced along a drilling in the crankshaft to the big-end bearings where it escapes and lubricates the cylinder walls, main bearings and other internal engine parts.

The oil pressure between the oil pump and crankshaft is controlled by means of the oil pressure release valve. After lubricating the engine, oil falls to the sump, where it is scavenged through the sump filter, and returned to the oil tank by the action of the oil pump scavenge plunger. The oil pump is designed so as to scavenge a greater quantity of oil than is supplied by the feed plunger; thus ensuring that the crankcase does not become flooded.

Oil is supplied to the valve operating mechanism by means of a feed pipe which is connected to the scavenge pipe just below the oil tank. After travelling through the rocker spindles, the oil is diverted and is fed along the outsides of the spindles. When it reaches a notch on each rocker arm, it is ejected towards the push rods and ball pins, and then falls by gravity through the push rod cover tubes. Holes are provided in the tappet guide blocks to allow this oil to drain into the sump, from where it is subsequently scavenged.

A rear chain oiling device is incorporated in the neck of the oil tank, consisting of an adjustable metering jet.

SECTION AA2
RECOMMENDED LUBRICANTS

GEARBOX LUBRICATION

UNITED KINGDOM

Mobil	B.P.	Castrol	Esso	Shell	Texaco
Mobilube GX90	B.P. Gear Oil E.P.90	Castrol Hypoy 90 E.P.	Esso Gear Oil GP90/140	Shell Spirax 90 E.P.	Multigear E.P. 90

OVERSEAS

Mobil	B.P.	Castrol	Esso	Shell	Texaco
Mobilube GX90	B.P. Gear Oil E.P.90	Castrol Hypoy 90 E.P.	Esso Gear Oil G.P.90/140	Shell Spirax 90 E.P.	Multigear E.P. 90

LUBRICATION SYSTEM

SECTION AA4
CHANGING THE OIL AND CLEANING THE FILTERS

All machines produced after engine number H65573 incorporate an oil tank dip-stick. This is attached to the filler cap. The markings shown are "FULL" and "ADD ONE PINT". It is essential that the maximum level is not exceeded as excessive venting will occur through the oil tank breather due to a lack of air space. The oil tank capacity when correctly filled is 5½ pints. The dipstick is shown in Fig. AA2.

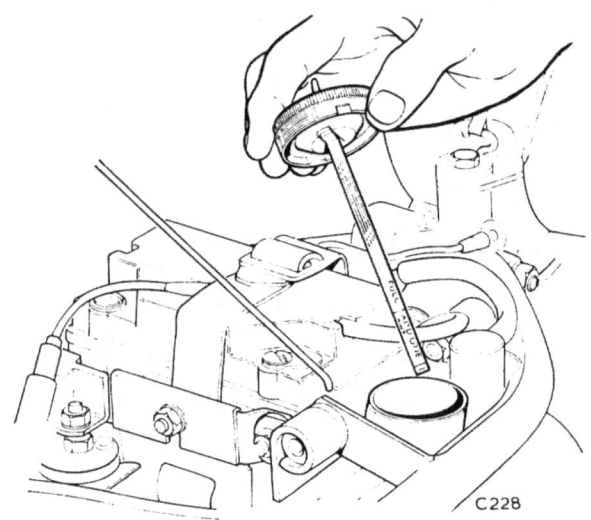

Fig. AA2. Oil tank dip stick

SECTION AA5
OIL PRESSURE

The oil pressure is controlled by means of the release valve which is situated at the front of the engine, adjacent to the timing cover.

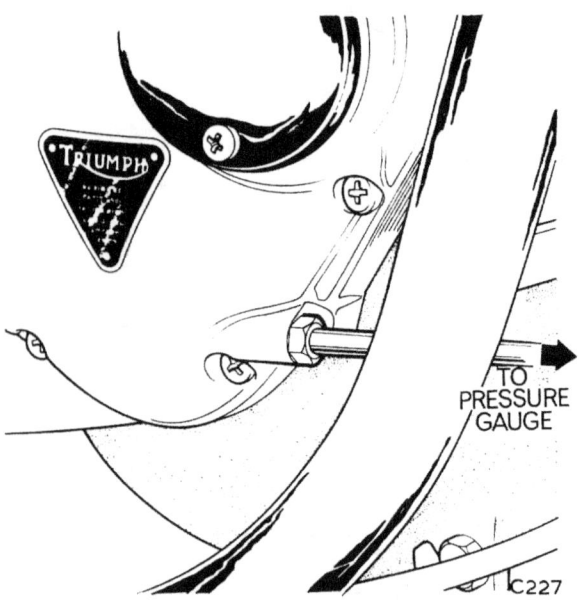

Fig. AA3. Oil pressure gauge take-off

When the engine is stationary there will be no oil pressure. When the engine is started from cold the pressure may be as high as 80 lb/sq. in., reducing when hot to the normal running figure of 65/80 lb/sq. in. At a fast idle when hot, pressure should be 20/25 lb/sq. in. The pressure can only be checked by fitting an oil pressure gauge in place of the oil pressure light switch (See Fig. AA3).

If satisfactory readings are not obtained, check the following:—

(1) That the release valve is clean and that the piston has the correct working clearances in the body. (Refer to General Data).

(2) That the oil level in the tank is between the two lines on the dipstick.

(3) That the sump filter and oil tank filter are clean and not blocked.

(4) That the oil pump is functioning correctly, and that there is a supply of oil to the pump. Refer to Section A7 and A8 for checking the oil pump and oil pipes with junction block.

LUBRICATION SYSTEM

(5) That the drillings in the crankcase connecting the oil pipe junction block to the oil pump are clear.

(6) That the big-ends are not badly worn. (See General Data).

Excessive periods of slow running (such as in heavy traffic), or unnecessary use of the air slide during starting can cause dilution in the oil tank, and an overall drop in oil pressure due to the lower viscosity of the diluted oil.

Most lubrication and oil pressure problems can be avoided by regular attention to oil changes.

SECTION AA10B
CONTACT BREAKER LUBRICATION

After engine number H65573, the spindle of the automatic advance and retard mechanism is pre-lubricated. A process is used whereby the lubricating substance is baked onto the spindle. If any form of wet lubricant is brought into contact with the pre-lubricated spindle, a glutinous paste will be formed, which will cause the spindle to seize. However, it is still necessary to lubricate the four pivots (as shown in figure A8) with a few drops of clean engine oil.

Both felt cam lubricating wicks are impregnated with Shell Retinax "A" grease on assembly, and should have one or two drops of clean engine oil applied at intervals of 2,000 miles (3,200 kms).

SECTION AA18
LUBRICATING THE CONTROL CABLES

After engine number H65573 a lubrication nipple is incorporated in the clutch cable. This nipple is situated at the forward end of the petrol tank, and with the aid of a pressure feed oil can, light engine oil should be pumped into the cable until it is seen to escape at the clutch lever. (See Fig. AA4).

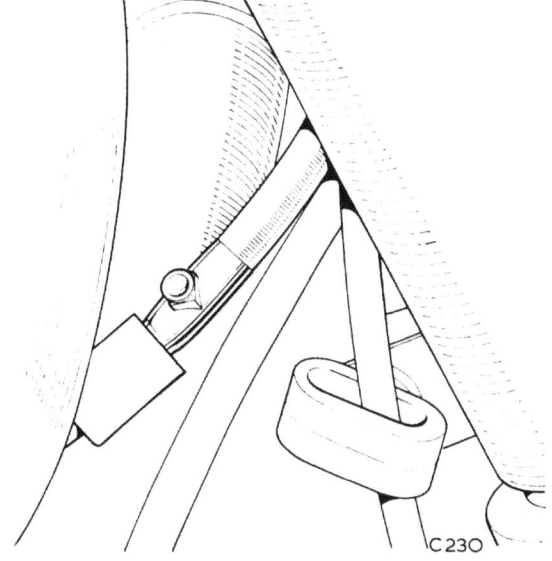

Fig. AA4. Clutch cable lubrication nipple

NOTES

SECTION B

ENGINE

DESCRIPTION	Section
REMOVING AND REPLACING THE ENGINE UNIT	B1
REMOVING AND REPLACING THE ROCKER BOXES	B2
INSPECTING THE PUSH RODS	B3
STRIPPING AND REASSEMBLING THE ROCKER BOXES	B4
ADJUSTING THE VALVE ROCKER CLEARANCES	B5
REMOVING AND REPLACING THE AIR CLEANER	B6
CARBURETTER—DESCRIPTION	B7
TWIN CARBURETTER ARRANGEMENT	B8
REMOVING AND REPLACING THE CARBURETTER (SINGLE AND TWIN)	B9
STRIPPING AND REASSEMBLING THE CARBURETTER	B10
INSPECTING THE CARBURETTER COMPONENTS	B11
CARBURETTER ADJUSTMENTS	B12
REMOVING AND REFITTING THE CYLINDER HEAD ASSEMBLY	B13
REMOVING AND REPLACING THE VALVES	B14
RENEWING THE VALVE GUIDES	B15
DECARBONISING	B16
RE-SEATING THE VALVES	B17
REMOVING AND REPLACING THE CYLINDER BLOCK AND TAPPETS	B18
INSPECTING THE TAPPETS AND GUIDE BLOCKS	B19
RENEWING THE TAPPET GUIDE BLOCKS	B20
REMOVING AND REFITTING THE PISTONS	B21
REMOVING AND REPLACING THE PISTON RINGS	B22
INSPECTING THE PISTONS AND CYLINDER BORES	B23
TABLE OF SUITABLE REBORE SIZES	B24
RENEWING THE SMALL END BUSHES	B25
REMOVING AND REPLACING THE CONTACT BREAKER	B26
REMOVING AND REPLACING THE TIMING COVER	B27
REMOVING AND REPLACING THE OIL PUMP	B28
EXTRACTING AND REFITTING THE VALVE TIMING PINIONS	B29
VALVE TIMING	B30
IGNITION TIMING—T.D.C. LOCATION, USING STROBOSCOPE	B31
STATIC IGNITION TIMING	B32
REMOVING AND REPLACING THE CAMSHAFTS ONLY	B33
DISMANTLING AND REASSEMBLING THE CRANKCASE ASSEMBLY	B34
STRIPPING AND REASSEMBLING THE CRANKSHAFT ASSEMBLY	B35
REFITTING THE CONNECTING RODS	B36
INSPECTING THE CRANKCASE COMPONENTS	B37
RENEWING THE MAIN BEARINGS	B38
RENEWING THE CAMSHAFT BUSHES	B39

ENGINE

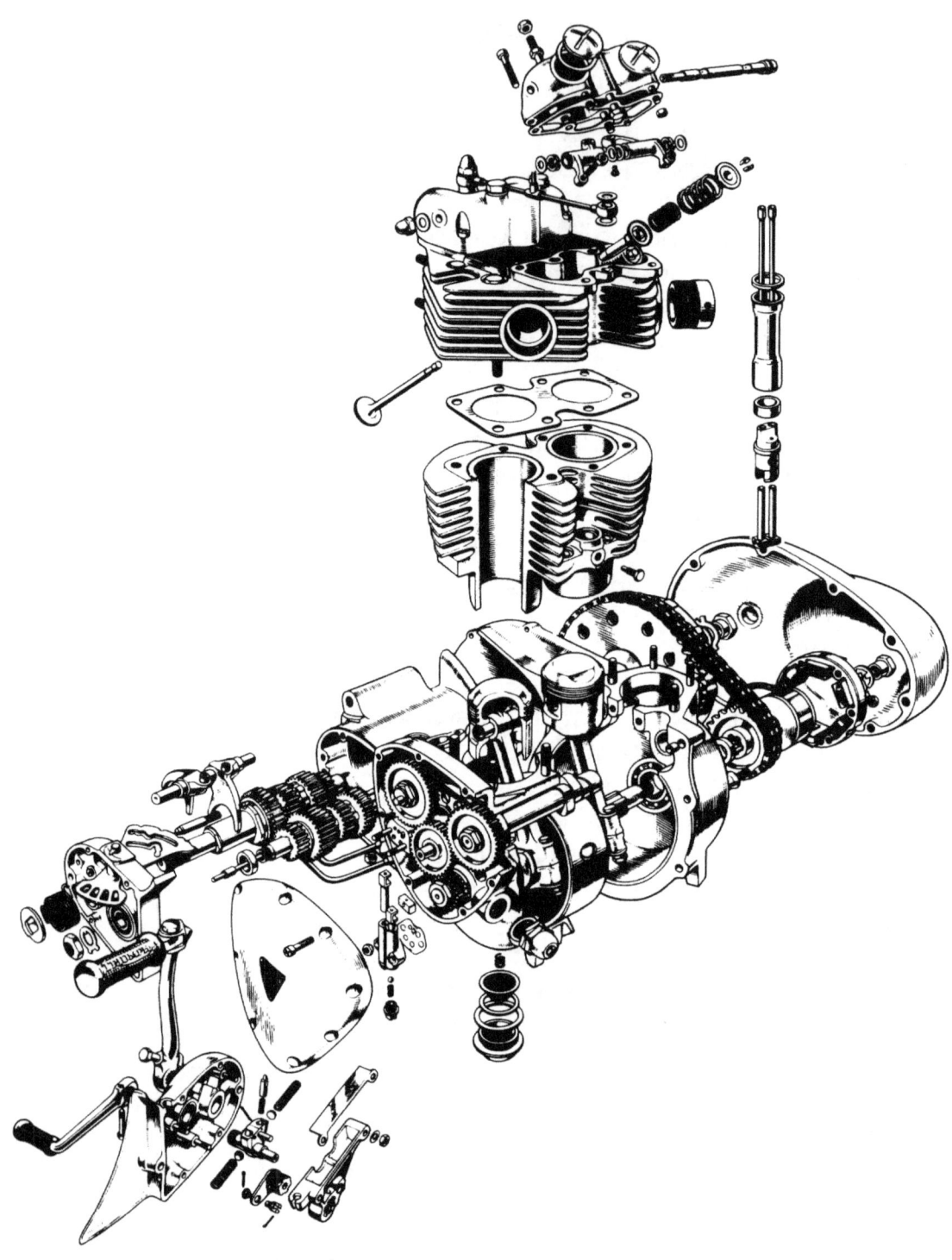

Fig. B1. Exploded view of the engine/gearbox unit

ENGINE

DESCRIPTION

The engine is of unit construction having two aluminium alloy mating crankcase halves, the gearbox housing being an integral part of the right half-crankcase and the primary chain case an integral part of the left half-crankcase.

The aluminium alloy cylinder head has cast in Austenitic valve seat inserts, and houses the overhead valves, which are operated by rocker arms housed in detachable alloy rocker boxes. Four aluminium alloy push rods operate the rocker arms, which are each fitted with adjusters, accessible when the rocker box inspection caps are removed.

The aluminium alloy die cast pistons each have two compression rings and one oil scraper ring. The connecting rods are of H Section in RR56 Hiduminium alloy on all current models and steel forgings on earlier 350 c.c. models with detachable caps, and incorporate steel-backed renewable "shell" bearings. Each of the connecting rod caps is machined from a steel stamping and held in position by means of two high tensile steel bolts, which are tightened to a predetermined extension figure to give the correct working clearance of the bearings on the crankshaft journals.

The inlet and exhaust camshafts operate in sintered bronze bushes which are housed transversely in the upper part of the left crankcase and in the crankcase on the right side. The inlet and exhaust camshafts are driven by a train of timing gears from the right end of the crankshaft. The inlet camshaft also operates the oil pump and rotary breather valve disc, whilst the exhaust camshaft drives the adjustable contact breaker, (which is fitted with an automatic advance and retard unit) and the tachometer drive gearbox (if fitted).

The two-throw crankshaft has a detachable shrunk-on cast-iron flywheel which is held in position by three high tensile steel bolts, locked by the use of "TRIUMPH LOCTITE" sealant and tightened to a predetermined torque figure.

The big end bearings are lubricated at pressure with oil which travels along drillings in the crankcase and crankshaft from the double plunger oil pump: oil pressure in the lubrication system is governed by means of the oil pressure release valve situated at the front of the engine, adjacent to the timing cover.

The cylinder barrel is made from a high-grade cast-iron and houses the press-fit tappet guide blocks.

Power from the engine is transmitted through the engine sprocket and primary chain to the shock absorbing clutch unit and four speed gearbox. Primary chain tension is governed by an adjustable rubber-pad chain tensioner which is immersed in the primary chain oil bath.

The electrical generator set consists of a rotor, which is fitted to the left end of the crankshaft, and a six coil stator which is mounted on three pillar bolts inside the primary chain housing.

Carburation is by an Amal monobloc carburetter with integral float chamber.

B ENGINE

SECTION B1
REMOVING AND REPLACING THE ENGINE UNIT

Remove the petrol tank (see Section E1). Remove both plug leads.

Disconnect the leads from the battery terminals and 'Lucar' connectors from the left and right ignition coils. Remove the top and bottom coil mounting bolts and distance pieces. The ignition coils will then be free to be removed. **Care should be taken not to damage the light alloy casing of the ignition coils; indentations caused to the outer casing may ultimately result in ignition failure.**

Unscrew the two nuts securing the torque stays to the cylinder head, remove the torque stay mounting bolt and withdraw the torque stays.

Disconnect the tachometer cable (if fitted) by unscrewing the union nut at the tachometer gearbox, and withdrawing the cable. (See Fig. B2).

Remove the bolts securing the switch panel to the frame, disconnect the "Lucar" connections from the ignition switch where necessary, and remove the panel. (Earlier models may have a socket on the wiring harness which should be disconnected from the back of the switch.)

Unscrew the two securing nuts and withdraw the carburetter complete with air cleaner. Remove any cable securing clips and place the carburetter well clear of the engine in a safe position.

Unscrew the two domed nuts which secure the rocker oil feed pipe to the rocker boxes by means of the centrally mounted oil feed bolts, which should now be withdrawn. Care should be taken not to bend the pipe excessively as this may ultimately result in a fracture.

To drain the oil tank remove the drain plug from the base of the oil tank and allow the oil to drain. The oil feed and return pipes should then be disconnected from the base of the oil tank.

At this stage it is advisable to drain the oil from the gearbox and primary chaincase by removing the respective drain plugs. The sump should also be drained; this can be done by unscrewing the hexagon headed filter drain plug situated underneath the engine adjacent to the bottom engine mounting lug.

Slacken off the clutch adjustment at the handlebar and withdraw the rubber cover from the clutch abutment at the gearbox. Unscrew the abutment and detach the clutch cable.

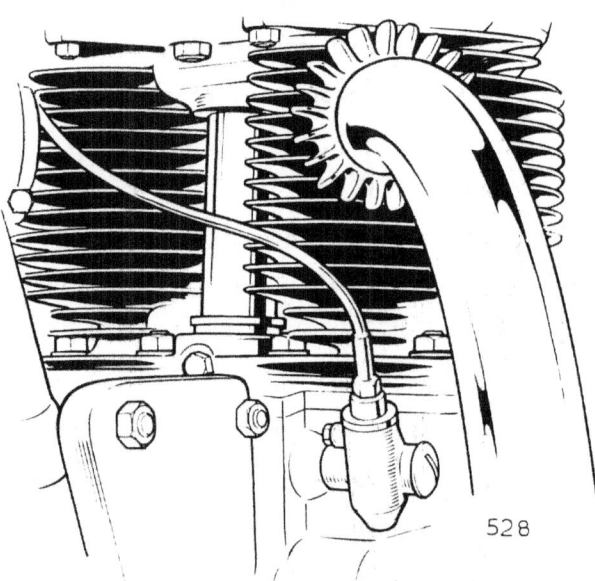

Fig. B2. Tachometer drive cable and adaptor

Slacken the left and right finned clip bolts, silencer clip bolts and the nuts securing the exhaust pipes underneath the engine. Drive the exhaust pipes free with a hide hammer. On earlier models where siamesed pipes are fitted, the pipe junction clip should also be slackened.

Remove the connecting link from the rear chain and withdraw the chain from mesh with the gearbox sprocket, then disconnect the generator leads underneath the engine (at the snap connectors). Unscrew the four bolts securing the

ENGINE

front engine plates to the frame and engine and withdraw the plates. Remove the stud which secures the underside of the engine to the frame, and the bolt securing the rear engine plates to the gearbox casing.

Finally to gain clearance for removal of the engine unit from the right, remove the following:—

(1) The two nuts which secure the right rear engine plate to the frame.

(2) The right rear engine plate.

(3) The left side front stud which secures the torque stay to the engine.

(4) The right footrest.

The engine is now free to be removed. It is recommended that removing the engine should be aided by the use of a hoist or the help of a second operator, due to the engine weight, which is approximately 105 lbs.

When refitting the engine to the frame, place the bottom frame bolt in position first. Then place the right rear engine plate in position and tighten the nuts finger tight. Finally place the front engine plate in position and when all bolts have been inserted, fully tighten up. When replacing the ignition coils, remember that the connector terminal end of each coil faces towards the rear of the machine. To ensure that the wiring harness is reconnected correctly, refer to the appropriate wiring diagram in Section H11.

Do not forget to fit the distance pieces on the coil mounting bolts, torque stay mounting bolts, and, in particular, the lowest engine mounting stud; also, attention is called to the lower panel mounting bolt on the left side of the machine.

For the correct grade and quantity of lubricant for the engine, gearbox and chaincase, see Section A2.

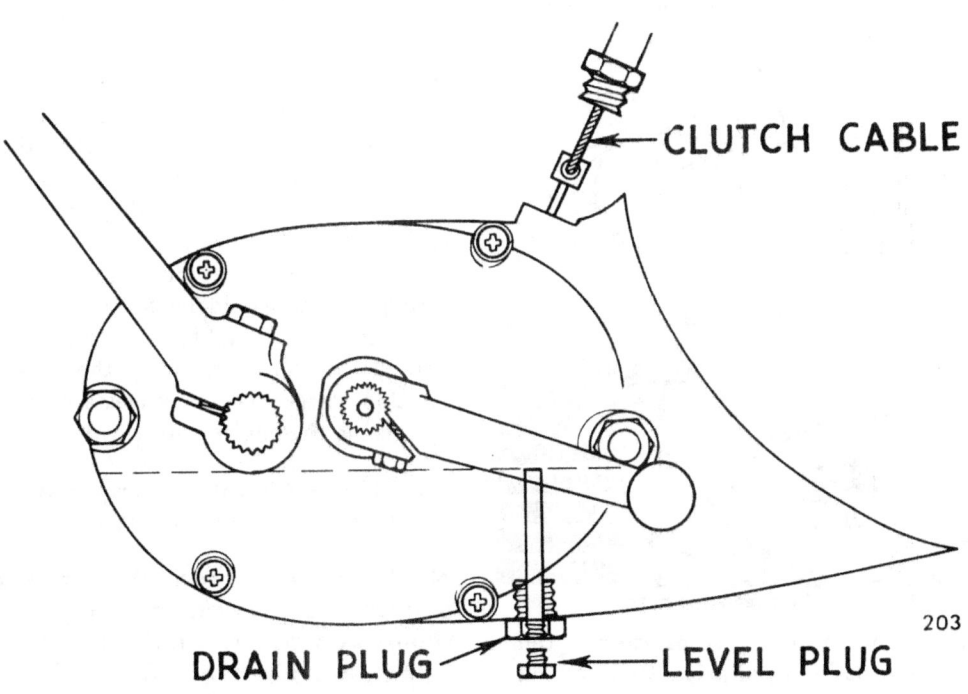

Fig. B3. Clutch cable adjustment and gearbox level and drain plugs

SECTION B2

REMOVING AND REPLACING THE ROCKER BOXES

Disconnect the leads from the battery terminals and remove the fuel tank as detailed in Section E1.

Disconnect the high tension cables and wiring harness from the left and right ignition coils. Remove the top and bottom coil mounting bolts and distance pieces. The ignition coils will then be free to be removed. Care should be taken not to damage the light alloy casings of the ignition coils as indentations may ultimately result in ignition failure.

Unscrew the two nuts securing the torque stay to the exhaust rocker box and remove the torque stay mounting bolt and distance pieces. The torque stays should then be removed.

Unscrew the two domed nuts which secure the rocker oil feed pipe to the rocker boxes by means of the centrally mounted oil feed bolts, which should now be withdrawn. Care should be taken not to bend the pipe excessively as this may ultimately result in a fracture. Remove the rocker inspection caps.

Fig. B4. Rocker box securing nuts

Unscrew the two nuts from the studs fitted to the underside of the exhaust rocker box. Remove the two Phillips screws on top of each rocker box, slacken all eight cylinder head bolts and unscrew the central cylinder head bolts. (Note that, at this stage the rocker box may rise slightly, due to a valve spring being compressed). The exhaust rocker box is now free to be removed. The above procedure also applies for the removal of the inlet rocker box.

Care should be taken to collect the six plain washers which are fitted (one beneath each of the underside securing nuts), as they sometimes adhere to the cylinder head flanges and may be subsequently lost.

After completion of the rocker box removal operation, the push rods should be withdrawn and stored in the order of their removal so that they can be replaced in their original positions. The junction surfaces of the rocker boxes and cylinder head should be cleaned for reassembly, by means of a soft metal scraper.

Replacement is a reversal of the above instructions, but remember to fit new gaskets between the rocker boxes and cylinder head.

When replacing the push rods place a small amount of grease into the bottom cup of each of the push rods, then locate the push rods, one at a time, by means of feeling the engagement of the tappet cup and the push rod ball end and then by testing the resistance to lifting caused by suction between the dome of the push rod and the tappet cup. When the push rods are correctly located, remove the sparking plugs and turn the engine over until the inlet push rods are level and at the bottom of their stroke. The inlet rocker box should then be assembled. Repeat this procedure for the exhaust rocker box. Remember that the four central cylinder head through bolts should be fitted first and that the underside nuts and Phillips screws are tightened last. Before finally clamping the rocker boxes in position, check that the valves are being operated by turning the engine over slowly.

Do not forget the distance pieces when refitting the torque stay and coil mounting bolts.

NOTE: It can be seen that the four central bolts also serve to retain the cylinder head and should be tightened first. The correct torque figures are given in GENERAL DATA, and sequence in figure B13.

Before fitting the central oil feed bolts and the rocker oil feed pipe the copper washers should be annealed by quenching in water from cherry red heat. Finally, remove any scale that may have formed. Annealing softens the copper thus giving it better sealing qualities.

ENGINE   B

SECTION B3

INSPECTING THE PUSH RODS

When the push rods have been removed, examine them for worn, chipped or loose end cups; also check that the push rod is true by rolling it slowly on a flat surface (such as a piece of plate glass).

Bent push rods are found to be the cause of excessive mechanical noise and loss of power and should be straightened if possible, or, preferably renewed.

SECTION B4

STRIPPING AND REASSEMBLING THE ROCKER BOXES

Removal of the rocker spindles from the rocker boxes is best achieved by driving out, using a soft metal drift. When the spindles are removed the rocker arms and washers can be withdrawn. All parts should be thoroughly cleaned in paraffin (kerosene) and the oil drillings in the spindles and rocker arms should be cleaned with a jet of compressed air.

Remove the oil seals from the rocker spindles and renew them.

If it is required to renew the rocker ball pins, the old ones should be removed by means of a suitable drift. New ones should then be pressed in with the drilled flat towards the rocker spindles.

To ensure an oil tight seal between the rocker box and cylinder head, in cases where an oil leak cannot be cured by fitting new gaskets, the joint surface of the rocker box should be linished to remove any irregularities.

An effective linish can be achieved by first extracting the rocker box studs (two nuts locked together on the stud should facilitate removal) then lightly rubbing the junction surface on a sheet of emery cloth mounted on a flat surface (such as a piece of plate glass).

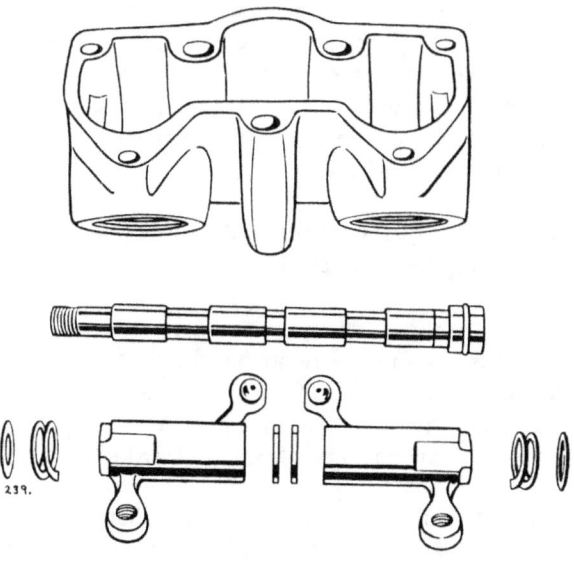

Fig. B5. Rocker box assembly

The following method of assembly incorporates the use of a home made alignment bar which can be made from a $\frac{7}{16}$ in. x 6 in. long bolt by grinding a taper at one end.

B7

ENGINE

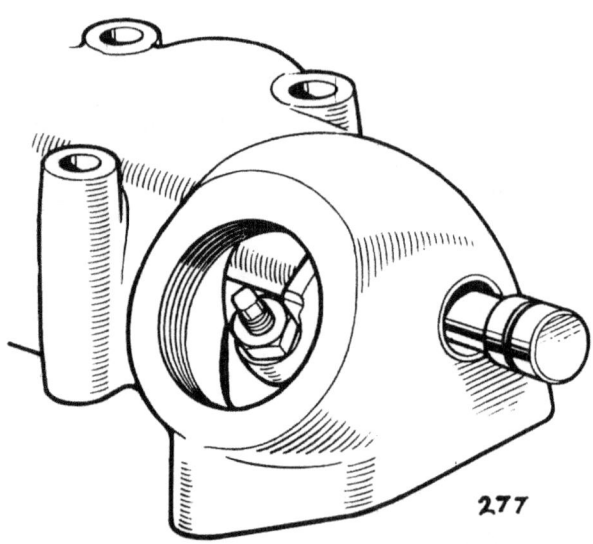

Fig. B6. Refitting the rocker spindle

Before commencing reassembly of each rocker box, note there is one plain washer in each box which has a smaller diameter bore. This is the thrust washer through which the smaller diameter of the spindle enters and is assembled last against the right hand inner face of the rocker box.

Smear the two plain washers with grease and place them one either side of the centre bearing boss. Place the left rocker arm in position, bringing it into line with the alignment tool and slide a plain washer and a spring washer (in the order shown in Fig. B5) into position. Carefully repeat this procedure for the other rocker arm and spring washer and slide the thrust washer with the smaller internal bore into position. Finally bring both rocker arms into line with the alignment bar.

Lubricate the spindle with oil and slide it (complete with oil seal) as far as possible into the rocker box, finally tapping it home with a hammer and soft metal drift (see Fig. B6).

SECTION B5

ADJUSTING THE VALVE ROCKER CLEARANCES

The valve rocker clearance should be checked and adjusted if necessary every 3,000 miles (4,800 kms). The correct clearance, for the type of camshaft employed, ensures that a high valve operating efficiency is maintained and that the valves attain their maximum useful lives.

NOTE: Adjustment should only be made when the engine is cold.

Access to the rocker arm adjuster screws and lock nuts is gained by removing the slotted inspection caps from the rocker boxes. Adjustment is aided by the tool kit spanners D361 ($\frac{3}{16}$ in. Whitworth spanner) and D362 (tappet key).

As it is difficult to insert a feeler guage between the rocker arm and the valve tip it is recommended that the clearance is set by using the pitch of the thread on the adjuster screw as a vernier in order to determine the correct setting. The thread is $\frac{5}{16}$ in. x 26 C.E.I. hence the pitch is ·038 in. Therefore $\frac{1}{4}$ turn of the adjuster screw represents ·010 ins. approximately. To set the valve rocker clearances proceed as follows:—

First, remove the left and right sparking plugs in order to relieve the compression, then slacken the four lock nuts securing the square headed adjuster screws; engage top gear.

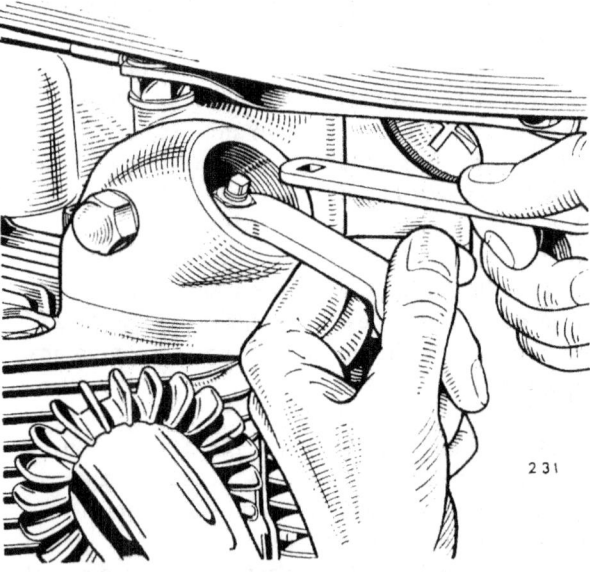

Fig. B7. Adjusting the valve rocker clearance

ENGINE

Inlet valves. Turn the rear wheel forwards until the right inlet valve is fully open whereupon the left inlet tappet will be resting on the base circle diameter of the cam form; the clearance for the left inlet rocker can now be set.

T90, T100SS, T100T (and later **5TA** from H40528). The clearance is ·002 in. (0·05 mm) and this means just the slightest perceptible movement of the rocker with a faint click when the clearance is taken up by moving the rocker with the fingers.

3TA and earlier **5TA**. The clearance is 0·010 in. (0·25 mm.) and the rocker should first be adjusted to zero clearance, that is free to move sideways with no vertical play. Now screw back the adjuster one quarter turn (one flat) and hold it in this position while tightening the locking nut.

Having adjusted the left inlet valve, turn the rear wheel forward until the left valve is fully open and repeat the procedure for the right inlet valve.

Exhaust valves. The procedure for adjusting the exhaust valves is the same as described for the inlet valves.

T90, T100SS, T100T (and later **5TA** from H40528). The clearance is ·004 in. (10 mm.) for these models. To obtain this clearance adjust the tappet to give nil clearance and then turn back the adjuster one eighth of a turn (half flat) on the squared adjuster. Hold the adjuster in this position whilst you tighten the lock nut. Repeat this procedure for the other exhaust valve.

3TA and earlier **5TA**. The clearance is ·010 in. (·25 mm.), exactly as for the inlet valves.

SECTION B6

REMOVING AND REPLACING THE AIR CLEANER

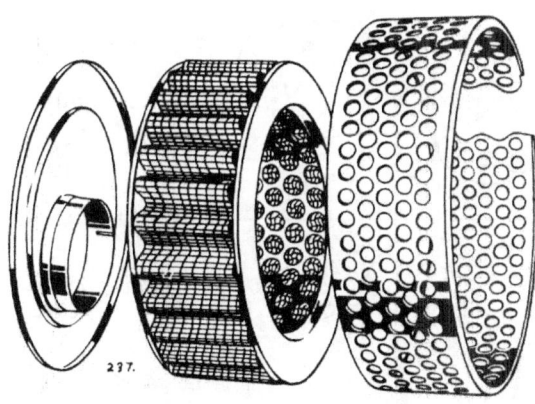

Fig B8 (a) The Air cleaner assembly

When the central circular clip is slackened it should be possible to slide the air cleaner off the carburettor adaptor, and withdraw it. If difficulty is encountered it is possible to remove the air cleaner by dismantling it. To do this remove the screw clip which secures the outer perforated case, then remove the back plate, filter and finally, slide the front plate from over the carburetter adaptor.

Models fitted with a dry felt type element should be carefully rinsed in parafin (kerosene) and allowed to drain thoroughly. Models incorporating paper type elements should be cleaned with a jet of compressed air. **Under no circumstances should this type of filter be soaked with oil.**

Replacement is the reversal of the above instructions but do not forget to tighten the perforated case clip and the circular clip securing the air cleaner to the carburetter.

Fig B8 (b) Inlet noise reduction air cleaner

Later T100R and T100C models built for the home and general export markets were fitted with inlet noise level reducing carburetter induction air filter chambers.

To gain access to the air filter element for cleaning or replacement, remove the three hexagon screws complete with lockwashers and detach the rear cover plate. Lift out the element, and where necessary, tap gently to remove dust, and clean with a jet of compressed air. Replacement is the reverse of the above.

Do not oil this type of element.

SECTION B7

CARBURETTER—DESCRIPTION

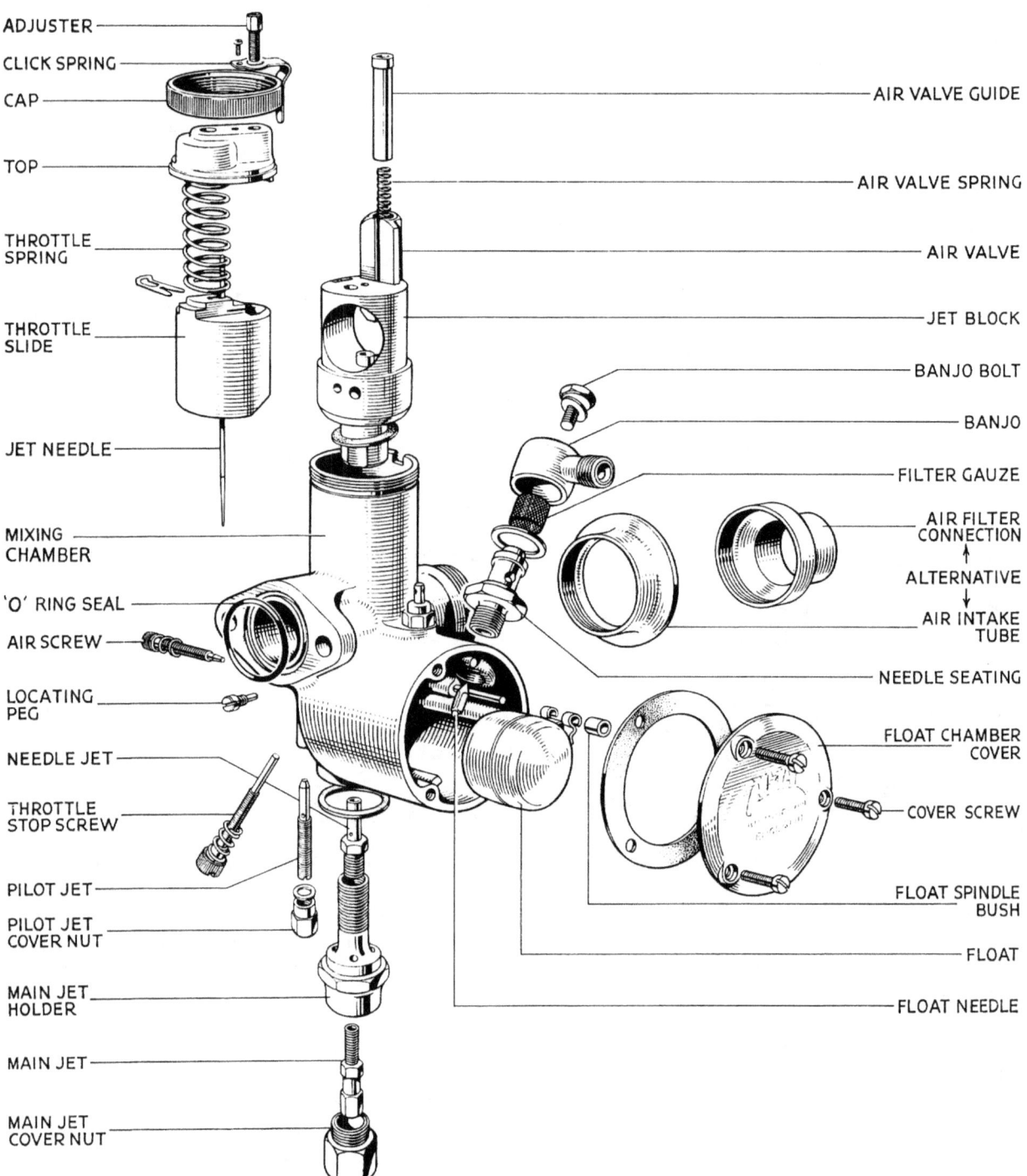

Fig. B9. Exploded view of carburetter

ENGINE

CONCENTRIC CARBURETTER TYPE 900
DESCRIPTION

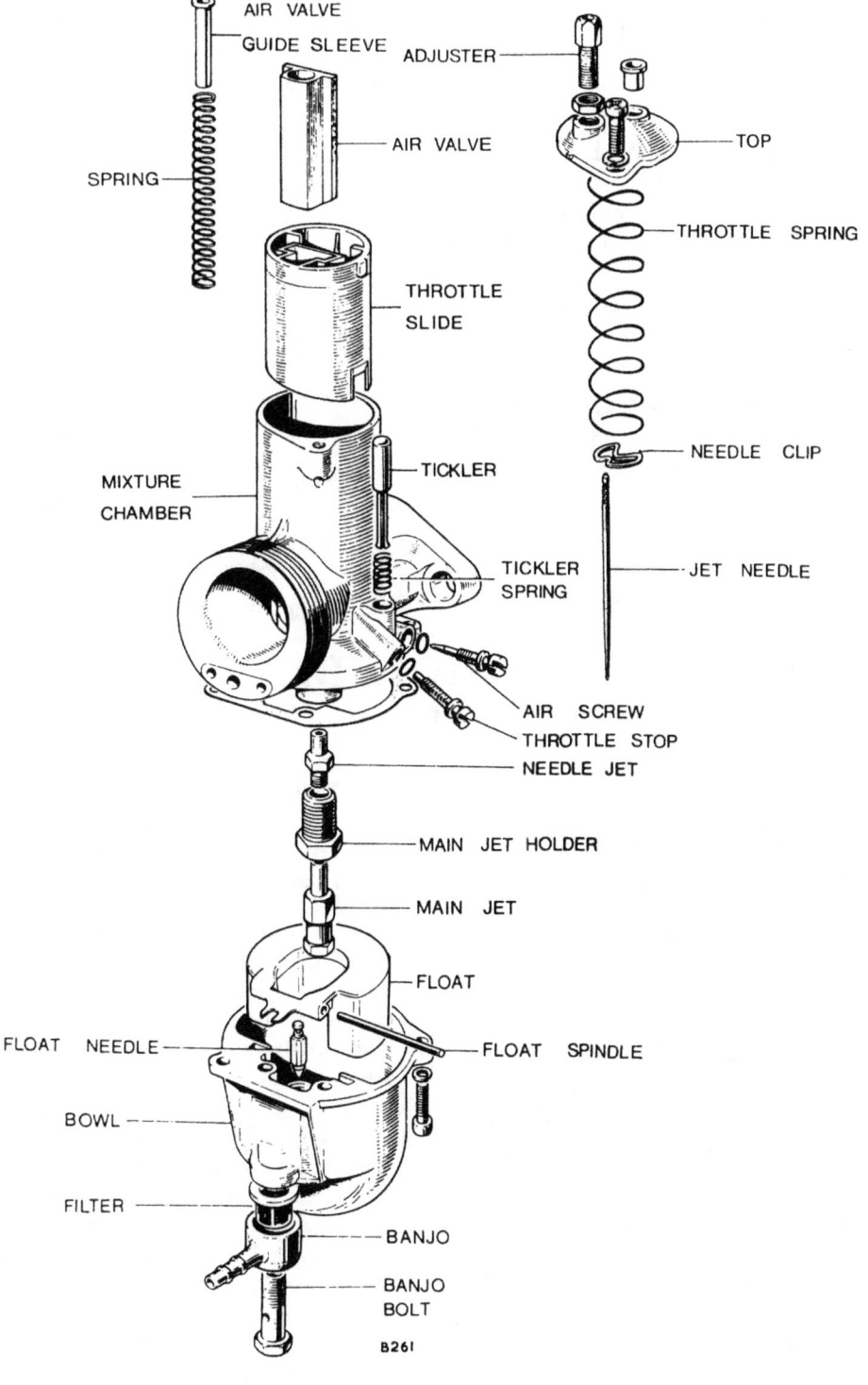

Fig. B9B Exploded view of carburetter

SECTION B8
TWIN CARBURETTER ARRANGEMENT

DESCRIPTION

The twin carburetters are of the monobloc variety, the right hand one being of the "chopped off" type, that is, without float chamber. The left hand carburetter is complete with the integral float chamber, both carburetters being fed from the one float chamber by means of a connecting pipe. There is a balance pipe fitted between the inlet manifolds to improve tickover.

THROTTLE CABLE

A "one into two" throttle cable is used. The single throttle cable from the twistgrip enters a junction box where it is fitted into a slide. The twin shorter carburetter cables are fitted to the other side of the junction box slide. Both the slide and junction box being made of plastic require no maintenance. See Fig. B10 for the order of assembly.

SETTING TWIN CARBURETTERS

The twin carburetters fitted to the T100T or T100R may require synchronisation and a simple method is as follows:—First adjust the cables from the junction box so that they have the minimum of free play.

Now start the motor and take off one plug lead and then adjust the pilot air screw and throttle stop screw in the OPPOSITE carburetter until the motor runs regularly. Replace the plug lead and repeat the process similarly for the other carburetter. With both plug leads replaced the tickover will be too fast and the stop screws should be lowered simultaneously until correct. It is most important the throttle slides lift simultaneously or the motor will run roughly, particularly when accelerating.

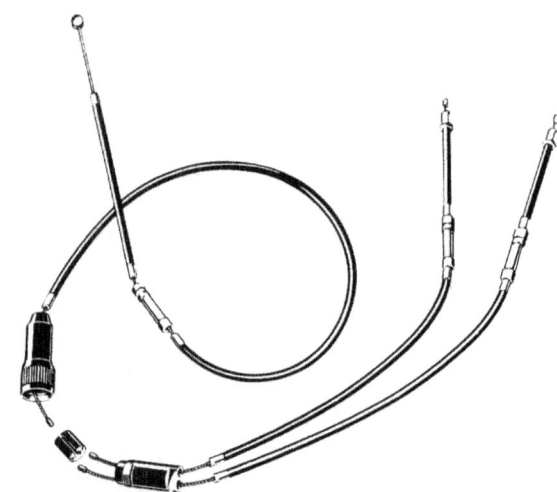

Fig. B10. T100T/T100R twin carburetter throttle cable

SECTION B9
REMOVING AND REPLACING THE CARBURETTER

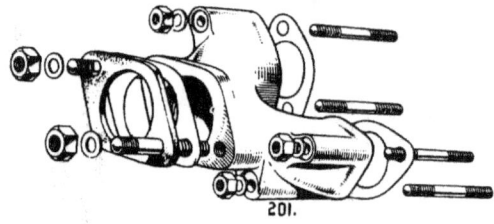

Fig. B11. Manifold assembly

SECTION B8(A) SINGLE CARBURETTER MODELS

First, remove the air cleaner as described in Section B6 above, then unscrew the serrated cap nut which is held in position by a ratchet spring at the top of the carburetter.

Ensure that the fuel taps are in the "OFF" position and disconnect the fuel pipes. Unscrew the two carburetter flange securing nuts then carefully withdraw the carburetter from over its mounting studs. As the carburetter is lowered the slide should be withdrawn and carefully wrapped in a piece of cloth until it is required to refit the carburetter.

The insulating block, paper washer and rubber "O" ring seal should be examined for damage which might impair their sealing qualities. If there is the slightest doubt about their serviceability, they should be renewed.

When replacing the carburetter, great care should be taken to ensure that the slide does not become damaged as it is lowered into the mixture chamber of the carburetter. This operation may require manipulation due to the slide having to locate over a peg and the needle; this must fit into the needle jet housing within the carburetter. In the event of great difficulty being encountered, check that the slot in the air slide is to the right then offer the air slide to the carburetter with the carburetter held in a vertical position. Ensure that the rubber "O" ring seal, insulating block and paper washer are correctly fitted, then slide the carburetter into position. Locate the cap and screw on the serrated cap nut. When refitting the carburetter securing nuts do not forget to fit the plain washers, and do not overtighten the nuts. Refitting continues as a reversal to the above instructions.

ENGINE B

SECTION B8(B) TWIN CARBURETTERS

Remove the Jubilee-type clips and take off both air filters. Ensure the petrol tap is turned off and disconnect the petrol pipe from the left hand carburetter, by removal of the union centre bolt. Keep the filter safely for re-use.

Remove the main jet covers and jet holders with fibre washers and the carburetter connecting pipe complete with both banjos.

Unscrew the serrated cap nuts which are held in position by ratchet springs at the tops of the carubretters. Remove the four carburetter securing nuts and washers, lift each carburetter off the mounting studs and keep the insulating blocks for re-use.

Proceed then as for section B8(A). Reassembly continues as a reversal of the foregoing.

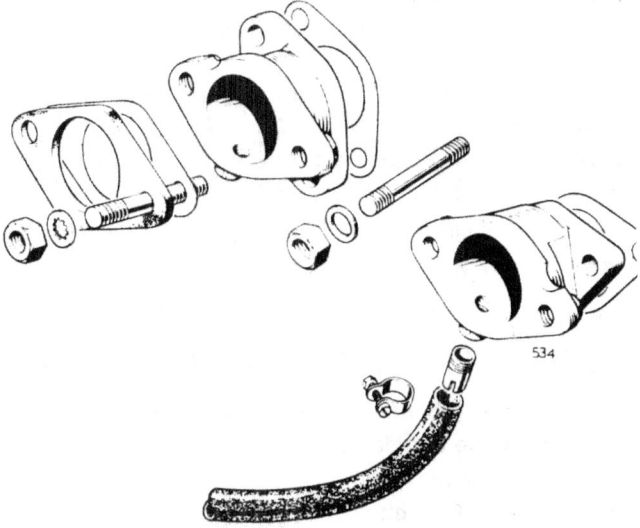

Fig.B12. Twin carburetter inlet manifolds

SECTION B10
STRIPPING AND REASSEMBLING THE CARBURETTER

When the carburetter is removed, disconnect the slide assembly from the throttle cable. To do this, first remove the needle retaining spring clip, then compress the slide return spring, pushing the nipple of the throttle cable down through the slot until it is free.

Unscrew three slotted screws and withdraw the float chamber cover and remove the float spindle bush and float; then withdraw the triangular sectioned float needle.

Unscrew the banjo bolt which secures the fuel pipe banjo connector to the float needle seating block and withdraw the banjo, filter and junction washers. Unscrew the needle seating block. Unscrew the tickler body then withdraw the tickler and spring.

Unscrew the air screw and throttle stop screw, then the main jet cover nut from the bottom of the body. Unscrew the main jet, main jet holder and needle jet. To release the jet block reinsert the main jet holder, until a few threads are engaged then tap it with a hide hammer. This will release the jet block upwards and through the carburetter body.

Unscrew the pilot jet cover, and unscrew the pilot jet. All that remains to be removed then is the hexagonal locating peg, the end of which can be seen protruding within the mixing chamber.

Thoroughly clean all parts in petrol (gasolene). Deposits on the carburetter body are best removed by a light grade wire brush. It is advisable to wash the parts several times each in a quantity of clean petrol, to avoid particles of dirt remaining. Allow the parts to drain, preferably using a jet of compressed air from such as a hand pump to ensure that oil holes and drillings are free from blockage.

Inspect the component parts for wear and check that the jets are in accordance with the recommended sizes given in GENERAL DATA.

Apart from one or two points that are mentioned below, reassembly is a reversal of the above instructions, referring to Fig. B9 for guidance.

Do not refit any fibre washer that looks unserviceable. It is advisable to purchase replacement washers before removing the carburetter.

When replacing the jet block, ensure that the fibre washer is in position; align the location flat in the jet block with the locating peg in the carburetter housing and drive the block home.

Finally, note that the float spindle bush fits on the outside end of the spindle, and that the float pressure pad is uppermost so that the float needle rests on it.

STRIPPING AND REASSEMBLING THE CONCENTRIC CARBURETTER

When the carburreter is removed, disconnect the slide assembly from the throttle cable. To do this pull back the return spring and remove the needle and needle clip. With the spring still retracted, push the cable through the slide and when the nipple is clear, across the figure of eight slot. The slide and return spring can now be removed.

To remove the air valve, push the valve and spring along with air cable until the cable nipple protrudes sufficiently out of its counterbore to be pushed out of the slot. The cable and spring can now be pulled clear of the valve.

Unscrew the petrol pipe banjo connection and remove the banjo and nylon filter.

B13

Unscrew two Phillips screws and remove the float bowl. The nylon float, spindle and triangular needle can now be withdrawn.

Unscrew the jet holder which will allow the main jet to be removed.

Unscrew the air adjusting screw and throttle stop screw.

Thoroughly clean all parts in petrol (gasoline) several times and dry with compressed air, or a hand pump, to remove any particles of dirt. Any external deposits are best removed with the use of a light wire brush. Reassemble in the reverse order, referring to Fig. B9 for guidance.

When refitting the float and needle valve, make certain that the recess on the valve is properly located in the "U" shaped slot in the float. Replace the float bowl sealing washer, and if necessary the two rubber "O" rings fitted to the adjusting screws.

SECTION B11
INSPECTING THE CARBURETTER COMPONENTS (CONCENTRIC & MONOBLOC)

The only parts liable to show wear after considerable mileage are the throttle valve slide, mixing chamber and the air slide (if fitted).

(1) Inspect the throttle valve slide for excessive scoring to the front area and check the extent of wear on the rear slide face. If wear is apparent the slide should be renewed. In this case, be sure to replace the slide with the correct degree of cut-away (see "General Data").

(2) Examine the air valve for excessive wear and check that it is not actually worn through at any part. Check the fit of the air valve in the jet block. Ensure that the air valve spring is serviceable by inspecting the coils for wear.

(3) Inspect the throttle return spring for efficiency and check that it has not lost compressive strength by measuring its length and comparing it to the figure given in "General Data".

(4) Check the needle jet for wear or possible scoring and carefully examine the tapered end of the needle for similar signs. Check the correct needle is in use. The needle for petrol is marked above the top groove "000". The needle for alcohol is marked "Z".

(5) In the case of monobloc carburetters examine the float needle for efficiency by inserting it into the inverted float needle seating block, pouring a small amount of petrol (gasoline) into the aperture surrounding the needle and checking it for leakage.

(6) Check the float bowl joint surface for flatness and flatten if necessary on emery paper on a perfectly flat surface.

(7) Ensure that the float does not leak by shaking it to see if it contains any fuel. Do not attempt to repair a damaged float. A new one can be purchased for a small cost.

SECTION B12
CARBURETTER ADJUSTMENTS

Throttle Stop Screw. This screw, which is situated on the right side of the carburetter sloping upwards and is fitted with a locking spring, should be set to open the throttle sufficiently to keep the engine running at a slow idle, when the twist grip is closed.

Pilot Air Screw. To set the idling mixture, this screw, which is situated on the right side, is also fitted with a locking spring, and should be screwed in to enrich the idle mixture or outwards to weaken it. As a guide to its approximate position, screw it in fully, then unscrew it approximately $2\frac{1}{2}$ turns.

The screw controls the suction on the pilot jet by metering the amount of air which mixes with the petrol.

Needle and Needle Jet. Carburation is governed by the cut-away and needle jet in varying degrees from when the throttle is just open to when it is approximately $\frac{3}{4}$ full throttle. The needle jet Machines are delivered from the factory with the needle in the specified position, and the needle position should not be varied from this setting.

Throttle Valve Cut-away. The amount of cut-away to the bottom of the throttle valve slide is indicated by a number marked on the slide, e.g. $376/3\frac{1}{2}$ means throttle type 376 with number $3\frac{1}{2}$ cutaway; a larger number such as 4 means that the throttle valve slide has a slightly larger cutaway and consequently gives a leaner mixture during the period of throttle opening through which a cutaway is effective, i.e. from just open to approximately $\frac{1}{4}$ throttle. Similarly, 3 indicates a slightly smaller cutaway and a slightly richer mixture.

Jet Sizes. The recommended jet sizes are given in GENERAL DATA and changing from these to any other size is left entirely to the discretion of the rider. The main jet is operative from approximately $\frac{3}{4}$ to full throttle; this is when the needle jet orifice ceases to have any reduction effect on the petrol

ENGINE   B

SECTION B13

REMOVING AND REFITTING THE CYLINDER HEAD ASSEMBLY

Proceed as detailed in Section B7 for removal of the rocker boxes and push rods.

Slacken the two finned clip bolts and the silencer clip bolts; slacken the exhaust pipe bracket nuts and drive the right hand exhaust pipe free with a hide mallet. Repeat the procedure for the left exhaust pipe.

Unscrew the four manifold securing nuts and withdraw the four plain washers. The manifold can be withdrawn from the cylinder head when the head is removed. In the case of twin carburetter models, each inlet manifold is secured by two socket headed screws, the manifolds being removed with the head.

Unscrew the four remaining cylinder head bolts, a turn at a time, until the load has been released, and then remove the cylinder head, sliding it forward to release the inlet manifold complete with carburetter.

If it is desired to remove the cylinder head simply as a unit to work on another part of the engine unit, it is unnecessary to remove the manifold(s) as well as the carburetter.

Remove the push rod cover tubes and renew the rubber seals as a matter of course.

The copper cylinder head gasket should be either renewed or reconditioned by annealing it to restore the sealing qualities of the copper. Annealing is achieved by heating the gasket to cherry red heat and quenching it in water; finally, remove any scale that may have formed by means of a piece of fine grade emery cloth.

REFITTING THE CYLINDER HEAD

Ensure that the junction surfaces of the cylinder block, gasket and cylinder head are clean. Grease the gasket and place it in position (check that all eight bolt holes are lined up) and locate the push rod cover tubes (complete with bottom oil seal and cup) onto the tappet guide block.

Lower the cylinder head (complete with top oil seal) into position and fit the four outer cylinder head bolts finger tight.

Replace the push rods in their original positions.

Carefully rotate the crankshaft until both of the inlet push rods are at the bottom of their stroke, then lower the inlet rocker box into position, ensuring that the push rods are engaged correctly, then fit the two central cylinder head single ended bolts finger tight. Screw in the two outer inlet rocker box Phillip screws and fit the two underside retaining nuts with plain washers. Repeat this procedure for the exhaust rocker box using the double ended type bolts which secure the torque stays. Refit the central oil feed bolts and rocker feed pipe described as in Section B2.

Tighten the eight cylinder head bolts in the order given in Fig. B14 and the torque settings given in GENERAL DATA. Finally tighten the remaining inlet and exhaust rocker box retaining nuts and bolts.

Reassembly then continues in the reverse order to the removal instructions. To obtain the correct valve rocker clearance settings, reference should be made to the GENERAL DATA Section.

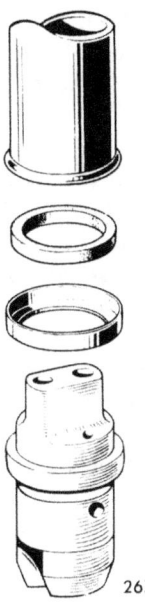

Fig. B13. Assembly of the push rod cover tubes

ENGINE

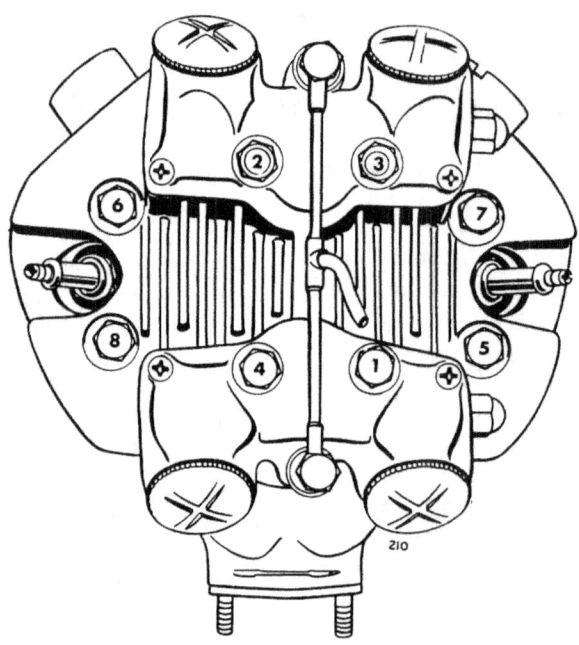

Fig. B14. Cylinder head bolt tightening sequence

SECTION B14

REMOVING AND REFITTING THE VALVES

Removal of the valves is facilitated by means of a "G" clamp type valve spring compressor. When the spring is compressed sufficiently, the split cotters can be removed with a narrow screwdriver, and the valve spring withdrawn when the compressor is released. As each valve is removed it should be marked so that it can be replaced in its original position.

NOTE: The inlet valves are marked "IN" and the exhaust valves "EX".

Fitting a new or reground valve necessitates seating by the grinding in process described in Section B17, but it does not necessitate recutting the cylinder head valve seat unless new valve guides have been fitted.

The valve springs should be inspected for fatigue and cracks, and check for wear by comparing them with a new spring or the dimension given in GENERAL DATA.

All parts should be thoroughly cleaned in paraffin (kerosene) and allowed to drain before reassembling.

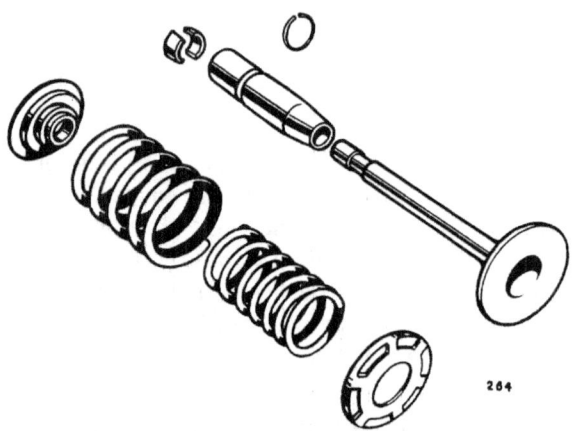

Fig. B15. Valve components

Assemble the inner and outer springs and top and bottom cups over the valve guide then slide the valve into position lubricating the stem with a small amount of graphited oil.

Compress the springs and slide the two halves of the split cotter into the exposed groove in the valve stem.

ENGINE B

SECTION B15

RENEWING THE VALVE GUIDES

The valve guides can be pressed or driven out using Service Tool Z16, with the cylinder head inverted on the bench. A suitable drift can be made by obtaining a 5 in. length of $\frac{1}{2}$ in. diameter mild steel bar (EN8) and machining one end to $\frac{5}{16}$ in. diameter for a length of 1 in.

The same method may be employed to fit the new guide, although the use of a press is recommended. In either case lightly grease the valve guide to assist assembly. Ensure that the guide is pressed in until the circlip is flush with the cylinder head.

Where new valve guides have been fitted it is necessary to recut the valve seats in the cylinder head and grind in the valves (see Section B17).

SECTION B16

DECARBONISING

It is not normally advisable to remove the carbon deposits from the combustion chamber and exhaust ports until symptoms indicate that decarbonising is necessary.

Such symptoms as falling off in power, loss of compression, noisy operation and difficult starting are all indications that decarbonising may be necessary.

When the cylinder head is removed unscrew the sparking plugs and clean them in paraffin (kerosene) or preferably have them grit blasted and checked. Before fitting the plugs, check that the gap setting is correct (see GENERAL DATA).

If special decarbonising equipment is not available then a blunt aluminium scraper or a piece of lead solder flattened at one end, should be used to remove the carbon deposits. Do not use a screw-driver or a steel implement of any kind on an aluminium surface.

When removing the deposits from the piston crown, a ring of carbon should be left round the periphery of the pistons to maintain the seal. Also the carbon ring round the top of the cylinder bores should not be disturbed. To facilitate this an old piston ring should be placed on top of the piston, level with the top surface of the cylinder block.

Remove the valve as described in Section B14 then remove the carbon deposits from the valve stems, combustion chamber and ports in the cylinder head. Remove all traces of carbon dust by means of a jet of compressed air or the vigorous use of a tyre pump, then thoroughly clean the cylinder head and valves in paraffin (kerosene). Finally, check the valves for pitting. If necessary, the valves can be ground in as shown in Section B17.

SECTION B17

RESEATING THE VALVES

Where the valve guides have been renewed or condition of a valve seat is doubtful, it is advisable to recut the cylinder head valve seat then grind in the valve, using a fine grade grinding-in paste.

It is important that the cylinder head valve seat and the valve guide bore should be concentric. For the purpose of recutting the valve seats the service tools shown in Section J1 are available.

The valve seat cutting operation should be carried out with the greatest care, and only a minimum amount of metal should be removed.

After the seats have been recut, they should be blended to give an even seating of $\frac{3}{32}$ in. (2·4 mm.).

Examine the face of the valve to see if it is pitted, scored or damaged. If necessary, the face can be reground, but excessive regrinding is not advisable for this adversely affects the heat transference properties of the valve and will ultimately result in critical pocketing.

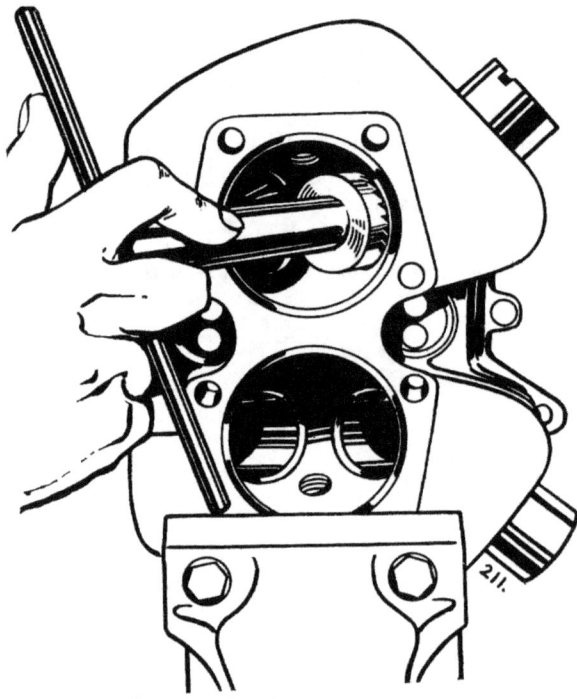

Fig. B17. Cutting the valve seats

The stem of the valve should be inspected for wear or scuffing and if either is pronounced, the valve should be renewed.

To grind in the valve use a fine grade carborundum grinding-in paste. Place a small amount evenly on the valve seat and place the valve in its guide with a holding tool attached.

Use a semi rotary motion, occasionally lifting the valve and turning it through 180 degrees. Continue this process until a uniform seal results. Wash the parts in paraffin (kerosene) to remove the grinding paste. Apply a smear of engineers marking blue to the seat of the valve. Rotate the valve through one revolution and inspect the seat. Successful valve grinding will give an unbroken ring of blue on the valve seat.

Alternatively, assemble the springs and split cotters and pour a small amount of paraffin (kerosene) into the ports. It should not penetrate the seating for at least 10 seconds if a good seal has been achieved.

Prior to reassembling the cylinder head, ensure that all traces of blue and grinding paste are removed by thoroughly washing in paraffin (kerosene).

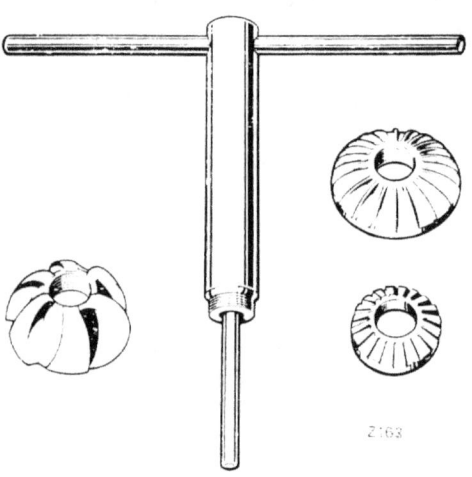

Fig. B16. Valve seating tools

ENGINE

SECTION B18

REMOVING AND REPLACING THE CYLINDER BLOCK AND TAPPETS

Wedge a disused shock absorber rubber, or a suitable retainer between the inlet and exhaust tappets to prevent the tappets from falling through the tappet block into the crankcase when the cylinder block is removed.

Turn the engine over until the pistons are at T.D.C. and unscrew the eight cylinder base nuts. Raise the cylinder block sufficiently to insert "non-fluffy" rag into the crankcase mouth. Remove the cylinder block carefully and ensure that the tappets or any broken piston rings do not fall into the crankcase.

Remove the tappets from the cylinder block storing them in the order of their removal, and thoroughly clean all parts in paraffin (kerosene). It is important that the tappets are replaced in their original positions; failure to observe this may result in subsequent excessive tappet and cam wear.

Generally, when the cylinder block is removed, the machine has covered a considerable mileage. It is therefore prudent to fit new piston rings and lightly hone the bores to break the "glaze" each time the cylinder block is removed. (See Section B22).

Reassembly is a reversal of the above instructions, but care should be taken to ensure that the cylinder block is correctly located over the two dowels in the crankcase. This will automatically place the machined side of flange against the timing cover.

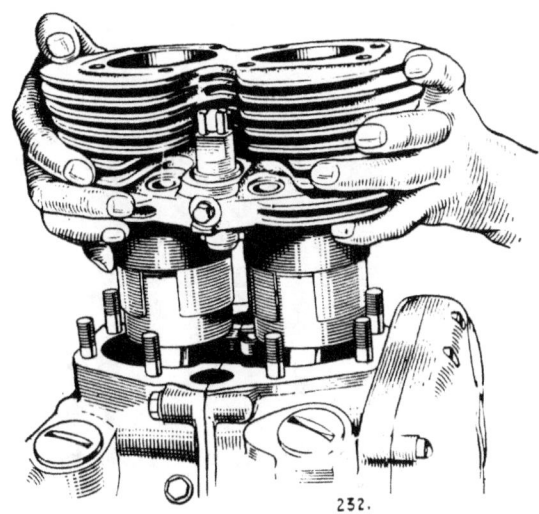

Fig. B18. Refitting the cylinder block

The tappets should be well lubricated prior to wedging them in their original positions in the tappet guide blocks. To facilitate an easy assembly of the cylinder block over the pistons, two collars part number Z130 (350 c.c.) or Z132 (500 c.c.) are required. The collars should be placed over the pistons to compress the piston rings, and withdrawn over the connecting rods when the pistons are sufficiently engaged in the block. Refit the eight cylinder base nuts.

SECTION B19

INSPECTING THE TAPPETS AND GUIDE BLOCKS

The base of the tappet is fitted with a "Stellite" tip. This material has good wear resisting qualities but the centre of the tip may show signs of slight indentations. If the width of the indentation exceeds $\frac{3}{32}$ in. then the tappets should be renewed.

It is not necessary to remove the tappet guide blocks for inspection purposes; the extent of wear can be estimated by rocking the tappet whilst it is in position in the guide block. It should be a sliding fit with a little or no sideways movement (see GENERAL DATA for working clearances).

Excessive play between the tappets and guide block may cause undesirable mechanical noise.

SECTION B20

RENEWING THE TAPPET GUIDE BLOCKS

Place the cylinder block in an inverted position on the bench. Remove the locking screw and drift out the guide block using service tool Z23.

To fit the new guide block, ensure the cylinder block is firmly supported by the base flange. Grease the outer surface of the guide block to assist assembly, then align the location hole in the guide block and cylinder block base, and drive in the guide block using service tool Z23, as shewn in Fig. B19, until the shoulder is flush with the flange. Do not attempt to align the tappet block by means of the ears on the guide block. They can easily be cracked.

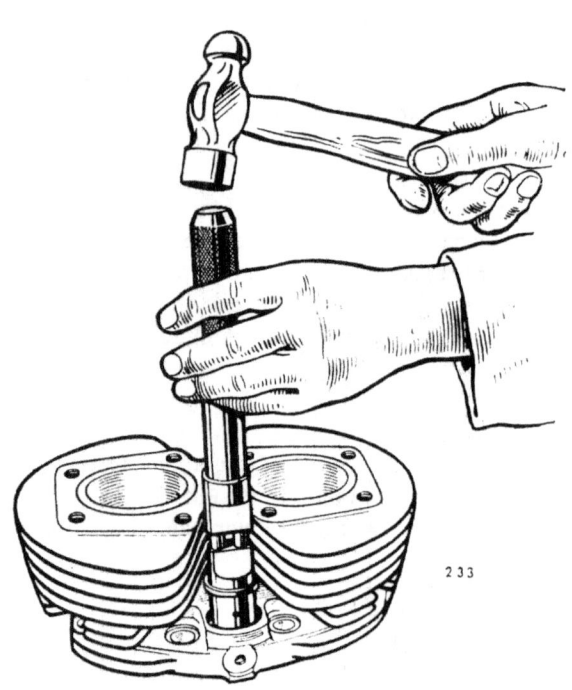

Fig. B19. Refitting a tappet guide block

ENGINE

SECTION B21

REMOVING AND REFITTING THE PISTONS

Remove the inner and outer circlips and press out the gudgeon pin with a suitable proprietary tool. The pistons are then free to be removed.

Alternatively the pistons may be removed by driving out the gudgeon pin with a suitable drift. However, this is not a recommended practice, and may result in a damaged piston or distorted connecting rod. **The need for care cannot be over-stressed when using this method to remove the gudgeon pin.** When the pistons are removed they should be suitably scribed inside so that they can be refitted in their original positions and facing the correct way round.

When refitting the pistons first place the inner circlip in position to act as a stop, then press the gudgeon pin into position using the proprietary tool.

It is advisable to renew the four circlips; this can be done for negligible cost.

If there is no alternative but to drive the gudgeon pin into position with a drift, the piston should be heated to 100 degrees centigrade (boiling water temperature) to assist assembly.

Finally, check that all the gudgeon pin retainer circlips are in position, and are correctly fitted This is extremely important.

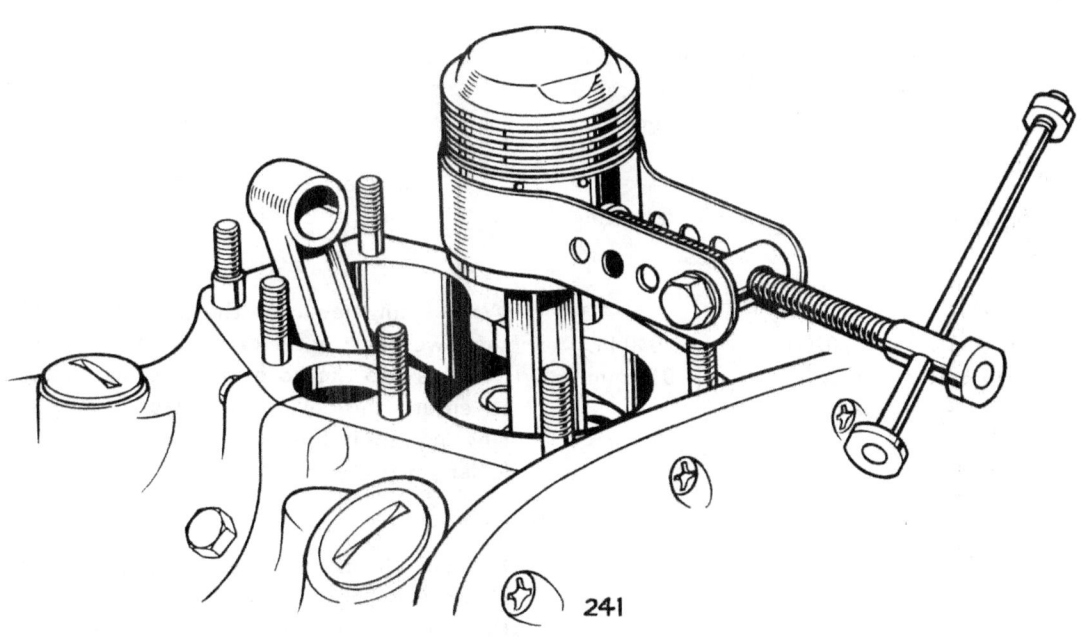

Fig. B20. Removing a piston

SECTION B22

REMOVING AND REPLACING THE PISTON RINGS

There should be little difficulty in removing piston rings, if the following procedure is adopted. Lift one end of the top piston ring out of the groove and insert a thin steel strip between the ring and piston. Move the strip round the piston, at the same time lifting the raised part of the ring upwards with slight pressure. The piston rings should always be lifted off and replaced over the top of the pistons.

If the piston rings are to be refitted the carbon deposits on the inside surface of the rings must be removed and the carbon deposits in the piston ring grooves must also be removed.

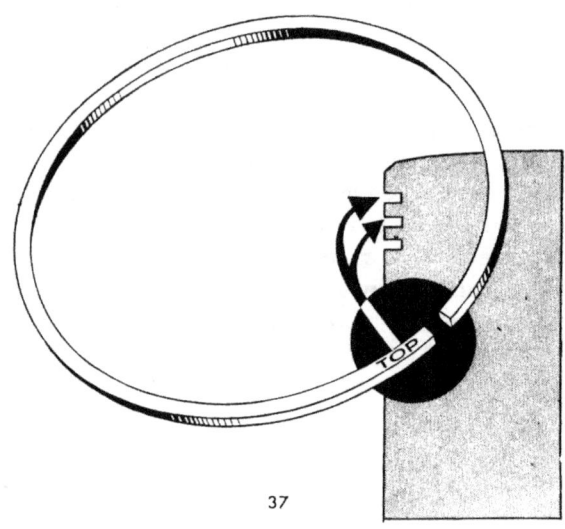

Fig. B21. Refitting a tapered piston ring

When fitting new piston rings, the bores must be lightly honed with a fine grade emery cloth so that the new piston rings can become bedded down properly. The honing should be carried out with an oscillatory motion up and down the bore until an even criss-cross pattern is achieved. The recommended grade of emery for this purpose is 300. Thoroughly wash the bores in paraffin (kerosene) and check that all traces of abrasives are removed.

Pistons and rings are available in the following oversizes:—

350 c.c.   ·010 in.   ·020 in.   ·040 in.
models   (0·254 mm.) (0·508 mm.) (1·016 mm.)

500 c.c.   ·010 in.   ·020 in.
models

Piston ring gaps when new are as follows:—

350 c.c. compression minimum ·008 in. (0·20 mm.)
model   ring   maximum ·010 in. (0·25 mm.)

         scraper   minimum ·008 in. (0·20 mm.)
         ring   maximum ·010 in. (0·25 mm.)

500 c.c. compression minimum ·010 in. (0·25 mm.)
models   ring   maximum ·014 in. (0·35 mm.)

         scraper   minimum ·010 in. (0·25 mm.)
         ring   maximum ·014 in. (0·35 mm.)

When fitting new rings the gap must be checked in the lowest part of the cylinder bore. The ring must lie square to the bore for checking purposes, and to ensure this, place the piston crown onto the ring and ease it down the bore. Check the gap with feeler gauges.

Refitting the piston rings is straight forward, but check that the two compression rings are fitted the right way up and that all the rings are fitted so that the gaps are staggered at 120° to each other.

The two taper compression rings are marked "top" to ensure correct assembly, and should be fitted with the "top" marking towards the cylinder head (see Fig. B21).

ENGINE

SECTION B23

INSPECTING THE PISTONS AND CYLINDER BLOCKS

PISTONS

Check the thrust areas of the piston skirt for signs of seizure or scoring.

The piston skirt is of a special oval form and is designed to have limited working clearance within the bores. The clearances are given in GENERAL DATA.

Prior to inspection, ensure that both the cylinder bores and pistons are clean and free from dirt, etc. Any deposits of burnt oil round the piston skirt can be removed by using a petrol (gasolene) soaked cloth.

NOTE: The top lands on 350 c.c. and 500 c.c. pistons have working clearances varying from .012 in. to .020 in. and thus allow the top piston ring to be viewed from above, and the piston to be rocked slightly. However, this is not critical; it is the skirt clearances that are all important.

CYLINDER BORES

The maximum wear occurs within the top half inch of the bore, whilst the portion below the piston ring working area remains relatively unworn. Compare the diameters, measured at right angles to the gudgeon pin, to obtain an accurate estimate of the wear. A difference between these figures in excess of ·005 in. (·13 mm.) indicates that a rebore is necessary. Compare the figures obtained with those given below so that an accurate figure for the actual wear can be determined.

An approximate method for determining the wear in a cylinder bore is that of measuring the piston ring gap at various depths in the bore and comparing with the gap when the ring is at the bottom of the cylinders. The difference between the figures obtained, when divided by three (an approximation of π) equals the wear on the diameters. As above, if the difference exceeds ·005 in. (·13 mm.), this indicates that a rebore is necessary.

SECTION B24

TABLE OF SUITABLE REBORE SIZES

350 c.c.	ins.	mms.
Standard	2·292	58·25
+·010 (·254 mm.)	2·302	58·504
+·020 (·508 mm.)	2·312	58·758
+·040 (1·016 mm.)	2·332	59·266
500 c.c.		
Standard	2·716	69·00
+·010 (·254 mm.)	2·726	69·254
+·020 (·508 mm.)	2·736	69·508
+·040 (1·016mm.)	2·756	70·00

SECTION B25

RENEWING THE SMALL END BUSHES

The small end bush wear, which normally is very slight, can be estimated when sliding the gudgeon pin through the bush. If it is in good condition the pin will be a sliding fit in the bush, with no play being in evidence. Renewal of the small end bush can be easily achieved by using the new bush 'C' to press out the old one. For this purpose a threaded bolt about 4 in. long 'A' and a $1\frac{1}{4}$ in. long piece of tube with an inside diameter of $\frac{7}{8}$ in 'B' will be required.

Place a suitable washer and the new bush onto the bolt, then offer it into the old bush. Place the piece of tube and a suitable washer over the bolt and screw the nut on finger tight. Centralise the bush and tube and align the oil way in the new bush with that in the connecting rod. When the nut is tightened the new bush will extract the old one.

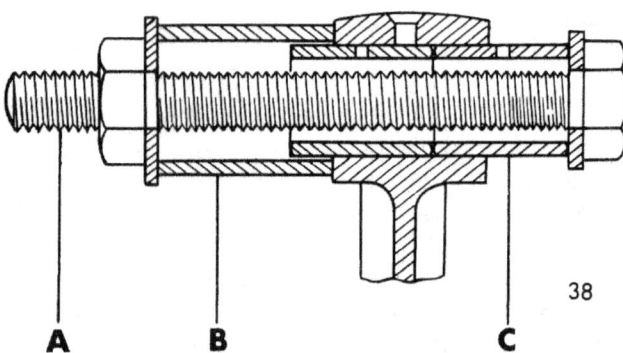

Fig. B22. Extracting a small end bush

Finally, ream the bore of the bush to the size given in GENERAL DATA, taking care not to allow any metallic particles to enter the crankcase. When reaming the bush, ensure that its bore is parallel with the big end bore.

SECTION B26

REMOVING AND REPLACING THE CONTACT BREAKER

The contact breaker mechanism is housed in the timing cover on the right of the engine and is driven by the exhaust camshaft. It consists of two sets of points (one per cylinder), two capacitors (condensers) and a fully automatic centrifugal drive advance and retard mechanism. The working parts are protected by a circular cover and gasket. The engine oil is prevented from entering the contact breaker cavity by means of an oil seal fitted to the inner wall of the timing cover. The complete contact breaker unit can be removed from the timing cover with the aid of service tool D484.

First, disconnect the leads from the battery terminal then remove the two screws and withdraw the outer cover and gasket. Remove the centre bolt and screw in service tool D484, until the cam unit is released from its locking taper in the camshaft. Unscrew the tool and remove the cam unit.

To completely detach the contact breaker unit it will be necessary to disconnect the two leads from the ignition coils and remove the appropriate frame clips so that the leads can be withdrawn through the holes in the crankcase and timing covers.

It is advisable to make a note of the degree figure which is stamped on the back of the cam unit, as this indicates the advance range, which is necessary to know for accurate static timing purposes.

Prior to replacing the cam unit it is advisable to add a small drop of lubricating oil to the pivot pins. The cam unit slot should be located on the peg in the camshaft and the centre bolt screwed in and tightened.

ENGINE

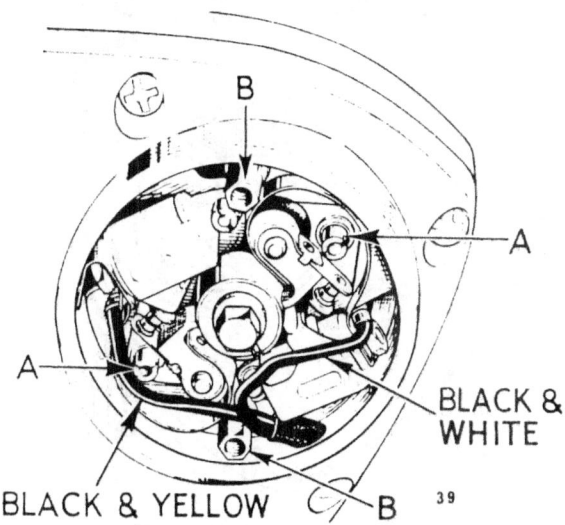

Fig B23 (a) Ignition contact breaker

To adjust contact breaker gaps slacken sleeve nuts 'A'. To rotate contact breaker base plate for setting ignition timing slacken pillar bolts 'B'.

The base plate should be repositioned so that the set of points with the black/yellow lead is rearmost and with the pillar bolts in the centres of the timing adjustment slots.

NOTE: Setting the ignition to the correct figure for the model, is fully described in Sections B31 and B32.

When the correct setting is achieved, ensure that the contact breaker bolts are tight, then fit the cover and gasket.

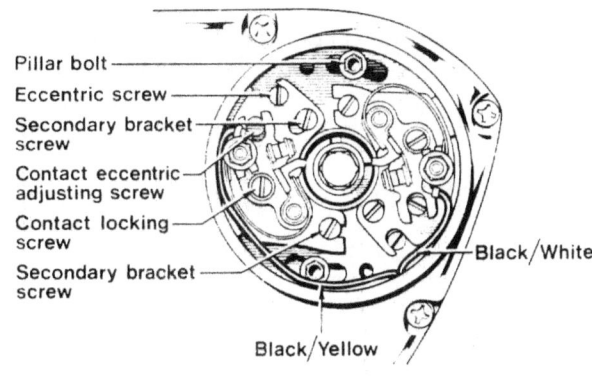

Fig B23 (b) Contact breaker – Type 6CA

SECTION B27

REMOVING AND REPLACING THE TIMING COVER

Remove the contact breaker as described in Section B26.

Unscrew the eight recessed screws which serve to retain the timing cover and if necessary tap the cover with a hide mallet until the cover is free. When the cover is removed, the contact breaker oil seal should be inspected for wear and replaced if necessary.

NOTE: The oil seal must be fitted with the 'open' face of the seal towards the timing gears.

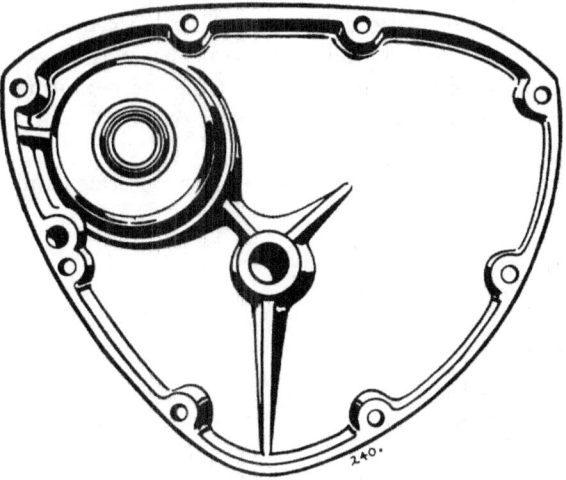

Fig. B24. Timing cover oil seal location

ENGINE

To replace the cover, first check that the contact breaker oil seal is facing in the correct direction (see Fig. B22) and then carefully clean the junction surfaces of the timing cover and crankcase and remove any traces of used jointing compound. Apply a fresh coat of a suitable proprietary jointing compound evenly over the timing cover junction surface. Screw the tapered adaptor pilot (service tool D486) into the exhaust camshaft and smear it with oil to assist assembly. Check that both the location dowels are in their correct positions, slide the cover into position and screw in the eight recessed screws.

Finally, replace the contact breaker assembly and reset the ignition timing as shown in Sections B31 and B32.

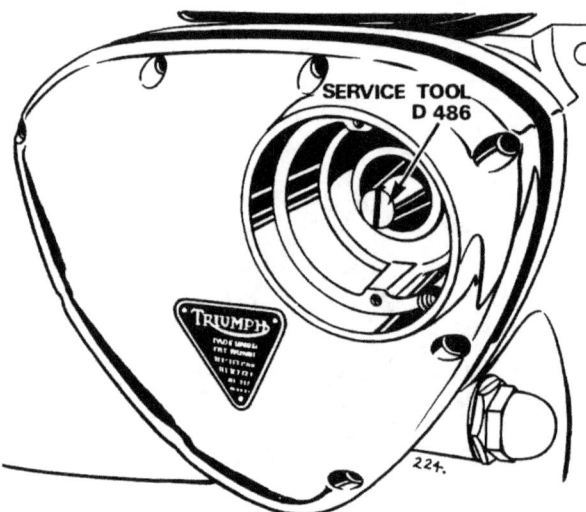

Fig. B25. Replacing the timing cover using service tool D486

SECTION B28

REMOVING AND REPLACING THE OIL PUMP

To remove the oil pump, first remove the contact breaker mechanism, and the timing cover as described in Sections B26 and B27. Unscrew the two nuts and the oil pump can be withdrawn complete with serrated washers from the mounting studs. The paper gasket should be renewed.

Full details concerning inspection, testing and rectification of the oil pump are given in Section A6.

When replacing the oil pump, care should be taken to ensure that the new gasket is fitted correctly, i.e., the holes in alignment with the holes drilled in the crankcase, and that the serrated washers are replaced before tightening down the securing nuts.

ENGINE

SECTION B29

EXTRACTING AND REFITTING THE VALVE TIMING PINIONS

Before attempting to remove any of the valve timing gears it is necessary to release the load on the camshafts caused by compressed valve springs. This should be done by removing the rocker boxes as detailed in Section B2, or may be achieved by sufficiently slackening the valve clearance adjuster screws; however, this is not always advisable as it may result in a push rod becoming disengaged.

Remove the contact breaker as detailed in Section B27.

Remove the timing cover as described in Section B27 and the oil pump as shown in Section B28. Select fourth (top) gear, apply the rear brake and unscrew the nuts retaining the camshaft and crankshaft, then withdraw the intermediate wheel.

NOTE: The camshaft pinion retainer nuts have LEFT-HAND threads. The crankshaft pinion retainer nut has a RIGHT-HAND thread.

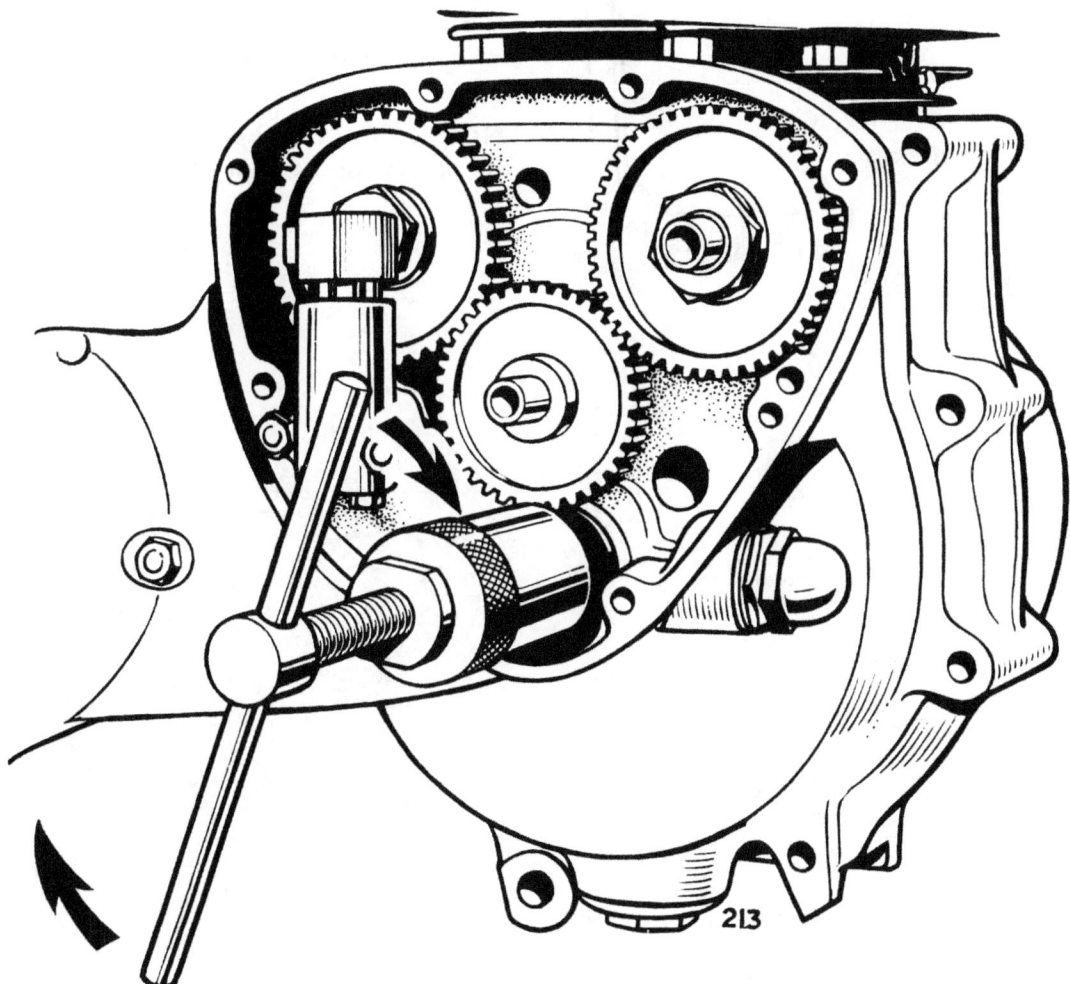

Fig. B26. Extracting the crankshaft pinion

CRANKSHAFT PINION

The crankshaft pinion is removed by using service tool Z89. To extract the pinion, first remove the pinion nut, then screw the extractor body onto the pinion and finally screw in the extractor bolt whereupon the pinion will be withdrawn from the crankshaft. Remove the key from the crankshaft and place it in safe keeping.

The crankshaft pinion can be refitted using a hollow drift to assemble it to the crankshaft. To do this smear the bore of the crankshaft pinion with grease to assist assembly, align the key and keyway and drive the pinion onto the crankshaft.

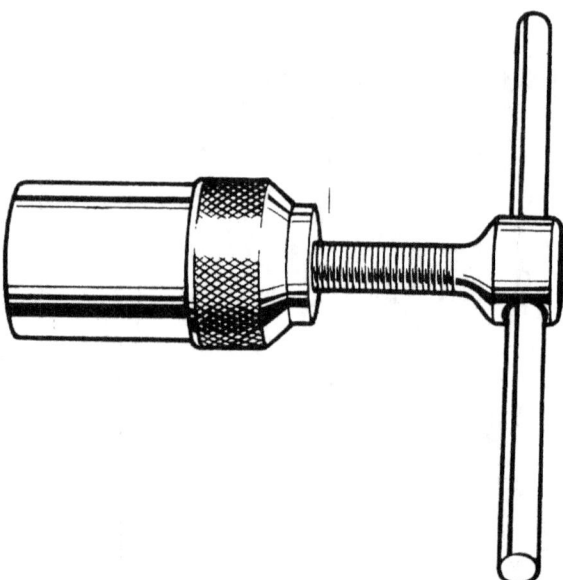

Fig. B27. Extractor tool Z89

CAMSHAFT PINIONS

To facilitate extraction and replacement of the camshaft pinions, extractor adaptor Z145 and replacer adaptor Z144 should be used in conjunction with existing service tool Z89.

To extract the pinion, first screw on the extractor body, then screw in the extractor bolt; the pinion will then be withdrawn from the camshaft (see Fig. B28).

In the case of the exhaust camshaft, extractor adaptor Z145 should be positioned in the end of the camshaft to avoid damage to the contact breaker location taper. A smear of grease applied to the adaptor should hold this in position. The location keys in each of the camshafts are a tight fit and may be left in position.

When replacing the pinions, first check that the keys are located correctly, see Section B30, then screw the replacer adaptor Z144 into the assembler bolt and onto the camshaft. The camshaft pinion should be lubricated to assist assembly and the body of the tool screwed onto it. When this is done, slide the pinion and body over the replacer bolt, align the key and correct keyway and screw on the replacer nut and washer, and draw the camwheel fully home with the replacer tool. Remove the tool and replace the exhaust camwheel nut.

NOTE: The camshaft nuts have a left hand thread and are stamped L H on the outer face.

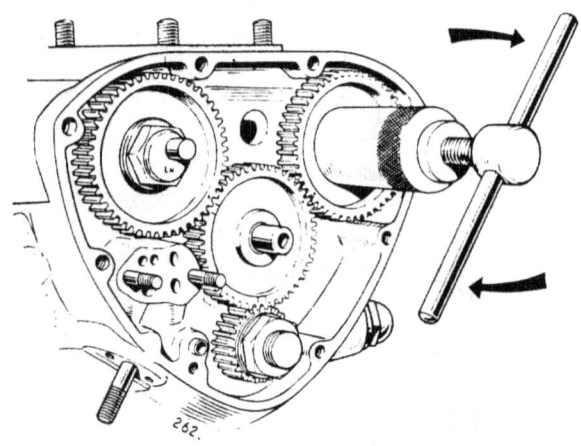

Fig. B28. Extracting camshaft pinion using service tool Z89

ENGINE

REFITTING THE INTERMEDIATE WHEEL

Turn the camshaft and crankshaft until the timing marks are towards the intermediate wheel spindle, then offer the wheel to the spindle with the timing marks aligned as shown in Fig. B30 and B31. Fourth gear should then be selected and the rear brake applied, so that the camshaft and crankshaft pinion retainer nuts can be tightened to the correct torque (see GENERAL DATA). Reassembly then continues as a reversal of the above instructions.

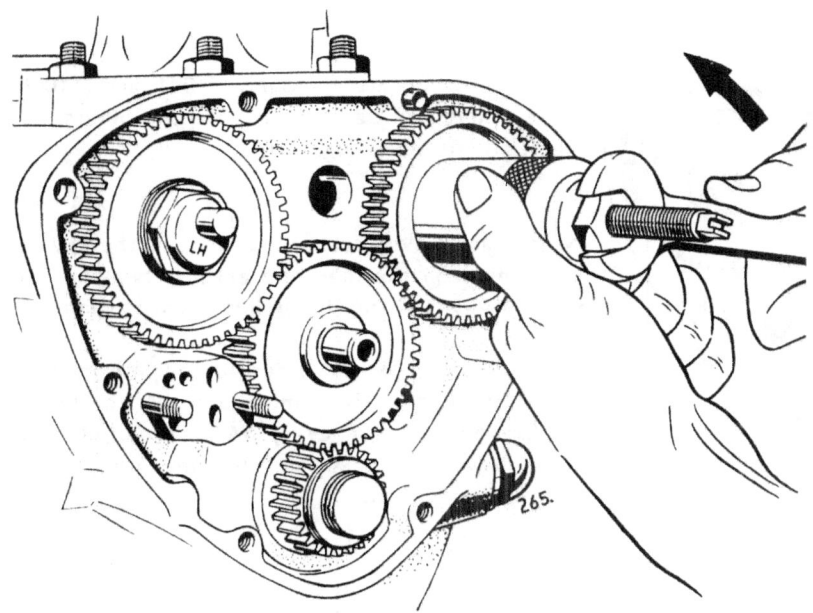

Fig. B29. Refitting the camshaft pinions

SECTION B30
VALVE TIMING

The valve timing is correct for single carburetter versions of models T90 and T100 when the intermediate wheel is assembled in the positions shown in Fig. B30, and the camshaft pinions are located by means of the keyway directly opposite the timing mark.

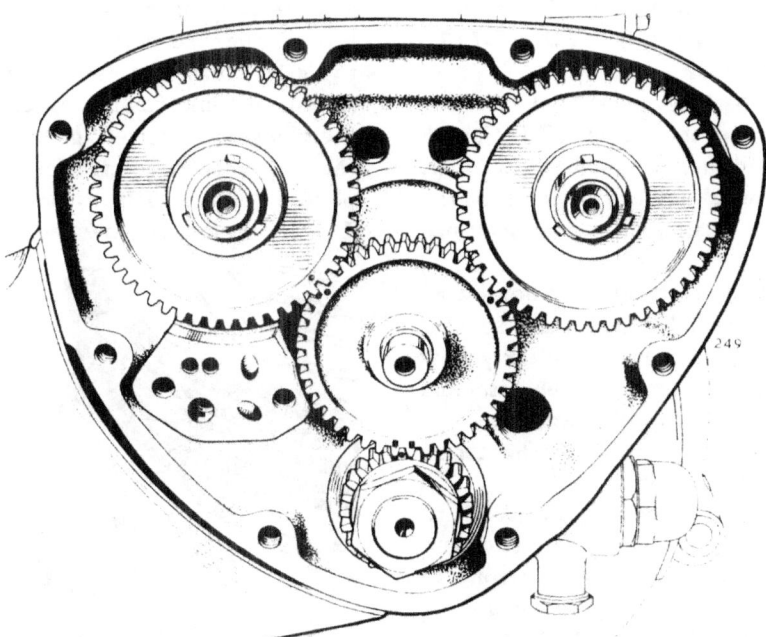

Fig. B30. Intermediate wheel location—Single carburetter models

(1) Exhaust camshaft pinion dot aligned with dot on intermediate wheel.
(2) Crankshaft pinion dot aligned with two dots on intermediate wheel.
(3) Inlet camshaft pinion dot aligned with dot on intermediate wheel.

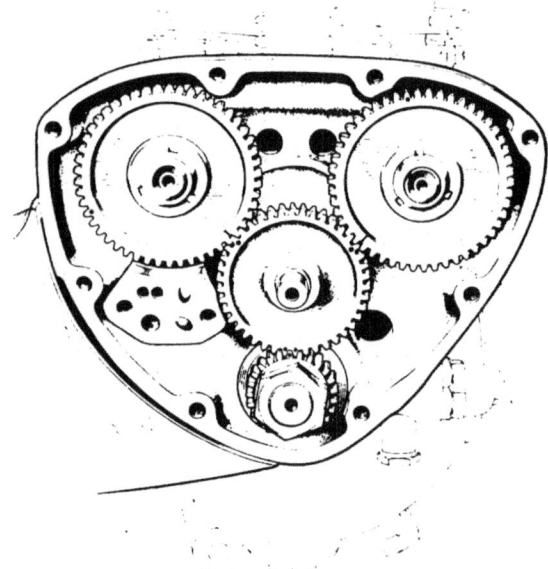

For twin carburetter models T100T and T100R, valve timing will be correct when the pinions are aligned as shown in Fig. B31.

Note that on twin carburetter models the keyway to be used on the inlet and exhaust camwheels is directly opposite the timing line in each instance.

It should be noted that, due to the intermediate wheel having a prime number of teeth, the timing marks only coincide every 94th revolution thus there is no cause for alarm if the timing marks will not readily re-align.

Fig. B31. Intermediate wheel location—Twin carburetter models

(1) Exhaust camshaft pinion line to single dot on intermediate wheel.
(2) Crankshaft pinion dot aligned with two dots on intermediate wheel.
(3) Inlet camshaft pinion line to single dot on intermediate wheel.

SECTION B31
IGNITION TIMING—INITIAL PROCEDURE

INITIAL ASSEMBLY OF THE CONTACT BREAKER MECHANISM AND AUTO ADVANCE UNIT PRIOR TO FINAL TIMING THE ENGINE

(1) Remove both sparking plugs and all four rocker box caps. Set the engine at T.D.C. with both valves closed in the right hand cylinder.
(2) Assemble the auto advance unit into the exhaust camshaft, locating on the camshaft peg where it is fitted.
(3) Assemble the C.B. plate, taking care not to trap the C.B. leads, assembling the plate so that the C.B. points connected to the black/yellow leads are located at 7 o'clock. Loosely assemble the hexagon pillar bolts and flat washers.
(4) Lock the auto advance cam into the taper, using the central fixing bolt.
   NOTE: When the degree disc is attached to the exhaust camshaft, the indicated setting and advance range will be half that of the engine, as the camshaft rotates at half engine speed.

ESTABLISHING TOP DEAD CENTRE POSITION

When setting the ignition timing, the T.D.C. position can be quickly found using workshop tool D571/2. The blanking plug on top of the crankcase immediately behind the cylinder block is removed and the body of the tool is screwed into its place. Having removed both sparking plugs and engaged top gear, rotate the rear wheel forwards until the pistons are just coming up towards T.D.C. Then the plunger is inserted in the body of the tool and the rear wheel is rotated forwards slowly until the plunger locates itself in the centre flywheel. The T.D.C. position has now been established.

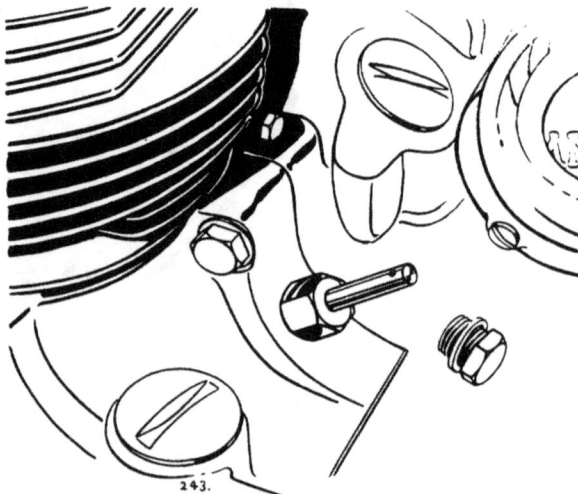

Fig. B32. Showing T.D.C. locating tool in use

ENGINE B

IGNITION TIMING USING A STROBOSCOPIC LIGHT

After establishing T.D.C. as described in Section B31, fit the timing disc adaptor shaft and timing disc into the camshaft auto advance unit and set the pointer, fixed to a convenient bolt on the engine to rear T.D.C.

NOTE: When using a stroboscope powered by 6 or 12 volt batteries as an external power source, do not use the machine's own battery equipment. (A.C. pulses in the low tension machine wiring, can trigger the stroboscope, and give false readings).

(1) Connect the stroboscope to the right hand spark plug lead and start the engine. Read the strobo-light on the disc, revving the engine up until the auto advance range is fully achieved. Check against the correct specification and adjust the C.B. back plate on its slots until the correct advanced timing is accurately set.

(2) Repeat for L.H. plug and adjust the accuracy of the spark on the C.B. points adjustment.

NOTE: To advance the spark, open the points, approximately 0·001 in. for each engine degree required, and to retard, close the points setting similarly. Minor adjustments to the left cylinder C.B. points gap setting, to ensure accurate ignition timing are permissible.

(3) Check back on the stroboscopic reading and slow tickover for range of advance on both cylinders, for efficient action of the auto advance unit, remembering the most important final setting is at fully advanced, both cylinders. Timing the engine stroboscopically with a timing disc ensures that both plugs are firing at exactly similar angular crank rotation (i.e. piston movement), at fully advanced ignition, that is at full power, thereby ensuring the smoothest, most vibration free engine running condition and ensuring maximum engine power output.

It also eliminates variations encountered in differing auto advance ranges due to possible non-standard components, uneven wear, etc., etc.

IGNITION TIMING USING A STROBOSCOPIC LIGHT

A stroboscope should be connected to the right hand sparking plug, and a power source.

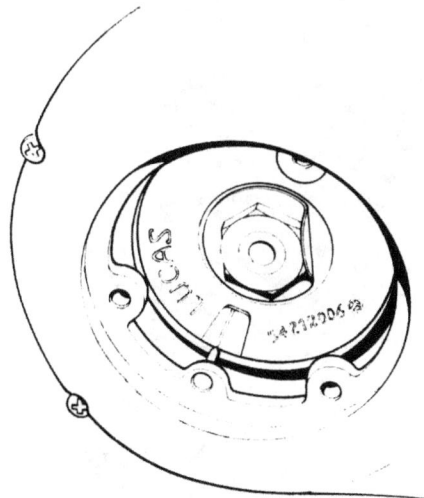

Fig. B 32(b). Showing ignition timing pin

NOTE: When using a stroboscope powered by six or 12 volt batteries as an external power source, do not use the machine's own battery equipment. (A.C. pulses in low tension wiring can trigger the stroboscope, and give false readings).

Start the motor, and direct the stroboscope beam at the rotor mark (see Fig. B32(b)). The rotor may have two timing marks, in which case the mark furthest from the keyway should be used, i.e. the mark nearest the word "Lucas".

Initial adjustment can be made by rotating the contact breaker back plate, and then locking the two hexagonal pillar bolts. Accurate setting is carried out by slackening the secondary bracket screws on the contact breaker (black/yellow side) and adjusting the eccentric screw until both scribed lines coincide when the engine is running at 2,000 r.p.m. or more. When an accurate setting has been achieved, retighten the secondary bracket screws.

Remove the crankshaft plug, and turn the engine through 360° (one revolution). Reposition the location plug in the 38° B.T.D.C. hole and re-connect the stroboscope to the left hand sparking plug. The previous procedure can now be repeated, bearing in mind that the contact breaker back plate must not be disturbed.

SECTION B32

STATIC IGNITION TIMING—TO BE USED ONLY WHERE A STROBOSCOPE IS NOT AVAILABLE

TO ESTABLISH THE ACCURATE STATIC IGNITION SETTING

(1) Check the General Data Section for the correct fully advanced ignition setting for the machine.

(2) Check the auto advance range stamped on rear of auto advance cam mechanism.

(3) Double the auto advance range and subtract the figure from the FULL ADVANCE setting for the machine. This is the correct STATIC SETTING for the engine.

(4) Use this figure for setting the position of the C.B. points opening, when assembling the contact breaker mechanism, using a degree plate or timing disc attached to the engine.

(5) Convert this figure in degrees to the equivalent piston movement B.T.C. if a timing stick is to be employed.

On machines where an engine camshaft peg is not fitted, rotate the auto advance mechanism until a position is reached where the rear set of C.B. points will just commence to open.

CONVERSION CHART—ENGINE DEGREE TO RELATIVE PISTON POSITIONS

Crankshaft position (B.T.D.C.)	Piston position (B.T.D.C.)	
Degrees	in.	mm.
7	·010	·25
8	·015	·38
9	·020	·51
10	·025	·64
11	·030	·76
12	·035	·89
13	·040	1·02
14	·048	1·22
15	·055	1·40
16	·060	1·52
17	·070	1·78
18	·080	2·03
19	·090	2·29
20	·100	2·54
21	·110	2·79

EXAMPLE OF STATIC SETTING CALCULATION

T100SS IGNITION TIMING=37° B.T.D. Fully advanced.

C.B. range stamped on auto advance cam=12°.
Twice 12°=24°
Full advance 37°−24°=13° B.T.C.

POSITIONING THE TIMING DISC WHERE THERE IS NO PROVISION FOR THE T.D.C. PLUNGER (Earlier models)

(1) Fit the timing disc adaptor shaft and timing disc into the camshaft auto advance unit, and set the pointer, fixed to a convenient bolt on the engine, to read T.D.C.

Engage top gear, and use a timing stick with a suitable mark which aligns along the top of the cylinder head fins at about 1 in. of piston movement. (For greater accuracy, use a Dial Test Indicator through the spark plug hole). Rotate the engine either side of T.D.C. by rocking the rear wheel, to exactly the same measured point of movement on the stick (or D.T.I.), setting the pointer so that it reads an equal number of degrees either side of T.D.C. on the degree disc.

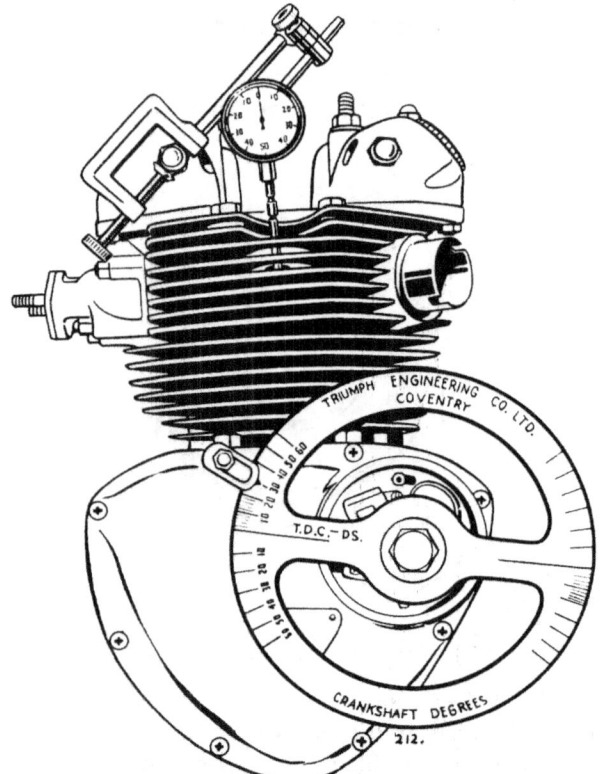

Fig. B33. Engine fitted with timing disc and dial test indicator

ENGINE

(1) Rotate the engine so that the fibre heel of the C.B. points have just passed beyond the ramp of the auto advance cam, and just reached the full open position. Set the point gap 0·015 in.

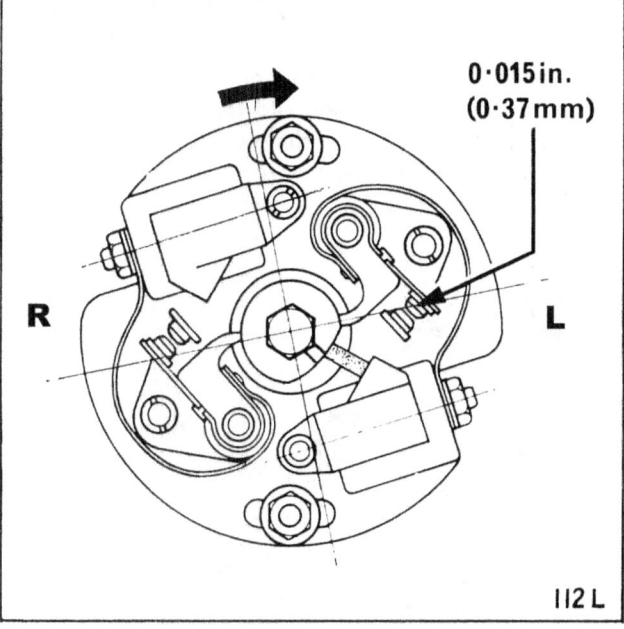

Fig. B34(b). Setting contact breaker point gap for the left cylinder (black/white) lead, illustrating the second position of the cam, where the points have just achieved the fully open position

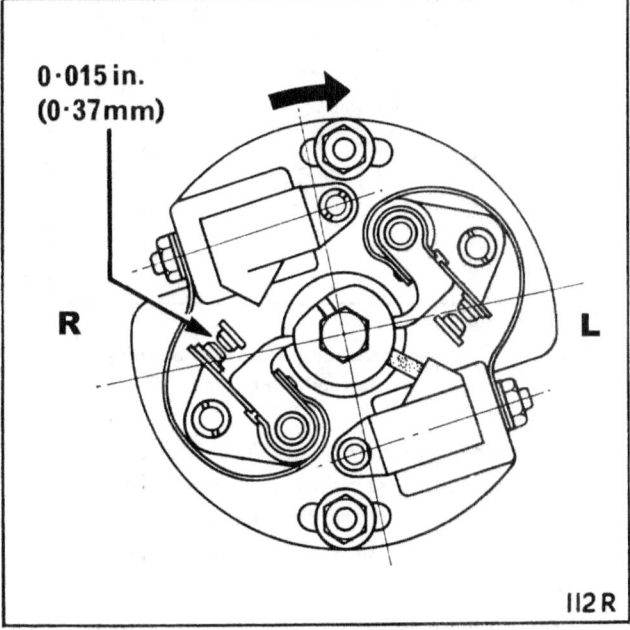

Fig. B34(a). Setting the contact breaker point gap for the right cylinder (black/yellow) lead, illustrating position of the cam where points are just fully open

If the machine is put in top gear, small increments in crank rotation and piston movement can be achieved by rotating the rear wheel slowly, and accurate piston T.D.C. established by "swinging" the engine either side of T.D.C. Mark the timing stick at T.D.C. Mark a second position on the timing stick ABOVE the T.D.C. mark appropriate to the specified timing for the machine, i.e. "piston movement before T.D.C.".

(2) Rotate the engine "forwards" through 360° and set the second set of points in the corresponding position on the cam. Set these points at a gap of 0·015 in.

(3) ROTATE ENGINE AND ESTABLISH ACCURATE T.D.C. (See Section B31 and foregoing)

(4) Rotate the engine "backwards" beyond this mark and then slowly reverse the rotation "forwards" until the timing mark is set in line with the top of the cylinder head fins. If a timing disc is employed, rotate the engine forwards until the correct "static setting" is achieved in crankshaft degrees.

ENGINE

(5) Rotate the C.B. back plate on its slots until a position is reached where the points just open (check using a battery and light, or an 0·0015 in. feeler gauge. Alternatively, if a battery is fitted to the machine and the ignition switch turned to "IGN", the position where the points open can be identified by the ammeter needle giving a "flick" back to zero).

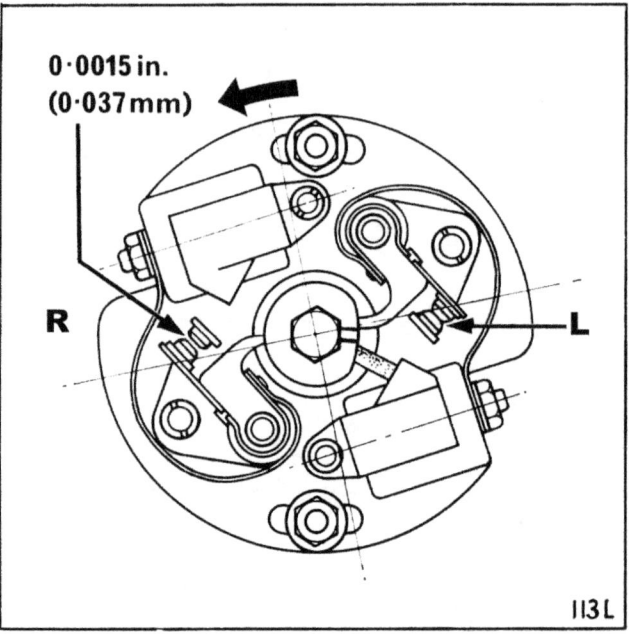

Fig. B35(b). Contact breaker points just opening on the left cylinder

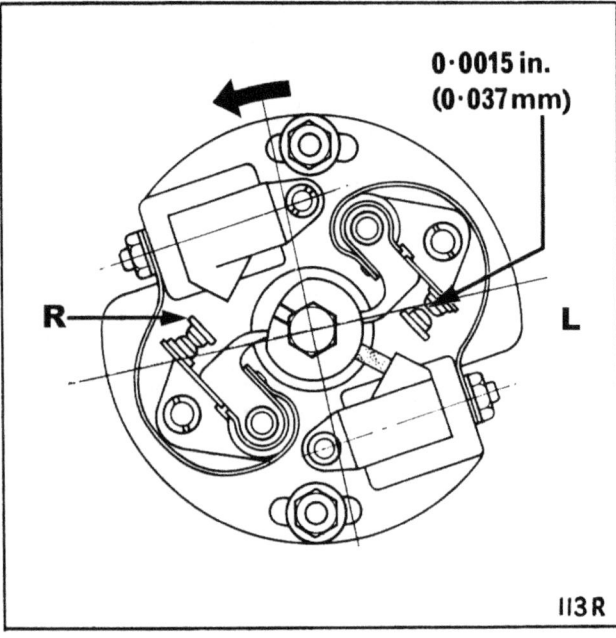

Fig. B35(a). Contact breaker points just opening on the right cylinder. With the engine set at the correct STATIC SETTING, the C.B. back plate assembly should be adjusted in the slots, to a position where the C.B. points just commence to open.

Rotate the engine through 360°. The other set of C.B. points should just have opened. If not, the accuracy of spark on the second set of C.B. points can be corrected by adjusting the points gap.

NOTE: To advance the spark, open the points, approximately 0·001 in. for each engine degree required, and to retard, close the points setting similarly. Minor adjustments to left cylinder C.B. points setting to ensure accurate ignition timing are permissible.

SECTION B33

REMOVING AND REPLACING THE CAMSHAFTS ONLY

It is not necessary to part the crankcases in order to replace the camshafts.

Remove the cylinder block and head (see Sections B13 and B18).

Remove the timing cover (see Section B27). Remove the oil pump by removal of the two conical nuts and locking washers. To avoid the loss of the engine oil, the necessary holes in the crankcase face can be blocked temporarily but it *is most essential* that these holes are cleared before the oil pump is refitted at a later stage. Extract the inlet and exhaust camwheels (see Section B29) and the camshaft retaining plates and screws will be seen.

The retaining plate screws are centre punched to lock them. A small drill should be used to remove the centre punch marks and the screws can be extracted, followed by the retaining plates.

At this stage the camshafts can be drawn out from the right hand side of the crankcases. Care must be taken that the breather disc and spring behind the inlet camshaft are not dropped into the engine.

When the new camshafts are fitted, place the rotary breather valve and spring into the camshaft bush then assemble both camshafts ensuring that the slot in the end of the inlet camshaft engages the projection of the breather disc valve. The camshaft retaining plates should be refitted, preferably using new screws. The screws should be centre punched and reassembly then proceeds as a reversal of the foregoing.

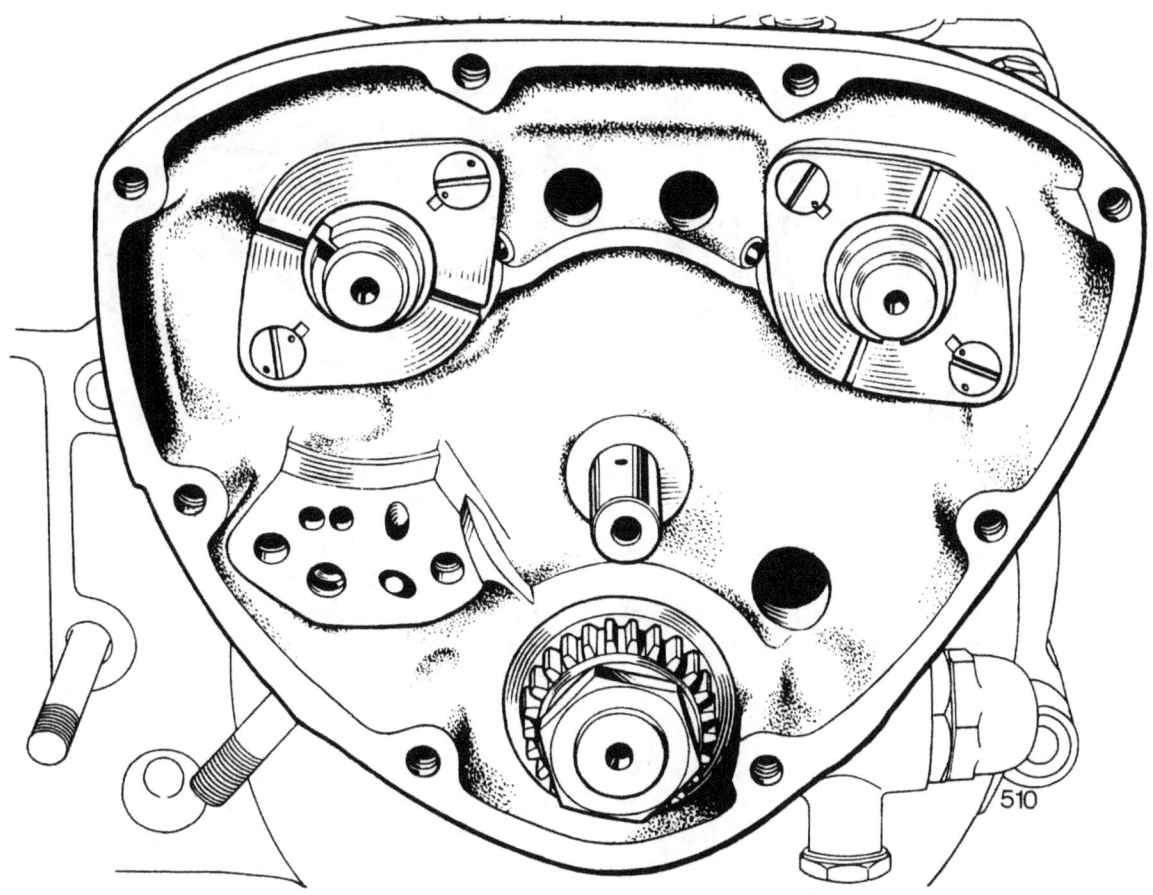

Fig. B36. Camwheels removed to show camshaft retaining plates

SECTION B34

DISMANTLING AND REASSEMBLING THE CRANKCASE ASSEMBLY

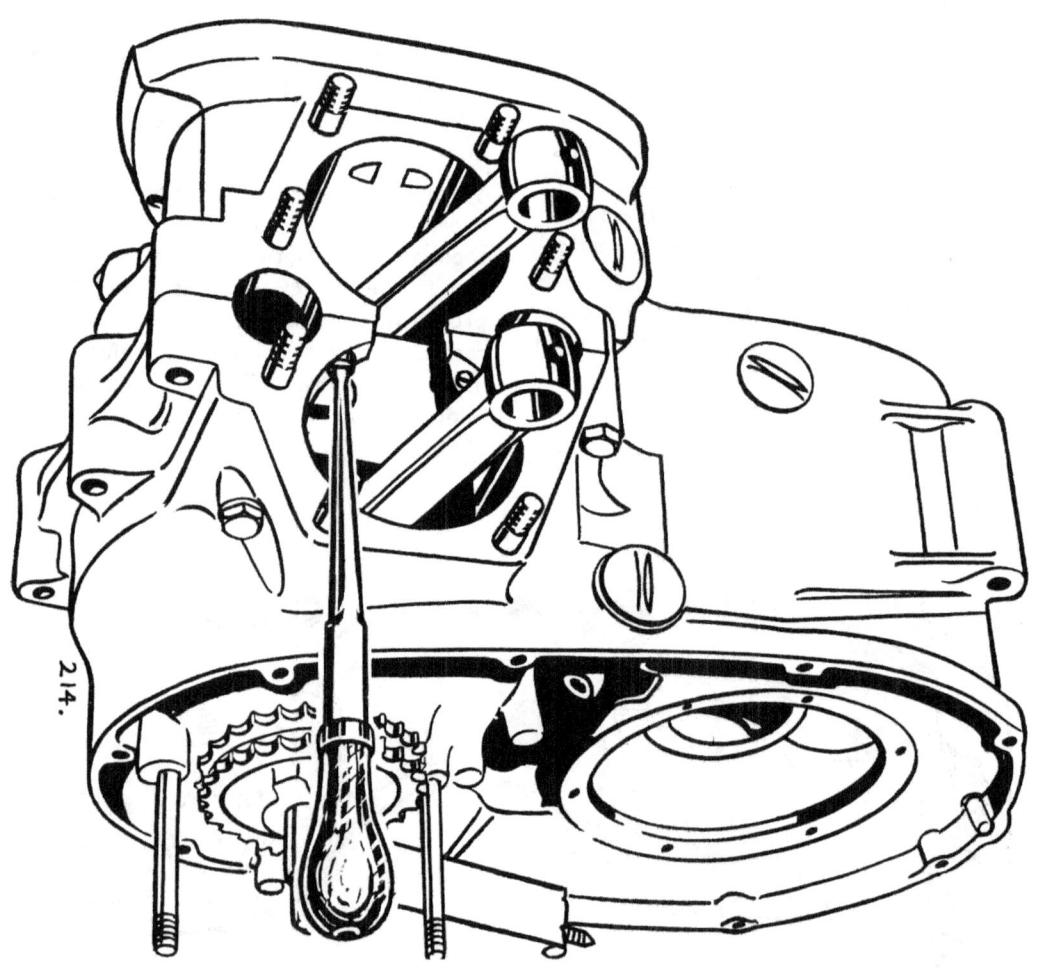

Fig. B37. Removing the crankcase junction screws

It is advisable to partially dismantle the engine unit whilst it is fitted to the motorcycle, then remove the remaining crankcase assembly and dismantle it on a work bench.

Proceed as described in Section B1 for removal of the engine unit, but leave the rear chain connected and the engine firmly mounted in the frame by means of the front and bottom engine mounting bolts. Remove the outer primary cover as shown in Section C3 then disconnect the generator leads underneath the engine (snap connectors). Unscrew the three nuts securing the stator and withdraw it from over the mounting studs. Do not try to withdraw the leads at this stage.

Remove the pressure plate and clutch plates as detailed in Section C4. Select fourth gear and apply the rear brake, then unscrew the clutch hub securing nut and extract the clutch hub as shown in Section C9. When the primary chain has been threaded over the stator the sleeve nut should be unscrewed and the stator leads withdrawn.

ENGINE

Remove the gearbox outer cover and dismantle the gearbox, (see Section D) remove the rocker boxes, cylinder head, block and pistons as shown in Sections B2, B13, B18 and B21 respectively, then disconnect the clutch cable and remove the carburetter.

Remove the C.B., timing cover and oil pump (Sections B26, B27 and B28) then extract the crankshaft pinion. If it is required to inspect or change the camshafts or bushes, the camshaft pinions should also be extracted.

Remove the front and bottom engine mounting studs, disconnect the rear chain and remove the crankcase assembly.

Grip the crankcase firmly in a vice by means of the bottom mounting lug and unscrew the bolt and two screws shown in Fig. B37. Remove the remaining stud at the front of the engine and also the two nuts adjacent to the gearbox housing. The crankcase halves may now be parted using extractor tool number Z151. When the halves are apart, withdraw the crankshaft assembly and store it carefully, then remove the rotary breather valve from within the inlet camshaft bush in the left half crankcase.

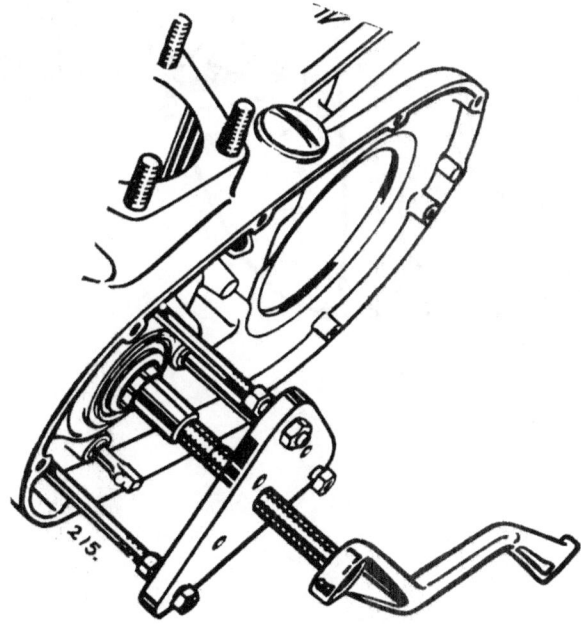

Fig. B38 Parting the crankcase halves

REASSEMBLY

Prior to reassembly, the junction surfaces should be carefully scraped clean, giving special attention to the location spigot and dowels.

Mount the left half crankcase on its side on two wooden blocks, or a bench with a hole in for crankshaft clearance, lubricate the main bearing and camshaft bushes. Place the rotary breather valve and spring into the camshaft bush, then assemble both camshafts ensuring that the slot in the end of the inlet camshaft engages the projection of the breather disc valve. Assemble the crankshaft carefully into position ensuring that it is right home in the bearing.

Apply a fresh coat of jointing compound to the junction surface of the left half crankcase then lubricate the main bearing and camshaft bushes in both halves of the crankcase. Position the con rods centrally and lower the right half crankcase into position over the crankshaft. When the halves are mated, check the crankshaft and camshafts for freedom of rotation. The crankshaft should revolve freely whilst the camshafts should offer little or no resistance to rotation by hand.

Refit the crankcase securing bolts and studs, and tighten them until they are just pinched up. Check that the cylinder block junction surface of the crankcase is level.

If there is a slight step between the two halves, this should be corrected by tapping the front and rear of the crankcase as required, until a level surface is achieved. The crankcase securing bolts should then be tightened, a turn at a time, to the torque figures given in GENERAL DATA.

Reassembly then continues as a reversal of the dismantling instructions. Prior to refitting the cylinder block, pour $\frac{1}{6}$ pint of oil into the crankcase.

SECTION B35

STRIPPING AND REASSEMBLING THE CRANKSHAFT ASSEMBLY

Grip the crankshaft conveniently in a suitable vice and place rag over any sharp edges to avoid the connecting rods becoming damaged. Mark the connecting rods, caps and crankshaft so that they can be replaced in their original positions.

Note the connecting rod, cap and nut are centre punched on initial assembly so that the cap may be refitted correctly relative to the connecting rod.

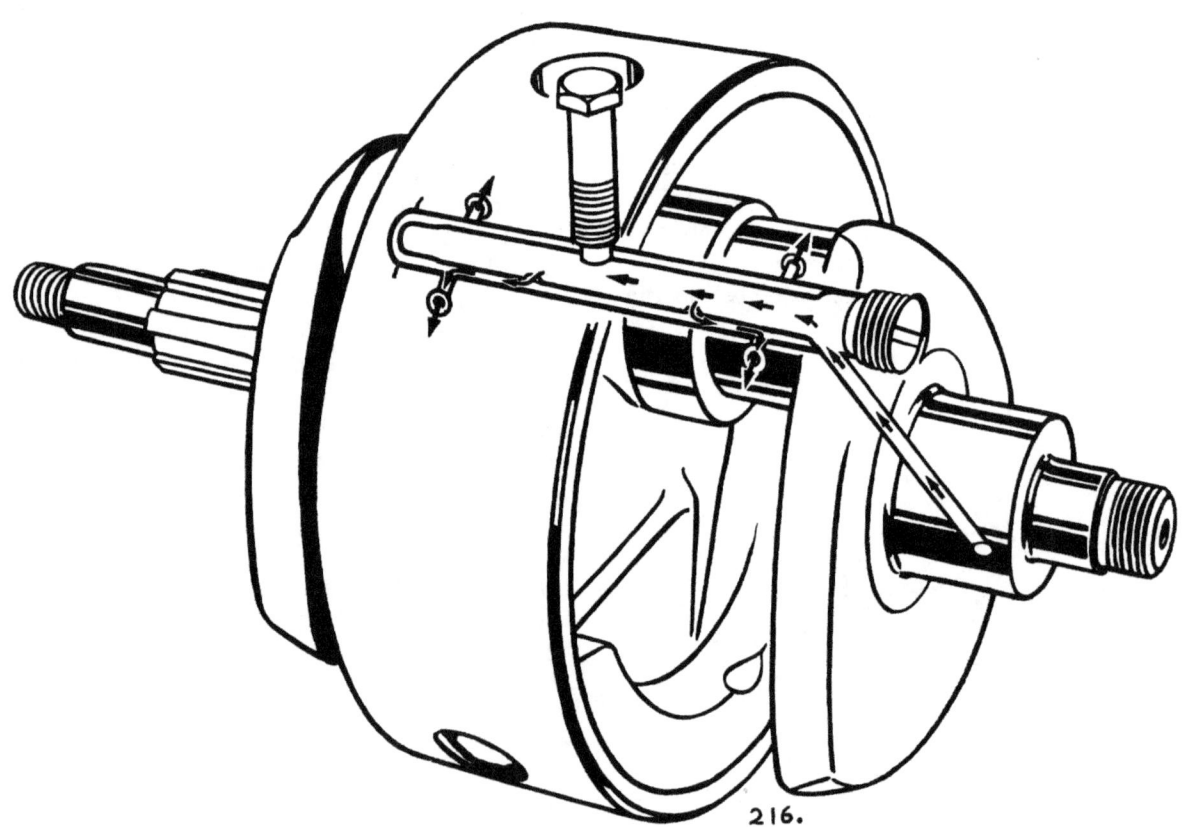

Fig. B39. Sectional view of crankshaft—showing oil tube

ENGINE

Unscrew the cap retainer nuts, a turn at a time to avoid distortion, then remove the caps and connecting rods. Refit the nuts to their respective bolts to ensure correct reassembly.

Using a large impact screw driver, unscrew the oil tube retainer plug from the right end of the big-end journal. If difficulty is encountered, drill an $\frac{1}{8}$ in. diameter hole to $\frac{1}{8}$ in. depth in the crankshaft, to remove the centre punched indentation which locks the oil tube retainer plug in position.

Unscrew the flywheel bolt adjacent to the big end journal, then withdraw the oil tube using a hooked rod located in the flywheel bolt location hole (see Fig. B39).

Thoroughly clean all parts in paraffin (kerosene) then clean the oil drillings using a jet of compressed air. Particular attention should be given to checking that each oil drilling is free from blockage.

To remove the flywheel unscrew the remaining two bolts and press out the crankshaft from the right (plain bearing) using a press which can give a load of up to five tons. (Ensure that there is a centre punch mark on the right side of the flywheel before removing; this enables the flywheel to be replaced in its original position).

Replacing the flywheel is best done when the oil tube is correctly located into position. Offer the oil tube into the crankshaft with the flywheel bolt holes in the tube and crankshaft aligned. Insert a flywheel bolt temporarily to locate the oil tube in position.

Apply a hydraulic type thread sealant to the crankshaft threads, and screw in the plug tightly. Centre punch the crankshaft opposite the slot so that the plug is locked in position.

To reassemble the flywheel it should be heated to 100° centigrade then placed over the crankshaft (which should be cold) with the centre punch mark to the right. It will be necessary to turn the flywheel through 180° to get it over the crankshaft web. Turn it to its correct position relative to the crankshaft as soon as this is achieved, and align the bolt holes.

The flywheel bolts should be tightened to the torque figure given in GENERAL DATA using Triumph Loctite Sealant to obviate any possibility of the bolts working loose.

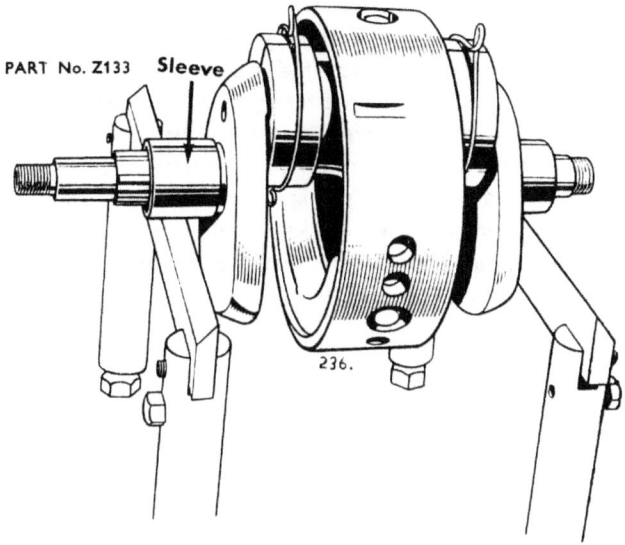

Fig. B40. Balancing the crankshaft (using sleeve Z133 on timing side)

If a new or reground crankshaft or a new flywheel has been fitted, the assembly should be rebalanced, using two service balance weights Z122 (490 grs. each). Place the assembly on two horizontal knife edges, resting it on the left and right main bearing diameters. Allow the assembly to come to rest, then mark the lowest point of the flywheel with chalk. Turn the assembly through 90° and if it returns to the same position drill a $\frac{3}{8}$ in. diameter hole centrally, adjacent to the chalk mark, to a depth of approximately $\frac{1}{2}$ in.

NOTE: A sleeve should be fitted over the L/H main bearing journal for this test. (See Fig. B40). Part No. Z133.

Repeat the balancing procedure, again making a chalk mark as necessary, and drill further holes until the assembly will come to rest in any position when placed on the knife edges. The drilled holes should have a distance of approximately $\frac{3}{4}$ in. between centres.

Finally, thoroughly wash the assembly in paraffin (kerosene) and check that the oil ways are free from blockage.

ENGINE

SECTION B36

REFITTING THE CONNECTING RODS

First, ensure that the connecting rod and cap and both the front and rear of the bearing shells are scrupulously clean, then offer the shells to the rod and cap and locate the shell tabs into their respective slots. Smear the bearing surfaces with oil and refit the rod and cap to their original journals, ensuring that the centre punch marks are aligned and that the tab location slots are adjacent (see Fig. B41).

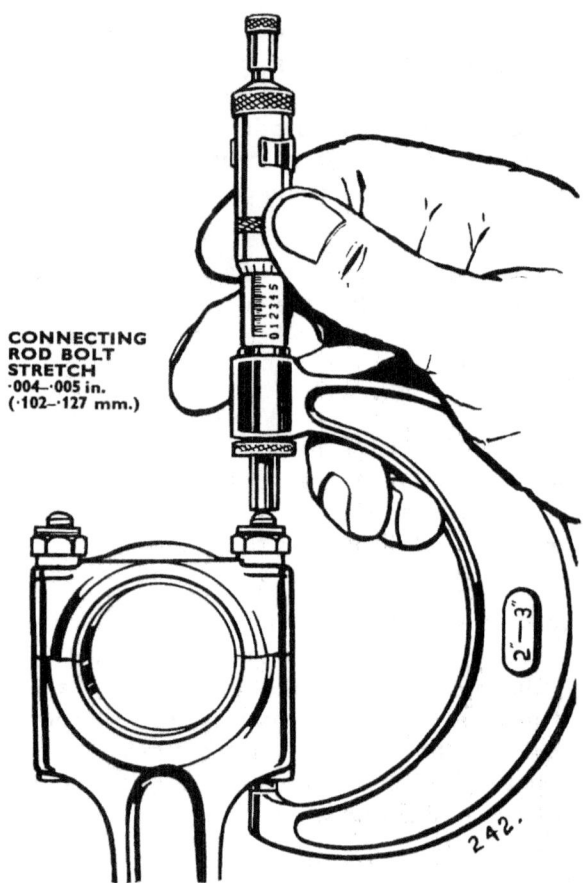

CONNECTING ROD BOLT STRETCH
·004–·005 in.
(·102–·127 mm.)

Fig. B42. Refitting the connecting rods

Refit the bolts and screw on the nuts, a turn at a time, until the centre punch marks on the rod and nut coincide. If new bolts or nuts are fitted then tighten to the given torque figure, or, preferably, the bolt extension figure given in Fig. B42.

Finally, force oil through the drilling in the right main bearing journal of the crankshaft with a pressure oil can until it is expelled from both big end bearings, thus indicating that the oil passages are free from blockage and full of oil.

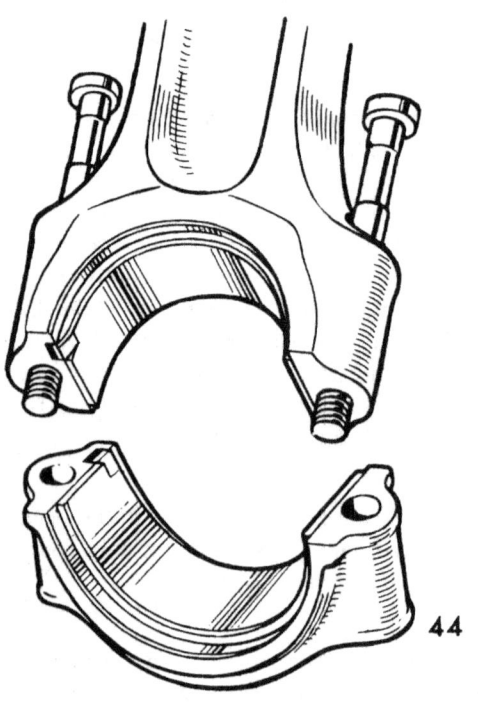

Fig. B41. Refitting the connecting rods

SECTION B37

INSPECTING THE CRANKCASE COMPONENTS

In preparation for inspection, thoroughly clean the crankcase halves, main bearings, crankshaft and connecting rods, etc., in paraffin (kerosene) and allow them to drain. If there is an air line accessible, then dry the components with a jet of compressed air and examine them as follows:—

(1) BIG END BEARINGS

The extent of wear to the big end journals can be determined by inspecting the bearing surfaces for scoring and by measuring the diameter of the journals. Light score marks can be reduced with smooth emery cloth but ensure that all parts are carefully washed after this operation.

Where a journal has been slightly scored the big end shell bearings should be renewed. If the scoring and wear is extensive the big end journals should be reground to a suitable size.

NOTE: The replaceable white metal big end bearings are pre-finished to give the correct diametral clearance. Under no circumstances should the bearings be scraped or the connecting rod and cap joint faces filed.

CRANKSHAFT AND BIG END JOURNAL DIAMETERS

	in.	mm.
Standard	1·4375 1·4380	36·512 36·525
—·010	1·4365 1·4370	36·258 36·271
—·020	1·4355 1·4360	36·004 36·017
—·030	1·4345 1·4350	35·750 35·763

(2) MAIN BALL BEARING (DRIVE SIDE)

Clean the bearing thoroughly in paraffin (kerosene), then dry it with a jet of compressed air. Test the ball race bearing for roughness by spinning. Check the centre race for side play and inspect the balls and tracks for any signs of indentation and pocketing.

(3) MAIN JOURNAL BEARING (TIMING SIDE)

The correct diameters of the main bearing and journal are given in GENERAL DATA.

A table of regrind sizes for the right main bearing journal and big end journals is given below, for which replacements are available.

The timing side plain bearing can be checked for wear by holding the right end of the crankshaft and moving it up and down. A more accurate method of determining wear on the bearing is to attach a dial test indicator to the intermediate gear spindle and locating the pointer onto the end of the crankshaft; by moving the crankshaft up and down the amount of wear will be indicated on the dial. Examine the bearing diameter on the crankshaft for wear, which will require regrinding if it has been scored in any way.

(4) CAMSHAFT AND BUSHES

The camshaft bushes normally show very little sign of wear until a considerable mileage has been covered. A rough check on the wear can be made by inserting the camshaft into the bearing and feeling the up and down movement. An exact check can be made by measuring the camshaft with a micrometer and measuring the camshaft bushes with calipers. The working clearance figures are given in GENERAL DATA. Wear on the cam form will be mainly centred on the opening flank of the cam and on the lobe of the cam. Particular attention should be given to these areas when examining the cam form for grooving. In a case where there is severe grooving both the camshaft and tappet followers should be renewed.

A method of estimating the extent of wear on the cam form is that of measuring the overall height of the cam and the base circle diameter. The difference is the cam lift. If all other aspects of the camshaft are satisfactory and the wear on the cam form does not exceed ·010 in., then the camshaft may be used for further service.

SECTION B38

RENEWING THE MAIN BEARINGS

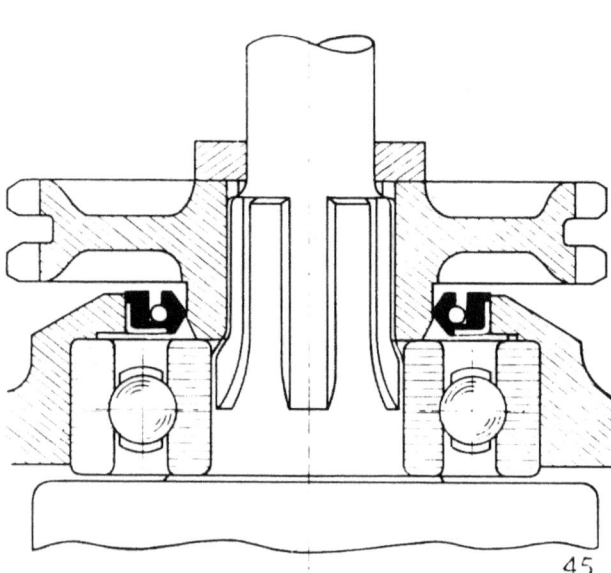

Fig. B43. Oil seal—left hand crankcase

To remove the left side bearing, heat the crankcase to approximately 100° centigrade and drive the bearing inwards using service tool Z14. The right side main bearing is of a bronze bush type and is removed by first removing the lock plate and then heating the crankcase to 100° centigrade, and then driving the bearing out using a suitable shouldered drift.

The oil seal can be removed from the left half crankcase by driving it outwards, in the opposite direction to the bearing after the bearing is removed. It is advisable to renew the oil seal, even if it does not appear badly worn.

To assemble the left bearing first ensure that the main bearing housing is clean, then heat the crankcase to approximately 100° centigrade and drive in the bearing using a tubular drift onto the outer race. Ensure that the bearing enters its housing squarely. If possible, use a press. Suitable dimensions for the drift are $2\frac{3}{4}$ ins. outside diameter by 6 ins. long.

To assemble the right main bearing, heat the crankcase to 100° centigrade and press the plain bearing into its housing. When the bearing has been located in the correct position allow the crankcase to cool and then the bearing has to be line reamed to give the correct clearance with the crankshaft journal. Workshop tool Z134 is available for line reaming the bearing and is utilised by bolting the crankcase halves together with the main bearings in place and inserting the reamer through the right main bearing and locating the pilot end of the reamer in the left main bearing and the cutter in the right main bearing. The reamer Z134 is also available in ·010, ·020 and ·030 in. undersizes.

When the bearings are in position, press the oil seal into place in the left half crankcase.

SECTION B39

RENEWING CAMSHAFT BUSHES

The inlet and exhaust camshafts are supported in the left half crankcase by two bronze bushes; in the right half crankcase the camshafts run directly in the wall of the crankcase. To remove the camshaft bushes in the left half crankcase, a tap is necessary. An ideal size is $\frac{7}{8}$ in. diameter by 9 Whitworth.

When a good thread has been cut in the old bush, heat the crankcase to 100° Centigrade and screw in a suitable bolt. Grip the bolt in a vice and drive the crankcase with a hide mallet until the bush is removed. Do not attempt to lever the bush out of position with the bolt or the case may be damaged. If the tap is used in place of the bolt, care must be taken not to give too hard a knock to the crankcase or the brittle tap may break. Retained behind the inlet camshaft bush is the breather valve supporting disc which is located by means of a peg. When renewing the bush ensure that the disc is located correctly on the peg. The sintered bronze camshaft bushes are machined to size before pressing in, therefore only the smallest amount of metal will need to be removed when they are renewed. See GENERAL DATA for reaming sizes and working clearances.

When reaming is completed, the crankcase must be thoroughly washed in paraffin (kerosene) and allowed to drain. Preferably, use a jet of compressed air to ensure that all swarf is removed.

SECTION BB

ENGINE

	Section
REMOVING AND REPLACING THE ENGINE UNIT	BB1
STRIPPING AND REASSEMBLING THE ROCKER BOXES	BB4
REMOVING AND REFITTING THE CYLINDER HEAD ASSEMBLY	BB13
RENEWING THE VALVE GUIDES	BB15
RESEATING THE VALVES	BB17
CONNECTING ROD SMALL END	BB25
REMOVING AND REPLACING THE TIMING COVER	BB27
EXTRACTING AND REFITTING THE VALVE TIMING PINIONS	BB29
REMOVING AND REPLACING THE CAMSHAFTS ONLY	BB33
STRIPPING AND REASSEMBLING THE CRANKSHAFT ASSEMBLY	BB35
REFITTING THE CONNECTING RODS	BB36
INSPECTING THE CRANKCASE COMPONENTS	BB37
RENEWING THE MAIN BEARINGS	BB38
RENEWING THE CAMSHAFT BUSHES	BB39

SECTION B (INCORPORATED IN SECTION BB)

ENGINE

REMOVING AND REPLACING THE TACHOMETER DRIVE BOX	B40
REMOVING AND REPLACING THE EXHAUST SYSTEM	B41
CONTACT BREAKER – TYPE 6CA	B42

SECTION BB1
REMOVING AND REPLACING THE ENGINE UNIT

On T100C and T100R machines fitted with Siba ignition coils it is possible to remove the engine unit without removing the coils. However they can be easily removed by unscrewing two nuts and bolts which attach the clamp brackets to the mounting bracket. All later variations in the range are fitted with Lucas 17M12 ignition coils. These are similar in shape and size to the Siba, and a similar practice should be adopted.

When removing or replacing the exhaust system which employs any form of balance connector, (either between the two exhaust pipes forward of the cylinder head, or forward of the silencers) refer to Section B41 which describes the procedure in detail.

The front engine plates are retained by studs, nuts and spring washers, and in order to remove the engine these must be removed.

SECTION BB4
STRIPPING AND REASSEMBLING THE ROCKER BOXES

After engine number H63307, rocker arms and spindles are equipped with a revised oiling system which directs a jet of oil towards the ball pin and push rod end cap. This avoids providing an oil hold through the centre of the rocker arm. (See Fig. BB1).

When replacing a ball pin it is unnecessary to select a particular position as previously.

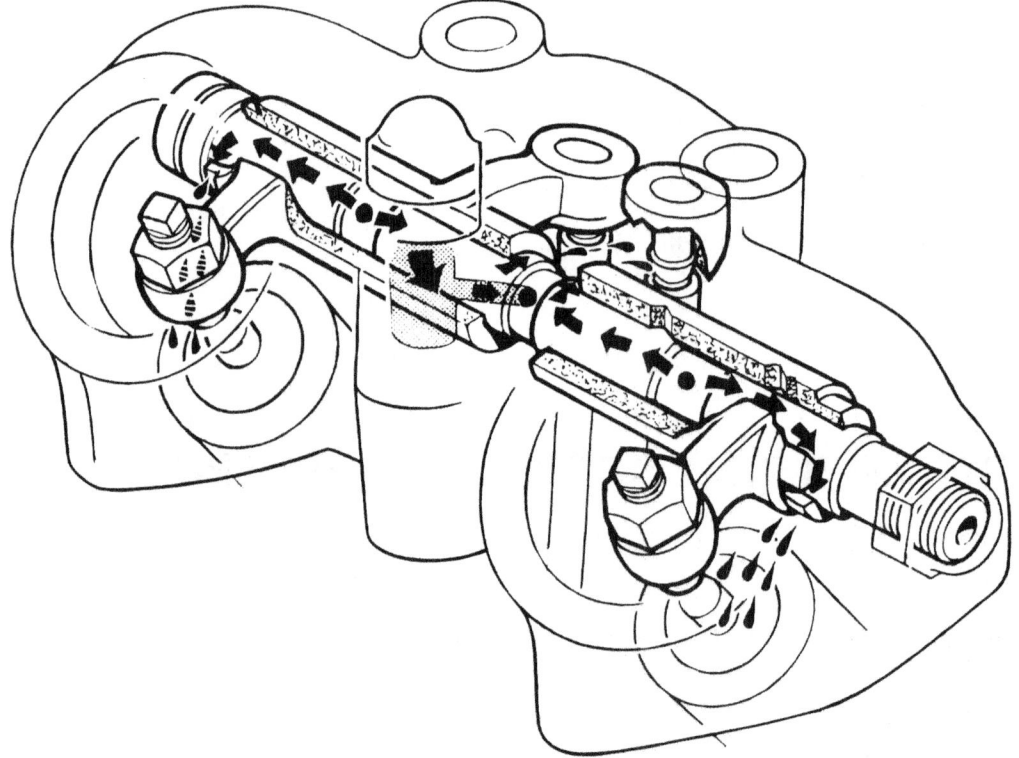

Fig. BB1. Oil feed through rocker gear

ENGINE   BB

SECTION BB13
REMOVING AND REFITTING THE CYLINDER HEAD ASSEMBLY

Refer to Section B41 when removing and replacing the exhaust system.

When refitting the cylinder head, ensure that both the upper and lower push rod tube "O" ring seals are replaced and in good condition (See Fig. BB2).

A red seal should be fitted at the lower end of the tube, and a block seal at the upper end.

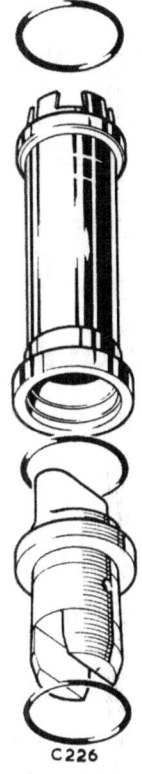

Fig. BB2. Push rod tube and seals

SECTION BB15
RENEWING THE VALVE GUIDES

A greatly improved workshop tool is now available for removing and replacing valve guides. It can be used on all models in the Triumph range, and employs a pulling action rather than drifting. Refer to Section JJ1 for an illustration and part number.

SECTION BB17
RESEATING THE VALVES

A revised set of valve seat cutters, blenders and an arbor pilot and tommy bars is now available. The set is designed for use on all models in the Triumph range.

Refer to Section JJ1 for an illustration and part number.

SECTION BB25
CONNECTING ROD SMALL END

After engine number H65573, no small-end bushes are fitted to the connecting rods.

Even after a very considerable mileage, little or no movement will be evident between the gudgeon pin and small-end eye.

For purposes of measuring, refer to the dimensions and tolerances given in General Data.

SECTION BB27
REMOVING AND REPLACING THE TIMING COVER

Remove the contact breaker as described in Section B26.

Pull the rubber boot away from the oil pressure switch, and disconnect the Lucar connector.

Unscrew eight "Pozidriv" screws that retain the timing cover, and if necessary tap the edge of the cover with a hide mallet to break the seal.

When the cover is removed the camshaft and crankshaft oil seals should be examined for signs of wear or cracking, and renewed if necessary. The camshaft seal can simply be pressed out, but a circlip must be removed before the crankshaft seal can be removed.

Remove the oil pressure switch and sealing washers (where fitted), and thoroughly clean all parts in

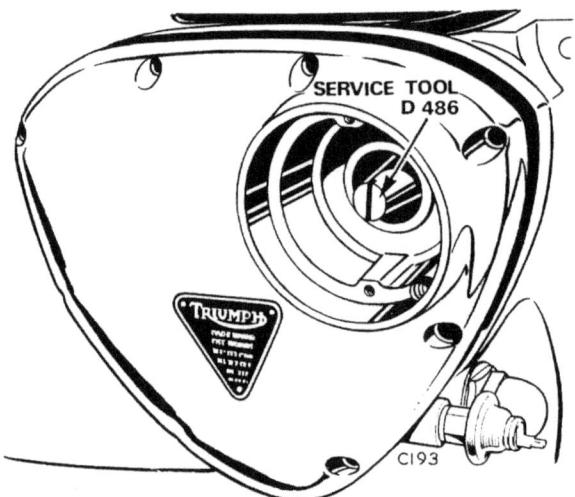

Fig. BB4. Oil seal protector in position

paraffin (kerosene). Clean the oilways with compressed air, and replace the oil pressure switch and washer.

When replacing either oil seal, refer to Fig. BB3 to ensure correct assembly.

To replace the cover, ensure that both joint faces are clean, and that all traces of old jointing compound have been removed. Apply a fresh coat of jointing compound. Screw the tapered oil seal pilot into the exhaust camshaft (pilot part number D486) and smear it with oil to assist assembly (see Fig. BB4). Slide the cover into position and replace eight "Pozidriv" screws. Reconnect the oil pressure switch, and replace the rubber boot. Finally replace the contact breaker, and reset the ignition timing as in Section B31 and B32.

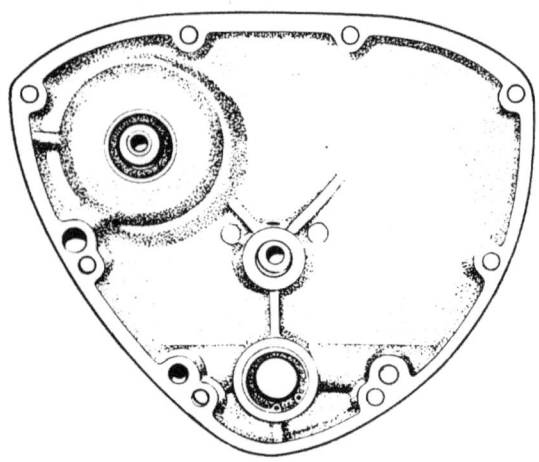

Fig. BB3. Timing cover oil seals

ENGINE

SECTION BB29
EXTRACTING AND REFITTING THE VALVE TIMING PINIONS

A camwheel extractor is now supplied under part number D2213 complete with adaptors to enable its use on all models in the Triumph range. For an illustration of the assembly refer to Section JJ1.

Procedure when using D2213:

To extract the inlet pinion, screw on the extractor body and then screw in the extractor bolt. The pinion will then be withdrawn (See Fig. BB5).

In the case of the exhaust pinion, the adaptor should be positioned on the end of the camshaft to avoid damaging the contact breaker location taper.

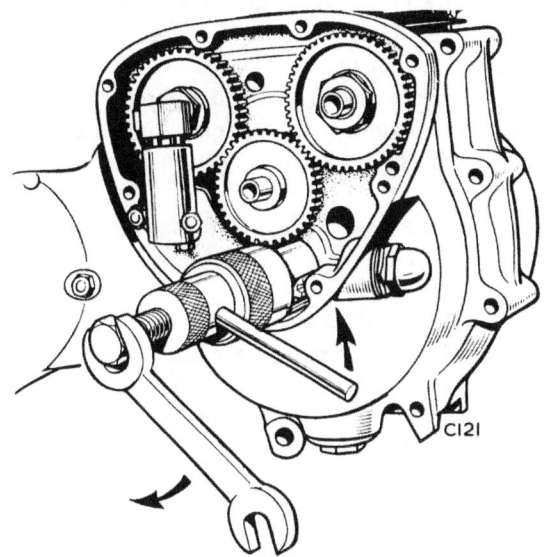

Fig. BB6. Removing the crankshaft pinion

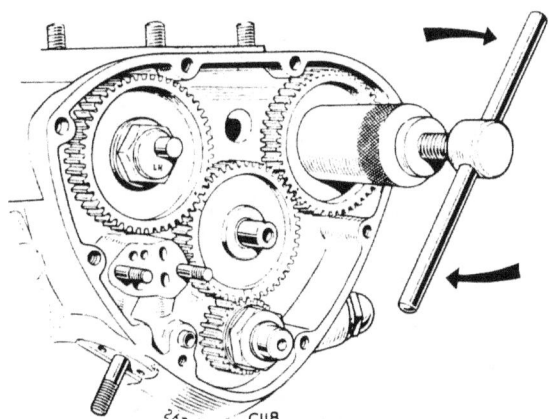

Fig. BB5. Removing a camwheel

A new service tool, part number 61-6019, is available to remove the crank shaft pinion. (See Fig. BB6).

When replacing the pinion, first check that the keys are located correctly in the camshafts. Screw the replacer adaptor onto the assembler bolt and onto the camshaft. Lubricate the camshaft to assist assembly, and slide the pinion over the assembler tool. Align the key to the keyway opposite the timing mark and screw on the replacer nut and washer (see Fig. BB7). Replace the camshaft nuts.

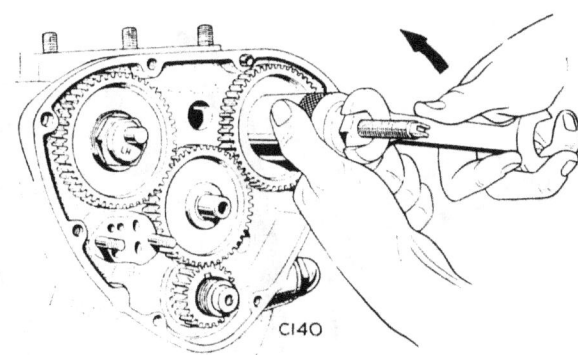

Fig. BB7. Replacing a camwheel

SECTION BB33
REMOVING AND REPLACING THE CAMSHAFTS ONLY

It is most important that the machine is leant over to the left before the camshafts are withdrawn. This will prevent both the breather disc and spring and the cam followers from falling into the crankcase.

SECTION BB35

STRIPPING AND REASSEMBLING THE CRANKSHAFT ASSEMBLY

During the 1969 season the centre punching of the connecting rod cap nuts has ceased. It is also advisable to disregard the centre punched dots on all previous machines, and tighten the nuts to the torque figure given in General data, or to the bolt stretch figure given in Section B36.

The crankshaft assembly showing the oilways is shown in figure BB8.

When rebalancing the crankshaft assembly, use two balance weights, part number Z122 (490 grs each) and fabricate two sleeves using the dimensions shown in Fig. BB9 to fit over the main bearing journals. Place the assembly on two horizontal knife edges, resting it on the left and right main bearing journals. Allow the assembly to come to rest, then mark the lowest point of the flywheel with chalk. Turn the assembly through 90 degrees and if it returns to the same position when released drill a $\frac{3}{8}$ in. diameter hole centrally, adjacent to the chalk mark, to a depth of approximately $\frac{1}{2}$ in. Repeat this procedure until the assembly will rest in any position without rolling. Allow approximately $\frac{3}{4}$ in. between each balance hole.

Finally wash the assembly thoroughly and clean the oilways using compressed air.

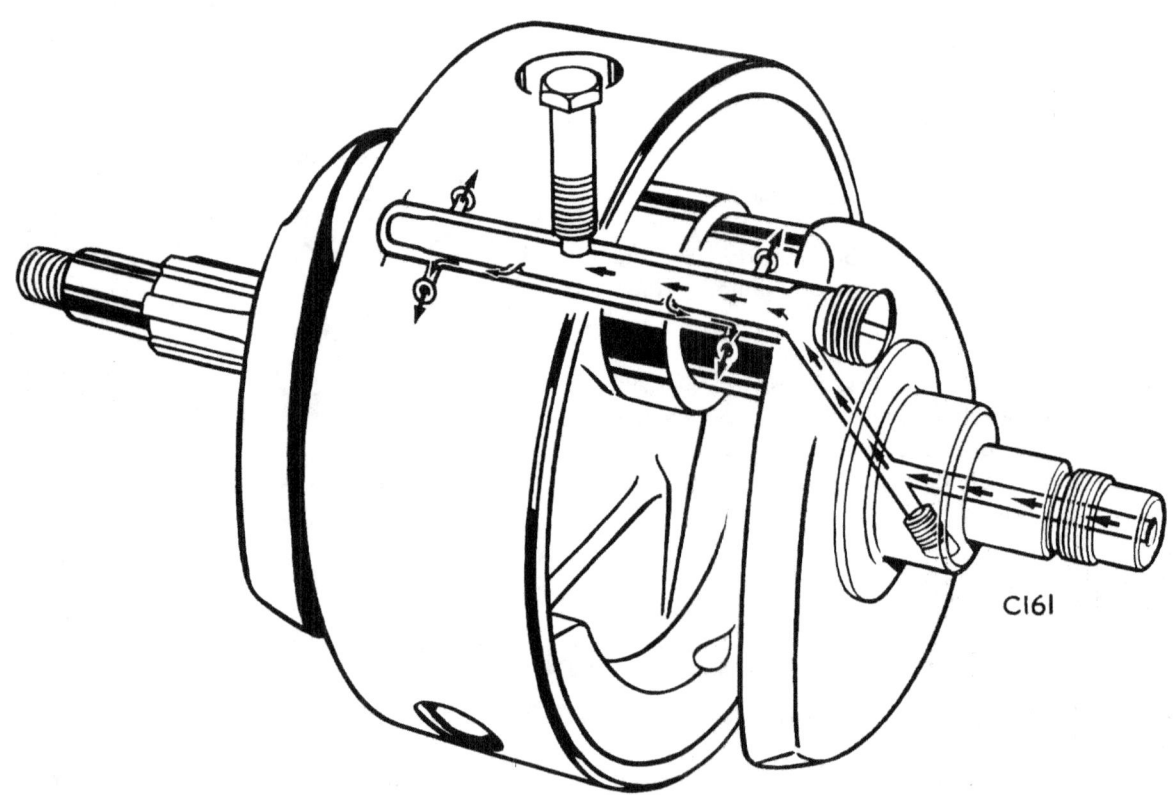

Fig. BB8. Crankshaft oilways

ENGINE

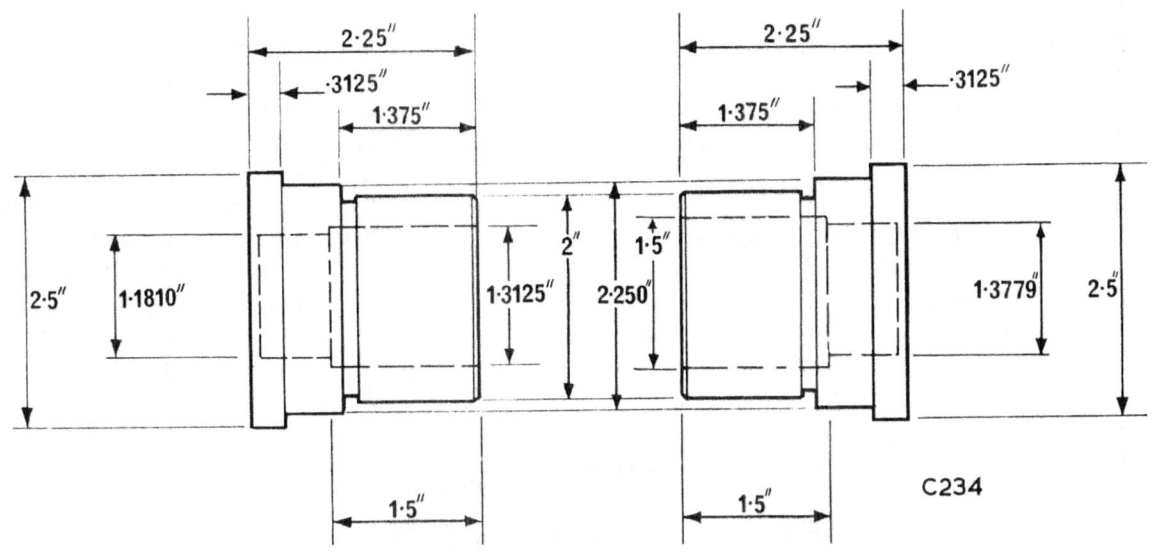

Fig. BB9. Crankshaft Balancing Sleeves

SECTION BB36
REFITTING THE CONNECTING RODS

1969 season machines have no centre punch markings on the connecting rod nuts, and therefore they must be tightened to either the torque figure given in General Data, or the bolt stretch figures shown in Section B36. It is advisable to disregard centre punch marks on any connecting rod nut used previously.

SECTION BB37
INSPECTING THE CRANKCASE COMPONENTS

Crankshaft and Big end journal diameters.

	Bearing Shell Marking	Suitable Crankshaft Journal Size	
	Standard	1·4375 in. 1·4380 in.	36·5125 mm. 36·5252 mm.
First regrind	—·010 in.	1·4275 in. 1·4280 in.	36·2585 mm. 36·2712 mm.
Second regrind	—·020 in.	1·4175 in. 1·4180 in.	36·0045 mm. 36·0172 mm.
Third regrind	—·030 in.	1·4075 in. 1·4080 in.	35·7505 mm. 35·7632 mm.

THE ABOVE CHART COMPLETELY SUPERSEDES THE CHART SHOWN IN SECTION B37.

Paragraph (2) **MAIN BALL BEARING (TIMING SIDE)**

A ball bearing is fitted in the timing side to replace the previous plain bearing.

(3) **MAIN ROLLER BEARING (DRIVE SIDE)**

Check that the rollers are in good condition and show no signs of wear, and check the outer race for signs of pitting and wear. There should be no "up and down" movement of the outer race when assembled onto the rollers and cage, but do not mistake movement when twisting the outer race from front to back, for this. The inner cage assembly should be a tight fit on the crankshaft, and the outer race should be a tight fit in the crankcase. A loose fitting bearing would tend to cause "rumble". The correct dimensions are given in General Data.

SECTION BB38
RENEWING THE MAIN BEARINGS

To remove the left side bearing (roller) outer spool from the crankcase, heat the crankcase to approximately 100°C and fit the expanding extractor tool part number 61-6060 (see Fig. BB10). Remove the bearing with the use of a press if possible, but otherwise a hammer and drift. The inner portion of the bearing can be withdrawn from the crankshaft with the use of a three-claw puller.

The oil seal can be removed from the crankcase by driving it outwards, in the opposite direction to the bearing. It is advisable to renew the seal even if it does not appear badly worn.

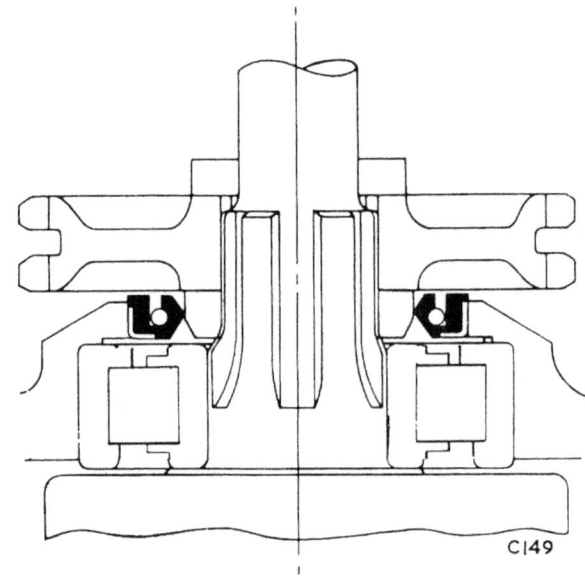

Fig. BB11. Left side crankcase oil seal

To remove the right side (ball) bearing, again heat the crankcase to approximately 100°C and drive the bearing inwards using a tubular drift and preferably a press.

To replace the left (roller) bearing, again heat the crankcase, and ensure that both the outer spool and housing are clean. It is advisable to apply a few drops of "Loctite" to the outside of the bearing, before replacing it. Ensure that the spool enters squarely and press it in using a suitable drift. After replacing the bearing spool, replace the oil seal, with the open face outwards. (See Fig. BB11).

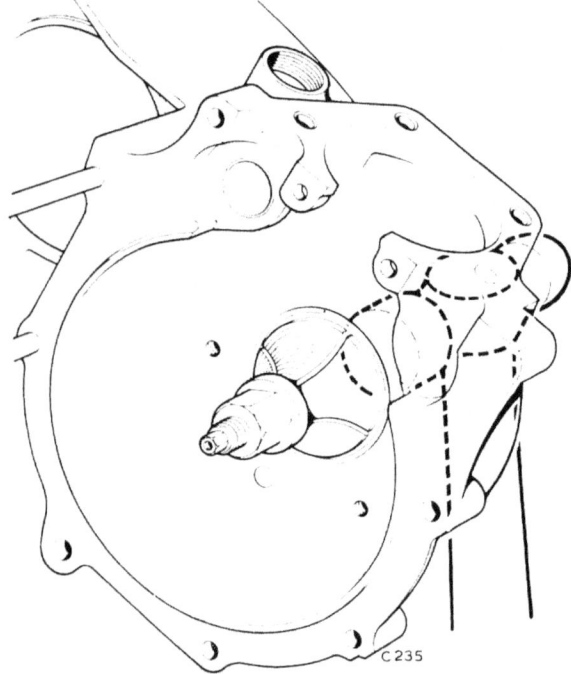

Fig. BB10. Removing the main bearing outer spool

Replace the right side bearing in a similar manner.

ENGINE

SECTION BB39
RENEWING THE CAMSHAFT BUSHES

Both the inlet and exhaust camshafts are supported in the left half crankcase by two pre-sized, steel backed split bushes. In the right half crankcase they run directly in the crankcase.

To remove the bushes in the left half, the split bush should be collapsed. This is achieved by inserting a very thin screwdriver at the split, between the bush and the crankcase. When collapsed, the bush can be extracted with a pair of thin nosed pliers.

The breather valve supporting disc is retained behind the inlet camshaft, located on a peg. When renewing the bushes it is essential that this disc is correctly positioned.

When refitting the bushes, heat the crankcase to approximately 100°C and press them in using a shouldered drift. The bushes should not require reaming, but if for any reason this is found necessary the correct dimensions and tolerances are given in General Data.

SECTION B40
REMOVING AND REPLACING THE TACHOMETER DRIVE BOX

Where the tachometer is fitted, there is a right angled drive gearbox as shown in Fig. BB12. When the large slotted end cap is removed and the engine turned over quickly the drive gear should be

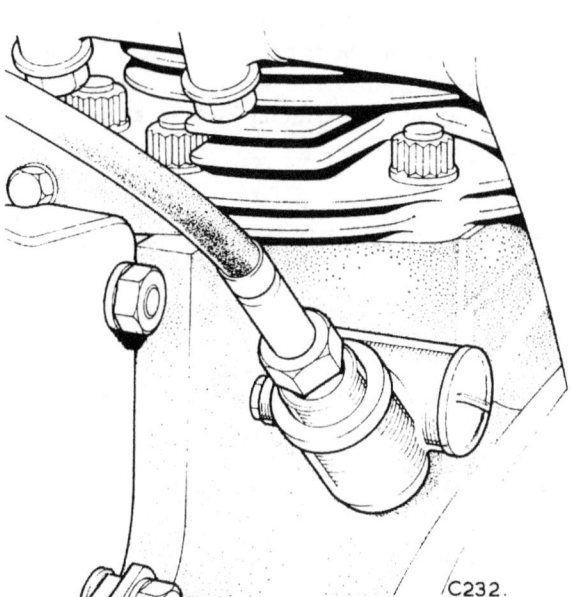

Fig. BB12. Tachometer drive gearbox

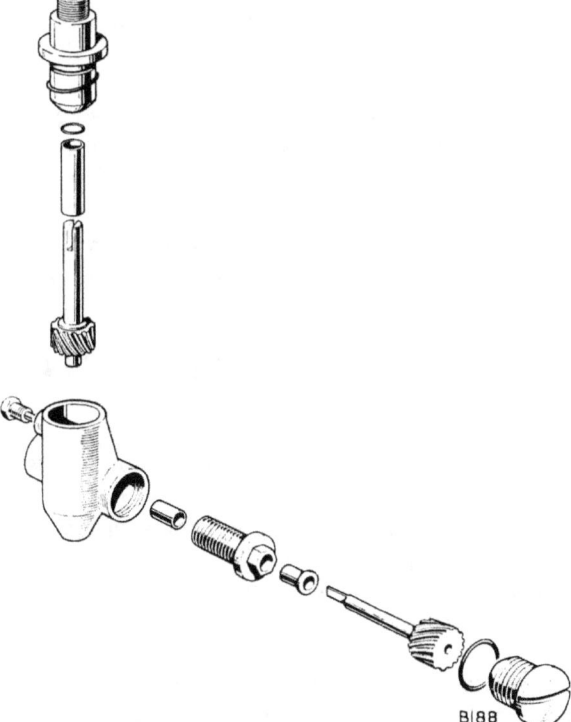

Fig. BB13. Tachometer drive gearbox exploded

ejected. If this is not successful the gear can be withdrawn with a pair of long nosed pliers. The centre bolt holding the gearbox to the crankcase will now be visible. A $\frac{7}{16}$ in. A.F. thin box spanner is required to release this. NOTE THAT THIS BOLT HAS A LEFT HAND THREAD.

The gearbox can now be withdrawn from the crankcase.

The cable, if still connected, should be unscrewed. If the driven gear and housing are to be removed, the locking pin must first be removed (see Fig. BB13).

The housing is a tight fit in the gearbox and will require "drifting" out using a soft metal drift.

It will be noted that a spade on the end of the driving gear spindle slots into a "thimble" which is permanently fitted into the end of the exhaust camshaft. If for any reason the thimble has become damaged, it can be replaced from outside the crankcase with a screwdriver slotted thimble, part number E9310.

The reassembly procedure for the gearbox is a reversal of the above, referring to Fig. BB13 for guidance.

SECTION B41

REMOVING AND REPLACING THE EXHAUST SYSTEM
T100S, T100T, T100R

To remove the exhaust system slacken the exhaust pipe to silencer clamp bolts, remove the 'cleveloc' nut and screw from both front brackets and slacken the finned cooling ring clamp bolts. Slacken four clamp bolts at the front cross-over pipe and slide inwards the outer sleeves, using a rubber mallet if necessary. Drive the exhaust pipes forward off the cylinder head stubs.

The silencers can be removed after unscrewing one bolt from behind each silencer hanger bracket. These bolts also serve to retain pillion footrests.

To refit the system, first fit the silencers with the brackets behind the hanger brackets, and replace the bolts, spring washers and pillion footrests. It is not advisable to tighten these at this stage. Ensuring that the finned cooling rings and exhaust pipe to silencer clamps are in position, replace both exhaust pipes using a rubber mallet to drive them into position. Replace the front bracket securing screws and nuts, ensuring that the screws are fitted from the front, but again do not tighten these. Lift the cross-over pipe, complete with sleeves into position, and slide the sleeves outwards over the exhaust pipe branches. Finally re-tighten all screws, bolts and nuts, ensuring that the finned cooling rings and exhaust pipes are fitted securely against the cylinder head to avoid any gas leakage.

REMOVING AND REPLACING THE EXHAUST SYSTEM
T100C

To remove the exhaust system, commence by removing the leg guard. This is achieved by removing two screws and washers which screw into captive nuts. The leg guard retaining clips can be removed complete with the screws, and the leg guard withdrawn.

It is advisable to remove the system in two sections, the first being the left and right exhaust pipes and brackets.

Slacken the finned cooling ring clamp bolts, and remove the bolt, 'cleveloc' nut and washer that secures the exhaust pipe rear brackets to the engine plate bracket. Slacken two exhaust to "H" connector clips and drive the exhaust pipes forward off the cylinder head stubs using a rubber mallet.

The second section to be removed is the silencer assembly. This is simply a matter of removing one nut, spring washer and bolt from the upper

ENGINE

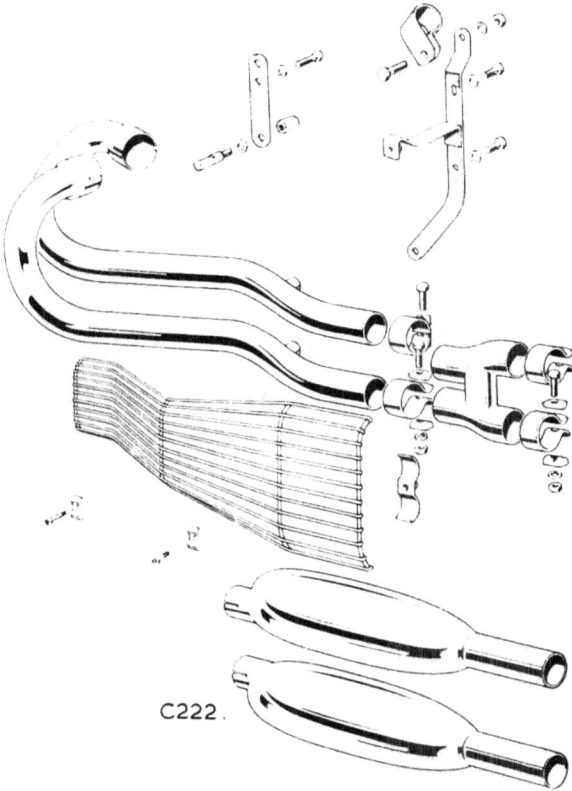

Fig. BB14. Exploded exhaust system T100C

assembly reference should be made to Fig. BB13 for guidance.

To replace the exhaust system, reposition the silencer assembly and replace the upper bolt, spring washer and nut, fitting the bolt from the outside, and the lower bolt spring washer and pillion footrest.

It is not advisable to tighten these bolts at this stage. Ensure that the cooling rings and "H" piece clamps are fitted, and refit the exhaust pipes, driving them onto the cylinder head stubs and into the "H" connector with a rubber mallet. Replace the bolt, nut and spring washer, which secure the exhaust pipe rear brackets to the engine plate bracket, but do not tighten them at this stage.

Secure the complete system by tightening the finned cooling rings, ensuring that both the rings and exhaust pipes are fitted securely against the cylinder head to avoid any gas leakage. Tighten the exhaust pipe to "H" connector clips, the exhaust pipe rear bracket bolt and the silencer upper and lower brackets.

Finally refit the leg guard; one screw, washer and clip should be fitted at the front of the leg guard and screwed into the double curved bracket which is fitted from behind the exhaust pipes, and the rear screw, washer and clips should be attached to the fixed silencer bracket.

mounting clips on the rear frame tube, and removing the pillion footrest, bolt and spring washer. The assembly is at this stage free to be removed.

If it is found necessary to dismantle the silencer

SECTION B42

CONTACT BREAKER – TYPE 6CA
(Fitted after eng no H57083)

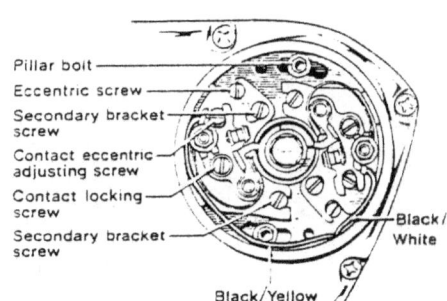

Fig. BB15 Contact breaker – Type 6CA

Contact breaker unit, Type 6CA

The contact breaker is contained behind the round chromium plated cover held by two screws on the right side of the motor. The nylon heels of the moving contacts may settle down initially and it is necessary to check both contact breaker gaps after 500 miles. After checking, apply 3 drops of clean motor oil to the lubricating felts.

To adjust the contact breaker gap, turn the motor with the starter pedal until the scribe mark on the cam aligns with the nylon heel of one set of points (see Fig. BB16). Measure the gap (0.015 in.) with feeler gauges. If they are outside the limits, slacken the slotted screw which secures the stationary contact and move the contact until the gap is correct, then tighten the slotted screw. Turn the motor forward until the second pair of contacts just open and adjust them in the same way.

Every 3,000 miles subsequently, inspect the contact breaker points and if they are burnt or pitted remove them from the base plates and clean them with fine emery cloth. Wipe with a clean cloth moistened with gasoline. Replace the contacts on the base plate making sure that any insulating washers are in their correct positions. Adjust the gap and then clean the second pair of contacts. Place a few drops of clean motor oil on the centrifugal automatic advance mechanism and one or two drops on the felt pad which lubricates the cam. Two drops of oil should also be applied to the spindle which supports the cam to prevent corrosion and possible seizure. Do not allow any oil on the contacts. Initially the lubricating felts are treated with Shell Retinax A grease and thereafter 3 drops of engine oil should be added to the wicks at 2,000 mile intervals.

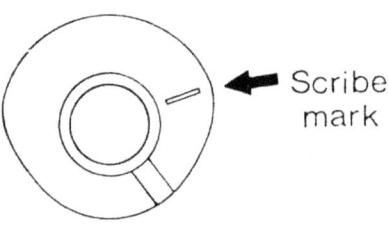

Fig. BB16

Showing point setting scribe mark.

SECTION C
TRANSMISSION

DESCRIPTION	Section
ADJUSTING THE CLUTCH OPERATING MECHANISM	C1
ADJUSTING THE PRIMARY CHAIN TENSION	C2
REMOVING AND REPLACING THE PRIMARY COVER	C3
REMOVING AND REFITTING THE CLUTCH PLATES	C4
INSPECTING THE CLUTCH PLATES AND SPRINGS	C5
ADJUSTING THE CLUTCH PRESSURE PLATE	C6
RENEWING SHOCK ABSORBER RUBBERS	C7
REMOVING AND REPLACING THE STATOR AND ROTOR	C8
REMOVING AND REPLACING THE CLUTCH AND ENGINE SPROCKETS	C9
INSPECTION OF THE TRANSMISSION COMPONENTS	C10
REAR CHAIN ALTERATIONS AND REPAIRS	C11

C | TRANSMISSION

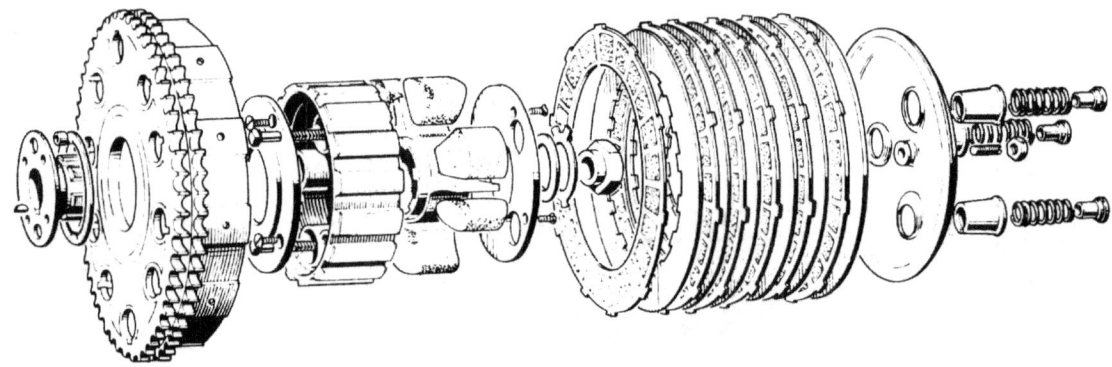

Fig. C1. General arrangement of clutch and shock absorber unit

DESCRIPTION

The clutch is of a multi plate type, using synthetic friction material on the bonded drive plates and incorporating a transmission shock absorber. The pressure on the clutch plates is maintained by three springs held in position by three slotted nuts.

The clutch is designed to operate in oil and it is essential that the oil level in the chaincase is maintained, otherwise the bonded segments of the driven clutch plates may burn and disintegrate under heavy loading. Always use the recommended grade of oil (see Section A2). If a heavier grade of oil is used the clutch plates will not readily separate when disengaged, which will cause a certain amount of difficulty when changing gear due to clutch drag.

The shock absorbing unit transmits the power from the clutch sprocket via the clutch plates to the gearbox mainshaft. Within the shock absorber unit the drive is transmitted through three large rubber pads to the three arm spider which is splined to the clutch hub; this in turn is located to the gearbox mainshaft by means of a taper and key. In addition, there are three rubber rebound pads. The total effect of the rubber pads is to reduce the variations in engine torque at low speeds, providing an extremely smooth transmission of power to the gearbox.

SECTION C1

ADJUSTING THE CLUTCH OPERATING MECHANISM

The clutch, which is situated within the outer primary cover on the left of the machine, can be adjusted by means of the handlebar adjuster, push rod adjuster and the pressure plate springs, the latter only being accessible for adjustment when the outer primary cover is removed. Section C6 fully describes adjusting the springs and pressure plate.

The clutch operating rod has $\frac{1}{16}$ in. (1·5 mm.) clearance between the clutch operating mechanism and the pressure plate. To achieve this remove the inspection cap from the centre of the primary cover,

then slacken the clutch cable handlebar adjustment right off.

Unscrew the hexagonal lock nut and screw in the slotted adjuster screw in the centre of the pressure plate until the pressure plate just begins to lift. Unscrew the adjuster one half turn and secure it in that position by retightening the locknut.

The clutch operating cable should then be re-adjusted, by means of the handlebar adjuster, until there is approximately $\frac{1}{8}$ in. (3 mm.) free movement in the cable.

TRANSMISSION

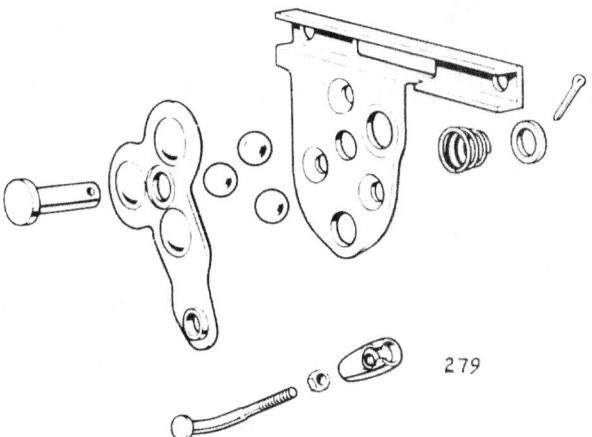

Fig. C2. Exploded view of clutch operating mechanism

Maladjustment of the clutch operating mechanism can be symptomised by a loud click when operating the clutch lever and/or the clutch cable becoming disconnected at the connector where the cable nipple joins the clutch mechanism operating spoke. In the former case adjustment of the clutch operating mechanism, as detailed above, will eliminate the noise. In the case where the clutch cable becomes disconnected at the gearbox, the clutch cable nipple and the spoke connector should be examined and renewed if necessary. This trouble may recur unless the adjustment procedure, as given above, is carefully followed. Full details of removal of the clutch operating mechanism are given in Section D2.

If the clutch is dragging and normal adjustment of the operating rod and operating cable produces no improvement, it will be necessary to remove the outer primary cover and check the pressure plate for true running as shown in Section C6.

To maintain a smooth and easy clutch operation, particular attention should be given to the recommended primary chain case oil change period (see Section A1) and clutch cable lubrication (see Section A17).

SECTION C2

ADJUSTING THE PRIMARY CHAIN TENSION

The primary chain is of the Duplex type and is non-adjustable as the centres of the engine mainshaft and gearbox mainshaft are fixed. Provision for take up of wear in the primary chain is made by means of a rubber-faced tension slipper blade below the lower run of the chain. The free movement in the chain can be felt with the finger after removing the top inspection plug adjacent to the cylinder block, with the engine stopped, of course.

The correct chain adjustment is ½ in. (12 mm.) free movement. To adjust the chain tension first place a drip tray underneath the chaincase and unscrew the hexagonal pillar bolt adjacent to the centre stand left hand lug.

Insert a medium screw driver and adjust the tension as required.

When adjustment is completed, check that the chaincase contains the recommended amount of oil (see Section A2).

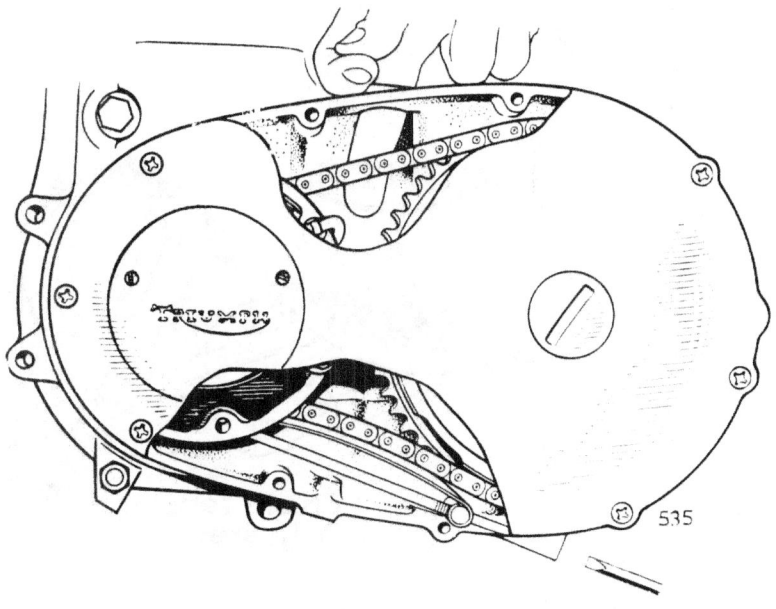

Fig. C3. Adjusting the chain tensioner

SECTION C3

REMOVING AND REPLACING THE PRIMARY COVER

On machines fitted with twin exhaust pipes slacken the left finned clip bolt, left silencer clip bolt and remove the nut and bolt securing the left exhaust pipe bracket underneath the engine. Remove the exhaust pipe by tapping in a forward direction with a rubber or hide mallet.

Slacken off the adjustment at the rear brake operating rod until the brake pedal is clear of the primary cover.

Unscrew the left footrest securing nut and withdraw the footrest.

Place a drip tray underneath the primary cover and remove the hexagonal pillar bolt adjacent to the centre stand lug and allow the oil to drain from the chaincase.

Unscrew and remove tension adjuster.

Remove the ten recessed screws from the periphery of the primary cover. Withdraw the cover and paper gasket and remove chain tensioner assembly.

Refitting the cover is the reversal of the above instructions but fit a new paper gasket. Fitting the gasket can be aided by smearing the crankcase joint surface with grease. It is not advisable to use a jointing compound for this application.

Finally, replace the drain plug and fibre washer and pour in the recommended quantities of oil. (See Section A2).

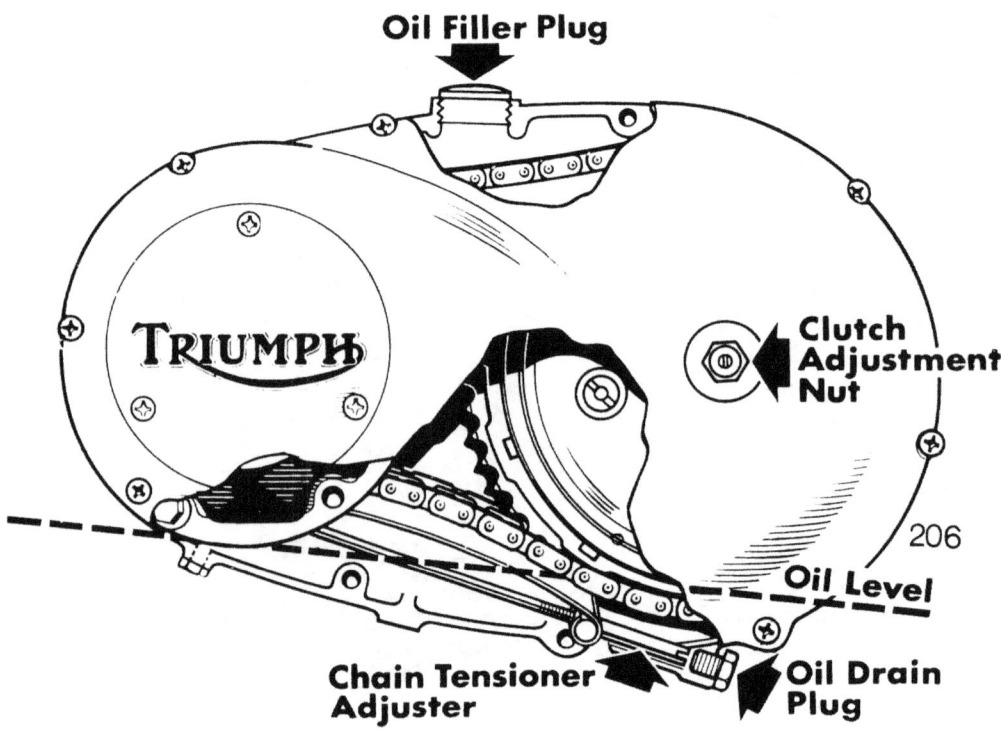

Fig. C4. Section through primary chaincase

SECTION C4

REMOVING AND REFITTING THE CLUTCH PLATES

Remove the outer primary cover as described in Section C3.

The three pressure plate springs are locked in position by means of location pips in the cups and on the drive adjuster nuts. To facilitate removal of the slotted adjuster nuts, insert a knife blade under the head of the nut whilst the nut is unscrewed using tool kit screw driver part number D364 or a screw driver of the type shown in Fig. C5. Withdraw the springs, cup and pressure plate assembly. Removal of the clutch plates is facilitated by means of two narrow hook tools which can be made from a piece of $\frac{1}{32}$ in. diameter wire by bending to form a hook at one end. Thoroughly clean all parts in paraffin (kerosene) and inspect the clutch springs and plates for excessive wear (see Section C5). When replacing the clutch plates remember that the innermost position is occupied by a bonded plate.

Ensure that the cups are located correctly and assemble the springs and nuts, then adjust the

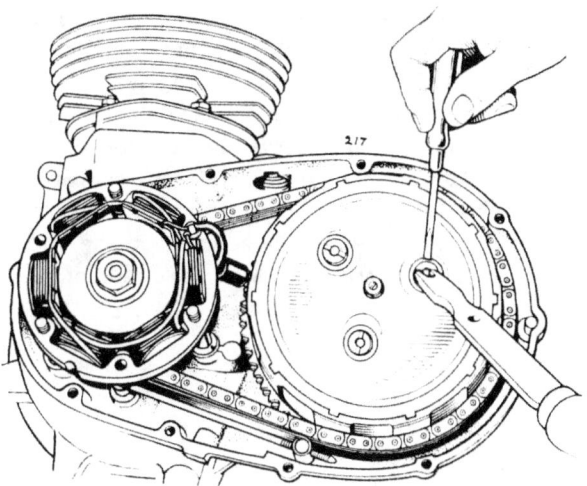

Fig. C5. Unscrewing the clutch spring nuts

pressure plate for true running as described below. Reassembly then continues as the reversal of the above instructions.

SECTION C5

INSPECTING THE CLUTCH PLATES AND SPRINGS

The bonded friction plates should be examined for excessive wear to the driving tags and the overall thickness of the clutch plates should be measured to determine the wear to the friction faces. If the reduction in thickness is more than ·030 in. (·75 mm.) the plate should be renewed. Check the fit of the driving tags in the clutch housing. The clearance should not be excessive.

Check the plain steel driven plates for flatness by placing the plates horizontally on a perfectly flat surface such as a piece of plate glass. It is not satisfactory to straighten buckled plates and they should be replaced with new plates.

Original finish on the driven plates is a phosphoric acid etched surface and hence the plates need not be polished. Check the fit of the plate on the shock absorber housing. The radial clearance should not be excessive.

Inspect the clutch springs for compressive strength by measuring the length of the spring and comparing it with the dimensions given in GENERAL DATA. If a spring has shortened more than ·1 in. (2·5 mm.) the complete set should be renewed. It is not advisable to renew just one or two springs as this may ultimately result in the pressure plate running unevenly.

SECTION C6

ADJUSTING THE CLUTCH PRESSURE PLATE

When the pressure plate is refitted or requires adjustment, the following procedure should be observed. With neutral selected, sit astride the machine, disengage the clutch, then depress the kickstarter pedal and observe the rotation of the pressure plate; it should revolve true relative to the clutch housing. If it does not do so, the three slotted nuts must be initially adjusted so the ends of the clutch pins are flush with the heads of the nuts.

The nut is prevented from unscrewing by a pip on the underside and to unscrew a nut, a narrow screw driver should be used to hold the spring away from the pip of the nut as shown in Fig. C5. When the nuts are flush with the end of the pins depress the kickstarter again and mark the high spot with chalk, then screw in the nearest nut about half a turn and try again. Repeat this procedure until the plate rotates evenly without wobbling.

SECTION C7

RENEWING SHOCK ABSORBER RUBBERS

When the primary cover and clutch plates are removed, access is gained to the shock absorber unit, which consists of a housing, paddle or spider, inner and outer cover plates and shock absorbing rubbers.

To remove the rubbers for inspection or renewal, first unscrew the three screws which retain the shock absorber cover plate and lever the plate free.

The shock absorber rubbers can be prised out of the position, using a sharp pointed tool, commencing by levering out the smaller rebound rubbers first.

When the three small rebound rubbers are removed the large drive rubbers will be free to be withdrawn.

If the rubbers show no signs of punctures or cracking etc., they can be refitted, but remember that a slight puncture in the rubber can ultimately result in the rubber disintegrating.

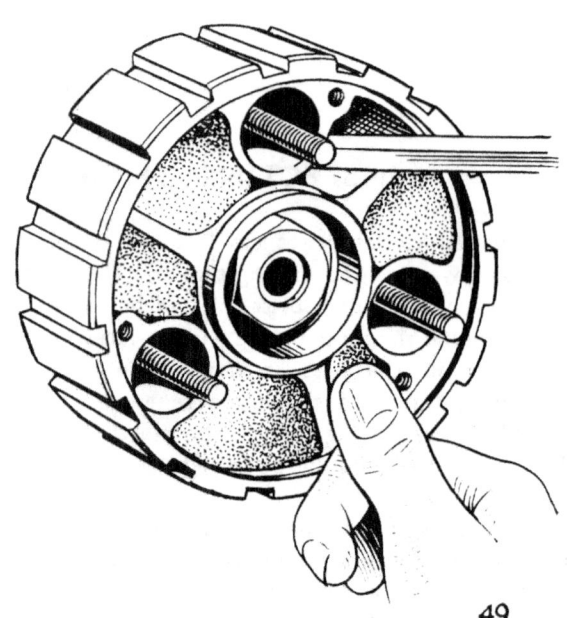

Fig. C6. Replacing the shock absorber rubbers

TRANSMISSION

To replace the shock absorber drive and rebound rubbers, first install all three of the larger drive rubbers in position as shown in Fig. C6. Follow through by inserting and replacing the smaller rebound rubbers. It may prove necessary to lever the shock absorber spider arms using a small tommy bar or similar to facilitate assembly, but with care this operation can be accomplished 'in situ' on the machine without the need for special tools or equipment, or necessity for removing the complete unit from the machine.

Although the rubbers are of an oil resistant type, it is not advisable to use oil or grease as an aid to reassembly as this may shorten the working life of the rubber.

Ensure that the three shock absorber outer cover screws are tight. Use a screw driver that engages the complete length of the screw slot. Apply Triumph Loctite to the screw threads before final assembly.

SECTION C8

REMOVING AND REPLACING THE STATOR AND ROTOR

First disconnect the stator leads from underneath the engine (snap connectors) then, with the primary cover removed, unscrew the three stator retaining nuts and withdraw the stator from over the mounting studs and unscrew the sleeve nut and the lead can then be withdrawn easily. To remove the rotor unbend the tab washer and unscrew the mainshaft nut using a box spanner and mallet, or, alternatively, select fourth (top) gear and apply the rear brake, then unscrew the nut.

Check the rotor carefully for signs of cracking or fatigue failure.

When replacing the rotor ensure that the key or sprocket peg is located correctly, then tighten the nut to the torque figure given in GENERAL DATA.

When refitting the stator, ensure that the side of the stator with the leads connecting the coils together is outermost, then tighten the retaining nuts to the torque figure given in GENERAL DATA SECTION. Insert the lead into the sleeve nut and connect the wires to those of the same colour code underneath the engine. Check that the position of the lead is such that it cannot foul the chain.

Finally, rotate the crankshaft and ensure that the rotor does not foul the stator. It should be possible to insert a feeler gauge of ·008 in. (·2 mm.) thickness between each of the stator pole pieces and the rotor.

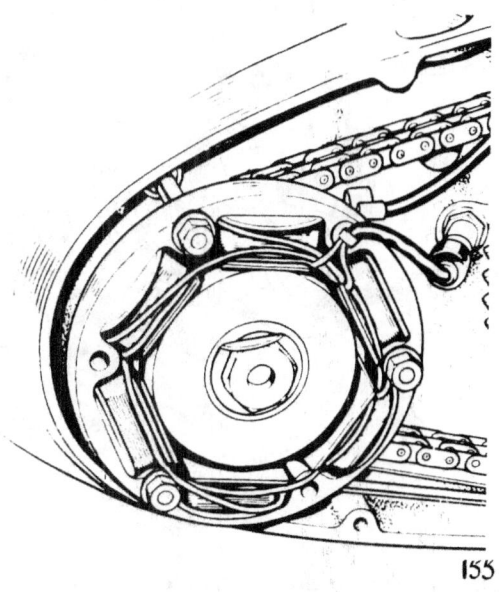

Fig. C7. Showing stator location on crankcase

SECTION C9

REMOVING AND REPLACING THE CLUTCH AND ENGINE SPROCKETS

Remove the primary cover as shown in Section C3, then remove the pressure plate and clutch plates, as shown in Section C4. Insert the locking plate Z13 into the clutch housing and remove the stator and rotor as described in Section C8. Remove the rotor key and distance piece. Remove the clutch securing self-locking nut and the cupped washer. It should be noted that machines before H.49833 have a tab washer and different cupped washer instead of a self-locking nut.

As the primary chain is of the endless type the clutch and engine sprockets have to be extracted simultaneously using extractor D662/3 and extractor tool Z151 as shown in Figs. C8 and C9. (Machines prior to H.49833 used extractor DA50/1).

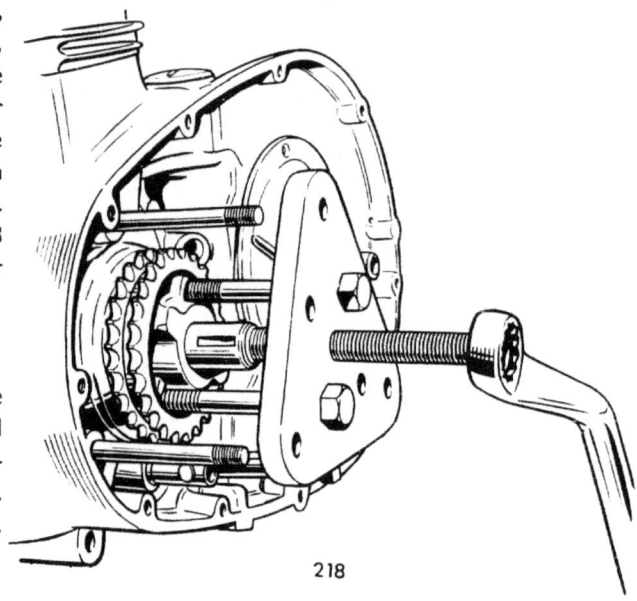

Fig. C9. Extracting the engine sprocket, using service tool Z151

Fig. C8. Extracting the clutch centre, using extractor D662/3 and locking plate Z13

Screw the body of the extractor into the clutch hub until the maximum depth of thread is engaged, then tighten the centre bolt until the hub is released. When this is achieved, assemble the engine sprocket extractor number Z151 and screw in the centre bolt to extract the engine sprocket.

Press out the hub from the shock absorber to release the sprocket, thrust washer, rollers and threaded pins.

Finally, remove the key from the gearbox mainshaft and check that the oil seal in the primary chain inner cover is a good fit over the high gear bush. To renew this oil seal the circular cover should be removed. When replacing the cover, use a new paper gasket and ensure that the oil seal is pressed in with the lip relative to the cover as shown in Fig. C10.

TRANSMISSION

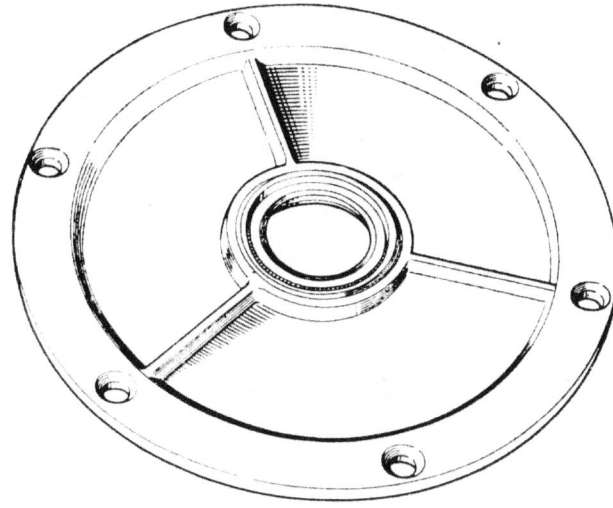

Fig. C10. Oil seal in gearbox sprocket detachable cover

Thoroughly clean all parts in paraffin (kerosene) and inspect them for wear or fatigue as shown in Section C10.

Grease the clutch hub and fit the thrust washer and 20 of the correct rollers. **Do not use** $\frac{1}{4}$ in. x $\frac{1}{4}$ in. rollers. Place the sprocket in position and press on the shock absorber complete with the three threaded pins. If the splines are loose use Triumph Loctite.

When replacing the primary chain and sprockets, ensure that the taper ground distance collar behind the engine sprocket has been replaced, and with the taper towards the crankshaft main bearing and the oil seal. With the gearbox mainshaft key carefully in position, locate the clutch hub onto the mainshaft taper and tap it slightly to lock it onto the taper.

Place the primary chain over the engine sprocket and offer the sprocket onto the crankshaft.

Place the clutch locking tool Z13 into the clutch plate housing and then refit the cup washer and self locking nut. Machines before H.49833 have a tab washer which must be flattened to the nut after tightening.

NOTE: The cup washer fits with the cup side out and the tab washer (if any in use) fits with the long tab located in the hole in the bore of the shock absorber spider.

Engage fourth gear, apply the rear brake and tighten the clutch securing nut to the torque figure given in GENERAL DATA.

Reassembly then continues as a reversal of the above instructions not forgetting to refit the rectangular section rotor locating key (or the sprocket dowel peg, where appropriate). Finally, replenish the chaincase with the recommended grade of oil (see Section A2).

Note: Alternatively, the clutch sprocket may be removed by prising out the 20 roller bearings and allowing the sprocket to move both outwards and forwards until it can be unmeshed from the primary chain. This alternative only applies if the shock absorber assembly can readily be detached from the hub to allow access to the rollers.

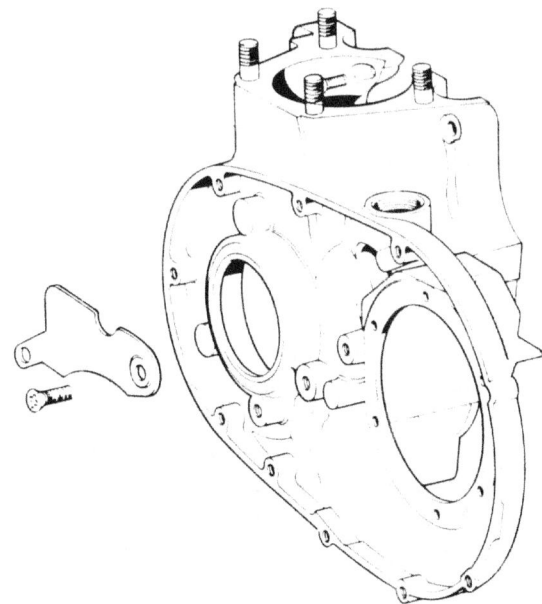

Fig. C11. Revised breather baffle plate.

Engine Breathing System

All machines commencing engine number KD27866 now incorporated a revised engine breather system, deleting the previous camshaft driven internal breather disc and vent. The engine drive shaft sprocket oil seal was no longer fitted (the engine now breathing directly into the primary chaincase-oil levels maintained by three additional small bore drillings in the crankcase wall), and the incorporation of a new breather baffle plate, installed to the rear of the clutch, connecting to a 'D' shaped breather vent pipe taken to the rear of the machine via an outlet stub attached to the upper inner chaincase. (See Section E21)

SECTION C10

INSPECTION OF THE TRANSMISSION COMPONENTS

(1) Inspect the primary chain for excessive wear of the rollers and pivot pins and check that the elongation does not exceed $1\frac{1}{2}\%$. To do this, first scribe two marks on a flat surface exactly 12 ins. (30·5 cm.) apart, then after degreasing or washing the chain in paraffin (kerosene), place the chain opposite the two marks. When the chain is compressed to its minimum free length the marks should coincide with the centres of two pivot pins 32 links apart. When the chain is stretched to its maximum free length the extension should not exceed $\frac{1}{4}$ in. (6·25 mm.).

Inspect the condition of the sprocket teeth for signs of hooking and pitting.

A very good method of indicating whether the chain is badly worn or not is to wrap it round the clutch sprocket and attempt to lift the chain from its seating at various points around the sprocket. Little or no lift indicates that both the sprocket and chain are in good condition.

(2) Check the fit between the shock absorber spider and the clutch hub splines. The spider should be a push fit onto the clutch hub and there should not be any radial movement.

Similarly check the fit of the engine sprocket splines onto the crankshaft. Again, there should not be any radial movement.

If either the spider or engine sprocket are tight fitting on the clutch hub and crankshaft respectively, there is no cause for concern as such a fit is to the best advantage.

(3) Check the clutch hub roller bearing diameter, the rollers themselves and the bearing of the clutch sprocket for excessive wear and pitting, etc. Measure the rollers, clutch hub and clutch sprocket bearing diameters and compare them with the dimensions given in GENERAL DATA.

If the diameters of the rollers are below the bottom limit, they should be renewed. When purchasing new rollers ensure that they are in accordance with the dimensions given in GENERAL DATA. In particular, check that the length is correct.

(4) Check that the shock absorber spider is a good working fit in the inner and outer retaining plate and that the arms of the spider have not caused excessive score marks on the inner faces of the retaining plate. A good idea is to check the working clearance by assembling the shock absorber unit without the rubbers.

(5) Inspect the clutch operating rod for bending, by rolling it on a flat surface such as a piece of plate glass. Check that the length of the rod is within the limits given in GENERAL DATA. This component should not be replaced with anything other than a genuine Triumph spare part. The ends of the rod are specially heat treated to give maximum wear resistance.

TRANSMISSION

SECTION C11

REAR CHAIN ALTERATIONS AND REPAIRS

If the chains have been correctly serviced, very few repairs will be necessary. Should the occasion arise to repair, lengthen or shorten the chain, a rivet extractor, as shown in Fig. C13, and a few spare parts will cover all requirements.

(1)

To shorten a chain containing an even number of pitches, remove the dark parts shown in Fig. 1 and replace by crank double link and single connecting link as shown in Fig. 2.

(2)

(3)

To shorten a chain containing an odd number of pitches remove the dark parts shown in Fig. 3 and replace by a single connecting link and inner link as shown in Fig. 4.

(4)

(5)

To repair a chain with a broken roller or inside link, remove the dark parts shown in Fig. 5 and replace by two single connecting links and one inner link as shown in Fig. 6.

(6)

Fig. C12. Rear chain alterations

The rivet extractor can be used on all motorcycle chains up to $\frac{3}{4}$ in. pitch whether the chains are on or off the chain-wheels.

When using the extractor:—

(1) Turn screw anti-clockwise to permit the punch end to clear the chain rivet.

(2) Open the jaws by pressing down the lever (see below).

(3) Pass jaws over chain and release the lever. Jaws should rest on a chain roller free of chain link plates (see below).

(4) Turn the screw clockwise until the punch contacts and pushes out the rivet end through the chain outer link plate. Unscrew the punch, withdraw the extractor and repeat the complete operation on the adjacent rivet in the same chain outer link plate. The outer plate is then free and the two rivets can be withdrawn from opposite sides with the opposite plate in position. Do not use the removed part again.

When the alterations are finished the chain should be lubricated as shown in Fig. A13.

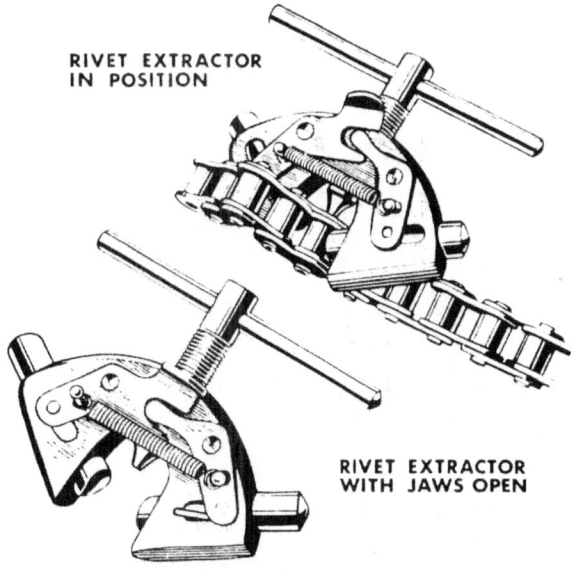

167 Rear chain rivet extractor

Fig. C13. Chain link rivet extractor, part number 167

NOTES

SECTION CC

TRANSMISSION

	Section
REMOVING AND REPLACING THE PRIMARY COVER	CC3
REMOVING AND REPLACING THE CLUTCH AND ENGINE SPROCKET	CC9

SECTION CC3
REMOVING AND REPLACING THE PRIMARY COVER

Refer to Section B41 of this Supplement which describes how to remove and replace the exhaust system.

SECTION CC9
REMOVING AND REPLACING THE CLUTCH AND ENGINE SPROCKET

A new extractor is available for removing the engine sprocket. This can be obtained under the part number D6046 (see Fig. CC1).

After engine number CC.18734, the location tabs are deleted from the clutch thrust washer, and to suit this condition the holes are deleted from the clutch hub. The bronze face of the thrust washer should be assembled towards the clutch sprocket.

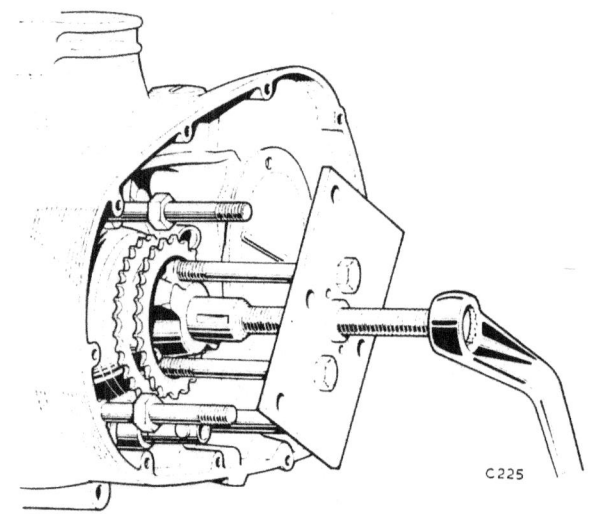

Fig. CC1. Removing the engine sprocket

SECTION D

GEARBOX

DESCRIPTION	Section
REMOVING AND REPLACING THE GEARBOX OUTER COVER ASSEMBLY	D1
DISMANTLING AND REASSEMBLING THE CLUTCH AND GEARCHANGE OPERATING MECHANISM	D2
RENEWING THE GEARCHANGE SPINDLE BUSH	D3
REMOVAL AND REPLACEMENT OF THE GEARBOX INNER COVER ASSEMBLY	D4
KICKSTARTER OPERATING MECHANISM	D5
DISMANTLING AND REBUILDING THE GEARBOX INNER COVER ASSEMBLY	D6
INSPECTION OF THE GEARBOX COMPONENTS	D7
REMOVING AND REPLACING THE GEARBOX HIGH GEAR	D8
RENEWING THE MAINSHAFT AND LAYSHAFT BEARINGS	D9
RENEWING THE GEARBOX SPROCKET WITHOUT DISMANTLING THE GEARBOX	D10

GEARBOX

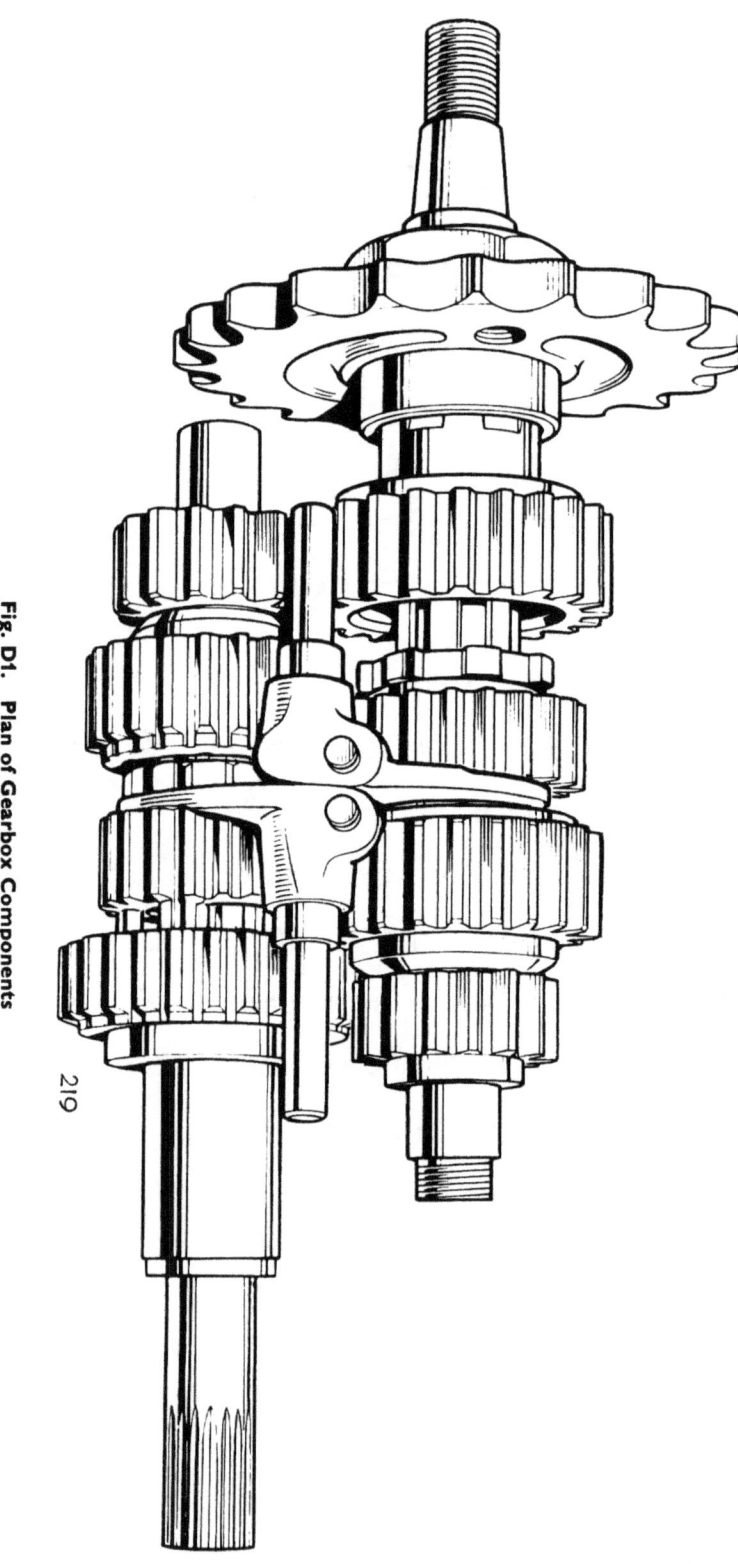

Fig. D1. Plan of Gearbox Components

GEARBOX

DESCRIPTION

The Triumph unit construction twin cylinder models are fitted with a four speed gearbox which is an integral part of the right half crankcase. The gearbox inner and outer covers are made of aluminium alloy DTD424 which gives the utmost strength and rigidity. Gears are manufactured from high quality nickel steel and subsequently case hardened and are designed to withstand heavy loading.

The mainshaft is supported by heavy duty ball races at each end and the layshaft by needle roller bearings which are pressed into the casing and kickstarter spindle respectively.

Note: 3TA and 5TA use bronze bushes to support the layshaft.

The clutch operating mechanism and footchange quadrant are both housed in the gearbox outer cover. The kickstarter pawl is housed in the inner cover, incorporated in the layshaft low gear.

To meet special demands for certain sporting events there are available alternative close ratio and wide ratio gears which enables the gearbox to be suitably converted for road racing and trials riding respectively. For details of the parts required for such a changeover, consult the appropriate Triumph Replacement Parts Catalogue.

SECTION D1

REMOVING AND REPLACING THE GEARBOX OUTER COVER ASSEMBLY

Slacken the right exhaust pipe finned clip bolt, silencer clip bolt and remove the nut and bolt securing the lower bracket of the right exhaust pipe underneath the engine. Remove the right exhaust pipe by driving it in a forward direction with a hide mallet. Unscrew the right footrest securing nut and remove the footrest.

Slacken off the clutch cable adjustment at the handlebar and remove the slotted adaptor from the abutment at the gearbox. Unscrew the abutment and disconnect the cable from the clutch actuating spoke. Place a drip tray underneath the gearbox and unscrew the gearbox filler plug and drain plug.

Engage fourth (top) gear. This will allow several otherwise difficult nuts to be unscrewed by subsequent application of the rear brake when required.

Unscrew the two nuts and four recessed screws from the periphery of the gearbox cover; remove the kickstarter lever. Grasp the footchange lever

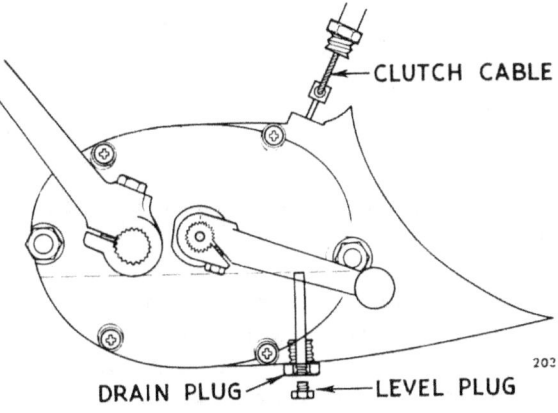

Fig. D2. Showing gearbox oil level and oil drain plugs

with the left hand, and holding a hide mallet in the right hand, tap the gearbox outer cover until it is withdrawn from the machine.

When the cover is removed, the gearchange mechanism and clutch operating mechanism will be accessible.

GEARBOX

Fig. D3. Gearbox outer cover, showing the clutch operating mechanism

Prior to refitting the outer cover ensure that the junction surface is clean and free from any deposits of old jointing compound, then thoroughly clean it in paraffin (kerosene). Apply a fresh coat of jointing compound to the junction surface, ensure that the two location dowels are in position, and the kickstart spindle return spring and spring plate are seated correctly.

Offer the outer cover to the gearbox and refit the nuts and screws. Refit the kickstart lever and replenish the gearbox with the correct amount of the recommended grade of oil (see Section A2).

Then reassemble the transmission, referring to Section A2 for the correct quantities and grades of lubricant for the primary chaincase and gearbox.

SECTION D2

DISMANTLING AND REASSEMBLING THE CLUTCH AND GEARCHANGE OPERATING MECHANISM

Unscrew the two nuts inside the gearbox outer cover and withdraw the cover plate and footchange return springs complete with the two thrust buttons and two distance pieces. Unscrew the countersunk screw which serves to retain the clutch operating mechanism and withdraw the assembly from the cover. Loosen the retaining bolt on the footchange lever and remove the lever from the shaft, whereupon the shaft can be withdrawn from the gearbox outer cover.

Remove the split pin from the clutch operating shaft, thus releasing the clutch operating balls. Withdraw the two split pins and disengage the plungers and springs from the gearchange quadrant and throughly wash all parts in paraffin (kerosene). Thoroughly dry all parts and check for wear, particularly whether the ball indentations have become pitted or elongated.

(1) Inspect the gearchange plungers for wear and ensure that they are a clearance fit in the quadrant. Check the plunger springs by comparing their lengths with the figures given in GENERAL DATA.

(2) Inspect the gear change pedal return springs for fatigue and if they show signs of corrosion due to condensation they should be renewed.

(3) Examine the gearchange quadrant bush for wear and possible ovality by inserting the quadrant into the bush and feeling the amount of play.

GEARBOX

(4) Check the tips of the plungers and the cut aways in the camplate for wear.

To reassemble the gearchange mechanism, first refit the springs, plungers and locating split pins then fit a new rubber "O" ring to the spindle and offer it to the outer cover bush using a smear of oil to assist assembly. Assemble the clutch operating

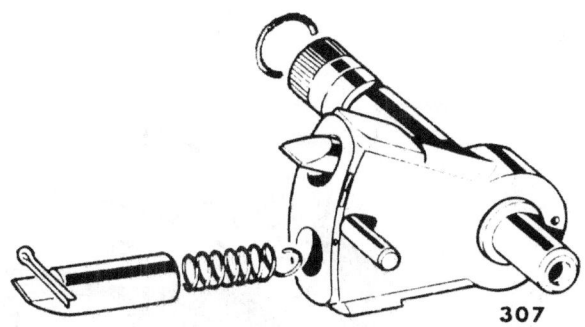

Fig. D5. Footchange operating mechanism

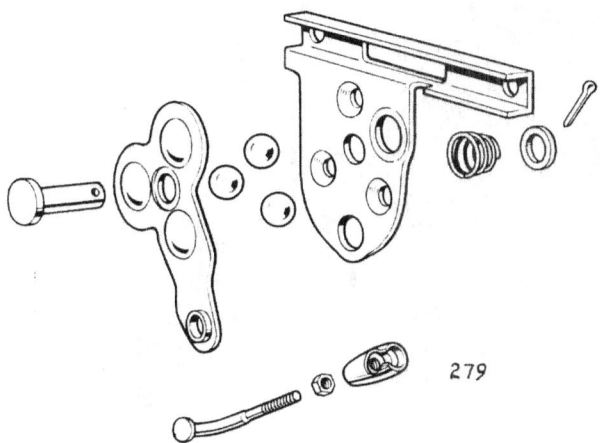

Fig. D4. Clutch operating mechanism

balls in their recesses and refit the shaft and clutch lever in the sequence shown in fig. D4, not forgetting to replace the spring and washer before inserting the split pin.

Refit the distance collar to the end of the footchange quadrant shaft then offer the clutch operating mechanism to the gearbox outer cover and secure it in place with the countersunk screw. Fit the distance pieces over the studs and refit the footchange return springs and thrust buttons. Finally, refit the return spring cover plate and tighten the retaining nuts.

SECTION D3
RENEWING THE GEARCHANGE SPINDLE BUSH

If it is found necessary to renew the gearchange spindle bush this should be done by completely stripping the outer cover of its assembly parts and heating it to 100°C., then driving the bush out using a shouldered drift made from $\frac{3}{4}$ in. dia bar, turned $\frac{5}{8}$ in. dia x $\frac{3}{4}$ in. long. Press in the new bush while the cover is still hot.

SECTION D4
REMOVAL AND REPLACEMENT OF THE GEARBOX INNER COVER ASSEMBLY

Remove the gearbox outer cover as shown in Section D1, leaving the gearbox with fourth (top) gear selected.

Remove the outer primary cover and dismantle the transmission as shown in Section C, not forgetting, finally, to remove the key from the gearbox mainshaft.

Bend back the tags on the lock washer and unscrew the mainshaft nut. This should be easily achieved with fourth (top) gear selected and the rear brake applied.

The gearbox inner cover is retained by two screws and the complete assembly can be removed by tapping the clutch end of the mainshaft with a hide hammer.

Using a pressure oil can, lubricate all the moving parts in the gearbox, then apply a fresh coat of joining compound to the gearbox junction surface. Replace the camplate index plunger and spring into its housing which is immediately adjacent to the high gear journal bearing. Position the camplate so that the selector fork rollers are placed midway along the camplate grooves and offer the complete inner cover assembly to the gearbox. Tap the inner cover with a hide mallet to locate the assembly over the studs and screw in the two retaining screws.

Fully tighten the two retaining screws and then replace the distance piece, tab washer and locking nut onto the mainshaft. Select fourth gear with the camplate, apply the rear brake and tighten up the mainshaft securing nut to the torque figure given in GENERAL DATA. Bend over the tab washer.

GEARBOX

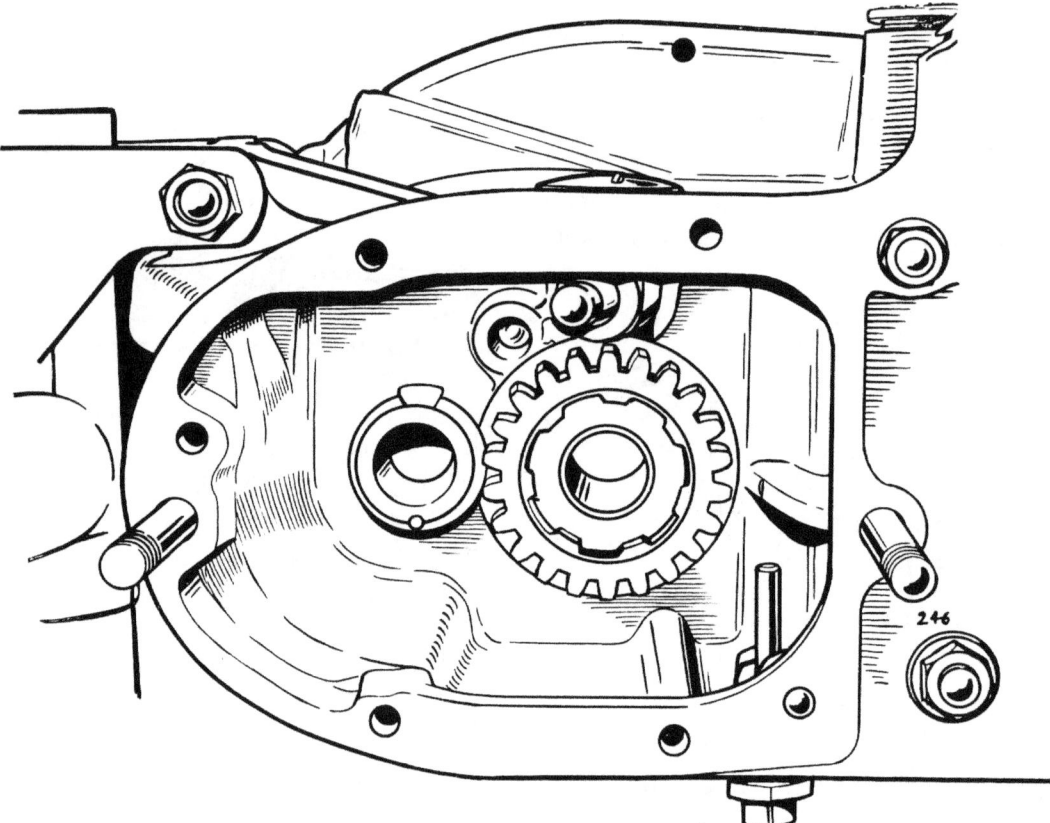

Fig. D6. Illustrating the location of the camplate plunger, layshaft bush and high gear

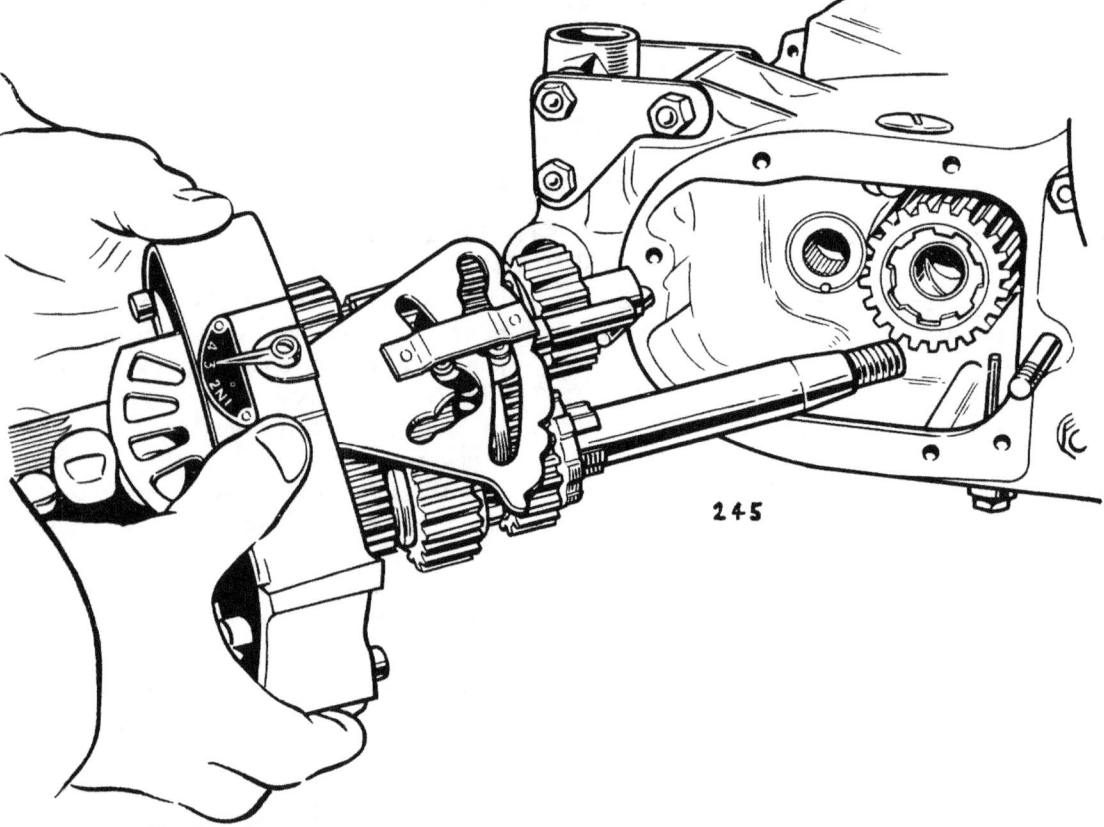

Fig. D7. Reassembling the gearbox inner cover assembly into the gearbox casing

GEARBOX

SECTION D5
KICKSTARTER OPERATING MECHANISM

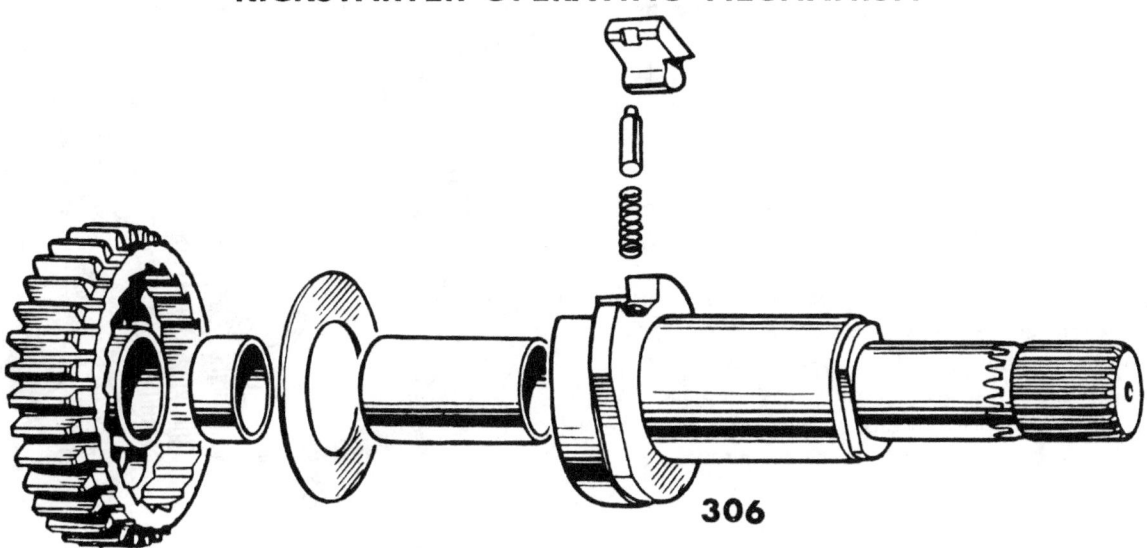

Fig. D8. Kickstart spindle pawl plunger and Spring assembly.

The kickstarter mechanism is contained within the gearbox inner cover and functions in combination with the layshaft low gear. When the layshaft is removed and the low gear disengaged, the kickstarter pawl, plunger and spring are released. Care must be exercised at this stage lest the spring and plunger are lost. Removal of the kickstart spindle is covered in Section D4.

When reassembling the kickstarter mechanism, it is advisable to refit the pawl, plunger and plunger spring in position, locate the assembly within the layshaft low gear, then check its operation to facilitate assembly. The kickstarter spindle can then be assembled to the inner cover when the gears and shafts are replaced.

SECTION D6
DISMANTLING AND REBUILDING THE GEARBOX INNER COVER ASSEMBLY

The camplate is withdrawn by removing the split pin and withdrawing the camplate spindle; lever off the kickstarter return spring, remove the spring and distance piece thus enabling the kickstarter spindle to be withdrawn from the inner cover. Remove the camplate index plunger and spring from the inside of the gearbox and place in safe keeping.

Withdraw the selector fork spindle and disengage the selector forks from the camplate. The layshaft can now be withdrawn from the inner cover leaving the mainshaft assembly, which should be removed by driving it out of the bearing with a hide hammer. Reassembly procedure continues as detailed below. Replace the layshaft thrust washer over the needle roller cage and retain in position with a smear of grease. Lubricate the mainshaft and layshaft captive gears, then assemble the mainshaft as shown in Fig. D1 onto the inner cover. Refit the plunger spring, plunger and kickstart pawl to the kickstarter spindle, insert the assembly into the inner cover, and slide the layshaft assembly into the the kickstart bearing. Do not forget to fit the mainshaft distance piece between the mainshaft assembly and the main bearing in the inner cover. Reposition the selector forks to the shafts as shown in Fig. D1 and insert the selector fork spindle to hold them in position. Assemble the camplate into the outer cover and locate the selector fork rollers in the camplate grooves. Fit the camplate spindle and locate with the split pin. The complete assembly is now ready to be reassembled to the gearbox inner cover. See Fig. D7. At this stage the camplate index plunger and spring must be refitted.

Note: Although the selector forks are very similar in appearance the rollers are offset and it is essential that the correct selector fork is fitted to its corresponding shaft, otherwise the gearbox will not be able to function properly. To check that the selector forks have been correctly positioned, operate the camplate manually prior to refitting the outer cover to the gearbox. When the camplate is moved to its full extent, both selector rollers should move to the full extremity of the camplate grooves in both directions. If the movement of either of the selector rollers is limited, the selector forks will have to be disengaged and their positions reversed.

Replace the distance piece over the kickstarter shaft, then secure the end of the kickstarter spring with the anchor screw. Use a screwdriver to tension the kickstarter spring and replace the return spring plate locating the hook on the spring with the lip on the return spring plate.

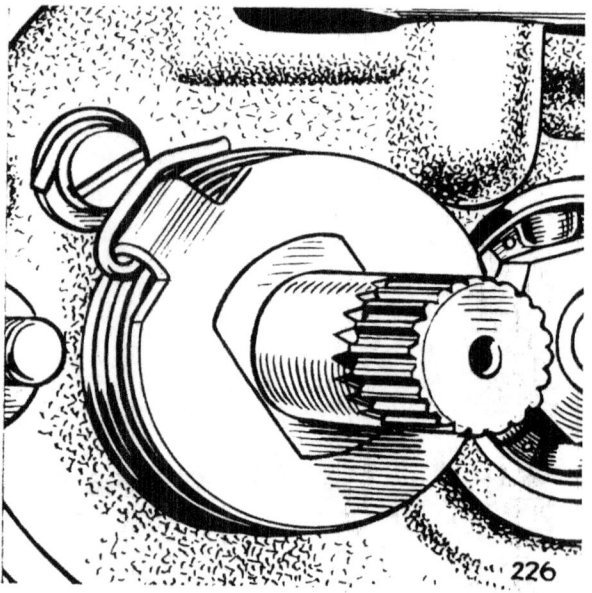

Fig. D9. Kickstart return spring location

SECTION D7
INSPECTION OF THE GEARBOX COMPONENTS

GEARBOX

(1) Inspect the gearbox housing and inner cover for signs of cracking and damage to the joint faces. Check that the location dowels are in position correctly in the gearbox inner cover. In preparation for reassembly, clean the junction surfaces of the gearbox, inner cover and outer cover of any previous deposits of jointing compound.

(2) Examine both the mainshaft and layshaft for signs of fatigue, damaged threads and badly worn splines. Check the extent of wear to the varying diameters of both shafts by comparing them with the figures given in GENERAL DATA. Examine the shafts carefully for signs of seizure. Excessive friction resistance and seizure will be indicated by local colouring of the shaft.

(3) Check the layshaft needle roller bearing by inserting the layshaft and feeling the amount of play. (3TA and 5TA models are fitted with a bronze bush).

(4) Inspect the gearbox mainshaft ball bearing races for roughness due to pitting or indentation of the ball tracks. An estimate can be made of ball wear by feeling the amount of side play of the centre track. It should not be possible to detect any appreciable movement by hand if the bearing is in good condition. The mainshaft should be a hand press fit in the inner cover bearing. Similarly the mainshaft high gear should be a good hand press fit in the opposite bearing.

(5) Examine the gears thoroughly for chips, fractured or worn teeth. Check the internal splines and bushes. Make sure that the splines are free on their respective shafts with no tendency to bind, and the bushes in the mainshaft high gear and layshaft low gear are not loose or excessively worn. Again, reference should be made to the dimensions given in GENERAL DATA.

(6) Check that the selector fork rod is not grooved and that it is a good fit in the gearbox casing and the inner cover. Inspect the selector fork running faces for wear. This will only have occurred if the gearbox is being continually used with a badly worn mainshaft bearing. The camplate rollers which fit on the selector fork are of case hardened steel and consequently wear should be negligible.

(7) The gear selector camplate should be inspected for signs of wear in the roller tracks. Excessive wear will occur if the mainshaft bearing has worn badly. Check the fit of the camplate spindle in its housing.

(8) Ensure that the camplate plunger works freely in the housing and that the moving parts are free from corrosion. To check if

GEARBOX D

the spring has become inefficient, measure its length and compare it with GENERAL DATA.

(9) Examine the mainshaft high gear bush for wear by inserting the mainshaft in it and feeling the amount of play. It is advisable to take micrometer readings of the mainshaft and compare them with caliper readings of the bush. If the clearance is excessively greater than the figure given in GENERAL DATA the bush should be renewed as shown in Section D9.

(10) Check that the kickstarter pawl and the layshaft low gear dogs are in good condition and have not become chipped or fractured.

SECTION D8

REMOVING AND REPLACING THE GEARBOX HIGH GEAR

The mainshaft high gear, in which the gearbox mainshaft runs, is located through the left hand main bearing and gearbox sprocket. The oil is prevented from leaving the gearbox through the main bearing by an oil seal which runs on a ground boss on the gearbox sprocket. To remove the mainshaft high gear and renew the oil seal it will be necessary to remove the sprocket. This can be done by removing the circular plate from the primary inner cover at the rear of the clutch prising the tab washer clear and unscrewing the large hexagonal gearbox sprocket nut. This operation is most easily achieved with the engine in the frame and the rear chain still in situ, and with the rear brake applied. If the engine unit has already been removed and is held in a vice, a short length of rear chain, wrapped round the sprocket and anchored to the work bench, will facilitate sprocket nut removal.

When the nut is removed, drive the high gear through into the gearbox using a hammer with a soft metal drift.

To remove the sprocket, disconnect the rear chain and remove it from around the sprocket, which can then be easily withdrawn through the aperture. To replace the new sprocket, firstly press the high gear into the bearing. Lubricate the ground tapered boss of the sprocket with oil and slide it on to the high gear. Replace the tab washer and screw on the securing nut finger tight.

Remesh the rear chain with the gearbox sprocket. Tighten the sprocket securing nut as tight as possible and bend over the tab washer.

SECTION D9

RENEWING THE MAINSHAFT AND LAYSHAFT BEARINGS

MAINSHAFT

The mainshaft ball bearings are a press fit into their respective housings and are retained by spring circlips to prevent sideways movement due to end thrust. To remove the right bearing, first lever out the circlip, then heat the cover to approximately 100°C. and drive out the bearing, using a suitably shouldered drift. The new bearings should be pressed or drifted in whilst the cover is still hot, using a suitable tubular drift onto the outer race (2½ ins. outside diameter by 6 in. long). Do not forget to refit the circlip.

To remove the high gear bearing on the left of the machine, first lever out the large oil seal (which must be renewed) then remove the retainer circlip. Carefully heat the casing locally to approximately 100C° then drive out the bearing from the right side by means of a suitably shouldered drift. Whilst the casing is still hot, drive in the new bearing, using a suitable tubular drift onto the outer race, then refit the circlip and press in the new oil seal.

Check the oil seal for cracking and wear. If there has been any signs of excessive oil leakage, renew it.

Drive the new oil seal up to the main bearing with the lip and spring towards the bearing.

GEARBOX

MAINSHAFT HIGH GEAR BUSH

If it is required to renew this bush, this can be done by pressing out the bush, using a suitable drift, which can be made from a 5 in. x ⅞ in. diameter piece of bar by machining a 13/16 in. x ¾ in. long pilot at one end. The bush must be pressed out by inserting the drift at the teeth end of the gear. The new bush must be pressed in with the oil groove in the bore of the bush at the teeth end. Finally, ream the bush to size. The pressed in bore size is given in GENERAL DATA.

LAYSHAFT

The right needle roller bearing, which is a light fit in the kickstarter spindle is removed simply by heating the kickstart spindle to approximately 100°C. and jarring the bearing free by striking the spindle on a block of wood. (On 3TA and 5TA models a floating bronze bush is fitted).

The left needle roller bearing is of the closed end type and is accessible from the left, through the sprocket cover plate aperture. The casing should be heated to approximately 100°C. and the bearing driven through into the gearbox, using a soft metal drift, taking care not to damage the bore into which the bearing fits. The new bearing must be carefully pressed in using the tool as indicated in Fig. D10, whilst the casing is still hot.

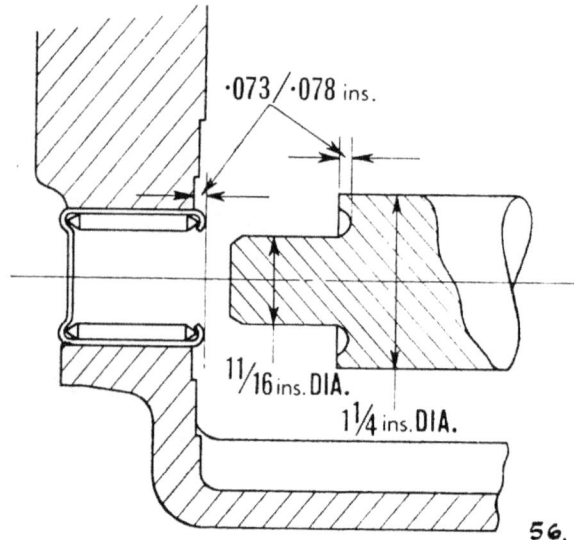

Fig. D10. Sketch of needle roller and drift

On 3TA and 5TA models the layshaft is supported on the left side by a plain bronze bush. To remove this, use a suitable drift from the inside to drive out the blanking plug. Heat the case to approximately 100°C. and drive the bush out, using a soft metal stepped drift. Whilst the casing is still hot the new bush can be pressed in or alternatively driven in, using the same drift as for removing. Fit a new blanking plug, using a proprietary sealant to ensure absolute oil tightness.

SECTION D10
RENEWING GEARBOX SPROCKET WITHOUT DISMANTLING THE GEARBOX

To gain access to the gearbox sprocket, first remove the left footrest and exhaust pipe and then remove the outer primary cover as shown in Section C3.

Remove the pressure plate, clutch plates and withdraw the shock absorber unit and clutch sprocket as shown in Section C9. Remove the key from the gearbox mainshaft and unscrew the six screws which serve to retain the circular cover.

Apply the rear brake, prise the tab washer away, then unscrew the gearbox sprocket securing nut. The rear chain may now be disconnected and the gearbox sprocket withdrawn through the aperature. Before fitting the new sprocket check that the gearbox oil seal is in good condition and that the rear chain is not excessively worn. Check the extension as shown in Section A13. If the old chain is to be retained for further use it should be thoroughly cleaned in paraffin and lubricated in a grease bath.

Lubricate the ground boss with oil and slide the sprocket over the gearbox mainshaft and high gear. When the sprocket is located on the splines, replace the tab washer, screw on the securing nut finger tight, then reconnect the chain. With the rear chain applied, tighten the nut until it is as tight as possible, and bend over the tab.

Smear the bronze bush protruding from the mainshaft high gear with oil and replace the circular cover plate, using a new paper gasket.

Finally, ensure that the oil seal is correctly engaged over the protruding bronze bush. Reassembly then continues as a reversal of the above instructions.

SECTION DD

GEARBOX

	Section
REMOVING AND REPLACING THE GEARBOX OUTER COVER ASSEMBLY	DD1

SECTION D (INCORPORATED IN SECTION DD)

GEARBOX

SEQUENCE OF GEARCHANGING	D11

SECTION DD1
REMOVING AND REPLACING THE GEARBOX OUTER COVER ASSEMBLY

Refer to Section B41 of this Supplement which describes the removal and replacement procedure of the exhaust system.

SECTION D11
SEQUENCE OF GEARCHANGING

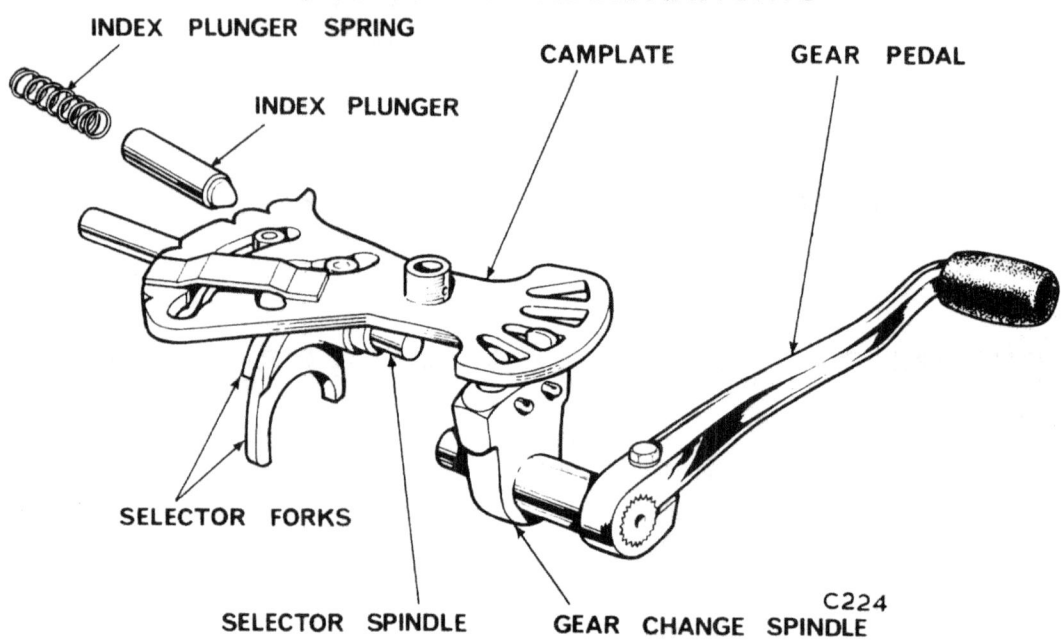

Fig. DD1. Gearchange mechanism

Fig. DD2. Gearbox in neutral position (note red line showing transmission of drive through the shafts and gears)

GEARBOX

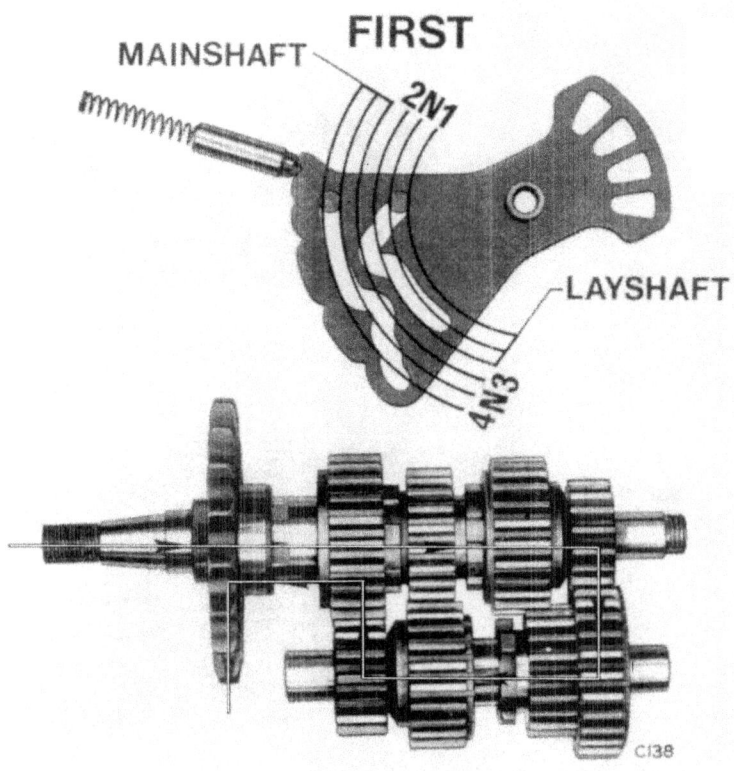

Fig. DD3. First gear

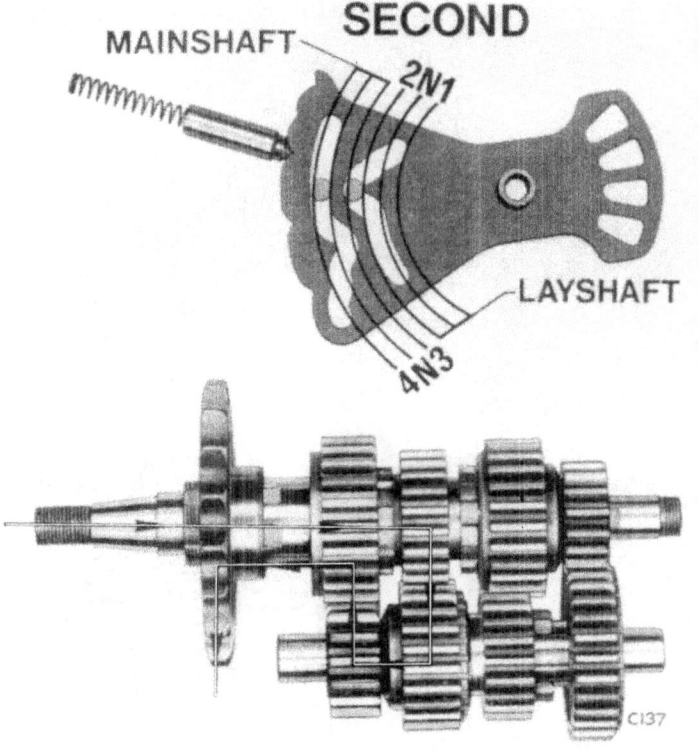

Fig. DD4. Second gear

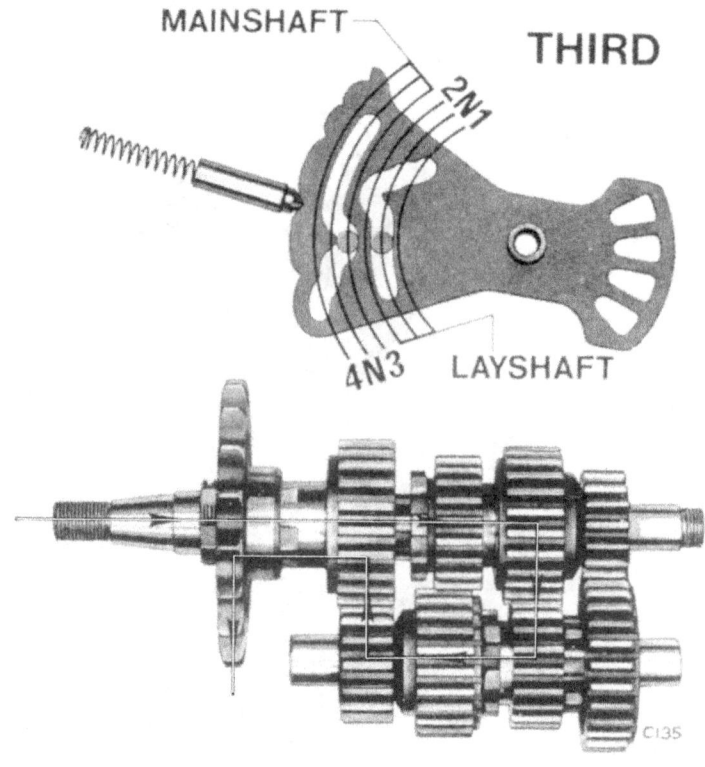

Fig. DD5. Third gear

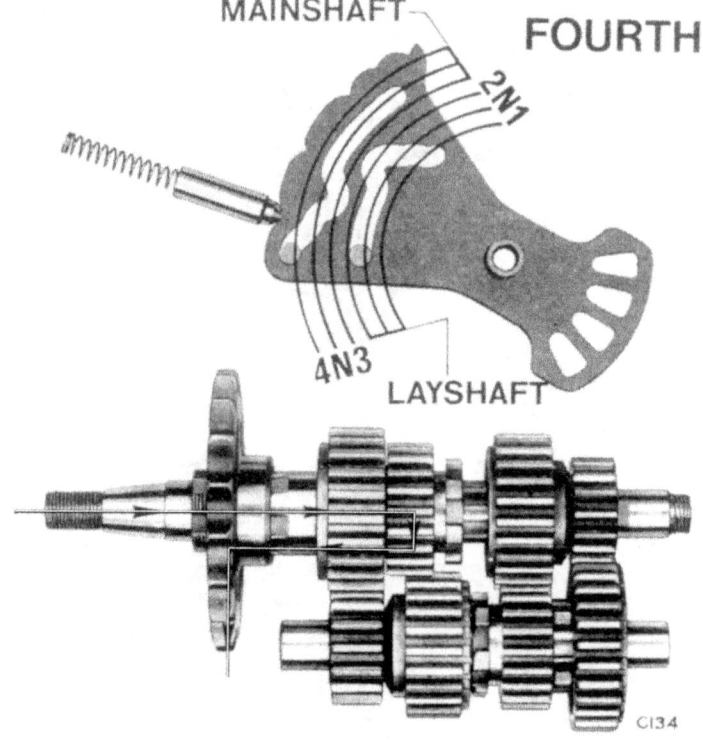

Fig. DD6. Fourth gear

SECTION E

FRAME AND ATTACHMENT DETAILS

	Section
REMOVING AND REFITTING THE FUEL TANK	E1
REMOVING AND REPLACING THE SWITCH PANEL	E2
REMOVING AND REPLACING THE TOOL TRAY	E3
REMOVING AND REPLACING THE BATTERY CARRIER ASSEMBLY	E4
REMOVING AND REPLACING THE OIL TANK	E5
REMOVING AND REPLACING THE ZENER DIODE	E6
REMOVING AND REPLACING THE RECTIFIER	E7
REMOVING AND REPLACING THE REAR MUDGUARD	E8
ADJUSTING THE REAR SUSPENSION	E9
REMOVING AND REFITTING THE REAR SUSPENSION UNITS	E10
STRIPPING AND REASSEMBLING THE SUSPENSION UNITS	E11
REMOVING AND REFITTING THE SWINGING FORK FROM ENGINE NUMBER H.49833	E12
REMOVING AND REFITTING THE SWINGING FORK UP TO H.49832	E13
RENEWING THE SWINGING FORK BUSHES	E14
REMOVING AND REFITTING THE REAR FRAME	E15
FRAME ALIGNMENT	E16
REPAIRS	E17
PAINTWORK REFINISHING	E18

VERY IMPORTANT

PLEASE NOTE THAT U.N.F. (UNIFIED) THREADS ARE BEING INTRODUCEDD PROGRESSIVELY THROUGHOUT THE FRAME GROUP. IT IS MOST IMPORTANT WHEN REPLACING NUTS, BOLTS AND THREADED PARTS THAT THE THREAD IS RECHECKED.

E — FRAME

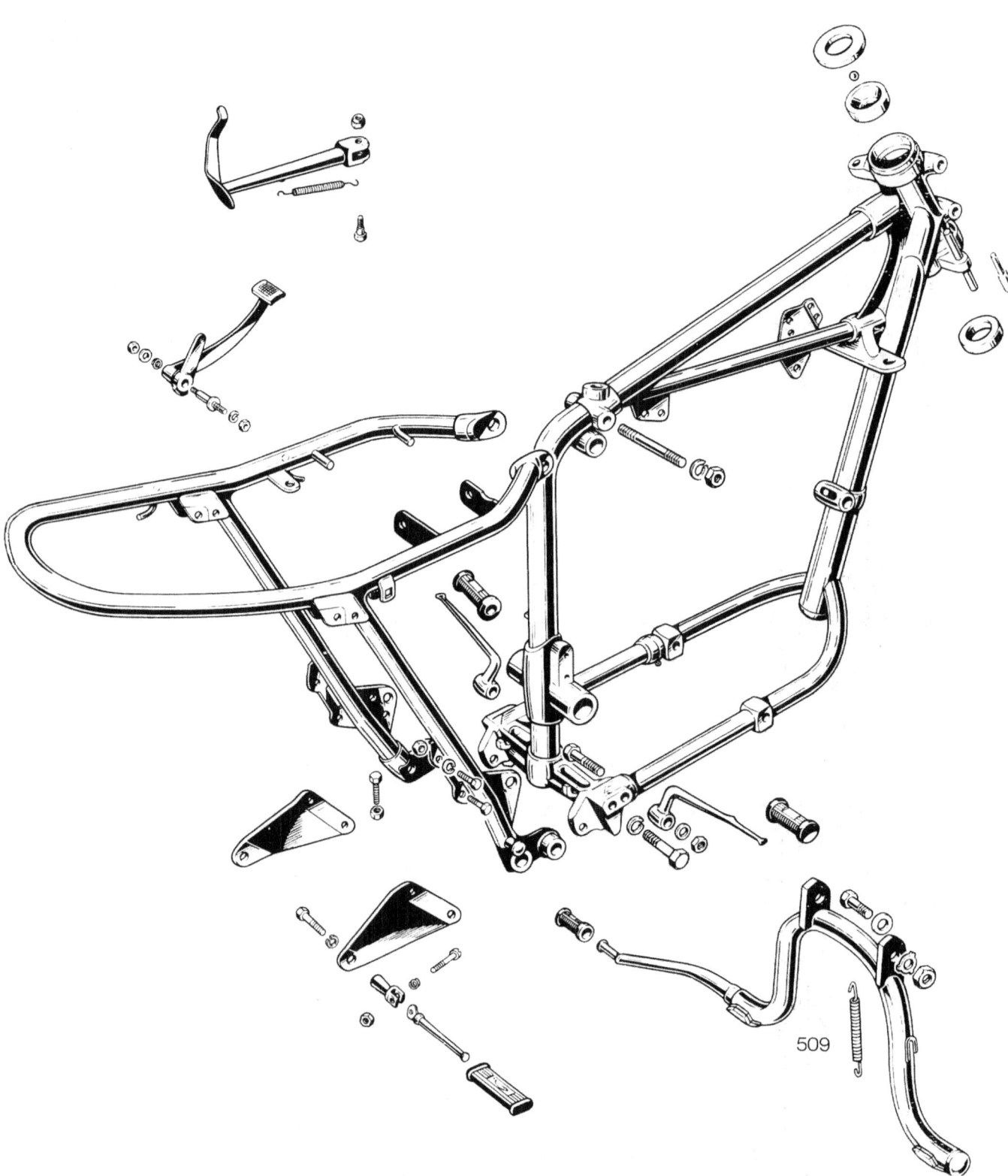

Fig. E1. General arrangement of front and rear frame assembly

FRAME

SECTION E1
REMOVING AND REPLACING THE FUEL TANK

Turn the fuel taps to the off position then unscrew the union nuts and disconnect the feed pipes. Raise the twin seat and detach the tank bolt locking wires.

PRIOR TO ENGINE NUMBER H.49833
Unscrew the four tank securing bolts and lift the petrol tank clear of the machine.

Replacing the tank is the reversal of the above instructions, but do not forget to fit the mounting rubbers on the front and rear tank securing bolts. The thick rubbers fit between the tank and frame brackets. The spigot rubbers are fitted with steel cups from below the frame brackets.

AFTER ENGINE NUMBER H.49833
Detach the locking wire from the front two tank bolts and remove the bolts. The rear tank bolt can then be removed and the tank lifted clear. On reassembly, at the rear tank bolt fit the thick rubber between the tank bracket and frame and the thin rubber and cap above the tank bracket. The order of assembly of the front rubbers is as for earlier machines.

Do not overlook to fit new bolt locking wires.

Do not overtighten the feed pipe union nut as this may result in failure of this part with subsequent fuel leakage.

SECTION E2
REMOVING AND REPLACING THE SWITCH PANEL

The switch panel on the left of the machine is secured by three point fixing. To remove the panel first disconnect the lead from the battery terminals, remove the battery, and then remove the two top mounting nuts. Unscrew the nut and bolt securing the bottom of the switch panel and lift the panel clear. Disconnect the "LUCAR" connectors from the ignition switch.

When the panel is free, the ignition switch can be detached by unscrewing the large retaining nut situated on the outside of the panel, and pushing the switch out of the panel.

Machines before H.49833 have the lighting switch on the switch panel also. On these machines, remove the rubber retaining band from the lighting switch and detach the plug socket connector. The lighting switch can then be removed by unscrewing the central recessed screw, withdrawing the knob and unscrewing the switch retaining nut.

When replacing the panel, ensure that the lighting socket is fully engaged. Replace the rubber band if the old one is perished. The pins in the socket are so arranged that they cannot be reconnected wrongly.

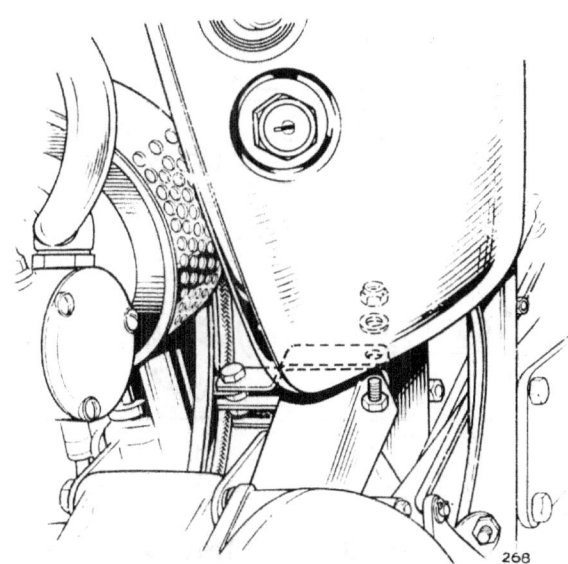

Fig. E2. Switch panel lower fixing bracket (prior to H.49833)

SECTION E3
REMOVING AND REPLACING THE TOOL TRAY

The plastic tool tray is mounted on two frame brackets by a bolt, nut and clamping washer arrangement at each end. Removal of the tray consists only in the removal of these two bolts.

Earlier models (prior to Eng. No. H.42328) incorporated a rectifier mounting bracket fitted below, and located on the left hand frame tool tray mounting bracket.

On these models an additional small diameter spacing washer was interposed between the tool tray top clamping washer and the frame bracket. Reassembly is the reverse of the above, but in the case of the earlier models, care must be taken to re-instal the small diameter spacing washer between the left hand clamping bolt washer, and the frame bracket, and to check the final installation of the rectifier, providing frame clearance to prevent electrical short circuiting.

E | FRAME

SECTION E4
REMOVING AND REPLACING THE BATTERY CARRIER ASSEMBLY

Disconnect the brown/blue negative lead from the battery. Part the red positive lead at the fuseholder, keep the fuse safely for further use and remove the battery equipment. Earlier 6v. models had no fuse in which case the positive lead should be disconnected at the battery. Remove the two top battery carrier fixing bolts from the cross straps. Prise the carrier upwards, from the cross straps, lifting the base of the carrier nearest the oil tank upwards, and towards the top of the oil tank.

To refit, the reassembly procedure is the reverse of the above. Do not overlook the refitting of the fuse (35 amp) into the fuseholder.

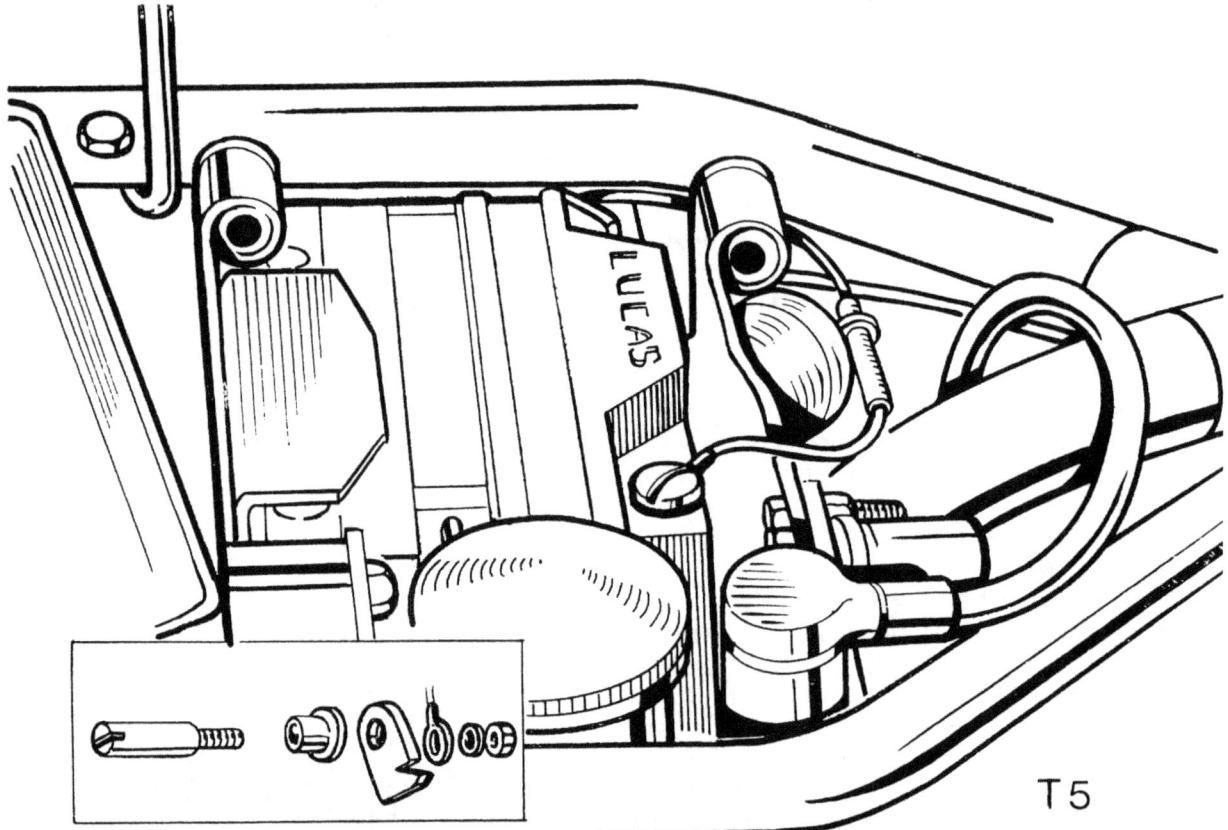

Fig. E3. Oil tank and battery carrier mounting

SECTION E5
REMOVING AND REPLACING THE OIL TANK

Unscrew the oil tank filler cap, place a drip tray underneath the oil tank and remove the drain plug, or, alternatively, unscrew the union nut and disconnect the oil feed pipe. Allow the oil to drain. Unscrew the large hexagon headed oil tank filter body from beneath the oil tank and thoroughly clean it in paraffin (kerosene).

Disconnect the oil return pipe, rocker feed, and chain oiler pipes from the oil tank and disconnect the oil breather pipe from the froth tower on top of the oil tank.

Remove the tool tray as detailed in Section E3.

Remove the battery carrier as detailed in Section E4 above.

Remove the battery carrier frame cross straps as detailed below. Disconnect and remove the top switch panel nuts on the left side of the cross straps, and then remove the attachment bolt and nut from the right end of each cross strap noting the position of the rubber washers. Withdraw each battery carrier frame cross strap from the left end spigot rubber bush.

Remove the two oil tank top bracket fixing nuts, disconnecting the seat check wire, and disengage the screwed studs clear of the frame brackets by pushing them through and out of the spigot rubber bushes in the oil tank top brackets.

FRAME

Swing the oil tank in towards the space above the gearbox, and lift the oil tank off the bottom spigot. If difficulty is encountered in this operation, finally remove the switch panel, as described in Section E2, and then unscrew the two tank bottom bracket mounting bolts and remove the bracket.

Reassembly is the reversal of the above instructions but remember to fit the bottom mounting rubber and also to connect the seat check wire to the rear top mounting bolt. When connecting the oil feed pipe union nut take care to avoid overtightening as this may result in failure of the union nut. When connecting the oil lines ensure that chafing of the rubber connections does not occur. Failure to observe this may result in rubber fragments entering the oil system and subsequently causing blockage.

Screw clips are fitted to prevent any possible oil leakage at the junction between the **connecting rubber and oil tank tube**. These clips should be carefully tightened.

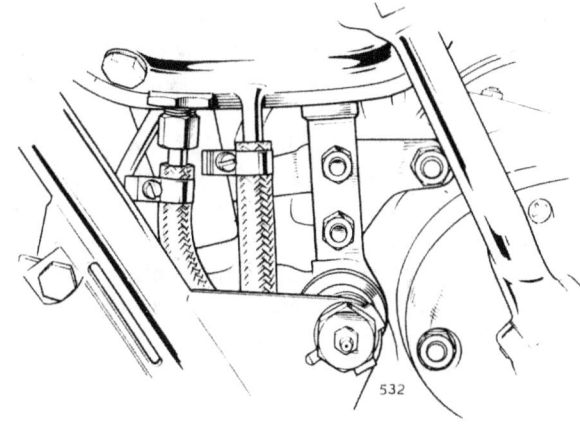

Fig. E4. Oil pipe clips

SECTION E6
REMOVAL AND REPLACEMENT OF THE ZENER DIODE AND HEAT SINK

Remove the switch panel as in Section E2. The heat sink and diode are then visible. The two holding bolts should be removed and the heat sink plate lifted clear. The Zener diode is secured only by one nut on the back which should be removed. The main harness spade terminal should be removed. When refitting, note that the Zener Diode nut must be retightened with extreme care. (Refer to retightening torque figure in GENERAL DATA) and the Zener diode red earthing (ground) lead must be fitted between the securing nut and the heat sink. **The earth (ground) lead must not be fitted between the face of the Zener Diode and the heat sink.**

Do not overlook the fitting of the crankcase breather pipe clip to the front heat sink bolt on reassembly (only after H.49833).

SECTION E7
REMOVAL AND REPLACEMENT OF THE RECTIFIER

Disconnect the battery negative lead. Remove the tool tray as described in Section E3. (On models prior to H42328 the rectifier will then be accessible as its mounting bracket attaches beneath the tool tray mounting bracket).

On later models, the rectifier bracket is attached to the battery carrier rear cross strap. Disconnect the three rectifier leads and remove the rectifier from its mounting bracket.

Refitting is the reversal of the above, but ensure the red earth (ground) tags are located under the central security bolt. When tightening the rectifier fixing nut, hold the rectifier by the TOP bolt, as shown in Fig. E5 to prevent damage to the rectifier itself.

Fig. E5. Removing the rectifier

SECTION E8
REMOVING AND REPLACING THE REAR MUDGUARD

Where a standard rear wheel is fitted, first remove the split link and disconnect the rear chain from the rear wheel sprocket. Unscrew the rear brake operating rod adjuster nut and remove the nut securing the torque stay to the anchor plate. Unscrew the wheel spindle nuts and withdraw the wheel. In the case of a quickly detachable rear wheel disconnect the speedometer drive cable, remove the wheel spindle, and withdraw the rear wheel. Slacken the rear number plate securing bolts and remove the two bolts securing the top clip and number plate. Remove the left and right panels (earlier models) or left panel only (late models) and remove the bottom bolt which secures the mudguard to the frame. Disconnect the rear light lead (two snap connectors adjacent to the rear mudguard), the rectifier leads and remove the two bolts securing the mudguard to the bridge. Remove the two bolts securing the lifting handles to the mudguard and carefully lower the mudguard at the same time allowing the lifting handle to pass underneath the number plate top bracket.

Replacement is a reversal of the above instructions but ensure that the electrical connections are coupled correctly and when reconnecting the rear chain, check that the nose of the spring connection link is facing in the direction of rotation.

SECTION E9
ADJUSTING THE REAR SUSPENSION

The movement is controlled by Girling combined coil spring and hydraulic damper units. The hydraulic damping mechanism is completely sealed but the static loading of the spring is adjustable.

There is a three position cam ring below the chromium plated dust cover and a "C" spanner is provided in the tool kit. To increase the static loading of the spring place the machine on the stand so that there is least load on the spring and use the "C" spanner to turn the cam; both units must be on the same notch whichever may be chosen.

The table below shows the spring rates and colour codes for various purposes.

	Rate lb./in.	Fitted Length (ins.)	Colour Code
Standard 3TA, 5TA T90, T100	130	8	Red/orange
	110	8	Red/red
	145	8	Blue/yellow

The standard lowest position is for solo riding, the second position is for heavier solo riders or when luggage is carried on the rear of the machine and third or highest position is for use when a pillion passenger is being carried.

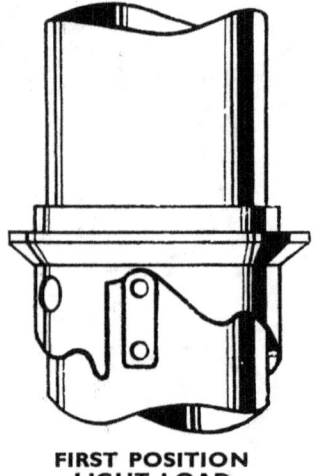

**FIRST POSITION
LIGHT LOAD**

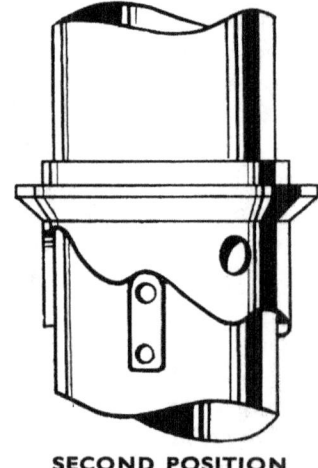

**SECOND POSITION
MEDIUM LOAD**

**THIRD POSITION
HEAVY LOAD**

Fig. E6. Adjusting the rear suspension units

FRAME

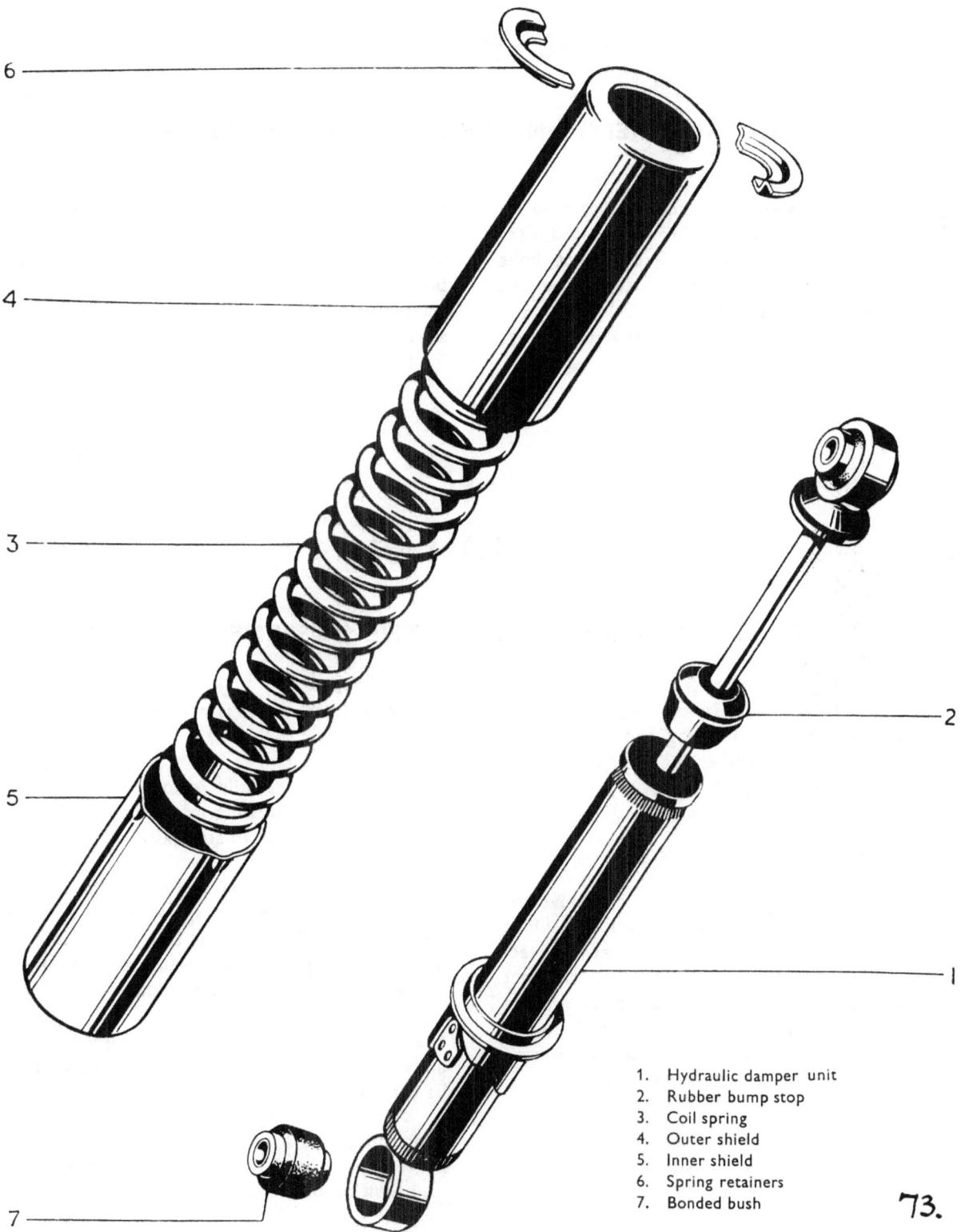

1. Hydraulic damper unit
2. Rubber bump stop
3. Coil spring
4. Outer shield
5. Inner shield
6. Spring retainers
7. Bonded bush

Fig. E7. Exploded view of the rear suspension unit

E　　　　　　　　　　　　FRAME

SECTION E10

REMOVING AND REFITTING THE REAR SUSPENSION UNITS

Removal of the suspension units is achieved by disconnecting the rear brake rod at the adjuster and removing the top and bottom pivot bolts whilst the machine is suitably mounted so that the rear wheel is off the ground.

When refitting the units, ensure that the bridge bracket fits in between the lifting handle and the frame prior to inserting the pivot bolts. It may be necessary to use an alignment bar to assist in bringing the holes into line. Finally the rear brake rod must be reconnected and the adjuster tightened as required.

SECTION E11

STRIPPING AND REASSEMBLING THE SUSPENSION UNIT

The suspension unit consists of a sealed hydraulic damper unit, outer coil spring and dirt shields. The static loading on the spring is adjustable and should be set according to the type of conditions under which the machine is to be used (see Section E8).

To dismantle the suspension unit and remove the spring, it is required to compress the spring whilst the semi-circular spring retainer plates are removed. To do this first turn the cam until it is in the light load position, then carefully grip the bottom lug in a vice. Take firm hold of the outer dirt shield and pull it until the spring is sufficiently compressed to allow the spring retainers to be removed.

The damper unit should be checked for leakage, bending of the plunger rod and damping action. Check the bonded pivot bushes for were and ensure that the sleeve is not loose in the rubber bush.

The bushes can be easily removed by driving out the old one and pressing in the new one using a smear of soapy water to assist assembly.

Squeaking coming from a suspension unit will probably be due to the spring rubbing on the bottom shield. To overcome this, smear some high melting point grease on the inside of the shield. Under no circumstances should the plunger rod be lubricated.

Note: For information concerning suspension units or spare parts, the local Girling Agent should be consulted.

Reassembly is a reversal of the dismantling procedure. Check that the cam is in the light load position before compressing the springs.

SECTION E12

REMOVING AND REFITTING THE SWINGING FORK FROM ENGINE NUMBER H.49833

The swinging fork pivots on bushes fitting over a hardened steel spindle. The spindle is a tight push in fit but is held in place by bolts through the rear frame side plates into the spindle. Removal of the swinging fork spindle necessitates swinging the rear frame assembly clear at the bottom but the spindle can be removed without a special extractor. Proceed as follows:—

Support the machine on the prop stand or on a box and disconnect the centre stand spring to facilitate later dismantling. Unscrew the rear brake adjuster off the rod. Remove the rear chain split link and remove the nut securing the torque stay to the rear brake anchor plate. Spring the torque stay clear of the anchor plate stud. Slacken the nut immediately to the rear of the left hand suspension unit bottom bolt and lift the rear of the chain guard. Disconnect the speedometer cable from the rear wheel drive. Remove the rear wheel as described in Sections F2 or F3. Disconnect the speedometer cable clips from the swinging fork. Disconnect the rubber pipe from the metal chain oiler pipe on the torque stay. Remove the exhaust pipes with silencers by slackening the finned cooling rings, removing the exhaust pipe bracket bolts, nuts and washers and releasing the silencers by taking off the pillion foot rests (where fitted) or the hanger bolts, nuts and washers.

Disconnect the stoplamp switch spring and pull out the snap connectors. Remove the suspension units (see Section E10). Take off the outer nut and remove the rear brake pedal complete with brake rod.

Unscrew both riders footrest retaining nuts and lift off the footrests after breaking them free of their tapers by a sharp upward blow. The footrest hanger bolts should then be withdrawn. Remove the nuts, spring washers and bolt securing the small front chainguard and front lower switch panel to the frame.

Remove the nuts and washers securing the oil tank lower mounting to the frame and tap the studs back through the lug. Note the position of the distance washer over the top stud between the oil tank bottom bracket and frame lug. Remove the mudguard forward bottom securing bolt. Slacken the top and remove the bottom nuts and bolts holding the rear to the front frame.

Remove both swinging arm spindle end bolts after tapping clear the tab washers. The right hand bolt is the one fitted with the grease nipple. The tab washers are then removed. Note for reassembly that the thin, angled tabs locate into the rear frame side plates. The rear frame assembly can now be pivoted on the top stud and supported in the raised position giving access to the swinging arm spindle. Take off the left and right distance pieces, noting that the thicker one fits on the chain side and that the right hand one has one side heavily ribbed. On reassembly the ribbed side must abut to the rear frame side plate.

The swinging arm spindle is free then to be removed. It is a tight push in fit and requires only a suitable shouldered drift and very light hammer blows to remove it. It will be noted that the chain side of the spindle has an extra hole to accommodate a 'C' spanner if this should prove necessary during reassembly.

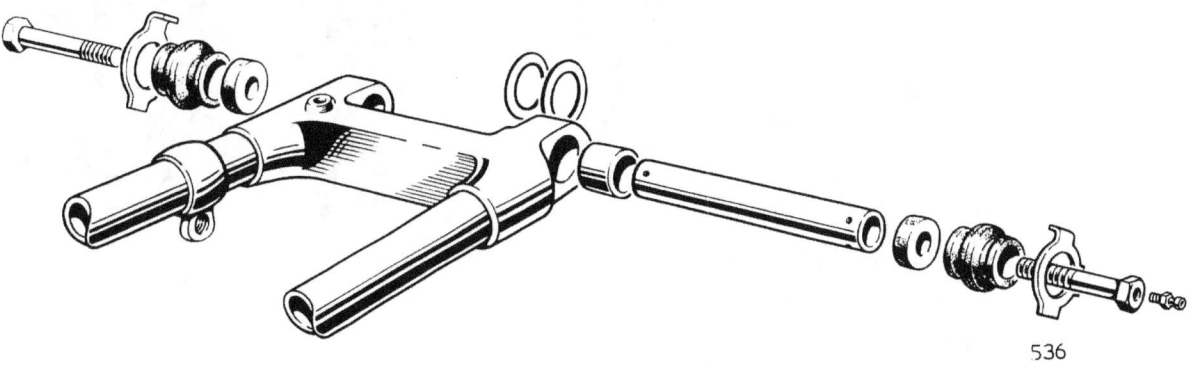

Fig. E8. Order of assembly-swinging fork components from engine number H.49833

FRAME

When refitting the swinging fork to the frame lug, the correct working clearance must be determined by fitting shims between the swinging fork pivot lug and the frame lug. Before fitting the swinging arm and spindle to the frame, scrape all paint from the inside faces of the swinging fork lugs, then using a number of shims and the spacing washer offer the swinging fork to the frame lug with the shims and spacing washer positioned immediately adjacent to the inside face of the swinging fork right lug in that order (the shims are available in ·003 and ·005 in. sizes). The correct working clearance is obtained when the swinging fork will just move under its own weight when fitted to the frame lug.

When the correct working clearance of the swinging fork has been determined, grease the swinging fork bushes and spindle and tap in the spindle from the left hand side.

When the spindle is correctly located, fill the inside with grease and replace the end caps and retaining rod and nut.

Use a pressure grease gun on the swinging fork grease nipple to completely fill the frame aperture until the grease is exuded from the swinging fork bushes.

Reassembly of the remainder of the machine then continues as a reversal of the dismantling instructions.

SECTION E13
REMOVING AND REFITTING THE SWINGING FORK UP TO ENGINE NUMBER H.49832

Unscrew the bolt at the front of the chainguard, disconnect the wires to the stop lamp switch, remove the stop lamp switch operating clip from the brake operating rod and remove the chainguard from the swinging fork.

Remove the two bolts which secure the suspension units to the swinging fork.

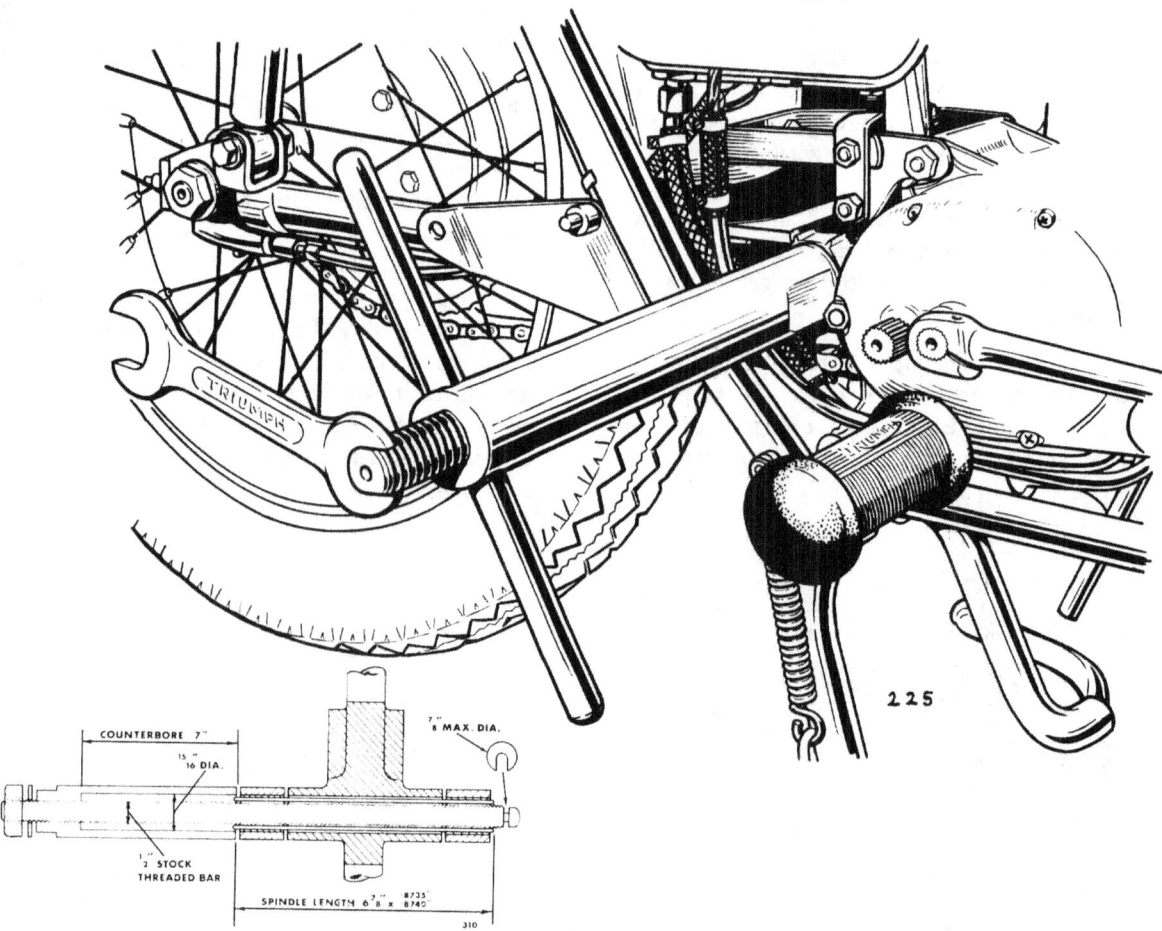

Fig. E9. Removing the swinging arm spindle

FRAME

To remove the spindle, remove the retaining rod and caps, then using a threaded extractor, draw the spindle out from the right side of the machine. A suggested extractor is shown in Fig. E8.

Disconnect the chain and remove the bolt securing the anchor stay to the brake back plate, then unscrew the brake operating rod adjuster nut.

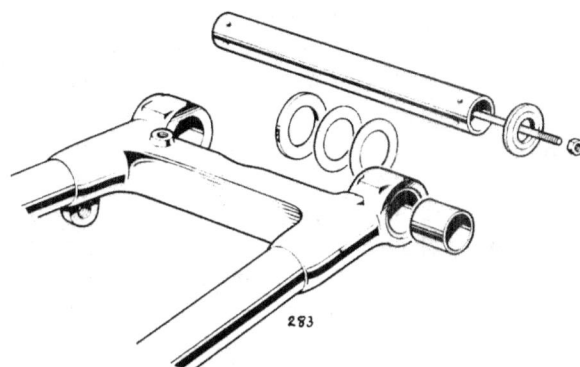

Fig. E10. Swinging fork components

Slacken the bolt at the rear of the chain guard and swing the chainguard upwards to allow the rear wheel to be removed when the speedo cable is disconnected and the spindle nuts slackened.

Remove the swinging fork from the frame lug and collect the shims and spacing washer.

Thoroughly clean all parts in paraffin (kerosene) and inspect for wear. The working clearance between the spindle and swinging arm bushes should not be excessive. If excessive wear is in evidence, the bushes will require renewing; for details of this see Section E14.

When refitting the swinging fork to the frame lug, the correct working clearance must be determined by fitting shims between the swinging fork pivot lug and the frame lug. Before fitting the swinging arm and spindle to the frame, scrape all paint from the inside faces of the swinging fork lugs, then using a number of shims and the spacing washer offer the swinging fork to the frame lug with the shims and spacing washer positioned immediately adjacent to the inside face of the swinging fork right lug in that order (the shims are available in ·003 and ·005 in. sizes). The correct working clearance is obtained when the swinging fork will just move under its own weight when fitted to the frame lug.

When the correct working clearance of the swinging fork has been determined, grease the swinging fork brushes and spindle and drive in the spindle from the left side of the machine using the same threaded extractor as used for dismantling.

When the spindle is correctly located, fill the inside with grease and replace the end caps and retaining rod and nut.

Use a pressure grease gun on the swinging fork grease nipple to completely fill the frame aperture until the grease is exuded from the swinging fork brushes.

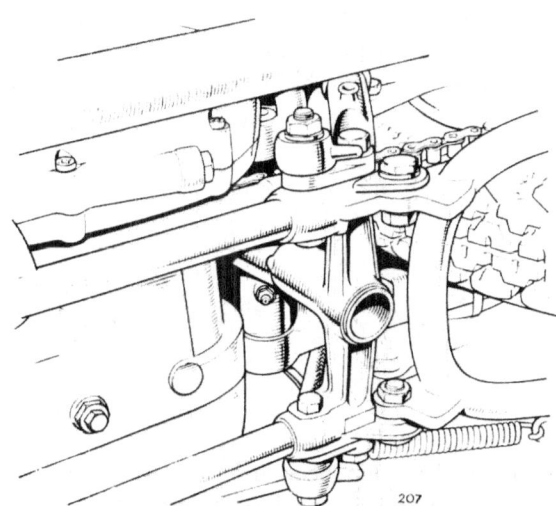

Fig. E11. Swinging fork lubrication nipple (prior to engine number H.49833)

Reassembly of the remainder of the machine then continues as a reversal of the dismantling instructions.

SECTION E14

RENEWING THE SWINGING FORK BUSHES

If the swinging fork bushes require renewing they should be remove by means of a drift inserted into the lugs.

New bushes are of the phosphor bronze type and when carefully pressed in, using a smear of grease to assist assembly, they will require line reaming to give the correct diametral clearance. If a press is not available the bush can be fitted by using a drift and hammer. The drift should be made from $\frac{31}{32}$ in. dia. bar, turned $\frac{7}{8}$ in. dia. x 1 in. at one end. Ensure that the bush enters squarely and that no burr is set up due to misalignment. Use Service Tool Z126 to line ream the swinging fork bushes. Bore sizes and working clearances are given in GENERAL DATA.

SECTION E15

REMOVING AND REPLACING THE REAR FRAME

Disconnect the leads from the battery terminals and remove the battery equipment. Unscrew the four bolts which serve to secure the twin seat hinges, then disconnect the check wire and remove the twin seat. Remove the switch panel, oil tank, rear wheel and rear mudguard as described in Section E2—E7 inclusive.

Slacken the finned clip bolts, silencer clip bolts and remove two nuts which serve to secure the exhaust pipes underneath the engine, then remove the exhaust pipes by tapping them in a forward direction with a hide or rubber mallet. Remove the left and right silencers, then remove both footrests by unscrewing the securing nuts and striking them with a hide mallet to release them from the locking tapers. Unscrew the two bolts which secure each of the pillion footrest brackets and withdraw the brackets and right hand bottom tyre inflator bracket from the rear frame. Unscrew the nut which secures the rear brake pedal and withdraw the pedal and operating rod from the machine. Remove the swinging arm spindle bolts and tab washers. Remove the centre stand bolts.

Finally, remove all frame clips, disconnect the wiring harness to the rear frame portion and unscrew the bottom left and right bolts which serve to secure the rear frame to the front frame, then remove the top securing stud. On removal of the two bolts which secure the rear suspension units to the rear frame, the rear frame can be removed from the machine by lifting it vertically upwards over the swinging fork.

Replacement is a reversal of the above instructions, but refer to the relevent wiring diagram in Section H13 when re-connecting the electrical units and wiring harness.

SECTION E16

FRAME ALIGNMENT

If the machine has been damaged in an accident the frame portions must be checked for correct alignment. In the following paragraph details are given of alignment checking for all parts of the frame (except in the telescopic fork which is dealt with in Section G).

Basic requirements for alignment checking are an engineer's checking table (surface area approximately 3 ft. x 5 ft.), adjustable height gauge (vernier type preferable) two "V" blocks, a set square and a suitable test bar as shown in the sketch (Fig. E11).

FRONT FRAME

It is essential that after setting, or checking, the front frame lug centre line is in a plane perpendicular to the plane of the swinging fork pivot lug centre line. It is also essential, that the remaining tubes and lugs are in their relative positions within the stated limits of accuracy.

The method of checking the front frame is that of securely fitting an adaptor bar of the type shown in Fig. E11 to the head lug. It is then required to support the bar and head lug on a plane parallel to, and approximately 6 in. (15 cm.) from, the checking table surface. For this purpose two 'V' blocks, packing pieces and two suitable 'G' clamps will be required. At the other end of the frame (swinging fork and rear frame removed) an adjustable pillar should be placed under the down tube adjacent to the swinging fork pivot lug. The height of the pillar can be determined by measuring the diameter of the tube which is to rest on it, halving the diameter and then subtracting it from the dimension between the head lug centre line and the table surface.

The frame centre line should now lie parallel to the checking table surface if the frame alignment is correct.

FRAME

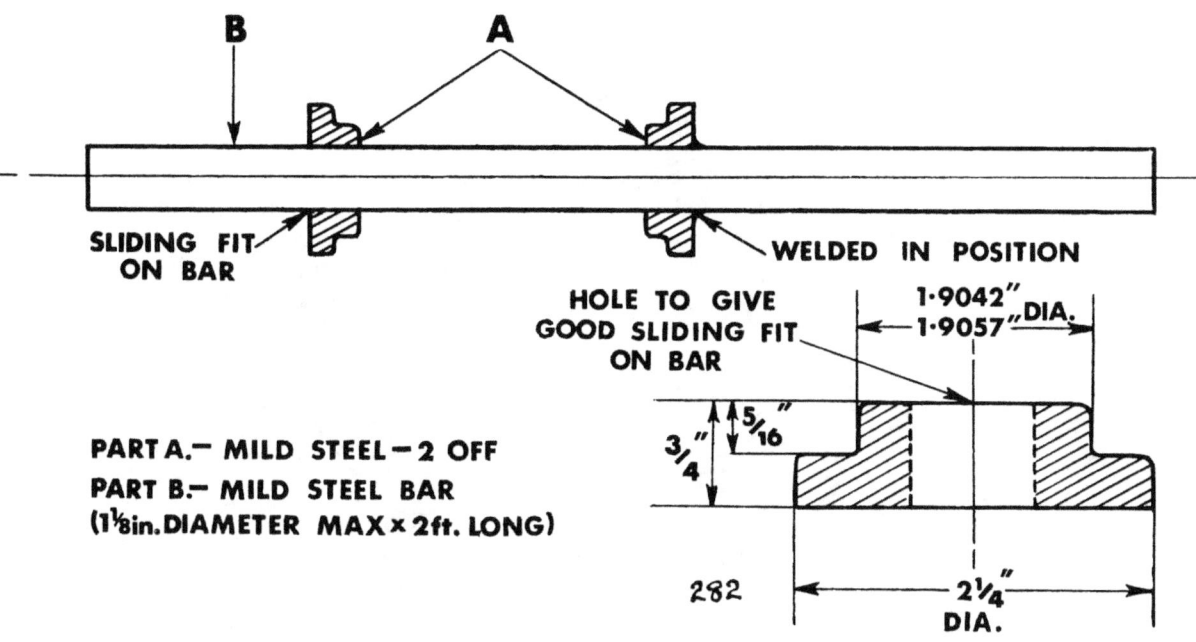

Fig. E12. Sketch of frame checking test bar

To verify this take height readings on the front down tube, top tube and rear down tube. See Figs. E13 and E14. Permissible maximum variation is $\frac{1}{32}$ in. (0·75 mm.).

Fit a swinging fork pivot spindle ground slightly undersize, to lie a free sliding fit in the lug and check the pivot lug for squareness using a set square and distance piece at the location points as shown in Fig. E14.

Then, using a set square, check that the bottom tubes are aligned by bringing the square to bear on them at the front and rear.

Using a steel rule measure the hole centres and compare the figures obtained with those given in Fig. E15.

REAR FRAME

The rear frame basically serves to mount the rear suspension unit and twin seat, etc., and it is only alignment between the top suspension unit support brackets with those on the swinging fork that is of most importance. The best means of checking rear frame alignment is that of fitting it to the front frame and taking readings as indicated in the following paragraph.

FRAME ASSEMBLY

Securely bolt the rear frame to the front frame and fit the swinging fork so that it can just be located by slight hand pressure. Mount the complete assembly horizontally on the checking table as described above, then take height readings at the swinging fork end and top and bottom suspension unit mounting brackets, referring to Fig. E15 for dimensions. These brackets should not be more than $\frac{1}{16}$ in. (1·5 mm.), out of line otherwise the suspension units will be working under excessive stress.

If, when frame alignment is completed, the amount of discrepancy is excessive and rectification is needed, then it is advisable to return the damaged part to the Service Department of Triumph Engineering Company. However, in the case of the swinging fork where the mis-alignment is not more than $\frac{1}{4}$ in. (6 mm.), measured at the tips of the fork ends, it may be possible to rectify this by the following means.

FRAME

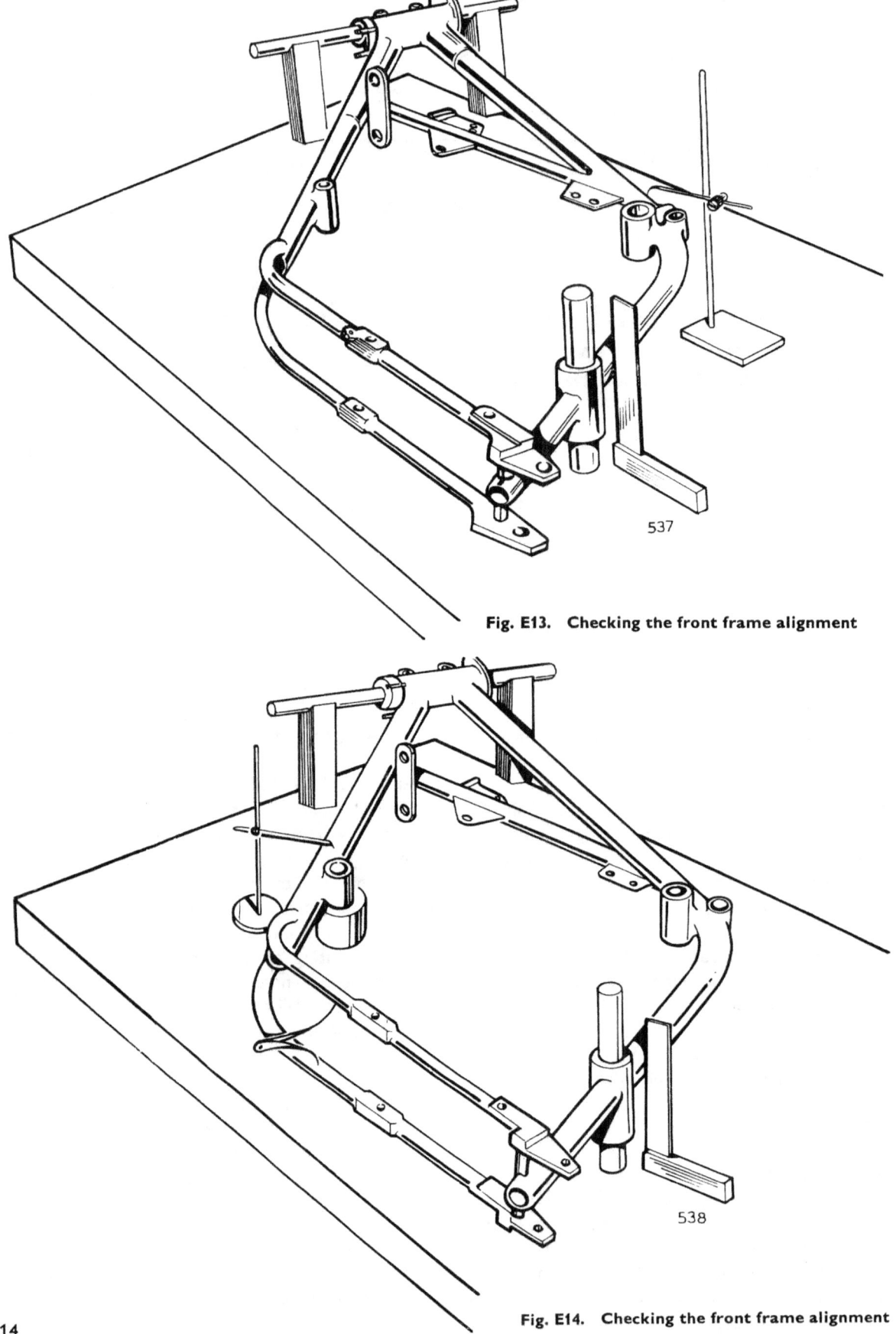

Fig. E13. Checking the front frame alignment

Fig. E14. Checking the front frame alignment

FRAME

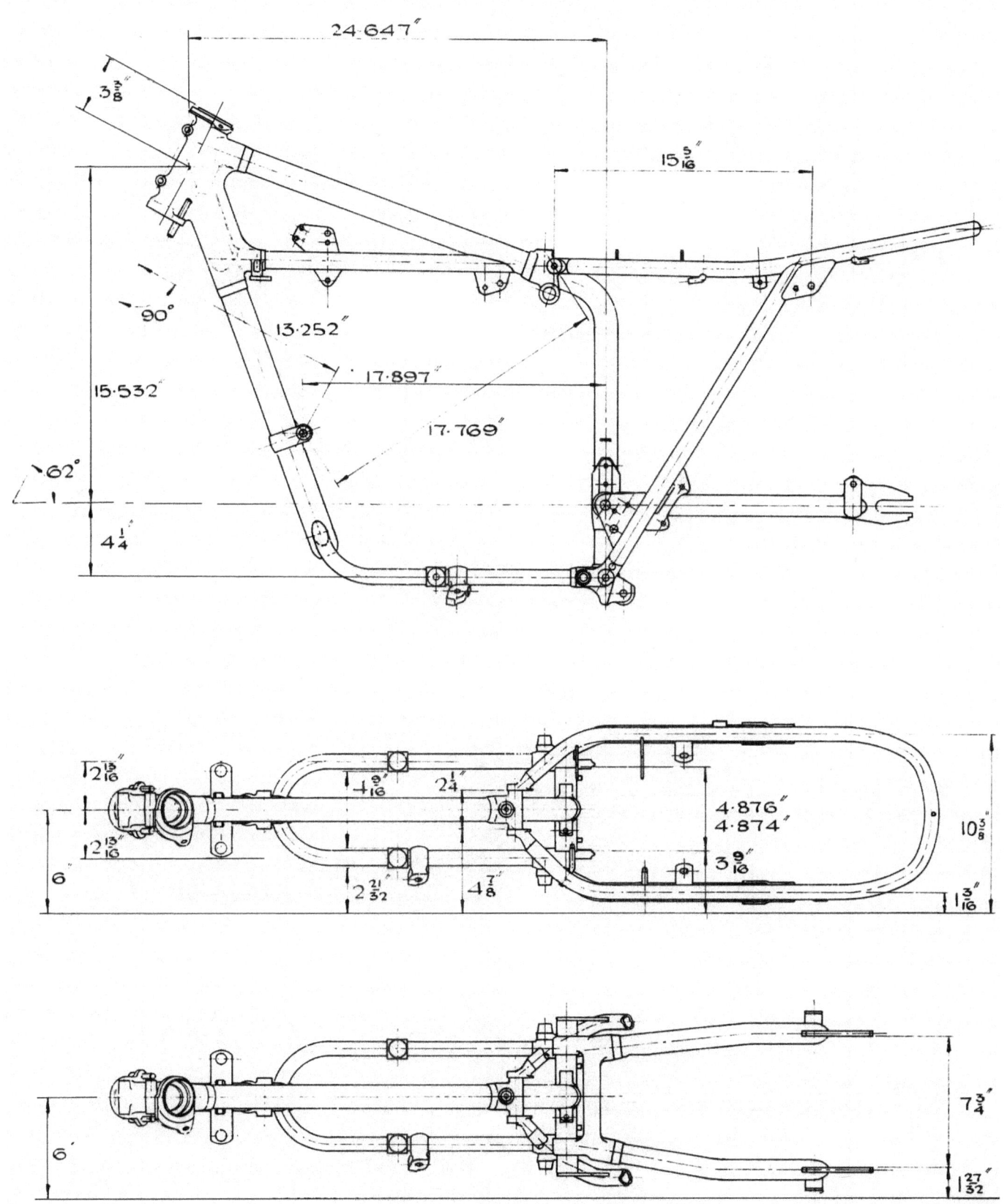

Fig. E15. Basic dimensions of the frame assembly from H49833

FRAME

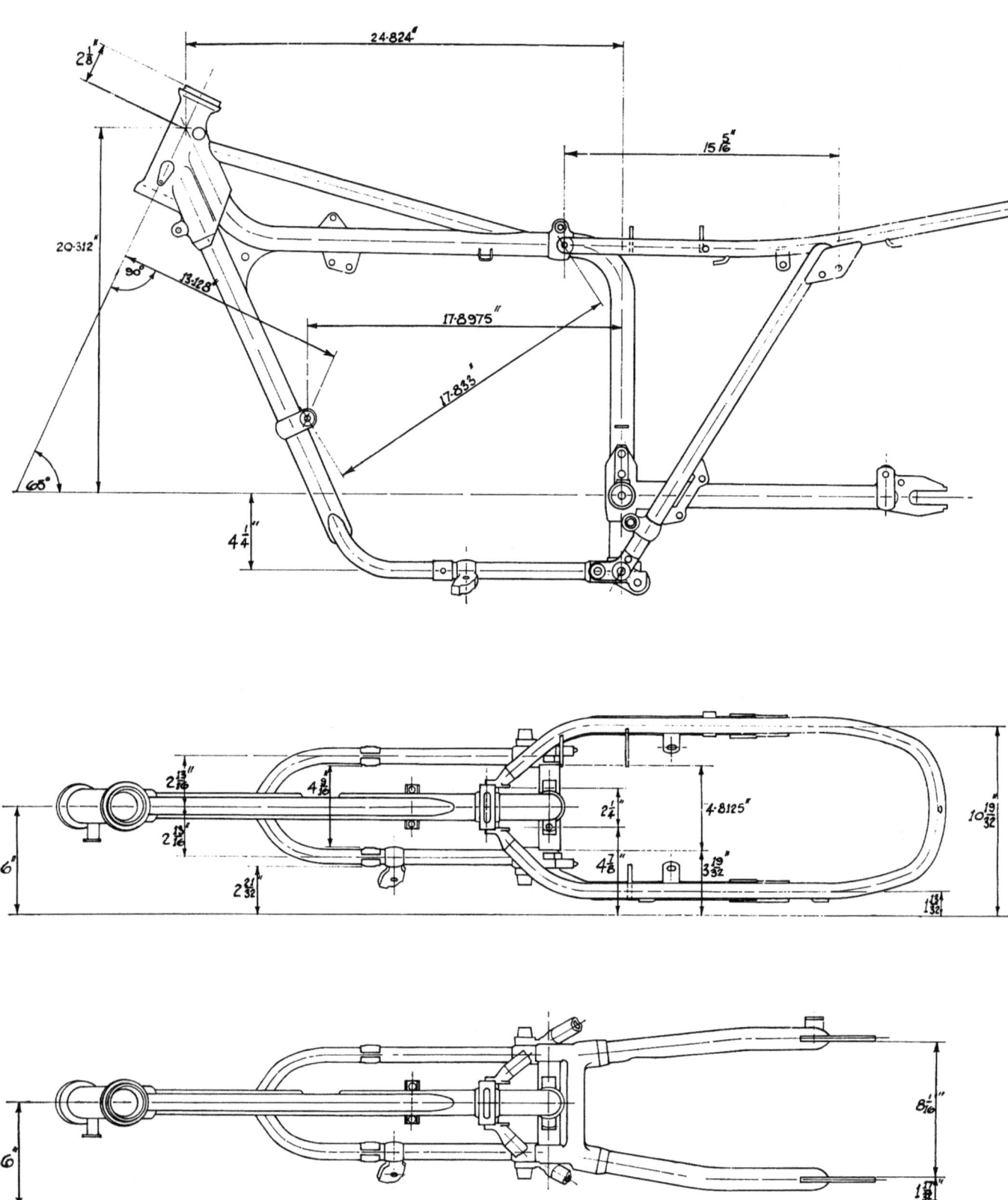

Fig. E15A. Basic dimensions of the frame assembly before H49833

FRAME

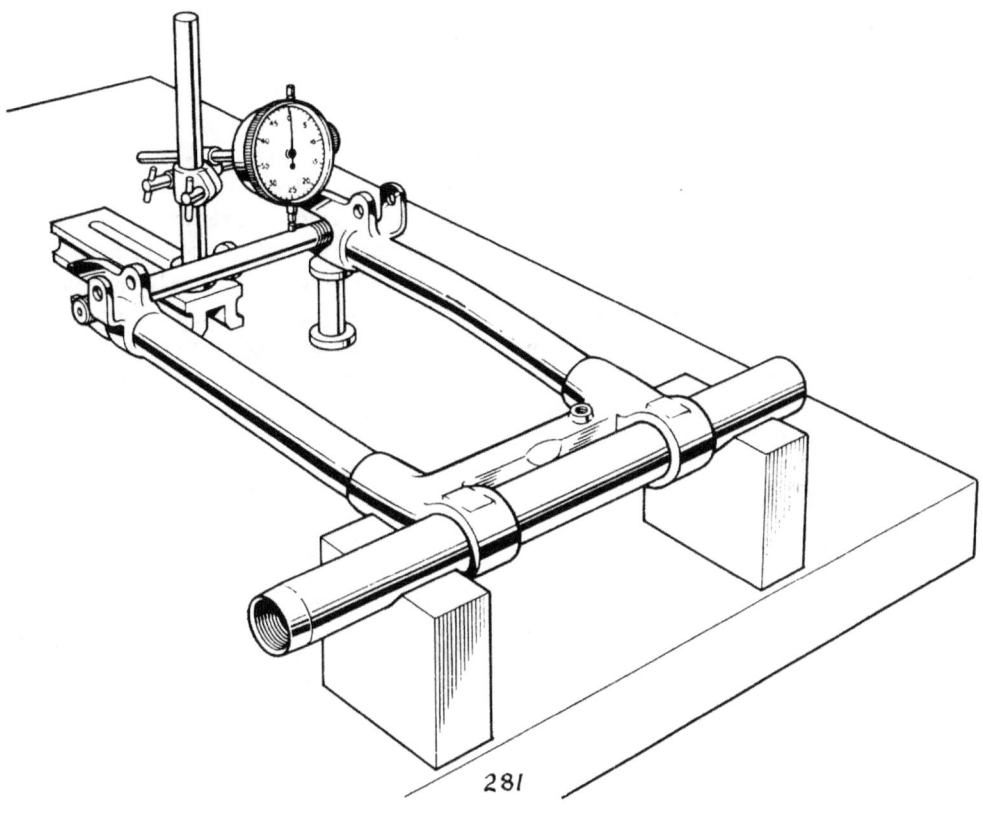

Fig. E16. Checking the swinging fork

SWINGING FORK

It is required to check that the centre line of the pivot spindle is in the same plane as the centre line of the rear spindle. To do this, first place a tube or bar of suitable diameter into the swinging fork bearing bushes, then mount the swinging fork on two 'V' blocks, one on either side, and clamp it lightly to the end of the checking table. Fit the rear wheel spindle into the fork end slots or, alternatively, use a straight bar of similar diameter, then support a fork end so that the swinging fork is approximately horizontal. Height readings should then be taken at both ends of the wheel spindle to establish any mis-alignment (Fig. E16).

Next, check that the distance between the fork ends is as given in Fig. E15.

It is now necessary to lever the fork ends in the correct direction until the wheel spindle can be inserted and found to be parallel with the pivot bush centre line. To do this, a bar of 4 ft. length x $1\frac{1}{4}$ in. diameter is required. It is now that great care is required. Insert the bar at the end of the swinging fork adjacent to the suspension unit mounting brackets so that it is over the high fork leg and under the low fork leg. Exert gentle pressure at the end of the bar then insert the spindle and re-check the alignment. Repeat this procedure using increased loads until the spindle height readings show that the swinging arm is now mis-aligned in the opposite sense. A small leverage now applied from the other side will bring the wheel back to parallel.

Note: Apply the leverage bar as near as possible to the suspension unit bracket, otherwise the tubes may become damaged. DO NOT USE THE THE FORK ENDS.

FRAME

SECTION E17

REPAIRS

Repairs covered in this section are simple operations requiring only a minimum of special tools. The type of repairs possible with these tools are those such as small dents to mudguards, panels etc., caused by flying stones or slight grooves which have not affected a large area or torn the metal. The tool required are shown below in Fig. E17.

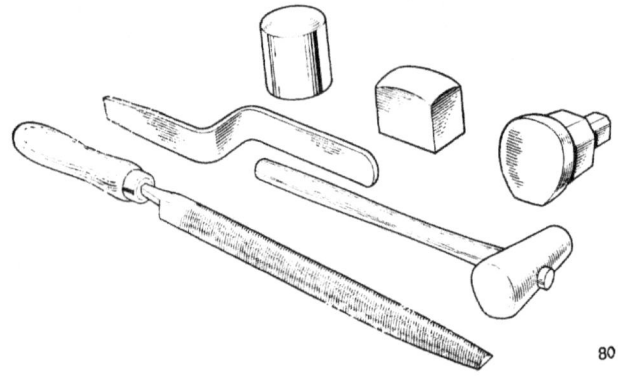

Fig. E17. Tools used for panel repairs

REMOVAL OF DENTS

To remove small dents a spoon and suitably shaped dolly block are required. A spoon can be made from a file by first normalising and removing the teeth and polishing the surface and cranking it as shown in Fig. E17.

Place the dolly block underneath the panel and hammer the dent carefully with a spoon until something like the original contour is achieved. Lightly file the surface to show any high spots there may be and use the dolly and spoon to remove them.

Note: Do not file more than is necessary to show up the high spots. Care should be taken to keep filing to a minimum otherwise serious thinning of the metal will occur.

Where denting has occurred without resultant damage to the paint work the dents may be removed whilst the paint work is preserved by careful use of a polished spoon and dolly block. Dents which are comparatively larger may be removed whilst the paint work is preserved by placing a sand bag against the outer surface and hammering the inside of the panel with a suitably shaped wooden mallet. A sand bag can be made from a piece of 18 in. square leather by folding it and packing it tightly with sand. Finally, finish off using a dolly block and polished spoon as required.

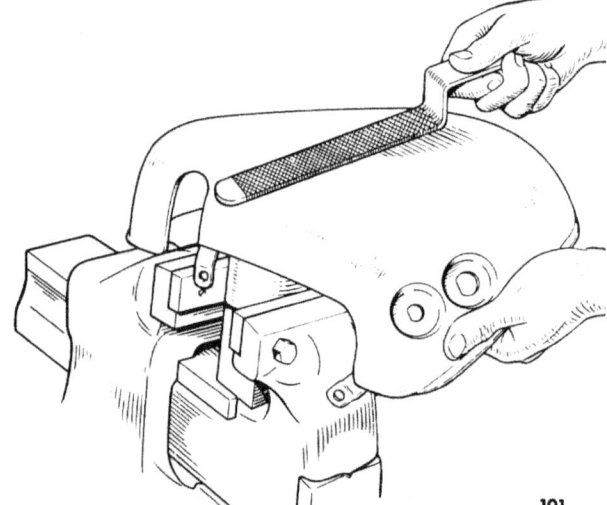

Fig. E18. Removing a dent with dolly block and spoon

Note: It is not advisable to use a hammer as hammer blows tend to stretch the surrounding metal, giving rise to further complications. Also, unless the aim is true, damage of a more serious nature may result.

Where a fuel tank has become damaged the repair work should only be entrusted to a competent panel beater, or return the tank to the Service Department—Triumph Engineering Company Ltd.

SECTION E18

PAINT WORK REFINISHING

PAINT STRIPPING

Except in cases where touching-up is to be attempted, it is strongly recommended that the old finish is completely stripped and the refinish is carried out from the bare metal. Paint stripper can be obtained from most paint stores and accessory dealers.

The stripper should be applied with a brush and allowed approximately 10 minutes to react. A scraper should be used to remove the old finish, then the surface cleaned with water using a piece of wire wool. Ensure that all traces of paint stripper are removed. If possible, blow out crevices with compressed air.

It is advisable to strip a small area at a time to avoid the stripper drying and also to enable easy utilising of the stripper.

Finally, the surface should be rubbed with a grade 270 or 280 emery cloth to give a satisfactory finish then washed off with white spirit or a suitable cleaner solvent.

PRIMING

A thin coat of cellulose primer must be sprayed onto the surface prior to application of an undercoat or stopper. Undercoat and stopper will not adhere satisfactorily to bare metals. It is advisable to thin the primer by adding one part cellulose thinners to one part primer. Ensure that the primer is dried before advancing further.

APPLYING STOPPER

Imperfections and slight dents in the surface may be filled with stopper, but rubbing down with wet and dry should not be attempted until the undercoat or surfacer has been applied.

Apply the stopper with a glazing knife in thin layers, allowing approximately 20 minutes for drying between each layer. After the last layer, allow the stopper about 6 hours (or over-night if possible) to dry. Heavy layers or insufficient drying time will result in surface cracking.

UNDERCOAT (SURFACER)

Most cellulose undercoats, also called surfacers, will suffice for a base for Triumph finishes. About two or three coats are required and should be sprayed on in a thinned condition using one part cellulose thinners to one part undercoat. Allow approximately 20 minutes between each coat.

If stopper has been applied the final layer of undercoat should be sprayed on after smoothing the surface with wet and dry abrasive as shown below.

WET AND DRY SANDING

After application of the undercoat, the surface should be rubbed down with 270 or 280 grade abrasive paper used wet. An ideal method is to have a rubber block approximately 3 in. x 2 in. x 1 in. around which to wrap the emery paper. However, this is only recommended for flat surfaces; where rapid changes of section occur, a thin felt pad is more useful.

The abrasive paper should be allowed to soak in cold water for at least 15 minutes before use. A useful tip is to smear the abrasive surface with soap prior to rubbing down. This will prevent clogging and should at least treble the useful life of the paper if it is washed thoroughly after each rub down.

When the surface is smooth enough, wash it thoroughly with water and dry off with a clean sponge.

If smoother surface than this is required it can be given another layer of undercoat and then the rubbing down procedure repeated using 320 or 400 grade of paper depending upon conditions.

FINISHING

Before spraying on the finishing coat the surface must be quite smooth, dry and clean. It is important that conditions are right when finish spraying is to be carried out otherwise complications may occur. Best conditions for outdoor spraying are those on a dry sunny day without wind. Moisture in the atmosphere is detrimental to paint spraying.

E   FRAME

The first coat should be thinned in the ratio of 50% cellulose thinners to 50% lacquer. Subsequent coats should have a higher proportion of thinners as shown below.

First coat 50% cellulose thinners 50% lacquer.
Second coat 60% cellulose thinners 40% lacquer.
Third coat 70% cellulose thinners 30% lacquer.
Fourth coat 80% cellulose thinners and 20% lacquer. Between each coat the surface may be flatted by hand with 320 or 400 grade of abrasive paper as required.

Allow at least 10 minutes between each coat and after the final coat leave over-night or 24 hours if possible. For most purposes the second coat of finish is more than adequate.

POLISHING

The final colour coat must be completely dry before cutting and polishing. Use a clean rag, rub down with brass polish or fine cutting paste and burnish to a high gloss using a clean mop before applying a suitable wax polish for protection and shine.

Note: Triumph supply only the finishing lacquers. These are available in quarter pint tins and Aerosol sprays or, for workshop use, one gallon tins.

FLAMBOYANT FINISHES

To regain the original depth of colour or shade, when applying flamboyant finishes, they must be applied onto the correct base colour e.g.

Finish	(Ser. Ref.)	**Base Colour**	(Ser. Ref.)
Kingfisher blue	K	Silver	V
Hi-Fi red	HF	Gold	G
Regal purple	P	Silver	V
Burnished gold	BG	Gold	G
Pacific blue	PB	Silver	V
Flame	F	Gold	G
Burgundy	B	Gold	G

METALLIC FINISHES

Sherbourne green (Service Ref. S.G.) is a metallic finish which needs no special base colour. This finish applies equally well either with a brown or white primer.

SECTION EE

FRAME

	Section
REMOVING AND REPLACING THE TOOL CARRIER...	EE 2(B)
ADJUSTING THE REAR SUSPENSION	EE 9
STRIPPING AND REASSEMBLING THE REAR SUSPENSION UNIT...	EE11
REMOVING AND REFITTING THE SWINGING FORK	EE12
REMOVING AND REPLACING THE REAR FRAME	EE15

SECTION E (INCORPORATED IN SECTION EE)

FRAME

FAIRING ATTACHMENT LUGS AND STEERING LOCK	E19
FITTING REPLACEMENT SEAT COVERS	E20
REVISED ENGINE BREATHER SYSTEM	E21

SECTION EE2(B)
REMOVING AND REPLACING THE TOOL CARRIER (LEFT PANEL)

Components are available to convert the toolbox retaining mechanism on machines after engine number H.57083 to eliminate any possibility of the plastic toolbox screw vibrating loose.

The components required are:—
- 1 off F11348 Spring clip
- 1 off F11379 Pop rivet
- 1 off F11377 Retaining washer

Remove the toolbox from the machine and position the spring clip as shown (see Fig. EE1). Using a No. 30 drill (0·1285 dia.) drill through the toolbox at the point shown. The clip should be fitted at the back of the toolbox and secured with the pop rivet which should also be fitted from behind.

The plastic screw must also be modified by filing four flats to the dimensions shown (see Fig. EE2).

Alternatively an already modified screw can be purchased under part number F11357.

When refitting the toolbox, the rubber washer should be fitted between the tool box and frame.

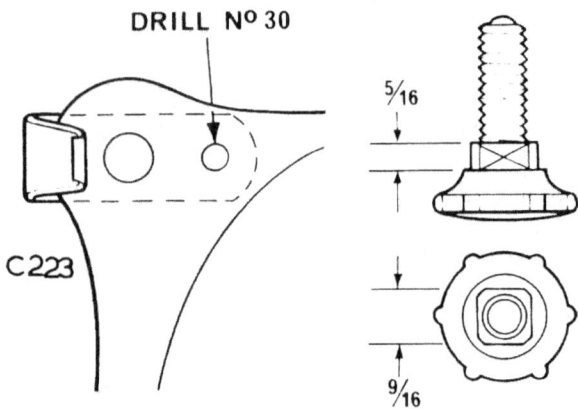

Fig. EE1. Position of clip   Fig. EE2. Dimensions of knob

SECTION EE9
ADJUSTING THE REAR SUSPENSION

The movement is controlled by a combined coil spring and hydraulic damper units. The damping mechanism is completely sealed, but the static loading of the spring is adjustable. There is a castellated, three position cam ring at the lower end of each unit. A "C" spanner is provided in the tool kit to either increase or decrease the load.

To adjust the units, place the machine on the centre stand, and turn the collar in the direction of arrow "A" to increase the static loading, and in the opposite direction to decrease it. Both units must be in the same position, whichever is chosen.

The lowest position or furthest in the opposite direction to the arrow is for solo riding, the second is for heavy solo riders or when luggage is carried on the rear of the machine, and the third or highest position (full rotation in direction of arrow "A") is for use when a pillion passenger is being carried.

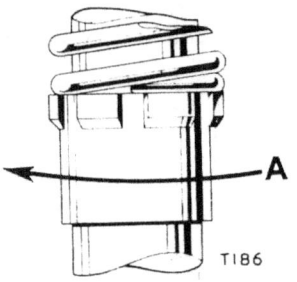

Fig. EE3. Static load adjuster

SECTION EE11
STRIPPING AND REASSEMBLING THE REAR SUSPENSION UNIT

The suspension units used on later machines are similar in construction to the early units except that no dirt shields are used, and the adjuster cam is enclosed.

To dismantle the unit merely grip the lower end in a vice, select the light load position on the adjuster, and depress the spring until the retainers can be removed.

The assembly procedure is a reversal of the above.

FRAME EE

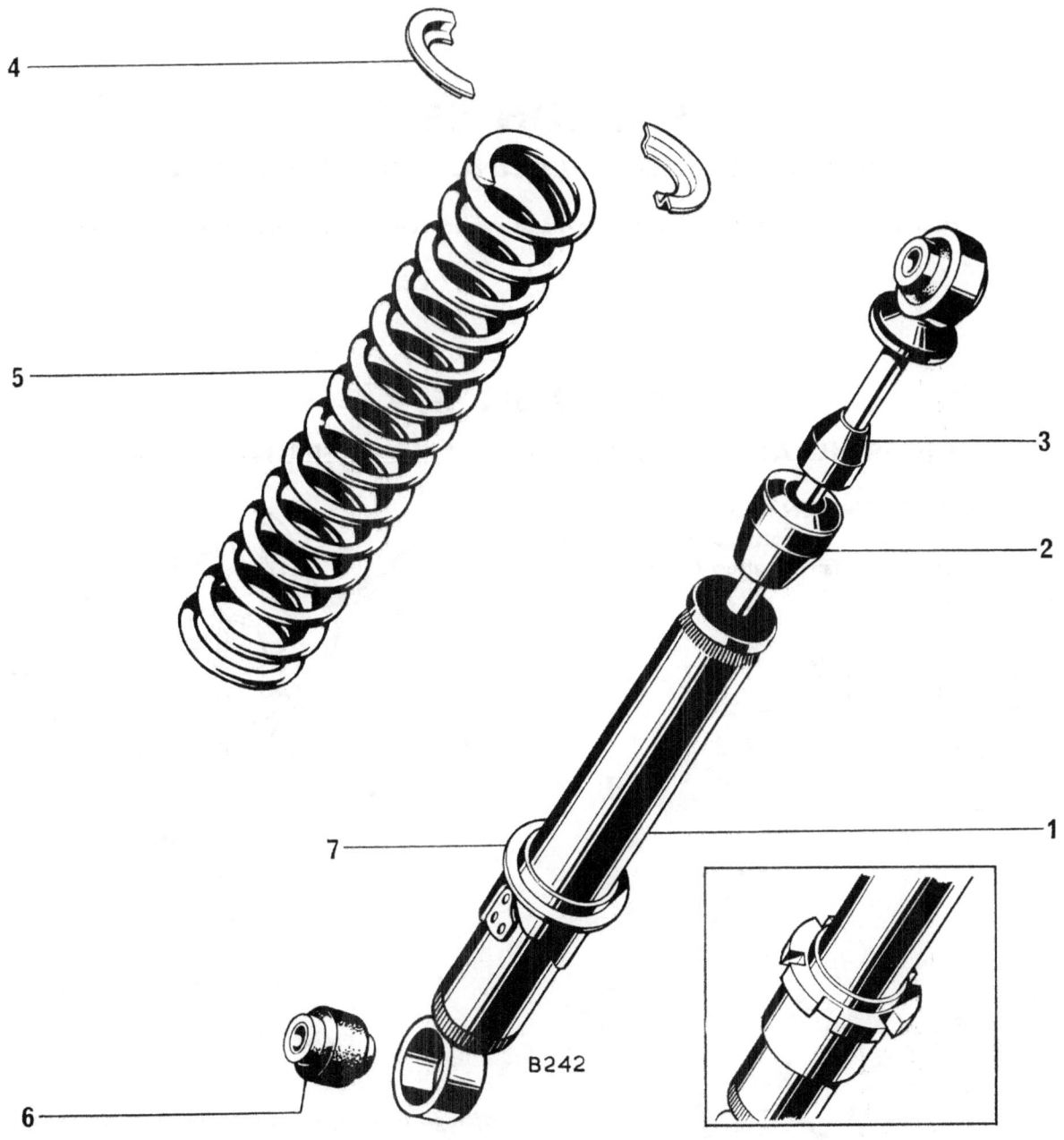

Fig. EE4. Exploded rear suspension unit (note later adjuster indented)

SECTION EE12
REMOVING AND REFITTING THE SWINGING FORK

Refer to Section B41 of this Supplement for the exhaust system removal and replacement procedure.

SECTION EE15
REMOVING AND REPLACING THE REAR FRAME

Refer to Section B41 of this Supplement for the exhaust system removal and replacement procedure.

SECTION E19
FAIRING ATTACHMENT LUGS AND STEERING LOCK

FAIRING ATTACHMENT LUGS
The two lugs shown in Fig. EE5 are fitted to facilitate mounting a fairing after the headlamp has been removed.

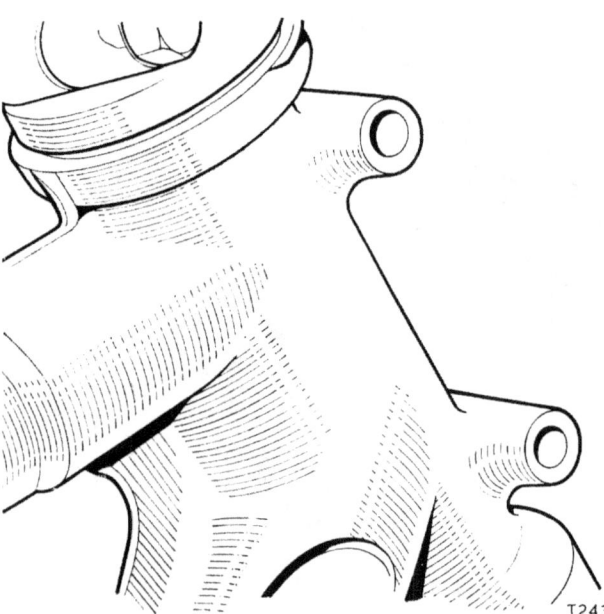

Fig. EE5. Fairing attachment lugs

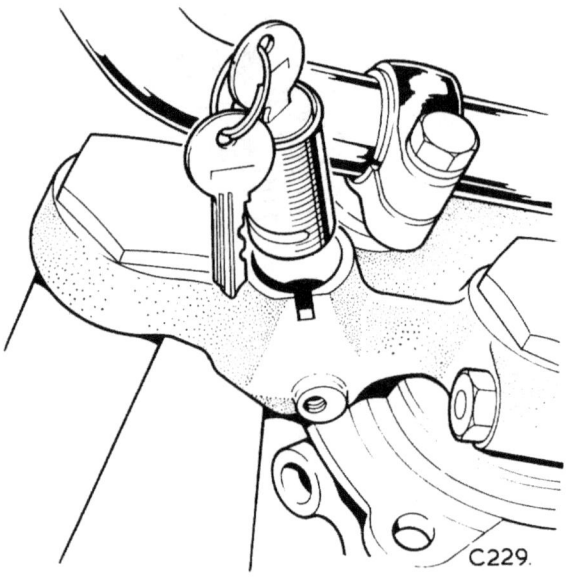

Fig. EE6. Steering lock

STEERING LOCK
A barrel type steering lock is fitted into the fork top lug. If for any reason the lock is to be removed, a grub screw (see Fig. EE6) must be removed, and the lock can be lifted clear. Note, however, that a blanking plug is fitted into the lug over the grub screw and this will have to be prised out to gain access to the screw. The slug is of lead, hammered into the screw hole and should be renewed after re-fitting the lock.

SECTION E20
FITTING REPLACEMENT SEAT COVERS

'Quiltop' twinseats have a cover retained by sprags which are part of the seat pan.

When fitting a replacement seat cover it is VERY IMPORTANT to first soak the complete cover assembly in hot water in order to soften the plastic, so that it can easily be stretched into place. After soaking the cover in hot water, wring out the excess water and you will find that the cover can very easily be stretched into place to give a neat fit without any wrinkles. This job is very difficult if you do not follow this suggested method.

Ideally the seat should be allowed to dry out in a warm place before being put back into service.

SECTION E21
REVISED ENGINE BREATHER SYSTEM

As described in Section C9 a revised engine breather system was introduced from engine number KD27866. This change also required the addition of a 'D' section breather pipe to be attached to the left side of the rear mudguard, connecting via a 'T' piece adaptor (from the oil tank vent pipe) to the chaincase breather outlet stub on the primary chaincase inner.

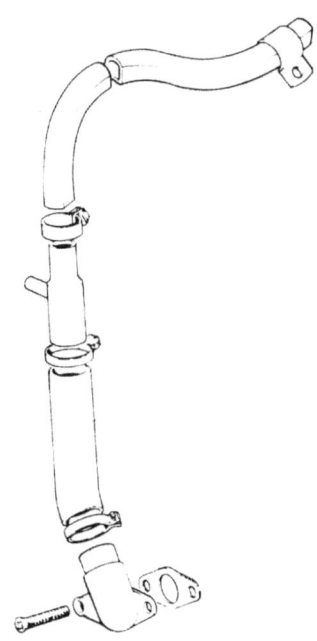

Fig. EE7. Revised engine breather system

NOTES

SECTION F

WHEELS, BRAKES AND TYRES

DESCRIPTION	Section
REMOVING AND REFITTING THE FRONT WHEEL	F1
REMOVING AND REFITTING THE REAR WHEEL	F2
REMOVING AND REFITTING THE QUICKLY DETACHABLE (Q.D.) REAR WHEEL	F3
FRONT AND REAR WHEEL ALIGNMENT	F4
BRAKE ADJUSTMENTS	F5
STRIPPING AND REASSEMBLING THE BRAKES	F6
RENEWING BRAKE LININGS	F7
REMOVING AND REFITTING THE WHEEL BEARINGS	F8
WHEEL BUILDING	F9
WHEEL BALANCING	F10
REMOVING AND REPAIRING TYRES	F11
SECURITY BOLTS	F12
TYRE MAINTENANCE	F13

F — WHEELS, BRAKES AND TYRES

SECTION F1

REMOVING AND REFITTING THE FRONT WHEEL

Place the machine with the front wheel approximately six inches off the ground. First, unscrew the handlebar front brake adjuster then disconnect the cable at the actuating lever on the brake plate. Unscrew the two wheel spindle cap bolts from the base of each fork leg and remove the wheel.

Refitting the wheel is the reversal of the above instructions but care should be taken to ensure that the anchor plate locates correctly over the peg on the inside of the right fork leg. Tighten the spindle cap bolts evenly a turn at a time.

SECTION F2

REMOVING AND REFITTING THE STANDARD REAR WHEEL

First unscrew the rear brake adjuster, and disconnect the rear chain. Slacken the bolt at the rear of the chainguard so that the chainguard can be swung upwards. Remove the nut securing the rear brake torque stay to the anchor plate, then slacken the left and right wheel spindle securing nuts. Disconnect the speedo cable and withdraw the rear wheel from the machine.

To refit the rear wheel first ensure that the spindle nuts are sufficiently unscrewed, then offer the wheel to the swinging fork. Locate the adjuster caps over the fork ends and then lightly tighten the wheel spindle nuts. Place the chain around the rear wheel sprocket and connect up the brake anchor plate torque stay. Refitting the chain may necessitate slackening off both the left and right adjusters. It is now necessary to ensure that the front and rear wheels are aligned. This is shown in Section F4 below. Finally, lock up the two spindle nuts, keeping pressure on the footbrake pedal, in order to centralise the brake shoes and the anchor plate. Ensure the torque stay securing nut is tight and reconnect the speedo cable.

SECTION F3

REMOVING AND REFITTING THE QUICKLY DETACHABLE WHEEL

The Q.D. Wheel is mounted on three bearings, two ball journal bearings being situated in the hub and one ball journal bearing in the brake drum. The wheel is quickly detachable by the simple method of splining the hub into the brake drum thereby eliminating the necessity of removing the rear chain, etc., when required to remove the wheel.

To remove the quickly detachable rear wheel, first disconnect the speedometer cable, then unscrew the wheel spindle from the right side of the machine and drop out the distance piece between the wheel and the fork end. Pull the wheel clear of the spline and the brake drum when the wheel can then be removed.

When replacing the wheel slight variations may be felt in the fit of the splines at various points. Select the tightest position and mark with a small spot of paint on the brake drum and corresponding spot on the hub to facilitate the replacement on future occasions. In addition there is a rubber ring which is assembled over the splines on the wheel and is in compression when the spindle is tight. This ring seals the spline joint and prevents abrasive wear at the joint. If it is perished or damaged fit a new one.

Replacement of the wheel is a reversal of the above instructions and if the chain adjuster is not altered it will not be necessary to re-check the rear wheel alignment. However, if this is necessary, full details are given in Section F4.

WHEELS, BRAKES AND TYRES

SECTION F4

FRONT AND REAR WHEEL ALIGNMENT

When the rear wheel has been fitted into the frame it should be aligned correctly by using two straight edges or battens about 7 ft. long. With the machine off the stand the battens should be placed along side the wheels, one either side of the machine and each about 4 in. from the ground. When both are touching the rear tyre on both sides of the wheel the front wheel should be mid-way between and parallel to both battens. Turn the front wheel slightly until this can be seen. Any necessary adjustment must be made by first slackening the rear wheel spindle nut, then turning the spindle adjuster nuts as required, ensuring that the rear chain adjustment is maintained. Refer to Fig. F1 for illustration of correct alignment. Note that the arrows indicate the adjustment required.

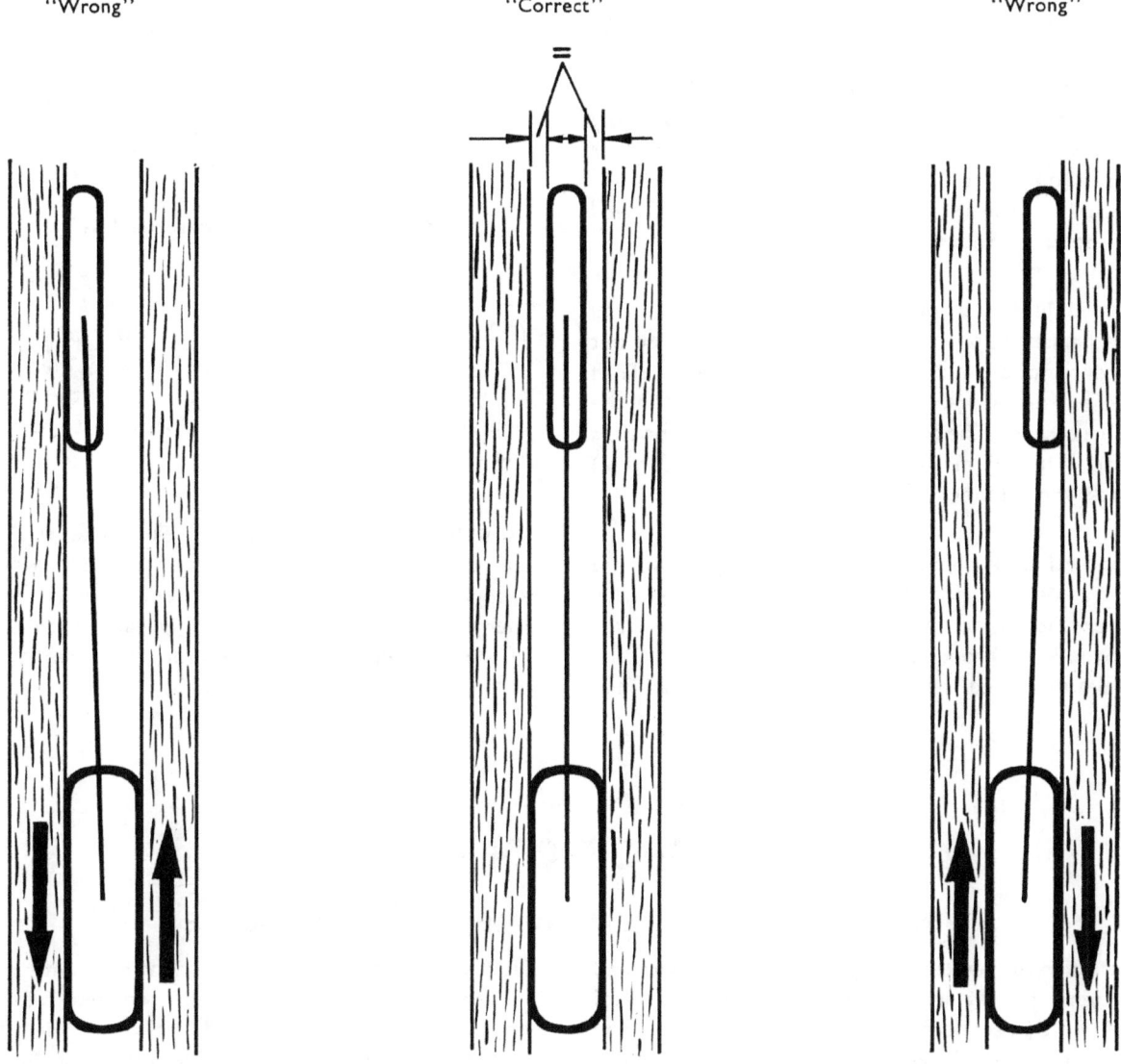

Fig. F1. Aligning the front and rear wheels

SECTION F5

BRAKE ADJUSTMENT

The front and rear brake shoes are semi-floating to allow them to self centralise on the fulcrum pin. In addition the front wheel brake shoe fulcrum pin is adjustable and is identified by a hexagonal nut just behind the fork bottom member on the anchor plate. To adjust, slacken the nut, apply full pressure to the front brake handlebar lever, and whilst holding this pressure, retighten the nut. This locks the fulcrum pin in the position which ensures the maximum area contact of the brake shoes within the brake drum.

Any wear on the brake shoe lining is indicated by the angular position of the brake operating lever when the brake is fully applied. Fig. F2 illustrates the limiting position before wear is obviously excessive. This applies to both front and rear brake operating levers. In this case the brake should be dismantled and the worn parts renewed as shown in Section F6.

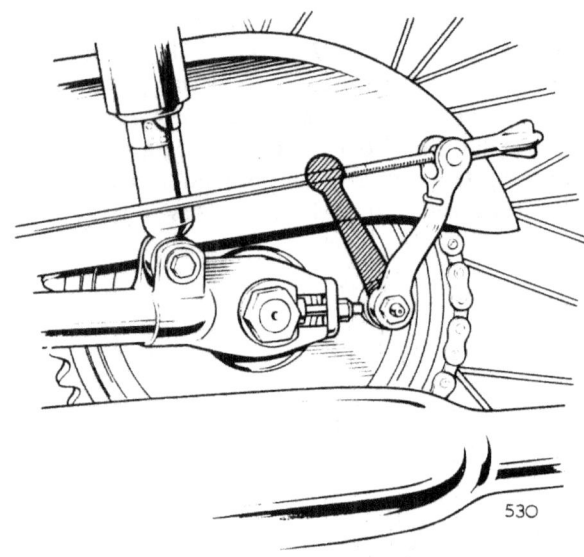

Fig. F2. Rear brake operating lever

The adjustment of the front brake operating mechanism is by means of a knurled adjuster nut incorporated in the handlebar abutment. Turn the nut anti-clockwise to take up the slack in the control cable. The correct adjustment is with not less than $\frac{1}{16}$ in. (1·5 mm.) and not more than $\frac{1}{8}$ in. (3 mm.) slack in the inner cable at the handlebar lever.

The rear brake pedal is adjustable for position and any adjustment for the pedal position to suit the rider should be made before adjusting the free movement. From the static position before the brake is applied there should be about half an inch (1·2 cm.) of free movement before the brake starts to operate. The actual adjustment is by means of a finger operated nut on the rear end of the brake operating rod. Turn the nut clockwise to reduce the clearance.

To centralise the shoes on the rear brake, slacken the left hand rear wheel spindle nut and whilst applying the rear brake, retighten the wheel nut; the bore of the anchor plate is greater than that of the spindle, and this allows the shoes maximum area contact with the drum.

SECTION F6

STRIPPING AND RE-ASSEMBLING THE BRAKE

Access to the brake shoes (front or rear) is obtained by removing the wheel and unscrewing the central nut which retains the brake anchor plate. If the brake operating lever is then turned to relieve the pressure of the shoes against the drum, the complete brake plate assembly can be withdrawn from the spindle.

Slowly release the lever and continue until the return spring can be removed, then take off the brake shoes by the method shown in Fig. F3. Remove the nut and washers securing the brake lever to the cam spindle and remove the lever. The cam spindle can then be easily withdrawn from the plate.

WHEELS, BRAKES AND TYRES

INSPECTION PROCEDURE

(1) Examine the anchor plate for cracks or distortion, particularly in the brake cam housing.

(2) Clean out the grease in the brake cam spindle and remove any rust with a fine emery cloth.

(3) Inspect the return springs for signs of fatigue and distortion. Renew them if necessary.

(4) Examine the brake drum for scoring or ovality. In the case of the rear wheel if the drum requires skimming it should be removed from the wheel. Do not skim more than ·010 in. from the drum. If the diameter exceeds more than given in the GENERAL DATA by more than ·010 in. the drum should be renewed.

In the case of the front wheel drum, scoring or signs of ovality can be removed by similar procedure but a large swing lathe of 18 in. or 19 in. diameter is required.

(5) Examine the brake shoes. The brake linings should be replaced immediately the rivets show signs of having worn level with the linings face, or the linings show signs of cracks or uneven wear. Replacement is described fully in Section F7. Also check that the brake shoes are not cracked or distorted in any way.

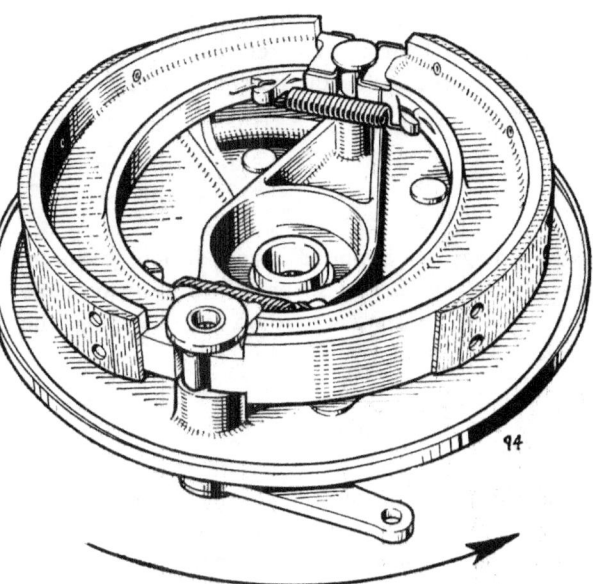

Fig. F4. Correct assembly of brake shoes onto front anchor plate. Arrow indicates direction of rotation

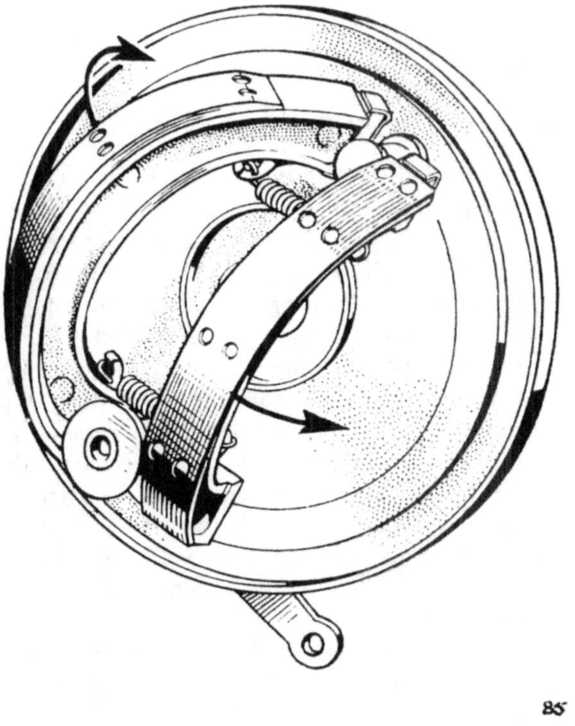

Fig. F3. Refitting brake shoes

To re-assemble the brake shoes to the brake anchor plate first place the two brake shoes on the bench in their relative positions. Fit the return springs to the retaining hooks, hook ends uppermost, then taking a shoe in each hand (see Fig. F3) and at the same time holding the springs in tension, position the shoes as shown over the cam and fulcrum pin and snap down into position by pressing on the outer edges of the shoes. Locate the brake lever in an anti-clockwise position and engage the return spring.

Note: When replacing the brake shoes, note that the leading and trailing brake shoes are not interchangeable in either the front or rear brake and ensure that they are in their correct relative positions as shown in Fig. F4.

Re-assembly then continues by placing the anchor plate over the wheel spindle and locking them with the spindle nut. Refer to Section F4 for final re-alignment of the wheel if this is found to be necessary.

F
WHEELS, BRAKES AND TYRES

SECTION F7
RENEWING THE BRAKE LININGS

The old linings can be removed by either drilling through the rivets with a suitable size drill (No. 23, ·154 in. diameter) or chiselling the lining off at the same time shearing through the brass rivet. Drilling is of course preferred and is best undertaken from the inside of the shoe to remove the peened over portion of the rivet.

New linings are supplied ready drilled, counter-bored and the correct shape. If no jig is available for riveting, a simple method of spreading the rivet is shown in Fig. F5.

Rivet the linings in the centre holes first, working towards the end: great care must be taken to ensure that the rivets are tight and that the linings do not lift between the rivets. After fitting, all sharp edges of the linings should be chamfered and the leading and trailing edges tapered off to the extent of $\frac{1}{8}$ in. deep x $\frac{1}{2}$ in. long.

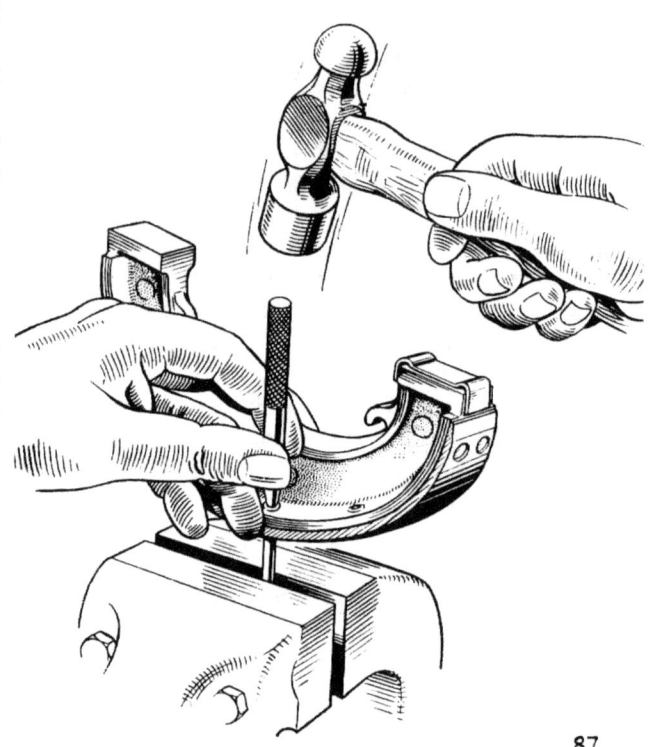

Fig. F5. Riveting lining onto brake shoe

SECTION F8
REMOVING AND REFITTING THE WHEEL BEARINGS

Access to the wheel bearings differs in front and rear wheels and therefore each wheel is dealt with separately in this section.

FRONT WHEEL

Remove the front wheel from the fork (see Section F1) and withdraw the front anchor plate from the brake drum. Unscrew the retainer ring (left hand thread) using service tool Z76.

The right bearing can be removed by using the spindle and driving through from the left side. Withdraw the backing ring and inner retaining disc. To remove the left bearing, spring out the circlip and insert the spindle from the right side, driving the bearing out complete with inner and outer grease retainer plates.

Fully clean all parts in paraffin (kerosene). Clean and dry the bearings thoroughly. Compressed air should be used for drying out the ball races. Test for end float and inspect the balls and races for any signs of pitting. If there is any doubt about their condition, the bearings should be renewed.

To refit the bearings, first insert the left inner grease retainer, bearing and outer dust cap, using a liberal amount of grease (see Section A2). Refit the spring circlip and insert the shouldered end of the wheel spindle from the right, using it as a drift to drive the bearing and grease retainer until they come up to the circlip. Re-insert the spindle the opposite way round and refit the right hand grease retainer disc and backing ring. Drive the right bearing into position well smeared with grease, then screw in the retainer ring (left hand thread) until tight.

Finally, tap the spindle from the left to bring the spindle shoulder up against the right bearing. Refer to Fig. F6 for correct layouts. Re-assembly then continues as a reversal of the above instructions.

WHEELS, BRAKES AND TYRES   F

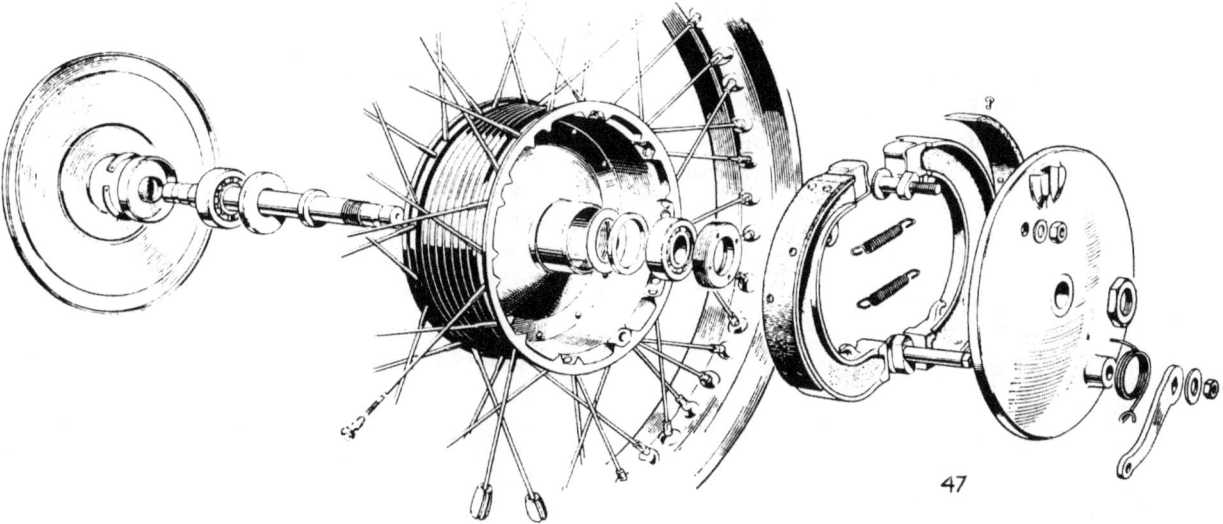

Fig. F6. Exploded view of front wheel bearing arrangement

REAR WHEEL (STANDARD)

Remove the rear wheel (see Section F2) then unscrew the anchor plate retainer nut and withdraw the brake anchor plate assembly. Withdraw the wheel spindle from the right complete with speedometer drive, then unscrew the *slotted screw which serves to lock the left bearing retainer ring. The retainer ring can then be unscrewed, using service tool Z76. So that the left bearing can be removed the central distance piece must be displaced to one side to allow a drift to be located on the inner ring of the left bearing. To do this, first insert a drift from the left and move the distance piece to one side so that the grease retainer shim collapses, as shown in Fig. F8. A soft metal drift should then be inserted from the right and the left bearing driven out. When this is done, withdraw the backing ring, damaged grease retainer and distance piece then drive out the right bearing and dust cap, using a drift of approximately $1\frac{5}{8}$ in. diameter.

Fully clean all parts in paraffin (kerosene) and clean and dry the bearings thoroughly. Compressed air should be used for drying out if possible. Test the end float and inspect the ball races for any signs of indentation or pitting. If the condition of the bearing is in doubt, it should be renewed.

The damaged grease retainer shim can be reclaimed for further service by carefully hammering it flat to restore its original shape. To refit the bearings first drive in the right inner grease retainer disc, the bearing and then press on the outer dust cap ensuring that the bearing and both cavities are well filled with grease. From the left, insert the distance piece, grease retainer shim, backing ring and having packed the bearing with grease, press it in the hub and bring the distance piece into line with the spindle. Screw in the retainer ring and tighten it with service tool Z76. Finally, tighten the locking screw to ensure that the bearing retainer ring is locked in position. Re-assembly then continues as a reversal of the above instructions, but do not forget to refit the outer distance piece before assembling the anchor plate and brake shoe assembly.

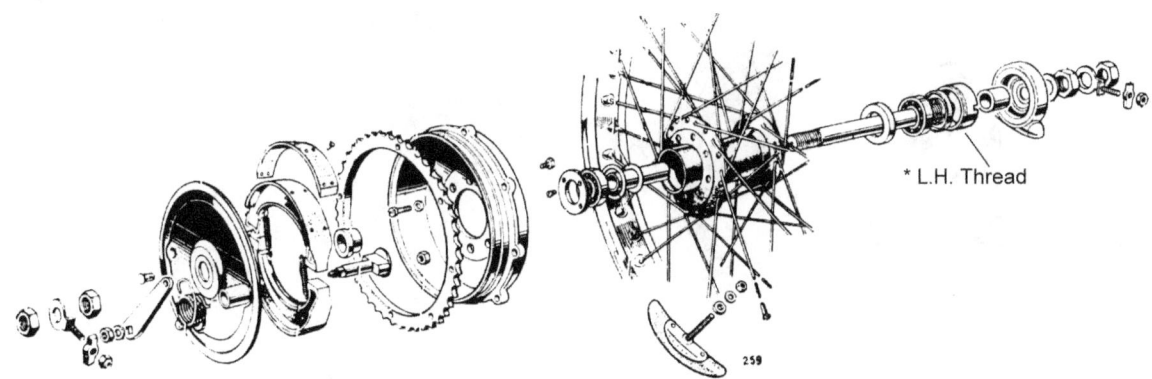

Fig. F7. Exploded view of rear wheel bearing arrangement

F7

REAR WHEEL (QUICKLY DETACHABLE)

Remove the wheel from the swinging fork as described in Section F3 and then unscrew the lock nut on the right side of the spindle sleeve and withdraw the speedometer drive from the wheel.

Fig. F8. Collapsing the left bearing grease retainer shim (standard and q.d. wheels)

The bearing sleeve is a sliding fit and is easily withdrawn. In order to remove the right bearing the central distance piece has to be displaced radially to allow a drift to be located on the inner ring of the right bearing. This is done by inserting a drift from the right and moving the centre distance piece radially so that the grease retainer shim collapses. Then insert a soft metal drift from the left and drive out the right bearing. Withdraw the backing ring, damaged grease retainer and distance piece; then, using a drift, drive out the left bearing and withdraw the other grease retainer.

Thoroughly clean all parts in paraffin (kerosene) and fully dry the bearings. Inspect the ball races for any signs of identation or pitting and renew if necessary.

On re-assembly of the hub, pack the bearings with grease and fit a new grease retainer. Re-assembly is now carried out in exactly the reverse manner described above.

Removal of the brake drum and sprocket assembly from the swinging fork is achieved by first disconnecting the rear chain, torque stay and brake operating rod, and then unscrewing the large nut from the spindle sleeve.

Remove the brake shoes and anchor plate assembly as described in Section F6. To remove the ball bearing from the brake drum, first press out the spindle sleeve and then remove the circlip from the brake drum. The retainer and felt washer can then be levered out to enable the bearing to be driven out. Care should be taken to avoid damage to the inner grease retainer when removing the bearing.

Clean the bearing in paraffin (kerosene) and check that there is not excessive play or that the race tracks are not indented or pitted. If in doubt, renew the bearing.

Re-assembly is a reversal of the above procedure referring to Fig. F9 for order of assembly and Section F3 for refitting the wheel to the swinging fork.

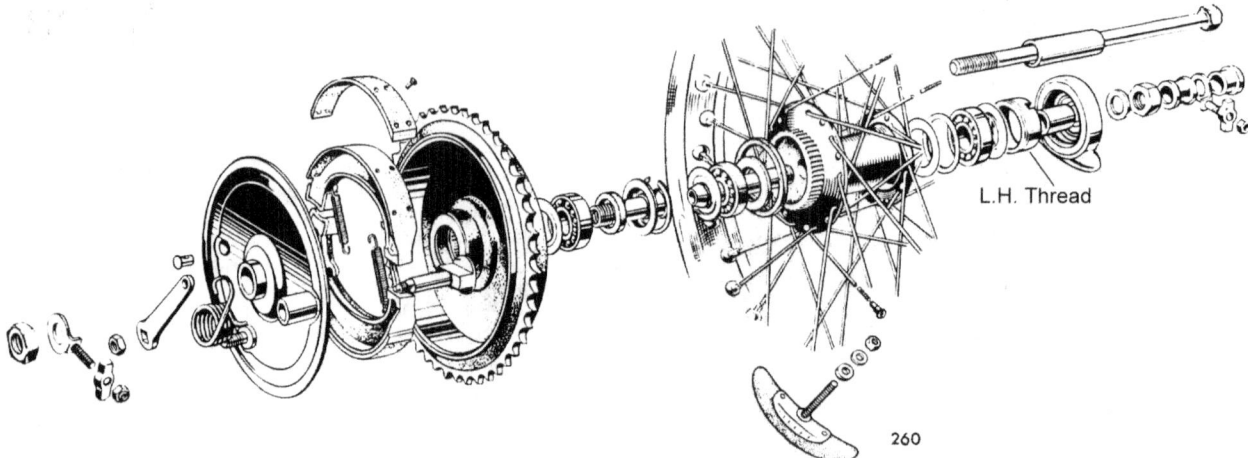

Fig. F9. Exploded view of Q.D. rear wheel

SECTION F9
WHEEL BUILDING

Wheel building, or adjustment to the spokes to realign the wheel rim should only be undertaken by a specialist and these notes are for the specialist, to enable him to follow Triumph practice. The main point to remember is that all Triumph wheels are built with the inside spokes on the brake drum side taking the braking strain. This means the inside spokes on the drum side are in tension when the brake is applied in the direction of forward motion.

The front wheel has 40 straight 8/10 gauge butted spokes and is single-cross laced, whilst the rear has 40 8/10 gauge butted spokes, and is double-cross laced.

A checking gauge suitable for Triumph wheels can be made from two pieces of mild steel bar as shown in Fig. F10 and this should be used to register from the edge of the hub or brake drum onto the wheel rim edge giving the relation indicated in the table.

This ensures the correct relation between the hub and rim centre lines.

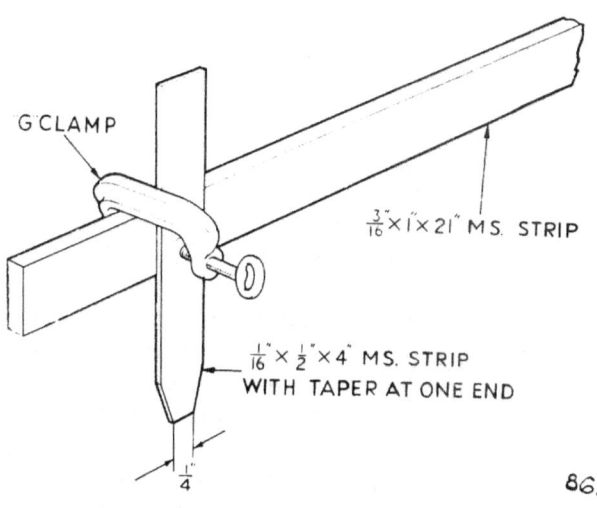

Fig. F10. Sketch of wheel building gauge

Wheel	Rim type	Loca-tion	Dimensions Inches	Dimensions mm.
Front: Standard T100T 8" brake	WM2 ,,	Drum ,,	$-\tfrac{1}{64}$,,	$-0\cdot 4$,,
Rear: Standard	WM2	Hub	$1\tfrac{7}{8}$	47·6
	WM3	Hub	$1\tfrac{3}{4}$	44·4
Q.D.	WM2	Hub	$1\tfrac{1}{16}$	27
	WM3	Hub	$\tfrac{7}{8}$	22·2

Table of "Dish" Dimensional Settings for Front and Rear Wheels

SECTION F10
WHEEL BALANCING

Wheel balancing is achieved by fitting 1 oz. or ½ oz. weights as required. All front wheels are balanced complete with tyre and tube before leaving the factory and if for any reason the tyre is removed, it should be replaced with the white balancing spot level with the valve. If a new tyre is fitted, existing weights should be removed and the wheel rebalanced, adding weights as necessary until it will remain in any position at rest. Make sure that the brake is not binding while the balancing operation is being carried out.

For normal road use it is not necessary for the rear wheel to be balanced in this way, but rear wheel balancing can be found to be advantageous under certain circumstances.

SECTION F11
REMOVING AND REPAIRING THE TYRES

To remove the tyre, first remove the valve cap and valve core, using the valve cap itself to unscrew the core. Unscrew the knurled valve securing nut and then place all parts where they will be free from dirt and grit. It is recommended that the cover beads are lubricated with a little soapy water before attempting to remove the tyres. The tyre lever should be dipped in this solution before each application. First, insert a lever at the valve position and whilst carefully pulling on this lever, press the tyre bead in the well of the rim diametrically opposite the valve position (see

Fig. F12. Removing the first bead of the tyre, using two tyre levers

Fig. F11. Removing the first bead of the tyre—Lever inserted close to valve whilst bead is pressed into well on opposite side of wheel

Fig. F11). Insert a second lever close to the first and prise the bead over the rim flange. Remove the first lever and reinsert a little further round the rim from the second lever. Continue round the bead in steps of 2 in. to 3 in. until the bead is completely away from the rim. Push the valve out of the rim and then withdraw the inner tube. To completely remove the tyre first stand the wheel upright and then insert a lever between the remaining bead and the rim. The tyre should be easily removed from the rim as shown in Fig. F12.

REFITTING THE TYRE

First place the rubber rim band into the well of the rim and make sure that the rough side of the rubber band is fitted against the rim and that the band is central in the well. Replace the valve core and inflate the inner tube sufficiently to round it out without stretch, dust it with French chalk and insert it into the cover with the valve located at the white balancing spot leaving it protruding outside the bead for about 4 ins. either side of the valve. At this stage it is advisable to lubricate the bead and levers with soapy water (see Fig. F13).

Fig. F13. Cover and tube assembled ready for refitting to the wheel

Squeeze the beads together at the valve position to prevent the tube from slipping back inside the tyre and offer the cover to the rim, as shown in Fig. F14, at the same time threading the valve through the valve holes in the rim band and rim. Allow the first bead to go into the well of the rim and the other bead to lie above the level of the rim flange.

WHEELS, BRAKES AND TYRES   F

Fig. F14. Refitting the tyre to the wheel. Note valve engaged in rim hole

Working from the valve, press the first bead over the rim flange by hand, moving forward in small steps and making sure that the part of the bead already dealt with, lies in the well of the rim. If necessary use a tyre lever for the last few inches, as shown in Fig. F15. During this operation continually check that the inner tube is not trapped by the cover bead.

Fig. F15. Levering the first bead onto the rim

Press the second bead into the well of the rim diametrically opposite the valve. Insert a lever as close as possible to the point where the bead passes over the flange and lever the bead into the flange, at the same time pressing the fitted part of the bead into the well of the rim. Repeat until the bead is completely over the flange, finishing at the valve position (see Fig. F16).

Fig. F16. Refitting the second bead over the wheel rim. Care must be taken not to trap inner tube

Push the valve inwards to ensure that the tube near the valve is not trapped under the bead. Pull the valve back and inflate the tyre. Check that the fitting line on the cover is concentric with the top of the rim flange and that the valve protrudes squarely through the valve hole. Fit the knurled rim and valve cap. The tyre pressure should then be set to the figure given in GENERAL DATA.

SECTION F12
SECURITY BOLTS

Security bolts are fitted to the wheel rim to prevent the tyre creeping on the rim when it is subjected to excessive acceleration or braking. Such movement would ultimately result in the valve being torn from the inner tube. There are two security bolts fitted to the rear wheel, which are equally spaced either side of the valve and thereby do not affect the balance of the wheels.

Note: The security bolt nuts must not be overtightened, otherwise excessive distortion may occur.

WHEELS, BRAKES AND TYRES

Where a security bolt is fitted the basic procedure for fitting and removing the tyre is the same, but the following instructions should be followed:—

(1) Remove the valve cap and core as described.

(2) Unscrew the security bolt nut and push the bolt inside the cover.

(3) Remove the first bead as described.

(4) Remove the security bolt from the rim.

(5) Remove the inner tube as described.

(6) Remove the second bead and tyre.

For refitting the tyre and inner tube:—

(1) Fit the rim band.

(2) Fit the first bead to the rim without the inner tube inside.

(3) Assemble the security bolt into the rim, putting the nut onto the first few threads (see F17).

(4) Partly inflate the inner tube and fit it into the tyre.

(5) Fit the second bead but keep the security bolt pressed well into the tyre, as shown in Fig. F18 and ensure that the inner tube does not become trapped at the edges.

(6) Fit the valve stem nut and inflate the tyre.

(7) Bounce the wheel several times at the point where the security bolt is fitted and then tighten the security bolt nut.

Fig. F17. Placing the security bolt in position

Fig. F18. Refitting the second bead with the security bolt in position

SECTION F13
TYRE MAINTENANCE

To obtain optimum tyre mileage and to eliminate irregular wear on the tyres it is essential that the recommendations given in tyre pressures and general maintenance are followed. The following points are laid out with this in mind.

(1) Maintain the correct inflation pressure as shown in GENERAL DATA. Use a pressure gauge frequently. It is advisable to check and restore tyre pressures at least once per week. Pressures should always be checked when tyres are cold and not when they have reached normal running temperatures.

(2) When a pillion passenger or additional load is carried, the rear tyre pressure should be increased appropriately to cater for the extra load.

(3) Unnecessary rapid acceleration and fierce braking should always be avoided. This treatment invariably results in rapid tyre wear.

(4) Regular checks should be made for flints, nails, small stones etc., which should be removed from the tread or they may ultimately penetrate and damage the casing and puncture the tubes.

(5) Tyres and spokes should be kept free of oil, grease and paraffin. Regular cleaning should be carried out with a cloth and a little petrol (gasolene).

(6) If tyres develop irregular wear, this may be corrected by reversing the tyre on the wheel to reverse its direction of rotation.

SECTION FF

WHEELS, BRAKES AND TYRES

	Section
STRIPPING AND REASSEMBLING THE BRAKES	FF5
REMOVING AND REFITTING THE WHEEL BEARINGS	FF8

SECTION FF5

STRIPPING AND REASSEMBLING THE BRAKES

FRONT BRAKE—TWO LEADING SHOE

Access to the front brake shoes is gained by removing the wheel (see Section F1). The brake plate is retained by a centre nut. This is recessed into the anchor plate and will require the use of 61-6062 box spanner. The brake plate assembly will then lift away complete. Holding the brake plate with one hand lift up one shoe as in Fig. FF1 until it is free. Disconnect one end of each brake return spring and lift away the second shoe. Release the spring clip from the pivot pin at each end of the lever adjustment rod and lift the pivot pins clear. Remove the brake cam nuts and washers and remove the return spring from the front cam. Finally prise off the levers in turn and the brake cams are free to be removed from the back of the anchor plate.

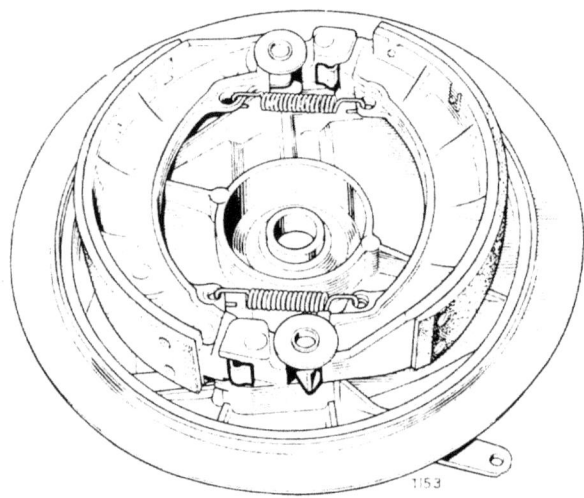

Fig. FF2. Correct assembly of shoes

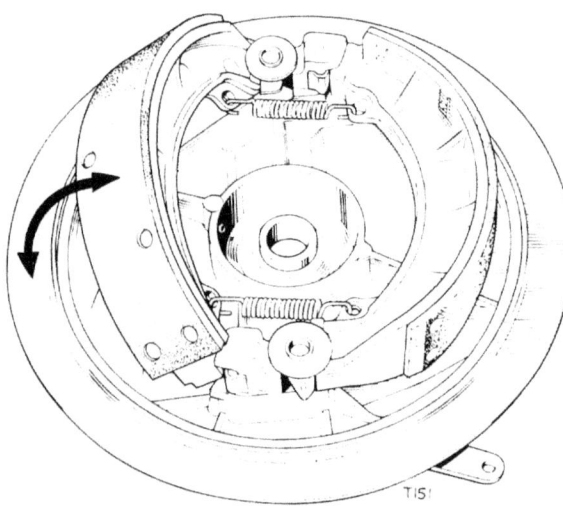

Fig. FF1. Removing or replacing brake shoe

To reassemble the brake shoes to the front anchor plate first grease the spindles lightly and refit both cams, wedge shape outboard on both. Refit the outside return spring to the front cam and then refit both brake cam levers (at a similar angle) and secure with the plain washers and nuts. Fit the abutment plates to the anchor plate, tag side towards the anchor plate.

Link the two shoes together with the return springs (the narrow end of the shoe abuts to the cam in each case). Both shoes fit with the radiused end to the pivot. Fit the first shoe to both the cam and abutmentpad then stretch the springs by grasping the second shoe and fitting it as shown in Fig. FF1.

The complete brake plate is now ready for fitting to the wheel. Replace the anchor plate over the wheel spindle and lock it home with the spindle nut, using spanner 61-6062.

At this stage it may be necessary to adjust the cam lever rod assembly. To do so the rod adjuster nut should be slackened (see Fig. FF3) and the rear pivot pin removed. The help of a second operator will be needed at this stage. Each cam lever should be applied until the shoes are in contact with the drum. The easiest method is by fitting a spanner to each cam nut.

The threaded fork end should be adjusted to accommodate the revised distance between the brake cam levers. The rod assembly should then be refitted, and the locknut retightened. Reconnect the brake cable and adjust as described in Section F5.

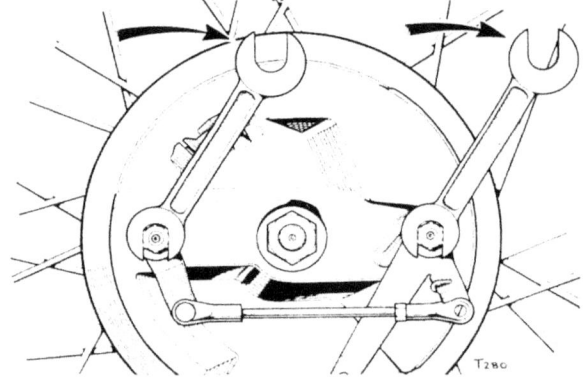

Fig. FF3. Adjusting Brake cam lever rod

WHEELS, BRAKES AND TYRES

SECTION FF8
REMOVING AND REFITTING THE WHEEL BEARINGS

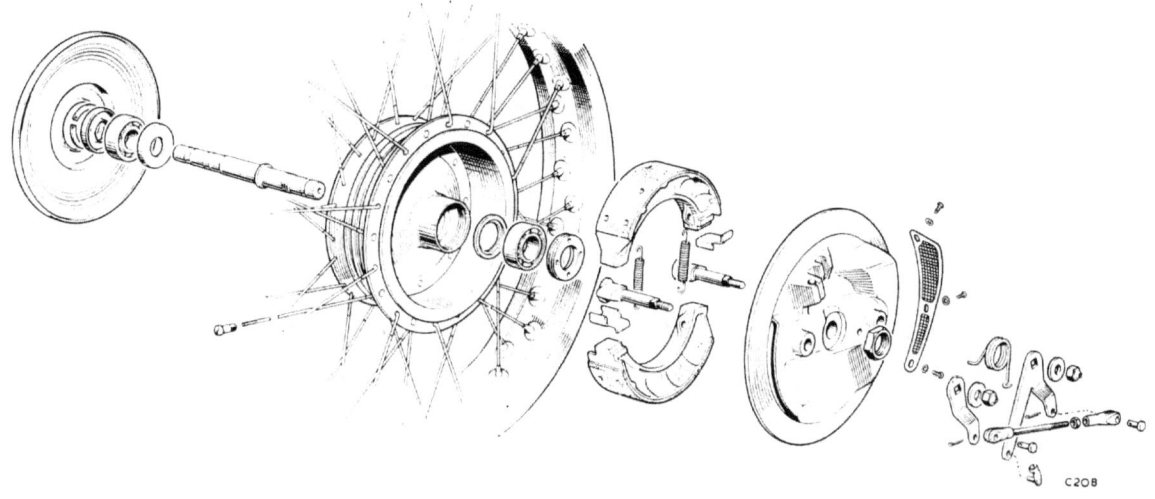

Fig. FF4. Exploded twin leading shoe front wheel

NOTES

SECTION G

TELESCOPIC FORKS

Section

DESCRIPTION:

REMOVING AND REFITTING THE HEADLAMP (T90 AND T100) G1

REMOVING AND REFITTING THE NACELLE TOP COVER (3TA AND 5TA) G2

REMOVING THE TELESCOPIC FORK UNIT G3

DISMANTLING THE TELESCOPIC FORK G4

INSPECTION AND REPAIR OF FORK COMPONENTS G5

RENEWING THE STEERING HEAD RACES G6

RENEWING THE FRONT OIL SEALS G7

REASSEMBLING AND REFITTING THE FORK UNIT G8

TELESCOPIC FORK ALIGNMENT G9

ADJUSTING THE STEERING HEAD RACES G10

CHANGING THE FRONT FORK MAIN SPRINGS G11

HANDLEBAR MOUNTINGS G12

THE HYDRAULIC DAMPER UNIT G13

TELESCOPIC FORKS

DESCRIPTION

The Triumph telescopic hydraulically controlled front forks require little attention other than an occasional check of the external nuts and bolts, etc., and the routine oil changes given in Section A1.

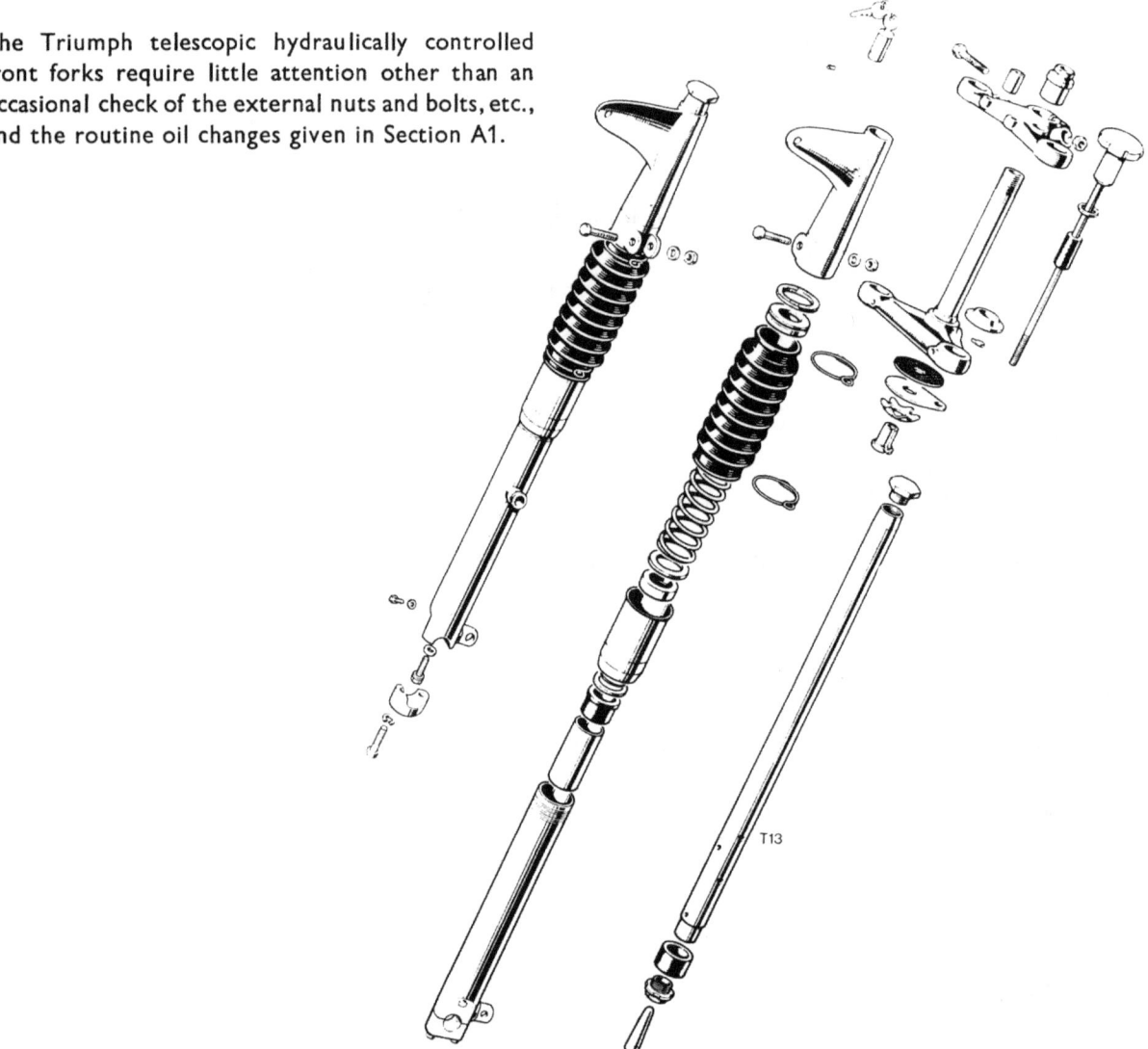

Fig. G1. Front fork assembly

SECTION G1

REMOVING AND REFITTING THE HEADLAMP (T90 AND T100)

Disconnect the leads from the battery terminals, then slacken the light unit securing screw at the top of the headlamp, until the light unit is released.

Disconnect the snap connector blocks from the wiring harness and then thread the dip switch leads and main harness leads through the grommet at the rear of the headlamp shell.

To remove the headlamp shell unscrew the left and right pivot bolts which secure the shell to the fork covers.

Refitting is the reversal of the above instructions but reference should be made to the wiring diagram in Section H13. Finally, set the headlamp main beam as shown in Section H8, Part A.

Do not tighten the headlamp pivot bolts over the torque setting given in GENERAL DATA.

TELESCOPIC FORKS G

SECTION G2

REMOVING AND REFITTING THE NACELLE TOP COVER (3TA AND 5TA)

Disconnect the leads at the battery terminals. Slacken the headlamp securing screw adjacent to the speedometer dial and lever off the headlamp. Disconnect the lead from the main bulb, pilot bulb and dip switch (4 snap connectors) and disconnect the headlamp earthing lead.

Remove the two adaptor rim securing screws and square nuts and withdraw the rim. Unscrew the two front and two rear top cover securing bolts and unscrew the left and right flash rear mounting screws.

Disconnect the front brake cable at the handlebar and thread it through the nacelle cover. Slacken off the clutch cable adjuster at the handlebar and lift the rubber sleeve at the gearbox and remove the slotted cable adaptor, then disconnect the clutch cable at the handlebar and thread it through the nacelle top cover. The nacelle cover can then be lifted to allow the drive cable and bulb holder to be disconnected from the speedometer.

Disconnect the ammeter terminal leads and detach the lighting switch and the ignition switch Bakelite connection plugs. The nacelle top cover is then free to be removed.

Refitting the cover is the reversal of the above instructions but reference must be made to the relevant wiring diagram in Section H11 to avoid incorrect connections being made. The blue/brown lead from the battery negative terminal should be connected to the ammeter positive terminal. To check that the ammeter is correctly connected, turn the ignition switch to "IGN" position. The ammeter needle should deflect to discharge. If it does not, reverse the ammeter terminal connections.

Finally, when the headlamp adaptor rim and light unit are refitted the headlamp main beam should be set as described in Section H8, Part A.

SECTION G3

REMOVING THE TELESCOPIC FORK UNIT

Removal of the front forks is best achieved by detaching the fork as a unit, removing the top lug only whilst the stanchions and middle lug assembly is lowered from the frame.

First, unscrew the small drain plugs at the bottom of the fork adjacent to the wheel spindle lug and drain the oil out by pumping the forks up and down a few times.

Place a strong wooden box underneath the engine so that the front wheel is about 6 ins. clear of the ground, then remove the wheel as shown in Section F1 (and front mudguard). Disconnect the speedometer cable (and tachometer cable where fitted). Remove the instrument bulbholders and bulbs. Note for reassembly the position of the red instrument earth (ground) lead. Unscrew and lift clear the steering damper knob complete with rubber sleeve and the plain washer. Remove the damper sleeve nut, spring plate and anchor plate. The anchor plate fits tightly on the lower end of the left steering stop peg and may require prising off. Remove the handlebars (see Section G12) after disconnecting the throttle, front brake and clutch cables from the controls. The handlebar can then be laid on the fuel tank if suitably protected or removed completely if the cut out switch and dip switch are unfastened. Detach the headlamp by dismantling as Section G2.

Nacelle models: Detach the nacelle top unit (or headlamp unit if fitted) and then detach the throttle cable and air control cable. The handlebar must then be removed (Section G12).

Remove the steering damper plate pivot bolt and then slacken the top lug pinch bolt and unscrew the sleeve nut with a suitable tommy bar. Unscrew the left and right stanchion cap nuts using spanner No. D220 (1½ in.—3·81 cm. across flats) and withdraw the two cap nuts.

Support the fork and then give the top lug a sharp tap on the underside until it is released from the stanchion locking tapers. The stanchion and middle lug assembly can then be lowered from the frame head lug. If care is taken, the top ball race can be left undisturbed and the lower race balls collected when the clearance is sufficient.

ALTERNATIVE METHOD, REMOVING FORK STANCHION ASSEMBLIES ONLY

Alternatively the fork stanchions can be removed whilst the middle lug, top lug and head races are left undisturbed. To facilitate extraction of the stanchions from the top and middle lugs in this case, service tool Z19 will be required. Remove the speedometer and tachometer, also the handlebar and cables as previously described. Remove the cap nuts, slacken the middle lug pinch bolts and then unscrew the two small hexagonal headed oil filler plugs (where fitted on nacelle models) from the stanchions. Screw in the adaptor plug Z19 and drive the stanchion until it is free to be withdrawn from the middle lug, as shown in Fig. G2. The middle lug, top lug and races can now be dismantled as required.

SECTION G4

DISMANTLING THE TELESCOPIC FORK

Remove the front fork from the frame head lug by the method shown in Section G3 and then grip the middle lug stem firmly in a vice and unscrew the two small hexagon headed oil filler plugs (where fitted) from the stanchions. Unscrew the two middle lug pinch bolts, withdraw the bottom nacelle covers, and remove the top and bottom gaiter securing clips if fitted.

Screw in service tool Z19, or an old cap nut, and drive the stanchions out of the middle lug. When the stanchions are removed, detach the spring covers, springs and top and bottom washers. It is advisable to renew the cork sealing washer when reassembling the forks.

Removal of the dust excluder sleeve nut is facilitated by service tool D527 which should be attached to the sleeve nut whilst the wheel spindle lug is held firmly in a vice. The sleeve nut has a right hand thread and should unscrew easily once the nut has been initially loosened by giving the spanner a sharp tap with a hide mallet.

Note: If the hydraulic damping unit shown in Fig. G13 is fitted, it will be necessary to remove them before the stanchions can be withdrawn from the bottom members. To do this, unscrew the hexagon headed bolt which can be seen counterbored into the wheel spindle lugs. It is sealed by means of an aluminium washer which should be withdrawn from the counterbore when the bolt is removed and placed in storage and refitted on assembly. **Do not remove these bolts if the hydraulic units are not fitted.**

When the dust excluder nut is removed, a few sharp pulls should release the stanchion, bush and damper sleeve assembly from the bottom members.

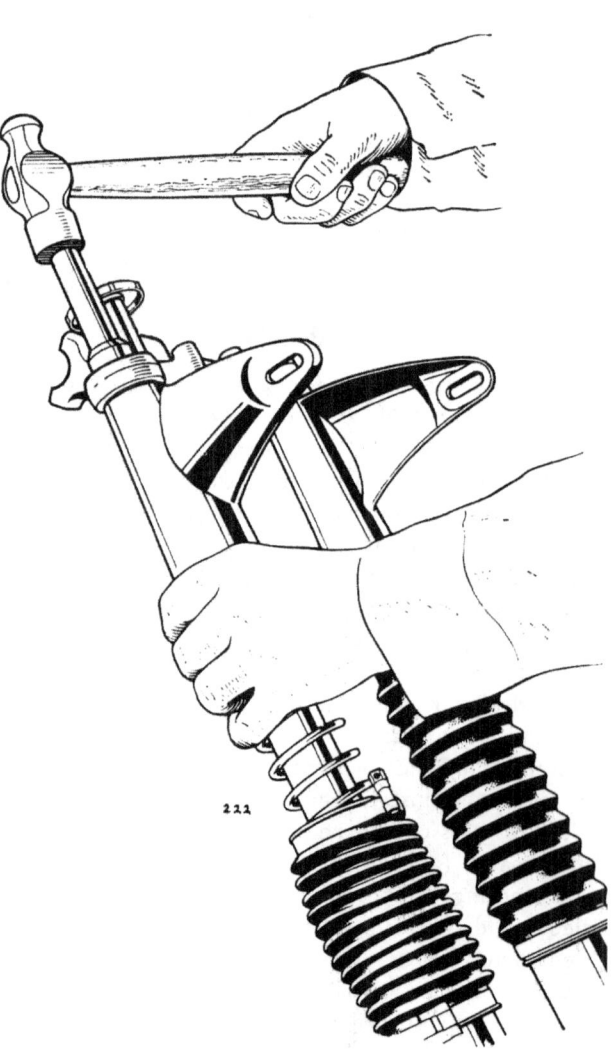

Fig. G2. Dismantling the telescopic fork using service tool Z19

SECTION G5

INSPECTION AND REPAIR OF FORK COMPONENTS

Telescopic fork components which have received minor damage may possibly be repaired without the need of new parts. The stanchions are the most vulnerable part to damage and correction is often possible if the damage is within the limits described below. The top lug and middle lug are malleable stampings and slight misalignment can also be corrected as described in the paragraphs below. The tools required in order that a thorough check of the various alignment can be made are an engineer's checking table, set square, adjustable calipers and a height gauge.

(1) Check the stanchions for truth by rolling them slowly on a flat checking table. A bent stanchion may be realigned if the bow does not exceed $\frac{5}{32}$ in. maximum. To realign the stanchion, a hand press is required. Place the stanchion on two swage "V" blocks at either end and apply pressure to the raised portion of the stanchions. By means of alternately pressing in this way and checking the stanchion on a flat table the amount of bow can be reduced until it is finally removed.

(2) Inspect the top lug by fitting both stanchions (if true) with the cap nuts tightened in position as shown in Fig. G3. Check that the stanchions are parallel to each other in both planes by laying the assembly on a checking table and taking caliper readings as shown. Using a set square, check that the stanchions are at right angles to the top lug.

Check the middle lug and stem for alignment by inserting the stanchions until $6\frac{1}{2}$ ins. (16·5 cm.) of the top of the stanchion protrudes above the top surface of the middle lug as shown in Fig. G4. Fit and tighten the pinch bolts in position and then lay the assembly on the checking table and with calipers check that the stanchions lie in parallel in the middle lug.

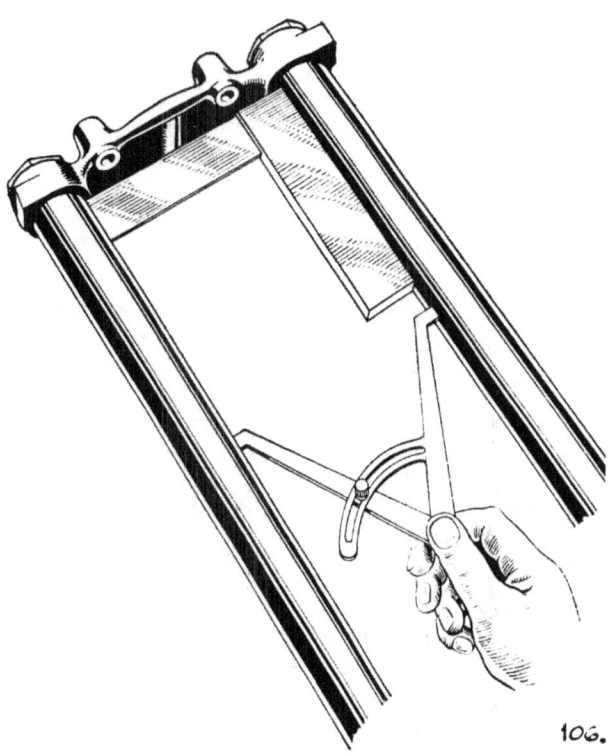

Fig. G3. Checking the top lug for alignment

The stanchions should also be checked for being parallel in the other plane by sighting along the checking table top. A set square should be used to check that the stanchions are at right angles to the middle lug.

The middle lug stamping is malleable and provided that the lug is not excessively distorted, it can be trued quite easily. Each time a distortion correction is carried out check that the assembly is true in both planes.

G TELESCOPIC FORKS

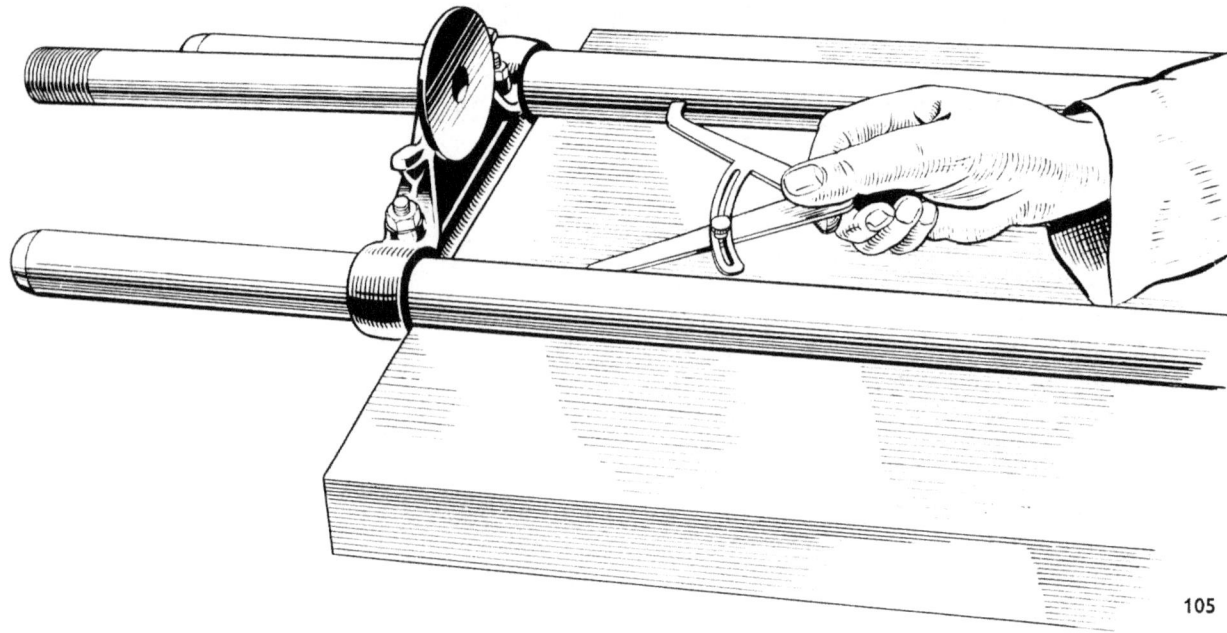

Fig. G4. Checking the stanchions and middle lug for alignment

(3) When the stanchions and middle lug assembly has been trued, the top lug can be used to check the position of the stem relative to the middle lug. For this purpose, the distance between the middle lug and top lug should be the same on either side and to achieve this the stanchions should be set in the middle lug to the figure given in Fig. G5. When the top lug is fitted the stem should be central in the top lug hole. If it is not, a long tube can be placed over the stem and used to press the stem in the correcting direction. When this is achieved, recheck the fork assembly to ensure that the original alignment has not been adversely affected.

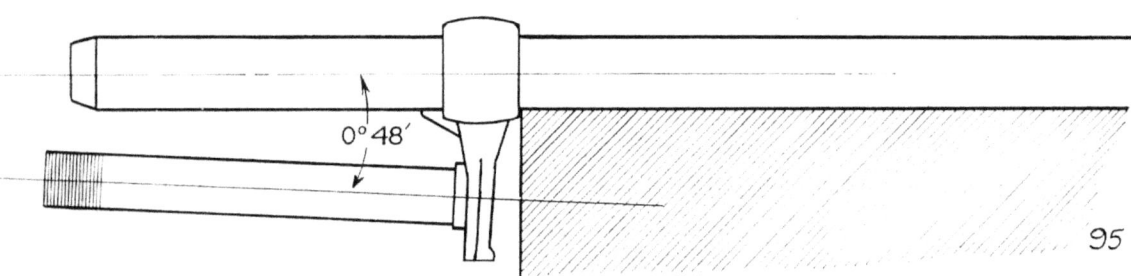

Fig. G5. Showing the correct angle between stanchion and stem centre lines

TELESCOPIC FORKS

(4) Check that the bottom members are not dented nor damaged in any way by inserting the stanchion and bottom bush assembly and feeling the amount of clearance of the bush within the bore of the bottom members. Any restriction on movement indicates that the bottom member is damaged and requires renewing. The wheel spindle lug can be checked for being at right angles to the bottom member by machining a $\frac{1}{4}$ in. groove in an $\frac{11}{16}$ in. diameter bar and bolting it in position in the wheel spindle lug. A square may then be used to check that the bar is perpendicular to the bottom member. If the degree of error is excessive, no attempt should be made to realign the wheel spindle lug; the bottom member should be renewed.

(5) Examine the top and bottom bushes for wear by measuring the bore diameter of the top bush and the outside diameter of the bottom bush and comparing them with the figures given in GENERAL DATA. Also, the bushes can be checked against their respective mating surfaces; put the top bush over the stanchion and at about 8 ins. from the bottom of the stanchion check the diametral clearance at the bush. An excessive clearance indicates that the bush requires renewing. As described above, the bottom bush can only be checked by fitting it to the stanchion and inserting the stanchion into the bottom member to a depth of about 8 ins. whilst the diametral clearance is estimated from the amount of play.

(6) Examine the main springs for fatigue and cracks and check that both springs are of approximate equal length and within $\frac{1}{4}$ in. (6·5 mm.) of the original length. The figures for the original length are given in GENERAL DATA.

(7) Inspect the cups and cones for wear in the form of pitting or pocketing. This will appear as a series of small indentations in the ball tracks and indicates that both the races and the balls require renewing.

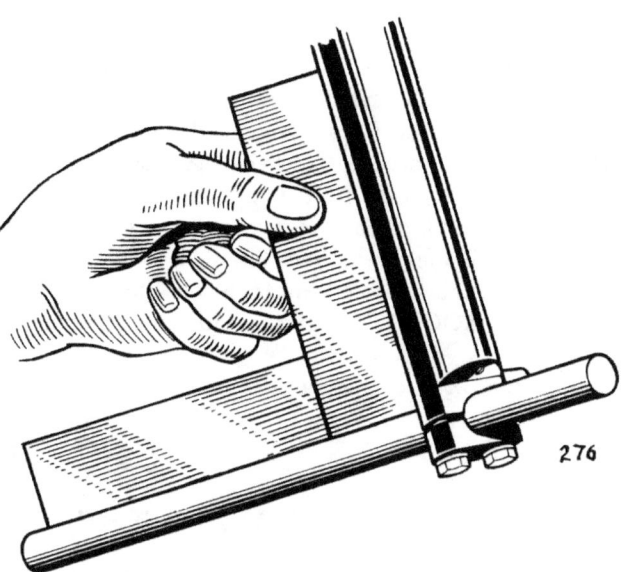

Fig. G6. Checking the bottom member wheel spindle lug for truth

The cups should be a tight interference fit into the frame head lug. Slackness there usually indicates that the head lug cup seatings are distorted. The bottom cone should be a tight fit onto the middle lug stem and the top cone and dust cap assembly should be a close sliding fit over the stem. Slackness of the cone on the stem indicates that the steering head races have not been in correct adjustment. In this case, if the new cone is not a tight fit over the stem, then either the middle lug assembly should be renewed or in certain cases a proprietary sealant may be used to secure the cone in position.

SECTION G6
RENEWING THE STEERING HEAD RACES

The cups can be driven out of the head lug from the inside by inserting a long narrow drift and locating it on the inner edge of the cups. When the cups are removed the bore of the head lug should be cleaned thoroughly and the new cups driven in by using a hammer and aluminium drift or a piece of hard wood interposed to check the blow. Care should be taken to ensure that the cup enters into the head lug squarely and that no burrs are set up due to misalignment. If there are signs of a loose fit between the cups and the frame headlug apply 'TRIUMPH LOCTITE' Sealant to locate securely.

The bottom cone can easily be removed from the stem by inserting levers on either side and prising the cone upwards. When it has been removed, clean the stem and remove any burrs with a fine grade file before fitting the new cones. To ensure that the new cone is driven in squarely, service tool number Z24 should be used. To assist in the assembly of the cone a small amount of grease may be smeared onto the middle lug stem. If the service tool is not available a suitable drift can be made from a piece of $1\frac{1}{16}$ ins. (2·7 cm.) inside diameter tube 9 ins. long. Note that when the new cups and cones are fitted, new balls must also be used. The correct quantity is 40 off $\frac{1}{4}$ in. diameter balls—20 top race and 20 bottom race.

SECTION G7
RENEWING THE FRONT FORK OIL SEALS

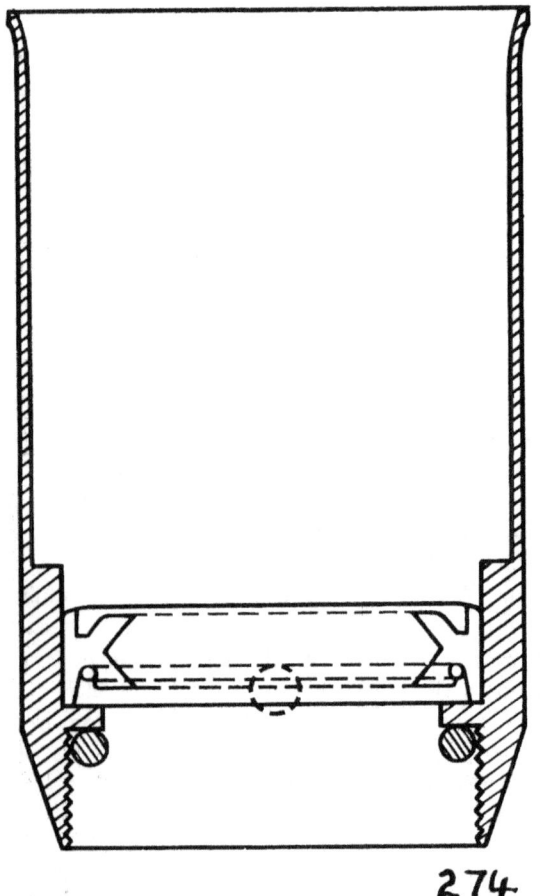

Fig. G7. Showing the location of the oil seal in the dust excluder nut

The front fork oil seal is pressed into the dust excluder sleeve nut and is freely accessible from both sides. The oil seal can be driven out by inserting a suitable drift and locating it on the oil seal at one end of the peripheral slots.

The new oil seal should be pressed in with the lip and spring side facing the threaded end of the sleeve nut and a check should be made to ensure that it is fully and squarely engaged.

SECTION G8

REASSEMBLING AND REFITTING THE TELESCOPIC FORK UNIT

To refit the oil restrictor if it has been removed, first slide it down inside the stanchion by using a piece of tubing about 2 ft. long and ½ in. (1·3 cm.) inside diameter, to grip the restrictor whilst several threads of the hexagon headed securing bolt are engaged. Do not forget to replace the aluminium sealing washer which fits over the securing bolt.

If hydraulic damper units are to be fitted, in place of the above oil restrictor, leave this part of the assembly procedure until later, as described in the text.

Screw in the small location (drain) plug and with the tubing rotate the restrictor until the location slot is aligned with the plug, then tighten the securing bolt. Do not forget to fit new fibre washers under each of the location plugs.

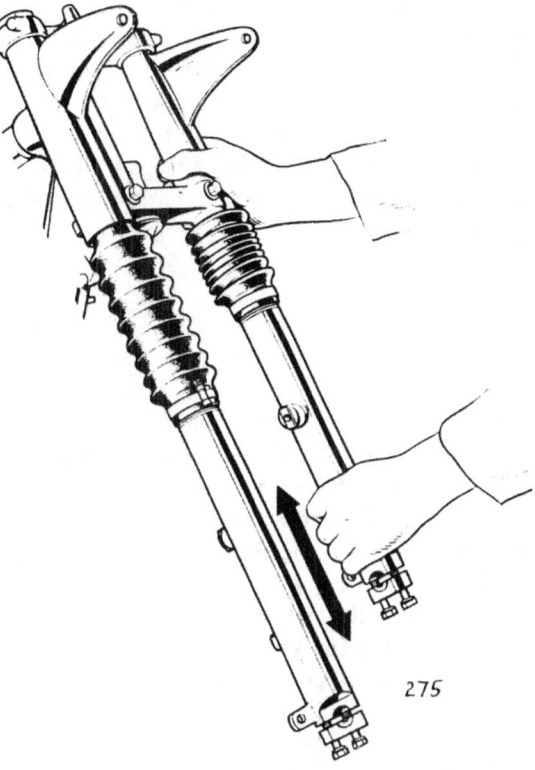

Fig. G8. Reassembling the telescopic fork

Assemble the stanchion to the bottom member and fit the damping sleeve, top bush and plain washer. Then screw on the dust excluder sleeve nut and oil seal assembly, having used jointing compound or other form of sealant on the outer member threads and hold the bottom member in a vice by means of the wheel spindle lug whilst the sleeve nut is tightened, using service tool D527.

When the stanchions are to be assembled into the middle lug in this condition on T90 and T100 models, fit the plain thrust washer, main spring, telescopic gaiter, spring abutment and cork washer over each stanchion first. On 3TA and 5TA models with nacelle, fit the plain washer, main spring, top cover, plain washer and cork washer in that order. The telescopic fork legs are now ready for assembly into the fork crown and stem.

Align the middle lug and top lug on the machine and position the left and right covers (nacelle covers on 3TA and 5TA models) and then insert the middle lug pinch bolt and fit the nuts finger tight.

TELESCOPIC FORKS

Offer the right stanchion assembly (with welded boss for front brake anchor plate location) and engage as much of the stanchion as possible in the middle lug. To pull the stanchion up to the top lug, service tool Z161 is required which should be inserted into the top lug and the plug adaptor screwed into the stanchion top. The stanchion can then be easily drawn up to the required level and when this is achieved temporarily tighten the pinch bolt, remove the tool and screw in the cap nut until several threads are engaged. Repeat this procedure for the left stanchion assembly and then remove both cap nuts.

The hydraulic damper units, if specified, should now be fitted. Offer each unit into the fork leg, until fully home. Fit the small location (drain) plug in the base of the bottom member and then engage the hexagon headed securing bolt having previously fitted a new aluminium washer, through the counterbore in the base of the bottom lug into the base of the damper unit. Rotate the damper unit until the slot engages in the location (drain) plug. Fully tighten the hexagonal securing bolt. Repeat for the other fork leg.

Thread the damper rod into the cap nut and lock in position with the underside locknut.

Pour $\frac{1}{3}$ pt. (190 c.c.) oil of the correct grade (see Section A2) into each fork leg.

Refit the cap nuts until several threads are engaged then slacken off the middle lug pinch bolt and fully tighten the cap nuts. On models with nacelle type front forks the stanchions will require turning prior to tightening the cap nuts so that the oil filler plug holes are accessible through the headlamp aperture. When this is achieved, adjust the steering head races as described in Section G10 and then tighten the sleeve nut pinch bolt and the two middle lug pinch bolts, to the torque figures given in GENERAL DATA.

Reassembly then continues as a reversal of the dismantling procedure, referring to Section H13 for the relevant wiring diagram and Section H8 to set the headlamp main beam.

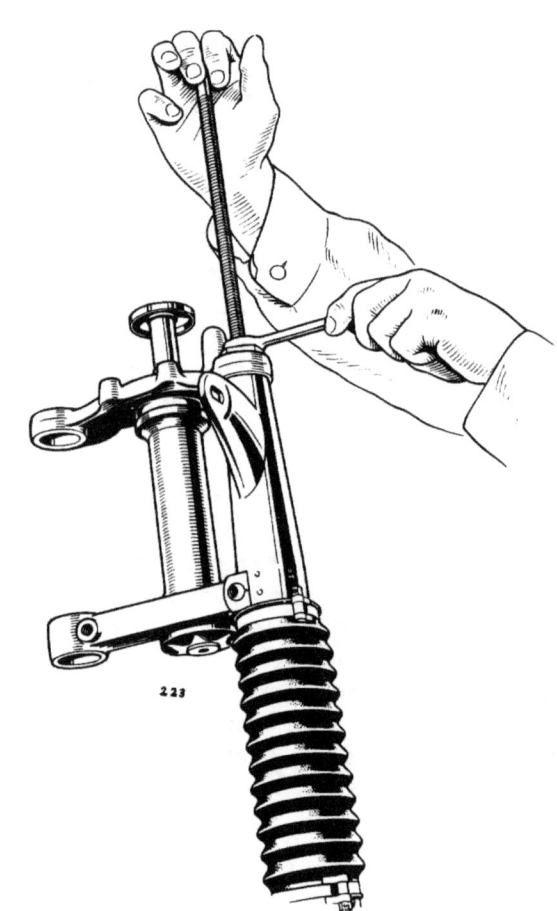

Fig. G9. Reassembling the telescopic fork using service tool Z161

SECTION G9

TELESCOPIC FORK ALIGNMENT

To facilitate checking the alignment of the telescopic fork legs there is available service tool Z103, the dimensions of which are shown in Fig. G10.

To check the front fork alignment, the front wheel and mudguard must be removed and a spare wheel spindle bolted in position. If a spare wheel spindle is not available use the wheel spindle removed from the front wheel as in Section F1.

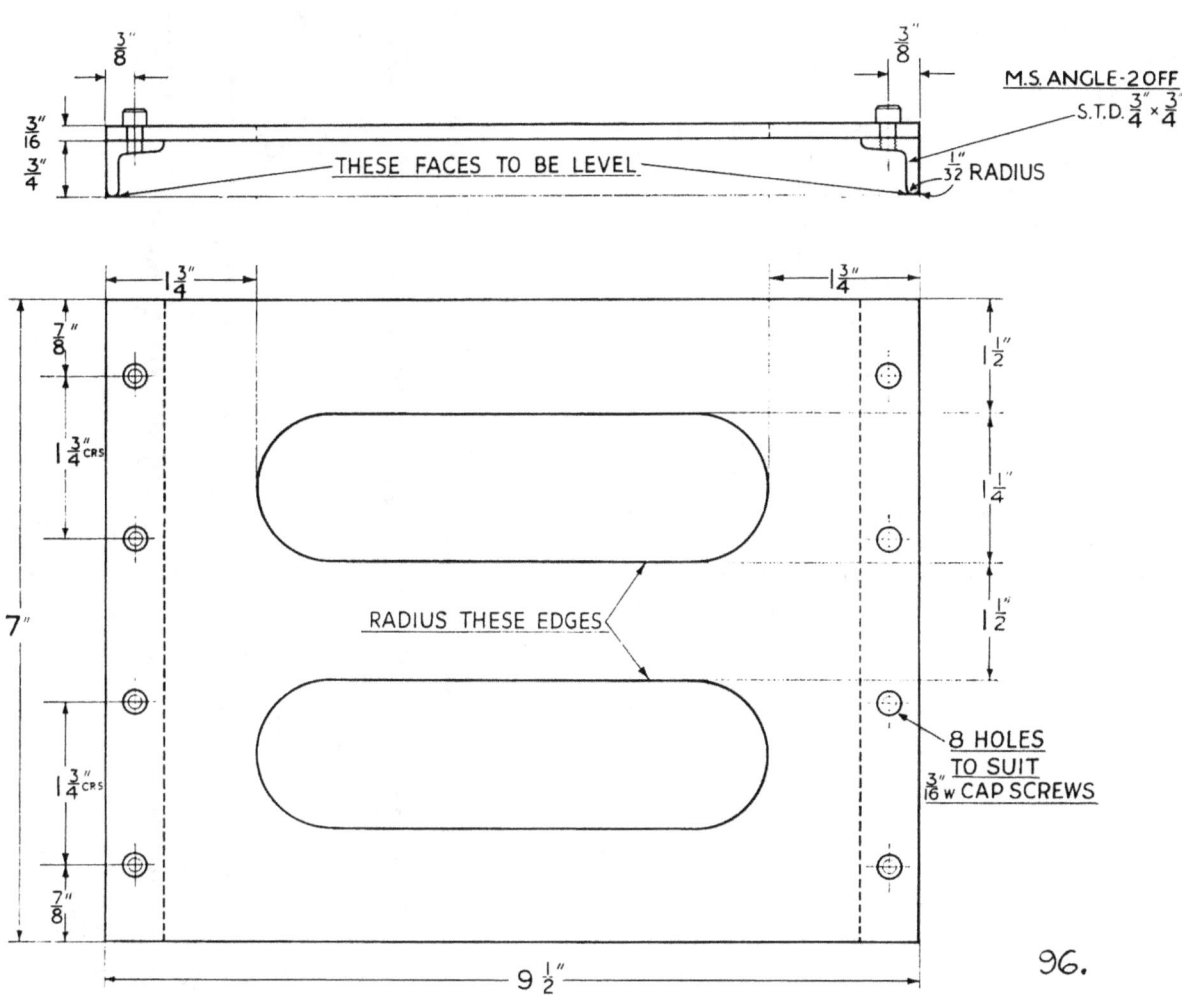

Fig. G10. Telescopic fork leg alignment guage service tool Z103

G   TELESCOPIC FORKS

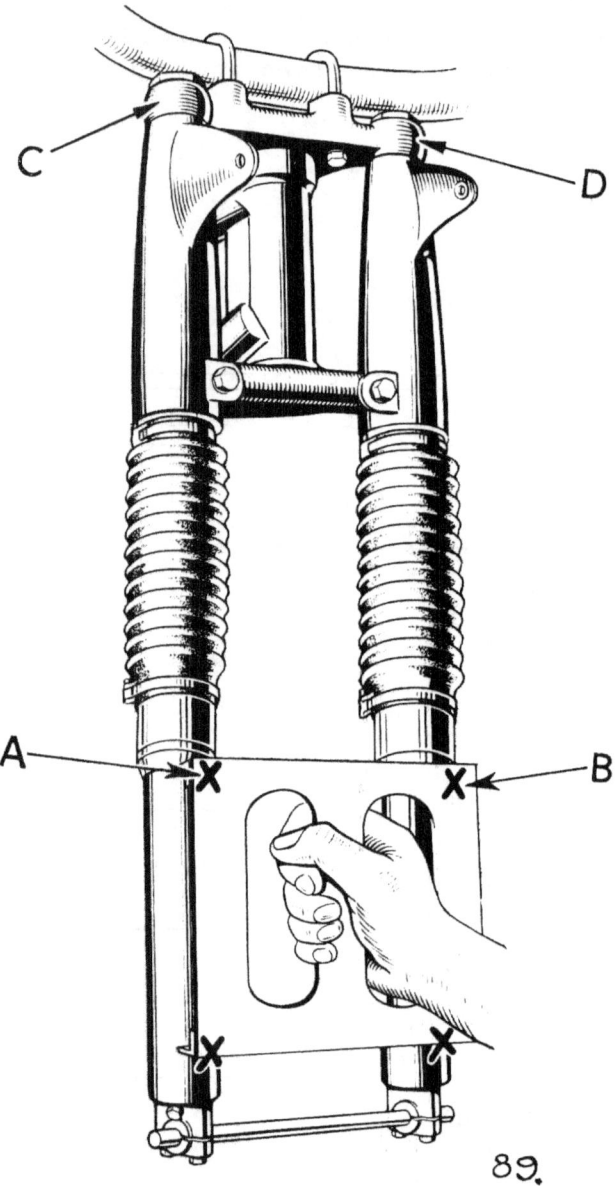

Hold the alignment gauge firmly against the fork legs as shown in Fig. G13 and check that the gauge contacts at all four corners. If the gauge does not make contact at point A then this indicates that point B is too far forward. To remedy this, slacken off the two middle lug pinch bolts and the stem sleeve nut pinch bolt and give point C a sharp blow using a hide mallet or a hammer used in conjunction with a soft metal drift. This allows the stanchion to rotate slightly and align itself within the fork lugs.

Check the alignment again with the gauge and again give correcting blows in the above mentioned manner until the amount of rock at any one corner does not exceed $\frac{1}{64}$ in. When this is achieved, tighten all three pinch bolts and then finally apply the gauge to check that tightening has not caused distortion.

Fig. G11. Checking the telescopic fork leg alignment with service tool Z103

TELESCOPIC FORKS   **G**

SECTION G10
ADJUSTING THE STEERING HEAD RACES

When a new machine has covered the 500 miles (running in period), or after new forks have been fitted, it will be necessary to check the steering head races for excessive play due to the balls, cups and cones bedding down.

Also, after long periods, the head races may require adjusting to compensate for any wear that may have taken place. The working clearance of the balls in the tracks of the cups and cones is controlled by the fork stem sleeve nut which is locked in position by means of a pinch bolt at the rear of the top lug. When the pinch bolt is slackened the sleeve nut can be turned to increase or decrease the head race working clearance.

Mount the machine with the front wheel clear of the ground and balance the front fork so that both the front and rear wheels are aligned. When the fork is tilted to either side of its central position, it should just fall to its full lock position. If the fork will do this then the head races are not overtight and conversely to check that they are not too loose, hold the top lug with the left hand (with the headlamp unit removed on models fitted with nacelle type front forks), and hold the top portion of the front mudguard in the right hand and then attempt to rock the fork. If there is any rock in evidence, then tighten the stem sleeve nut $\frac{1}{4}$ of a turn and check again. Continue in this way until the fork will not rock but will turn from lock to lock easily. When this is achieved, retighten the stem sleeve nut pinch bolt.

SECTION G11
CHANGING THE FRONT FORK MAIN SPRINGS

Removing the main springs on all models necessitates removal of the fork leg assemblies and for details of this see Section G3. Reassembly of the fork unit is covered in Section G8.

SECTION G12
HANDLEBAR MOUNTINGS
BEFORE ENGINE NUMBER H.49833

On all T90 and T100 models the handlebars are held in lugs on the fork crown and retained by 2 clamps, 4 bolts and 4 washers.

On nacelle models 3TA and 5TA "U" bolts are fitted over the handlebar and tensioned beneath the fork crown with 2 nuts and washers each.

AFTER ENGINE NUMBER H.49833

T90 and T100S models utilise rubber mountings for the handlebars. These take the form of threaded eyebolts fitted through metalastic bushes in the fork top lug. On this arrangement note that the hemispherical washer "A" is fitted with the rounded side towards the head lug. The washer "B" in Fig. G12 is radiused internally on one side only. The radius must be towards the head of the eyebolt.

T90 and T100S when fitted with a handlebar mounted windscreen or fairing must have the metalastic bushes replaced by steel bushes to render the handlebar rigid. The rigid bushes for this conversion are shown in Fig. G12.

U.S.A. models T100R and T100C have rigidly mounted handlebars as for machines prior to engine number H.49833.

Note that if a handlebar grip should be removed, on refitting, Bostik 1765 adhesive must be applied.

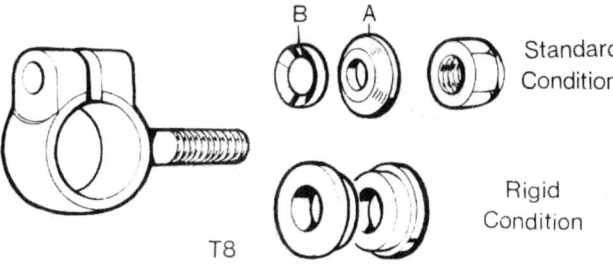

Fig. G12. Handlebar eyebolt mountings

SECTION G13

THE HYDRAULIC DAMPING UNIT

Fig. G13 shows an exploded view of the damping unit which may be fitted to certain types of telescopic front forks. To fit these units, two alternative stanchion cap nuts are required with a threaded hole into which the top of the damper unit rod screws. Locknuts are provided to secure the cap nut to the rod. Note that on a machine fitted with these damper units, if the rod should become detached from the cap nut for any reason, it must be remembered that it will fall back into the stanchion. Therefore when fitting the fork to the frame a check should be made to ensure that the operation of fitting the damper unit rod to the cap nut has not been forgotten.

The bottom of the damper unit is secured in the same way as the restrictor on standard machines (Section G8), i.e. by means of a hexagon headed bolt countersunk into the wheel spindle recess. To dismantle the unit, first grip the body carefully in a vice, then unscrew the adaptor nut (two flats) and withdraw the rod assembly. The cap is removed by unscrewing the locknut from the end of the rod and withdrawing the sliding fit oil restrictor cup.

When reassembling the damper, ensure that the pin is in position and when the locknut is tight, use a centre punch to prevent the nut subsequently unscrewing.

Ensure that the oil holes in the stem are free from blockage and refit the rod assembly to the body.

After assembly, test the unit for damping efficiency by immersing the lower end of the unit into oil and pumping the centre rod a few times. There should be little or no resistance on the down stroke and a good resistance on the up stroke.

Particularly when this damper assembly is fitted, a heavier grade of oil than that shown in Section A2 must **NOT** be used.

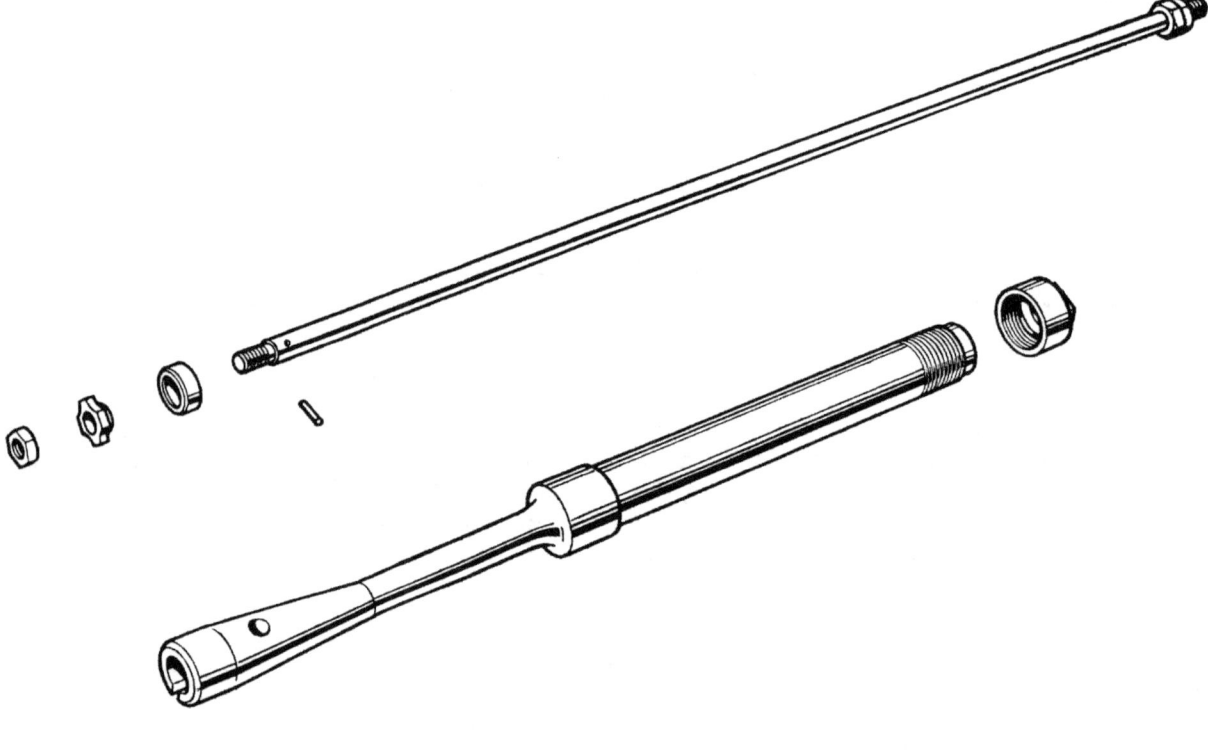

Fig. G13. Exploded view of telescopic fork internal hydraulic damper unit assembly

SECTION GG

TELESCOPIC FORKS

	Section
REMOVING AND REFITTING THE HEADLAMP	GG1
REMOVING THE TELESCOPIC FORK (ALTERNATIVE METHOD, REMOVING STANCHIONS ONLY)	GG3
DISMANTLING THE TELESCOPIC FORK	GG4
REASSEMBLING AND REFITTING THE TELESCOPIC FORK	GG8
TELESCOPIC FORK ALIGNMENT	GG9

SECTION G (INCORPORATED IN SECTION GG)
TELESCOPIC FORKS

FORK STANCHION MODIFICATION	G14

GG TELESCOPIC FORKS

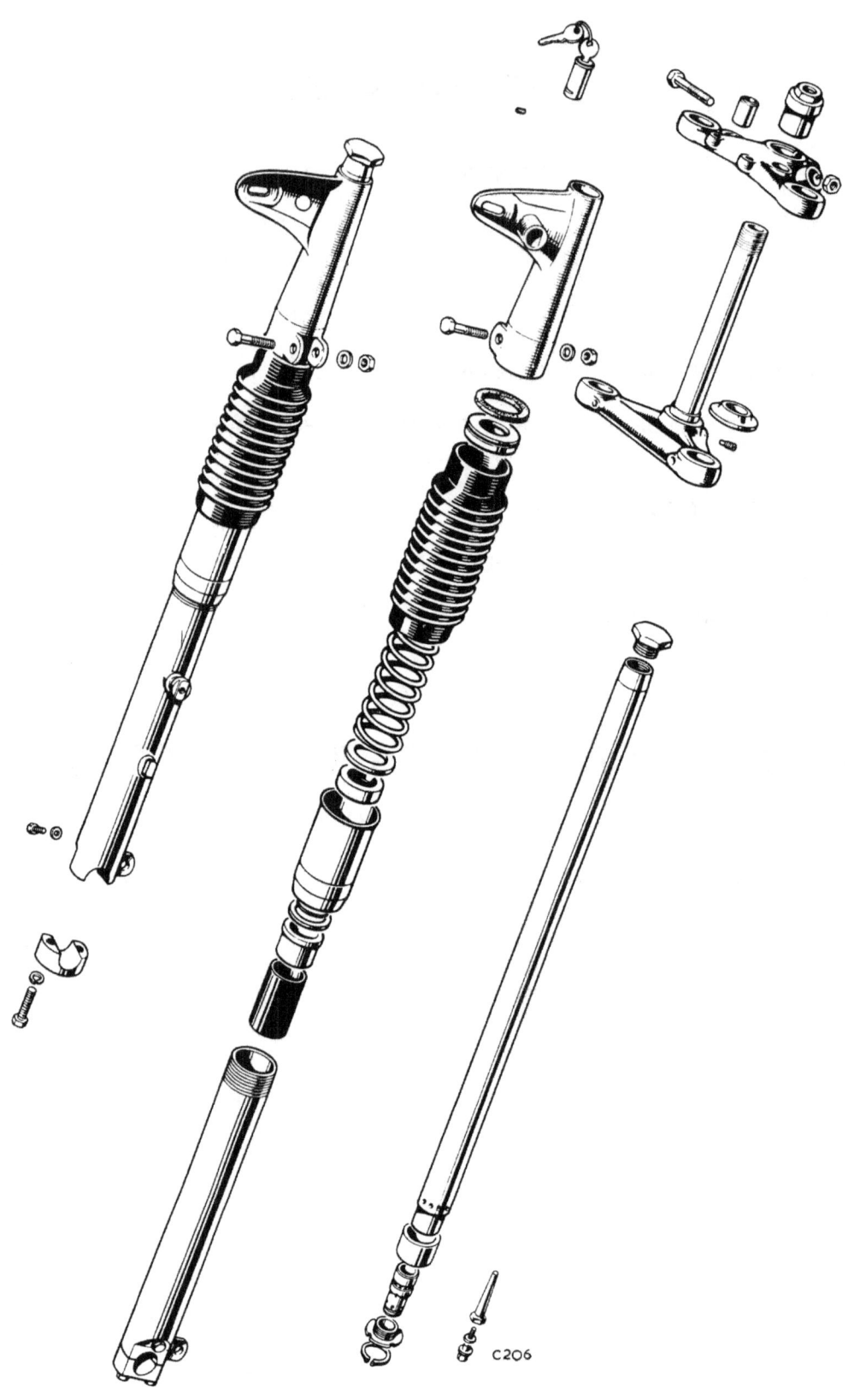

Fig. GG1. Exploded telescopic fork

GG2

TELESCOPIC FORKS

SECTION GG1
REMOVING AND REFITTING THE HEADLAMP

Disconnect one double snap connector and three single snap connectors to release the dipswitch. Withdraw the bulb holder complete with two wires from the red warning light, and disconnect one red snap connector and one blue/white snap connector to isolate the green warning light.

Withdraw the "Lucar" connectors from the lighting switch, unscrew the ammeter terminals and disconnect two red wires from the back of the double snap connector which connects to the headlight bulb holder. Withdraw the harness and dipswitch wires through the headlamp grommet.

SECTION GG3
REMOVING THE TELESCOPIC FORK
ALTERNATIVE METHOD, REMOVING FORK STANCHIONS ONLY

A service tool, part number 61-3824, is available for removing and replacing fork stanchions.

To remove a stanchion, remove the nut and collar from the tool, screw the tool into the stanchion and drive downwards (see Fig. GG2).

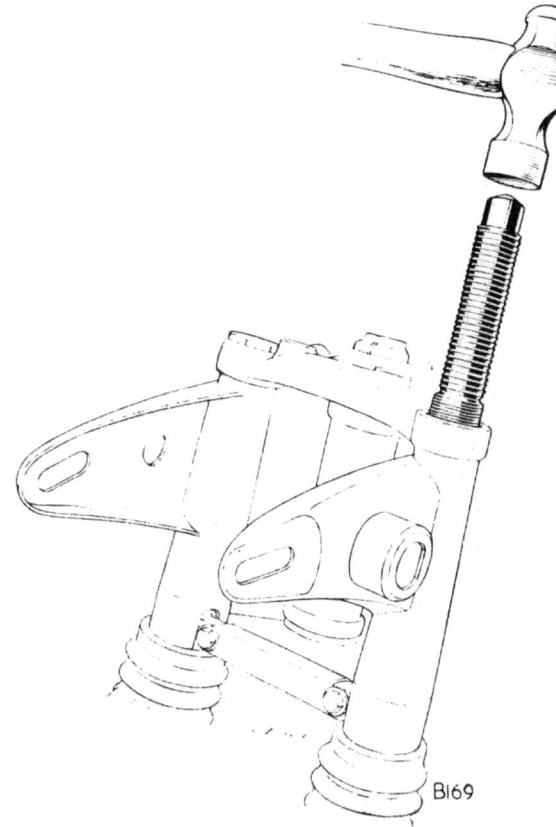

Fig. GG2. Removing a stanchion

SECTION GG4
DISMANTLING THE TELESCOPIC FORK

Service tool, part number 61-3824, is available for removing and replacing the fork stanchions (see Fig. GG2).

SECTION GG8
REASSEMBLING AND REFITTING THE TELESCOPIC FORK

When replacing the stanchions, service tool 61-3824 is available. This should be screwed into the top of the stanchion, and as much stanchion as possible should be pushed through the middle lug. Fit the collar and nut, and turn the nut clockwise to pull the stanchion upwards into the top lug (see Fig. GG3).

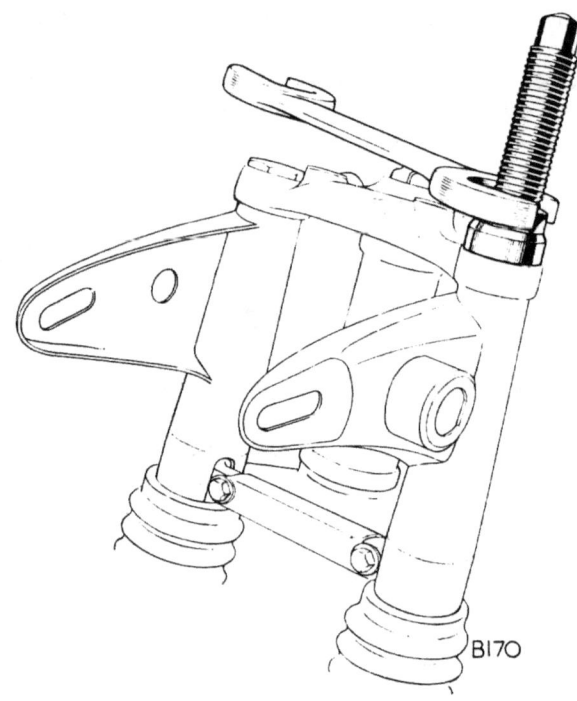

Fig. GG3. Replacing a stanchion

SECTION GG9
TELESCOPIC FORK ALIGNMENT

The front fork assembly fitted to machines after H.65573 is slightly wider than previous forks.

To check the legs for alignment, service tool 61-6025 is available, the dimensions of which are shown in Fig. GG4.

TELESCOPIC FORKS GG

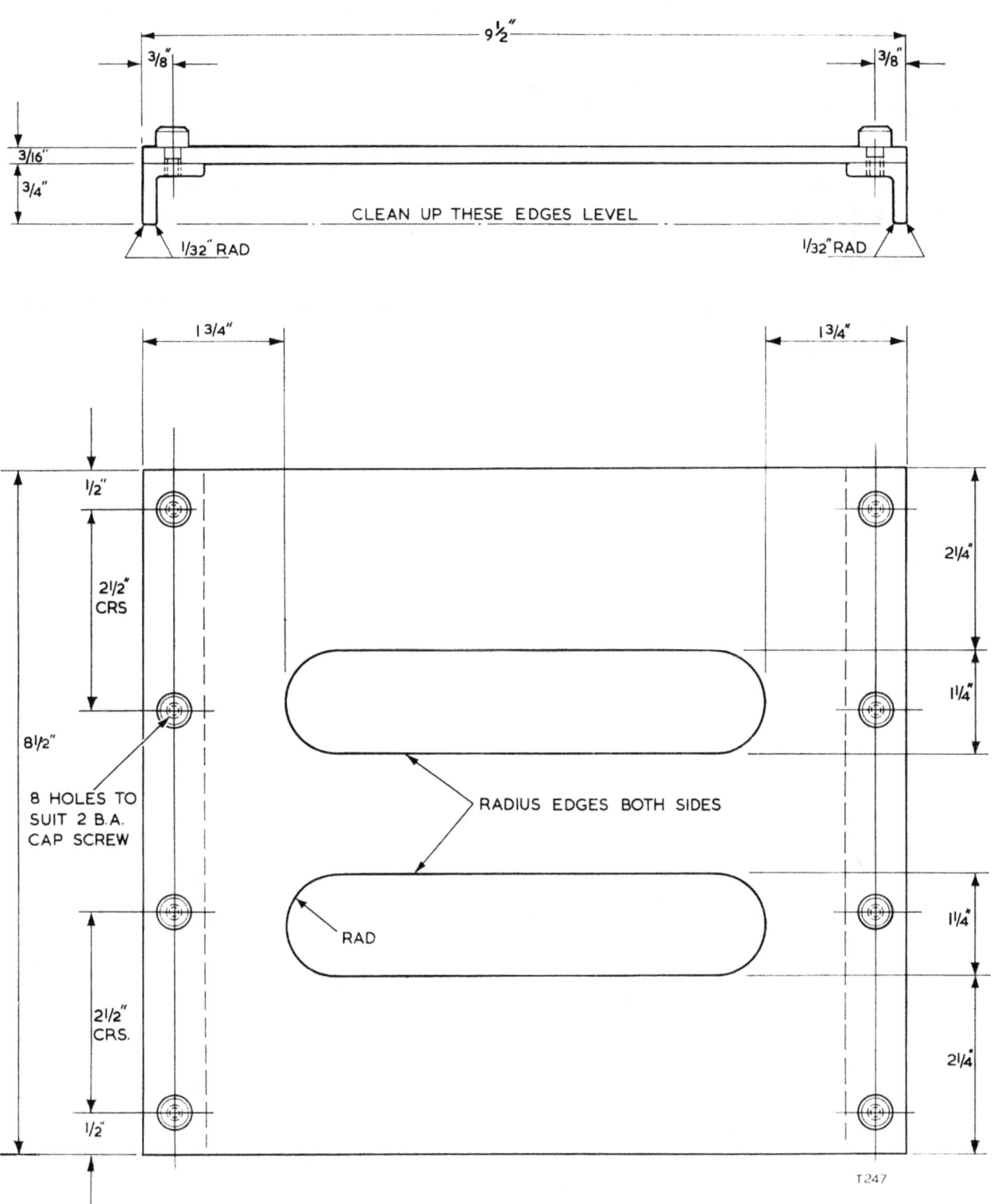

Fig. GG4. Dimensions of fork alignment gauge

GG5

SECTION G14
FORK STANCHION MODIFICATION

Machines produced after engine number AC.10464 are fitted with stanchions which incorporate two additional drilled holes. This modification improves the fork action.

Machines manufactured between engine numbers H.57083 and AC.10464 can be modified by drilling two $\frac{5}{64}$ in. diameter holes in the stanchion at the positions shown in Fig. GG5.

The correct quantity and grade of oil remains at 200 c.c. of S.A.E.20.

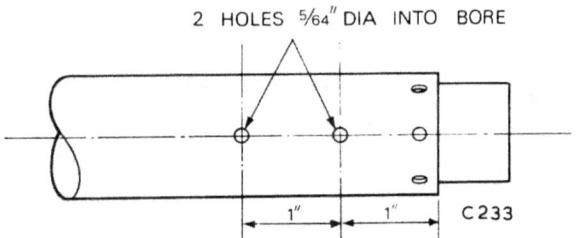

Fig. GG5. Position of additional holes in stanchion

SECTION H

ELECTRICAL SYSTEM

INTRODUCTION

BATTERY INSPECTION AND MAINTENANCE ... H1
    DESCRIPTION
    (a) DRY CHARGED BATTERIES
    (b) ROUTINE MAINTENANCE

COIL IGNITION SYSTEM ... H2
    DESCRIPTION
    (a) CHECKING THE LOW TENSION CIRCUIT FOR CONTINUITY
    (b) FAULT FINDINGS IN THE LOW TENSION CIRCUIT
    (c) IGNITION COILS
    (d) CONTACT BREAKER
    (e) CHECKING THE HIGH TENSION CIRCUIT
    (f) CHECKING THE EMERGENCY STARTING CIRCUIT

SPARKING PLUGS ... H3

CHARGING SYSTEM ... H4
    DESCRIPTION
    (a) CHECKING THE D.C. INPUT TO BATTERY
    (b) CHECKING THE ALTERNATOR OUTPUT
    (c) RECTIFIER MAINTENANCE AND TESTING
    (d) CHECKING THE CHARGING CIRCUIT FOR CONTINUITY
    (e) MAKING A 1 OHM LOAD RESISTOR

ZENER DIODE CHARGE CONTROL ... H5
    PROCEDURE FOR TESTING ON THE MACHINE

A.C. IGNITION (E.T.) AND A.C. LIGHTING SYSTEMS ... H6
    DESCRIPTION
    (a) A.C. IGNITION
    (b) TESTING THE A.C. IGNITION SYSTEM
    (c) CHECKING THE A.C. ALTERNATOR OUTPUT
    (d) DIRECT LIGHTING SYSTEM

ELECTRIC HORN ... H7

HEADLAMP ... H8
    DESCRIPTION
    BEAM ADJUSTMENTS

TAIL AND STOPLAMP UNIT ... H9

FUSES ... H10

IGNITION CUT-OUT (KILL) BUTTON ... H11

WARNING LAMPS ... H12

WIRING DIAGRAMS ... H13
    COIL IGNITION (12V) FROM H49833 (USA)
    COIL IGNITION (12V) FROM H49833 (HOME)
    COIL IGNITION (12V) UP TO H49832 (HOME AND EXPORT)
    COIL IGNITION (12V) WITH NACELLE
    A.C. IGNITION (E.T.) MODELS
    COIL IGNITION (6V) MODELS
    COIL IGNITION (6V) POLICE MODELS WITH BOOST SWITCH

ALTERNATOR AND STATOR DETAILS (Specifications and Output Figures) ... H14

ELECTRICAL SYSTEM

INTRODUCTION

The electrical system is supplied from an alternating current generator contained in the primary chaincase and driven from the crankshaft. The generator output is then converted into direct current by a silicon diode rectifier. The direct current is supplied to the 12 ampere/hour battery equipment on 6 volt machines, or on 12 volt machines to a 12 volt 8 ampere/hour battery or two 6 volt 8 ampere/hour batteries connected in series, with a Zener diode in circuit to regulate the battery current.

The current is then supplied to the ignition system which is controlled by a double contact breaker driven direct from the exhaust camshaft. The contact breaker feeds two ignition coils, one for each cylinder.

Coil ignition machines subsequent to ENGINE NUMBER H40528 have been fitted with 12 volt electrical equipment with no separate 'EMERGENCY START' facility. There is however, sufficient voltage available to start the machine when a discharged battery is in circuit.

On 6 volt machines prior to H40528 where the 'EMERGENCY START' facility is provided the emergency position of the ignition switch supplies output direct from the generator through one pair of contacts and one ignition coil to enable the engine to be started. As soon as the engine has been started, the ignition switch must be returned to the normal 'IGN' position, or burning of the contact breaker points will occur.

The routine maintenance needed by the various components is set out in the following sections. All electrical components and connections including the earthing points to the frame of the machine must be clean and tight.

SECTION H1
BATTERY INSPECTION AND MAINTENANCE
DESCRIPTION

Battery models ML9E, MLZ9E and MK9E, MKZ9E are six volt units and a single 12 volt battery model PUZ5A, or two of the 6 volt type are connected in series on some models, to give 12 volts. The battery containers are moulded in translucent polystyrene through which the acid can be seen. The tops of the containers are so designed that when the covers are in position, the special anti-spill filler plugs are sealed in a common venting chamber. Gas from the filler plugs leaves this chamber through an elbow-shaped vent pipe union which can be inserted into one of the alternative sealed outlets. Polythene tubing may be attached to the vent pipe union to lead the corrosive fumes away from any parts of the machine where they might cause damage.

H1. PART A. DRY CHARGED BATTERIES

Battery modesl ML9E, MK9E and PU5A are supplied either dry and uncharged or filled and charged, while models MLZ9E, MK9E and PUZ5A are supplied dry-charged. To prepare one of the above types of battery for service, first discard the vent hole sealing tapes and then pour into each cell pure dilute sulphuric acid of appropriate specific gravity to THE COLOURED LINE. (See table a). Allow the battery to stand for at least one hour for the electrolyte to settle down, thereafter maintain the acid level at the coloured line by adding distilled water.

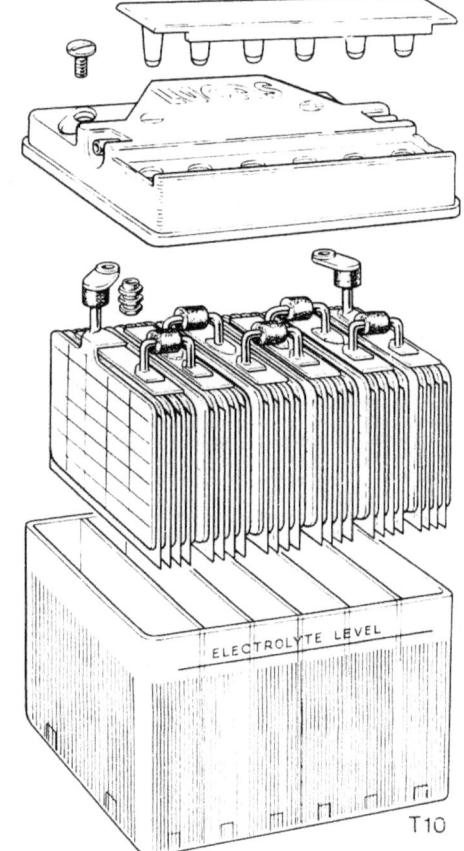

Fig. H1. Exploded view of battery

ELECTRICAL SYSTEM

H1. PART B. ROUTINE MAINTENANCE

Every week examine the level of the electrolyte in each cell. Lift the battery out of the carrier so that the coloured filling line can be seen. Add distilled water until the electrolyte level reaches this line.

Note. On NO account should the ML9E or MLZ9E batteries be topped up to the separator guard but only to the COLOURED LINE.

PUZ5A batteries should be topped up until the electrolyte level is just above the plates.

With this type of battery, the acid can be reached by a hydrometer, which would indicate the state of charge.

Great care should be taken when carrying out these operations not to spill any acid or allow a naked flame near the electrolyte. The mixture of oxygen and hydrogen given off by a battery on charge, and to a lesser extent when standing idle, can be dangerously explosive.

The readings obtained from the battery electrolyte should be compared with those given in table (a). If a battery is suspected to be faulty it is advisable to have it checked by a Lucas Depot or Agent.

(a) SPECIFIC GRAVITY OF ELECTROLYTE FOR FILLING BATTERIES ML9E, MLZ9E MK9E, MKZ9E, PUZ5A and PU5A

U.K. and Climates normally below 90°F (32·2°C)		Tropical Climates over 90°F (32·2°C)	
Filling	Fully charged	Filling	Fully charged
1·260	1·280/1·300	1·210	1·220/1·240

Every 1,000 miles (1,500 k.m.) or monthly, or more regularly in hot climates the battery should be cleaned as follows. Remove the battery cover and clean the battery top. Examine the terminals: if they are corroded scrape them clean and smear them with a film of petroleum jelly, such as vaseline. Remove the vent plugs and check that the vent holes are clear and that the rubber washer fitted under each plug is in good condition.

(b) MAXIMUM PERMISSIBLE ELECTROLYTE TEMPERATURE DURING CHARGE

Climates normally Below 80°F (27°C)	Climates between 80–100°F (27–38°C)	Climates frequently above 100°F (38°C)
100°F (38°C)	110°F (43°C)	120°F (49°C)

Notes.

The specific gravity of the electrolyte varies with the temperature. For convenience in comparing specific gravities, they are always corrected to 60°F., which is adopted as a reference temperature. The method of correction is as follows:

For every 5°F. below 60°F. deduct ·20 from the observed reading to obtain the true specific gravity at 60°F. For every 5°F. above 60°F., add ·020 to the observed reading to obtain the true specific gravity at 60°F.

The temperature must be indicated by a thermometer having its bulb actually immersed in the electrolyte and not the ambient temperature. To take a temperature reading tilt the battery sideways and then insert into the electrolyte.

SECTION H2
COIL IGNITION SYSTEM

DESCRIPTION

The coil ignition system comprises two ignition coils and a contact breaker fitted in the timing cover and driven by the exhaust camshaft. The ignition coils are mounted underneath the fuel tank one either side of the main tank tube. Access to the coils is achieved by removing the fuel tank as shown in Section E1. Apart from cleaning the coils, in between the terminals and checking the low tension and high tension connections, the coils will not require any other attention. Testing the ignition coils is amply covered in H2 Part C below whilst testing the contact breaker is described in H2 Part D.

The best method of approach to a faulty ignition system, is that of first checking the low tension circuit for continuity as shown in H2 Part A, and then following the procedure laid out in H2 Part B to locate the fault(s).

Failure to locate a fault in the low tension circuit indicates that the high tension circuit or sparking plugs are faulty, and the procedure detailed in H2 Part E must be followed. Before commencing any of the following tests, however, the contact breaker and sparking plugs must be cleaned and adjusted to eliminate this possible source of fault.

ELECTRICAL SYSTEM

H2 PART A. CHECKING THE LOW TENSION CIRCUIT FOR CONTINUITY

To check whether there is a fault in the low tension circuit and to locate its position, the following tests should be carried out:—

Disconnect and remove the fuel tank (Section E1) removing the white lead which connects the "S.W." terminals of the left and right ignition coils. Then, with the wiring harness white lead connected to the S.W. terminal of the left ignition coil only, turn the ignition switch to the "IGN" position. Slowly crank the engine and at the same time observe the ammeter needle, which should fluctuate between zero and a slight discharge, as the contacts open and close respectively.

Disconnect the wiring harness white lead from the left ignition coil and connect it to the S.W. terminal of the right ignition coil and then repeat the test. If the ammeter needle does not fluctuate in the described way then a fault in the low tension circuit is indicated.

First, examine the contact breaker contacts for pitting, piling or presence of oxidation, oil or dirt, etc. Clean and ensure that the gap is set correctly to ·014 in.–·016 in. (·35–·40 mm.) as described in Section B31.

H2 PART B. FAULT FINDING IN THE LOW TENSION CIRCUIT

To trace a fault in the low tension wiring, turn the ignition switch to "IGN" position and then crank the engine until both sets of contacts are opened, or alternatively, place a piece of insulating material between both sets of contacts whilst the following test is carried out.

For this test, it is assumed that the fuel tank is removed and the wiring is fully connected as shown in the appropriate wiring diagram, Section H11. With the aid of a D.C. volt meter and 2 test-prods (volt meter 0–10 volts for 6 volt machines, and 0–15 volts for 12 volt electrical systems), make a point to point check along the low tension circuit starting at the battery and working right through to the ignition coils, stage by stage, in the following manner, referring to the relevant wiring diagram in Section H13.

Note. On 12V machines it will be necessary to disconnect the Zener Diode before the test is carried out. To do this remove the white lead from the Diode centre terminal.

(1) First, establish that the battery is earthed correctly by connecting the volt meter across the battery negative terminal and the machine frame earth. No voltage reading indicates that the red earthing lead is faulty (or the fuse) blown, where fitted). Also, a low reading would indicate a poor battery earth connection.

(2) Connect the volt meter between the left ignition coil S.W. terminal and earth and then the right ignition coil S.W. terminal and earth. No voltage reading indicates a breakdown between the battery and the coil S.W. terminal, or that the switch connections or ammeter connections are faulty.

(3) Connect the volt meter between both of the ammeter terminals in turn and earth. No reading on the "feed" side indicates that either the ammeter is faulty or there is a bad connection along the brown and blue lead from the battery, and a reading on the "battery" side only indicates a faulty ammeter.

(4) Connect the volt meter between ignition switch input terminal and earth. No reading indicates that the brown and white lead has faulty connections. Check for voltage at the brown/white lead connections at rectifier, ammeter and lighting switch terminals No's 2 and 10.

(5) Connect the volt meter across ignition switch output terminal and earth. No reading indicates that the ignition switch is faulty and should be replaced. Battery voltage reading at this point but not at the ignition coil S.W. terminals indicates that the white lead has become "open circuit" or become disconnected.

(6) Disconnect the black/white, and black/yellow leads from the C.B. terminals of each ignition coil. Connect the volt meter across the C.B. terminal of the left coil and earth and then the C.B. terminal of the right coil and earth. No reading on the volt meter in either case indicates that the coil primary winding is faulty and a replacement ignition coil should be fitted.

(7) With both sets of contacts open reconnect the ignition coil leads and then connect the volt meter across both sets of contacts in turn. No reading in either case indicates that there is a faulty connection or the internal insulation has broken down in one of the condensers (capacitors).

If a capacitor is suspected then a substitution should be made and a re-test carried out.

(8) Finally, on machines with 12V electrical systems, reconnect the Zener Diode white lead and then connect the volt meter between the Zener Diode centre terminal and earth (with ignition "ON"). The volt meter should read battery volts. If it does not the Zener Diode is faulty and a substitution should be made. Refer to Section H5 for the correct procedure for testing a Zener Diode on the machine. Ignition coil check procedure is given in Section H2 Part C.

ELECTRICAL SYSTEM   H

H2 PART C. IGNITION COILS

The ignition coils consist of primary and secondary windings wound concentrically about a laminated soft iron core, the secondary winding being next to the core. The primary winding usually consists of some 300 turns of enamel covered wire and the secondary some 17,000–26,000 turns of much finer wire—also enamel covered. Each layer is paper insulated from the next in both primary and secondary windings.

To test the ignition coil on the machine, first ensure that the low tension circuit is in order as described in H2 Part A above then disconnect the high tension leads from the left and right sparking plugs. Turn the ignition switch to the "IGN" position and crank the engine until the contacts (those with the black/yellow lead from the ignition coil) for the right cylinder are closed. Flick the contact breaker lever open a number of times whilst the high tension lead from the right ignition coil is held about $\frac{3}{16}$ in. away from the cylinder head. If the ignition coil is in good condition a strong spark should be obtained. If no spark occurs this indicates the ignition coil to be faulty.

Repeat this test for the left high tension lead and coil by cranking the engine until the contacts with the black/white lead from the left ignition coil are closed.

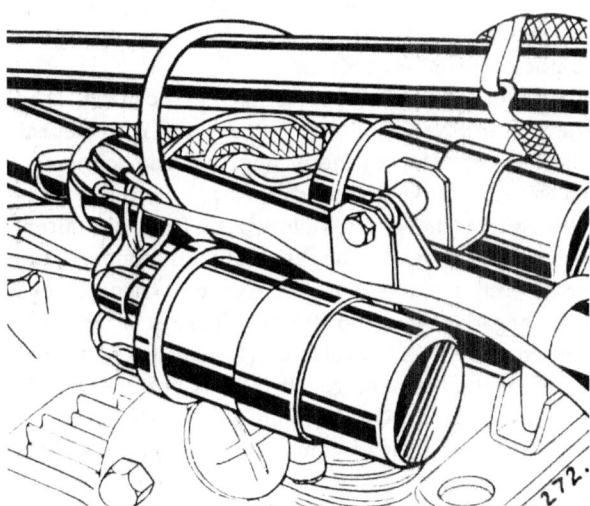

Fig. H2. Ignition coils in position on machine

Before a fault can be attributed to an ignition coil it must be ascertained that the high tension cables are not cracked or showing signs of deterioration, as this may often be the cause of mis-firing, etc. It should also be checked that the ignition points are actually making good electrical contact when closed and that the moving contact is insulated from earth (ground) when open. It is advisable to remove the ignition coils and test them by the method described below.

BENCH TESTING AN IGNITION COIL

Connect the ignition coil into the circuit shown in Fig. H3 and set the adjustable gap to 8 mm. for MA6 coils and 9 mm. for MA12 types. With the contact breaker running at 100 r.p.m. and the coil in good condition, not more than 5% missing should occur at the spark gap over a period of 15 seconds. The primary winding can be checked for short-circuit coils by connecting an ohmeter across the low tension terminals. The reading obtained should be within the figures quoted below (at 20°C).

Coil	Primary Resistance	
	Min.	Max.
MA6	1·8 ohms.	2·4 ohms.
MA12	3·0 ohms.	3·4 ohms.

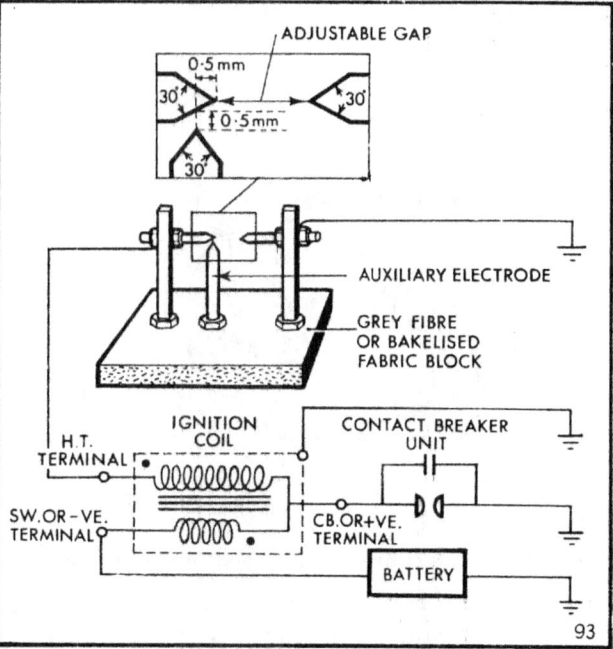

Fig. H3. Ignition coil test rig

H2 PART D. CONTACT BREAKER

Faults occurring at the contact breaker are in the main due to incorrect adjustments of the contacts or the efficiency being impaired by piling, pitting or oxidation of the contacts due to oil etc. Therefore, always ensure that the points are clean and that the gap is adjusted to the correct working clearance as described in Section B31.

H ELECTRICAL SYSTEM

To test for a faulty condenser, first turn the ignition switch to "IGN" position and then take voltage readings across each set of contacts with the contacts open. No reading indicates that the condenser internal insulation has broken down. Should the fault be due to a condenser having a reduction in capacity, indicated by excessive arcing when in use, and overheating of the contact faces, a check should be made by substitution.

Particular attention is called to the periodic lubrication procedure for the contact breaker which is given in section A10. When lubricating the parts ensure that no oil or grease gets onto the contacts.

If it is felt that the contacts require surface grinding then the complete contact breaker unit should be removed as described in Section B25 and the moving contacts disconnected by unscrewing the securing nuts from the condenser terminals. Grinding is best achieved by using a fine carborundum stone or very fine emergy cloth, afterwards wiping away any trace of dirt or metal dust with a clean petrol (gasoline) moistened cloth. The contact faces should be slightly domed to ensure point

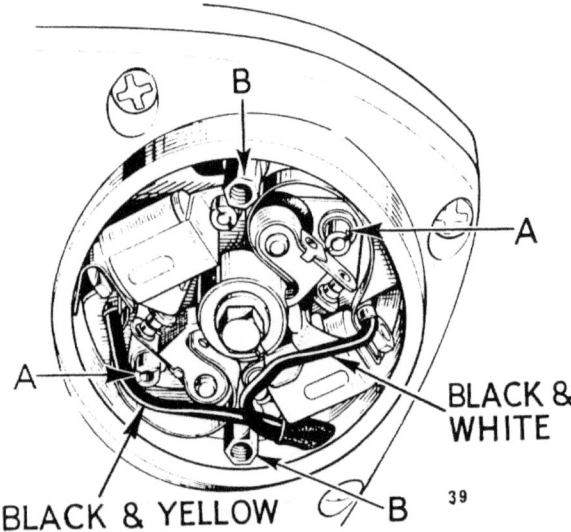

Fig. H4. Contact breaker and condenser assembly

contact. There is no need to remove the pitting from the fixed contact. When re-fitting the moving contacts do not forget to refit the insulating shields to the condenser terminals and apply a smear of grease to the C.B. cam and moving contact pivot post. Lubricate the one felt pad.

H2 PART E. CHECKING THE HIGH TENSION CIRCUIT

If ignition failure or mis-firing occurs, and the fault is not in the low tension circuit, then check the ignition coils as described in Part C. If the coils prove satisfactory, ensure that the high tension cables are not the cause of the fault.

If a good spark is available at the high tension cable, then the sparking plug suppressor cap or the sparking plug itself may be the cause of the fault. Clean the sparking plug and adjust the electrodes to the required setting as described in Section H3 below and then re-test the engine for running performance. If the fault recurs then it is likely the suppressor caps are faulty and these should be renewed.

H2 PART E CHECKING THE EMERGENCY START CIRCUIT

Machines subsequent to ENG. No. H40528 are not provided with an EMERGENCY START circuit, the 12 volt electrical equipment being so arranged to provide sufficient electrical output to start the engine, even with a fully discharged battery in circuit.

For machines prior to ENG. No. H40528 incorporating EMERGENCY START facilites, the following check procedure should be adopted.

First, ensure that the contact breaker and sparking plug gap settings are satisfactory and then remove the contact breaker cover and place a small piece of insulating card between each set of contacts. Connect a D.C. voltmeter (0–15V) with the positive lead to earth and negative lead to the moving contact spring of the front set of contacts. A resistor is not required for this test.

Turn the ignition switch to "IGN" position. The voltmeter should indicate battery voltage. Repeat the test with the voltmeter negative lead connected to the rear moving contact spring.

Disconnect the green/yellow lead from the alternator (underneath the engine) and connect the voltmeter positive to green/yellow harness lead and negative lead to frame. Turn the ignition switch to "EMG" position. The voltmeter should indicate battery voltage. If it does not the green/yellow lead to No. 17 ignition switch terminal, and black/white lead connecting ignition coil C.B. (+) terminal to ignition switch terminal No. 15 should be checked. Reconnect alternator lead. Finally, disconnect the battery, and then connect an A.C. voltmeter (0–15V) between the front moving contact spring and frame. With ignition switch in "EMG" position, (both contacts still insulated with card) attempt to kickstart the engine. The A.C. voltmeter should deflect to about 7 to 10 volts. If it does not, the alternator should be checked as shown in Section H4 Part B.

ELECTRICAL SYSTEM

SECTION H3

SPARKING PLUGS

It is recommended that the sparking plugs be inspected, cleaned and tested every 3,000 miles (4,800 km.) and new one fitted every 12,000 miles (20,000 km.).

To remove the sparking plugs a box spanner ($\frac{13}{16}$ in. (19·5 mm.) across flats) should be used and if any difficulty is encountered a small amount of penetrating oil (see lubrication chart Section A2) should be placed at the base of the sparking plug and time allowed for penetration. When removing the sparking plugs identify each plug with the cylinder from which it was removed so that any faults revealed on examination can be traced back to the cylinder concerned.

Due to certain features of engine design the sparking plugs will probably show slightly differing deposits and colouring characteristics. For this purpose it is recommended that any adjustments to carburation etc., which may be carried out to gain the required colour characteristics should always be referred to the left cylinder.

Examine both plugs for signs of oil fouling. This will be indicated by a wet, shiny, black deposit on the central insulator. This is caused by excessive oil in the combustion chamber during combustion and indicates that the piston rings or cylinder bores are worn.

Next examine the plugs for signs of petrol (gasoline) fouling. This is indicated by a dry, sooty, black deposit which is usually caused by over-rich carburation, although ignition system defects such as a discharged battery, faulty contact breaker, coil or condenser defects, or a broken or worn out cable may be additional causes. To rectify this type of fault the above mentioned items should be checked with special attention given to carburation system. Again, the left plug should be used as the indicator. The right plug will almost always have a darker characteristic.

Over-heating of the sparking plug electrodes is indicated by severely eroded electrodes and a white, burned or blistered insulator. This type of fault is usually caused by weak carburation, although plugs which have been operating whilst not being screwed down sufficiently can easily become overheated due to heat that is normally dissipated through to the cylinder head not having an adequate conducting path. Over-heating is normally symptomised by pre-ignition, short plug life, and "pinking" which can ultimately result in piston crown failure. Unecessary damage can result from over-tightening the plugs and to achieve a good seal between the plug and cylinder head a torque wrench should be used to tighten the plugs to the figure quoted in "General Data".

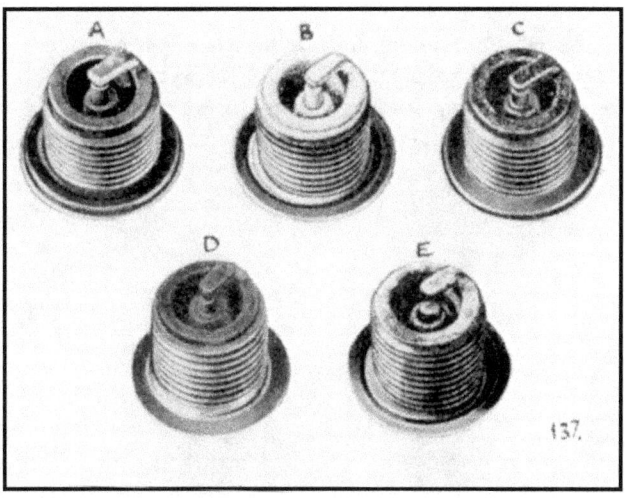

Fig. H4(a) Sparking plug diagnosis

A plug of the correct grade will bear a light flaky deposit on the outer rim and earth electrode, and these and the base of the insulator will be light chocolate brown in colour. A correct choice of plug is marked A. B shows a plug which appears bleached, with a deposit like cigarette ash; this is too 'hot-running' for the performance of the engine and a cooler-running type should be substituted. A plug which has been running too 'cold' and has not reached the self-cleaning temperature is shown at C. This has oil on the base of the insulator and electrodes, and should be replaced by a plug that will burn off deposits and remove the possibility of a short-circuit. The plug marked D is heavily sooted, indicating that the mixture has been too rich, and a further carburation check should be made. At illustration E is seen a plug which is completely worn out and badly in need of replacement.

To clean the plugs it is preferable to make use of a properly designed proprietary plug cleaner. The maker's instructions for using the cleaner should be followed carefully.

When the plugs have been carefully cleaned, examine the central insulators for cracking and the centre electrodes for excessive wear. In such cases the plugs have completed their useful life and new ones should be fitted.

Finally, before re-fitting the sparking plugs the electrodes should be adjusted to the correct gap setting of ·020 in. (·5 mm.). Before refitting sparking plugs the threads should be cleaned by means of a wire brush and a minute amount of graphite grease smeared onto the threads. This will prevent any possibility of thread seizure occurring.

If the ignition timing and carburation settings are correct and the plugs have been correctly fitted, but over-heating still occurs then it is possible that carburation is being adversely affected by an air leak between the carburetter, manifold and the cylinder head. This possibility must be checked thoroughly before taking any further action. When it is certain that none of the above mentioned faults are the cause of over-heating then the plug type and grade should be considered.

Normally the type of plugs quoted in "General Data" are satisfactory for general use of the machine, but in special isolated cases, conditions may demand a plug of a different heat range. Advice is readily available to solve these problems from the plug manufacturer who should be consulted.

Note.—If the machine is of the type fitted with an air filter or cleaner and this has been removed it will affect the carburation of the machine and hence may adversely affect the grade of sparking plugs fitted.

SECTION H4

CHARGING SYSTEM

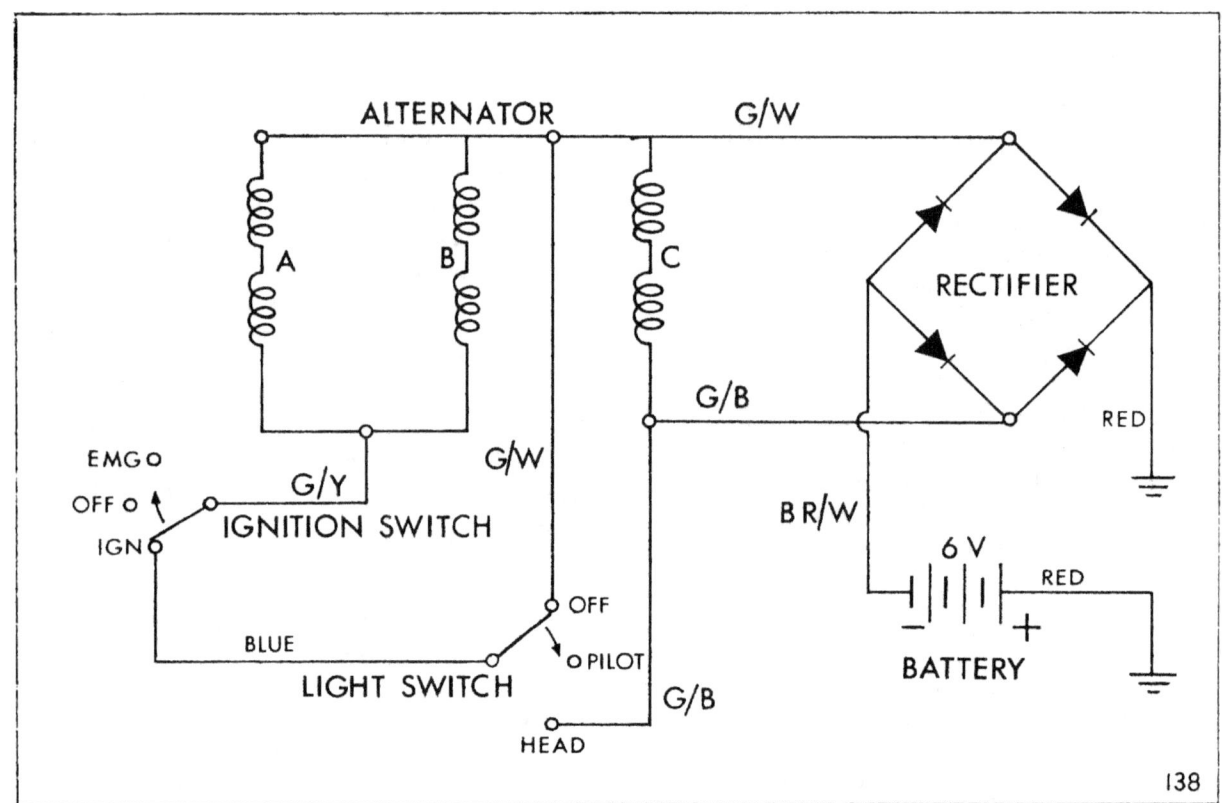

Fig. H5. Schematic illustration of 6 volt charging circuit

ELECTRICAL SYSTEM

DESCRIPTION—6 VOLT AND 12 VOLT CIRCUITS

The charging current is suppled by the alternator, but due to the characteristics of alternating current the battery cannot be charged direct from the alternator. To convert the alternating current to direct current a full wave bridge rectifier is connected into the circuit.

6 VOLT MODELS

On 6 volt systems it is not satisfactory to have just this arrangement for battery charging, due to the varying applied load on the alternator, i.e. lights, state-of-charge of battery, etc. Hence to overcome the problem of variations in load, the output from the alternator has to be governed to meet requirements. This is achieved by interconnecting the generating coils and switch terminals as shown in the diagram on previous page in Fig. H5. With the lighting switch in "OFF" position the coils A and B are short circuited and flux induced interacts with the rotor flux maintaining minimum output. With the switch in PILOT position the coils A and B are open circuited and the flux interaction is thereby reduced causing coil C to give increased "medium" output. With the switch in HEAD position the coils A, B and C are connected in parallel, giving maximum output.

12 VOLT MODELS

On models with a 12 volt electrical system and Zener Diode charge control, the alternator leads are connected differently. The alternator gives full output, all the alternator coils being permanently connected across the rectifier. (See Fig. H6). Excessive charge is absorbed by the Zener Diode which is connected across the battery. To ensure that back-leakage does not occur, the Zener Diode is connected to the battery, through the ignition switch so that there is no possibility of the battery discharging through the Diode. Always ensure that the ignition switch is in the "OFF" position whilst the machine is not in use.

To locate a fault in the charging circuit, first test the alternator as described in H4 Part B. If the alternator is satisfactory, the fault must lie in the charging circuit, hence the rectifier must be checked as given in Part C and then the wiring and connections as shown in Part D.

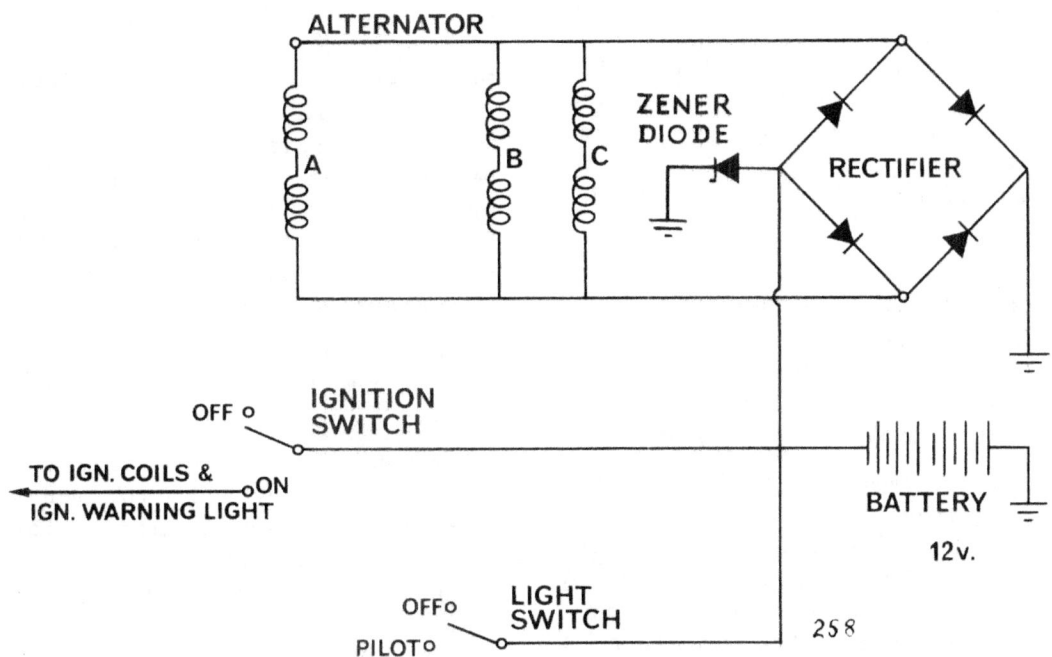

Fig. H6. Schematic illustration of 12 volt charging circuit

ELECTRICAL SYSTEM

H4 PART A. CHECKING THE D.C. INPUT TO BATTERY

For this test the battery must be in good condition and a good state of charge, therefore before conducting the test ensure that the battery is up to the required standard, or alternatively fit a good replacement battery.

Connect a D.C. ammeter (0–15 amp.) in series between the battery main lead (brown/blue) and battery negative terminal and then start the engine and run it at approximately 3,000 r.p.m. (equivalent to 45 m.p.h. in top gear).

Note.—Ensure that the ammeter is well insulated from the surrounding earth points otherwise a short circuit may occur.

Operate the lighting switch and observe the ammeter readings, for each position of the switch. The observed figures should not be less than those tabulated in Fig. H27 for the particular model. If the readings are equal to or higher than those given, then the alternator and charging circuit are satisfactory. If the readings are lower than those quoted, then the alternator must be tested as described in Part B below.

H4 PART B. CHECKING THE ALTERNATOR OUTPUT

Disconnect the three alternator output cables underneath the engine and run the engine at 3,000 r.p.m. (equivalent to 45 m.p.h. in top gear).

Connect an A.C. voltmeter (0–15 volts) with 1 ohm load resistor in parallel with each of the alternator leads in turn as shown in the table, Fig. H27, and observe the voltmeter readings. A suitable 1 ohm load resistor can be made from a piece of nichrome wire as shown in Section H4 Part E.

From the results obtained, the following deductions can be made:—

(i) If the readings are all equal to or higher than those quoted for the particular model then the alternator is satisfactory.

(ii) A low reading on any group of coils indicates either that the leads concerned are chafed or damaged due to rubbing on the chains or that some turns of the coils are short circuited.

(iii) Low readings for all parts of the test indicates either that the green/white lead has become chafed or damaged due to rubbing on the chain(s) or that the rotor has become partially demagnetised. If the latter case applies, check that this has not been caused by a faulty rectifier or that the battery is of correct polarity, and only then fit a new rotor.

(iv) A zero reading for any group of coils indicates that a coil has become disconnected, is open circuit, or is earthed.

(v) A reading obtained between any one lead and earth indicates that coil windings or connections have become earthed.

If any of the above mentioned faults occur, always check the stator leads for possible chain damage before attempting repairs or renewing the stator.

It is beyond the scope of this manual to give instruction for the repair of faulty stator windings. However, the winding specification is given in the table, Fig. H27 for those obliged to attempt repair work.

H4 PART C. RECTIFIER MAINTENANCE AND TESTING

The silicon bridge rectifier requires no maintenance beyond checking that the connections are clean and tight, and that the nut securing the rectifier to the frame is tight. It should always be kept clean and dry to ensure good cooling, and spilt oil washed off immediately with hot water.

Note.—The nuts clamping the rectifier plates together must not be disturbed or slackened in any way.

When tightening the rectifier securing nut, hold the spanners as shown in Fig. H7, for if the plates are twisted, the internal connections will be broken. Note that the circles marked on the fixing bolt and nut indicate that the thread form is $\frac{1}{4}$ in. U.N.F.

Fig. H7. Refitting the rectifier

ELECTRICAL SYSTEM

TESTING THE RECTIFIER

To test the rectifier, first disconnect the brown/white lead from the rectifier centre terminal and insulate the end of the lead to prevent any possibility of a short circuit occurring, and then connect a D.C. voltmeter (with 1 ohm load resistor in parallel) between the rectifier centre terminal and earth.

Disconnect the alternator green/yellow lead and reconnect to rectifier green/black terminal by means of a jumper lead.

Note.—Voltmeter positive terminal to frame earth (ground) and negative terminal to centre terminal on rectifier.

Ensure that all the temporary connections are well insulated to prevent a short circuit occurring then turn the ignition switch to "IGN" position and start the engine.

With the engine running at approximately 3,000 r.p.m. (approximately 45 m.p.h. in top gear) observe the voltmeter readings. The reading obtained should be at least 7·5V minimum on 12V and 6V machines.

(i) If the reading is equal to or slightly greater than that quoted, then the rectifier elements in the forward direction are satisfactory.

(ii) If the reading is excessively higher than the figures given, then check the rectifier earthing bolt connection. If the connection is good then a replacement rectifier should be fitted.

(iii) If the reading is lower than the figures quoted or zero readings are obtained, then the rectifier or the charging circuit wiring is faulty and the rectifier should be disconnected and bench tested so that the fault can be located.

Note that all of the above conclusions assume that the alternator A.C. output figures were satisfactory. Any fault at the alternator will, of course, reflect on the rectifier test results. Similarly any fault in the charging circuit wiring may indicate that the rectifier is faulty. The best method of locating a fault is to disconnect the rectifier and bench-test it as shown below:

BENCH TESTING THE RECTIFIER

For this test the rectifier should be disconnected and removed. Before removing the rectifier, disconnect the leads from the battery terminals to avoid the possibility of a short circuit occurring.

Connect the rectifier to a 12 volt battery and 1 ohm load resistor, and then connect the D.C. voltmeter in the V2 position, as shown in Fig. H8. Note the battery voltage (should be 12V) and then connect the voltmeter in V1 position whilst the following tests are conducted.

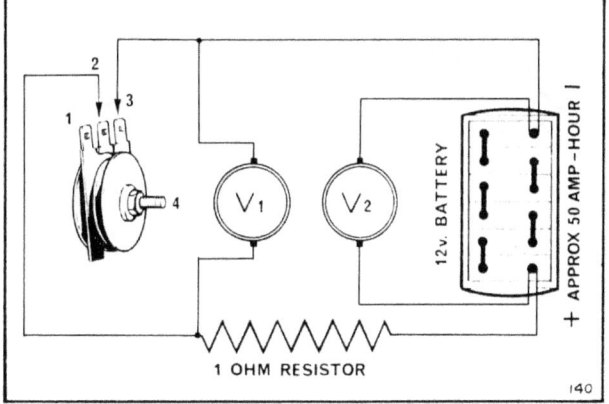

Fig. H8. Bench testing the rectifier

A voltmeter in position V1 will measure the volt drop across the rectifier plate. In position V2 it will measure the supply voltage to check that it is the recommended 12 volts on load.

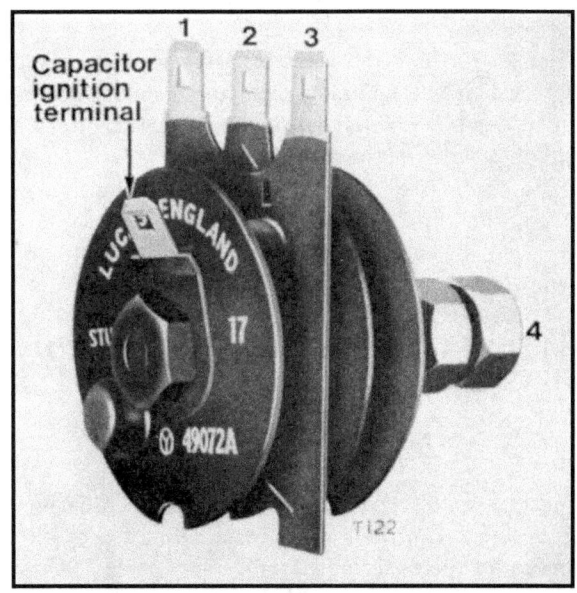

Fig. H9. Rectifier—showing terminal connections for bench tests 1 and 2

ELECTRICAL SYSTEM

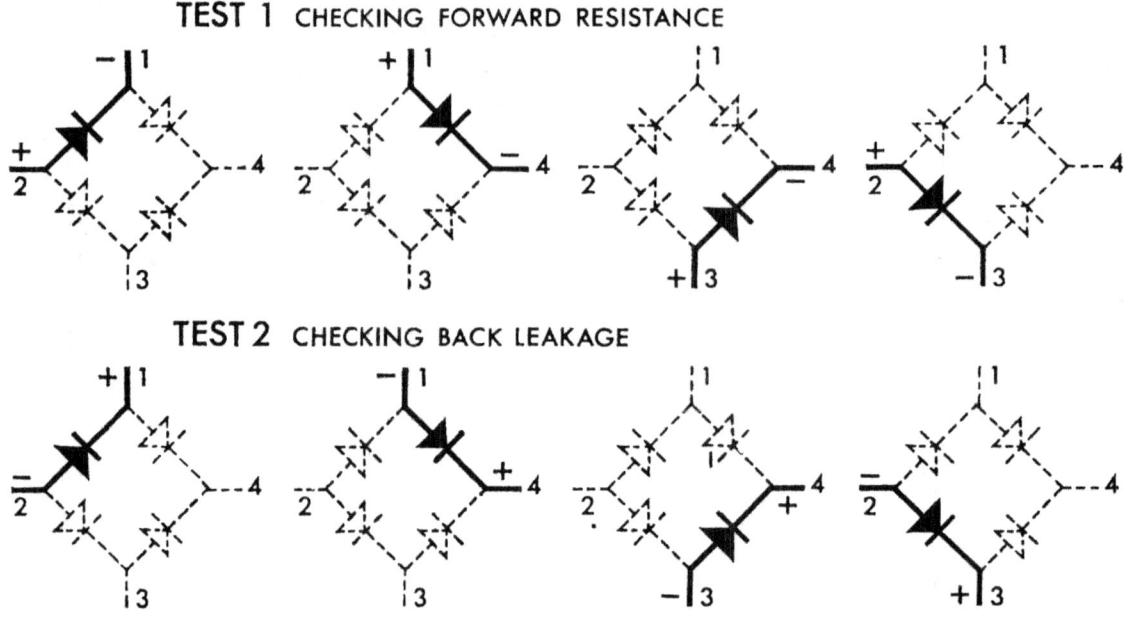

Fig. H10. Rectifier test sequence for checking foward resistance and back leakage

Test 1. With the test leads, make the following connectings but keep the testing time as short as possible to avoid overheating the rectifier cell: (a) 1 and 2, (b) 1 and 4, (c) 3 and 4, (d) 3 and 2. Each reading should not be greater than 2·5 volts with the battery polarity as shown.

Test 2. Reverse the leads or battery polarity and repeat Test 1. The readings obtained should not be more than 1·5 volts below battery voltage (V_2) (i.e. 10·5 volts minimum).
If the readings obtained are not within the figures given, then the rectifier internal connections are shorting or aged and the rectifier should be renewed.

H4 PART D. CHECKING THE CHARGING CIRCUIT FOR CONTINUITY

6 VOLT MACHINES

These three tests utilise the machine's own battery to test for continuity or breakdown in the A.C. section of the charging system.
For this series of tests, the battery must be in a good state of charge and the **ALTERNATOR LEADS MUST BE DISCONNECTED** at the snap connectors underneath the engine, so that there is no possibility of demagnetising the rotor.

(i) First, check that there is voltage at the rectifier centre terminal by connecting a D.C. voltmeter, with 1 ohm load resistor in parallel, between the rectifier centre terminal and earth (remember (+ve) positive earth (ground)). The voltmeter should read battery volts. If it does not, there is a faulty connection in the wiring and tests 1, 3 and 4 in H2 Part B should be carried out to locate the fault.

(ii) Connect the green/yellow lead from the wiring harness (underneath the engine) to the rectifier centre terminal lead (brown/white), by means of a jumper lead, and turn the ignition switch to "IGN" position. Connect a D.C. voltmeter with load resistor in parallel between the green/white lead at the rectifier and earth (frame). With the lighting switch at "OFF" positions the voltmeter should read battery volts. If it does not the leads to ignition switch terminals 16 and 18 should be checked and also the leads to lighting switch terminals 4 and 5 must be checked.

ELECTRICAL SYSTEM

(iii) Connect the green/yellow lead from the wiring harness (underneath the engine) to the rectifier centre terminal, by means of a jumper lead, as in test (ii). Turn the ignition switch to "IGN" position and the lighting switch to HEAD position, and connect a D.C. voltmeter (with 1 ohm resistor in parallel) between green/black lead at rectifier and earth. The voltmeter should read battery voltage. If it does not, the leads to ignition switch terminals 16 and 17 should be checked and the leads to the lighting switch terminals 5 and 7 should also be checked. With the lighting switch in 'Pilot' position no reading should be obtained between green/black and earth or green/white and earth at the rectifier.

12 VOLT MACHINES

On 12 volt machines the electrical circuit is so arranged that all six alternator coils are connected in parallel so that the full alternator output is available irrespective of the lighting switch position. This also makes an emergency start system unnecessary and it is therefore possible to use a simplified wiring circuit.

First check that there is voltage at the battery and that it is correctly connected into the circuit +ve earth (ground). Ensure that the fuse has not blown.

(1) Check that battery voltage is reaching the rectifier central terminal (brown/white lead). If it is not, disconnect the alternator leads (green/black, green/white and green/yellow) at the snap connectors under the engine unit.

(a) Fit a jumper lead across the brown/white and green/yellow connections at the rectifier, and check the voltage at the snap connector. This test will indicate whether the harness alternator lead is open circuit.

(b) Repeat this test at the rectifier for the white/green lead.

(2) If no voltage is present at the rectifier central terminal (brown/white), check the voltage at the ammeter terminal. If satisfactory, it indicates that the brown/white wire is open circuit. If not, the ammeter is open circuit.

(3) If no voltage is present at either ammeter terminal, then the brown/blue wire from the battery (—ve) is open circuit.

H4 PART E. CONSTRUCTING A ONE-OHM LOAD RESISTOR

The resistor used in the alternator tests must be accurate and constructed so that it will not overheat otherwise the correct values of current or voltage will not be obtained.

A suitable resistor can be made from 4 yards (3¾ metres) of 18 S.W.G. (·048 in. (i.e. 1·2 m.m.) dia.) NICHROME wire by bending it into two equal parts and calibrating it as follows:—

(1) Fix a heavy gauge flexible lead to the folded end of the wire and connect this lead to the positive terminal of a 6 volt battery.

(2) Connect a D.C. voltmeter (0-10V) across the battery terminals and an ammeter (0-10 amp) between the battery negative terminal and the free ends of the wire resistance, using a crocodile clip to make the connection.

(3) Move the clip along the wires, making contact with both wires until the ammeter reading is numerically equal to the number of volts shown in the voltmeter. The resistance is then 1 ohm. Cut the wire at this point, twist the two ends together and wind the wire on an asbestos former approximately 2 inches (5cm.) dia. so that each turn does not contact the one next to it.

SECTION H5

ZENER DIODE CHARGE CONTROL (12 VOLT MACHINES ONLY)

DESCRIPTION

The Zener Diode output regulating system which uses the 6-coil alternator connected permanently across the rectifier, provides automatic control of the charging current. It will only operate successfully on a 12 volt system where it is connected in parallel with the battery as shown in the wiring diagram (Section H13). The Diode is connected through the ignition switch to prevent any leakage when the motor cycle is not in use.

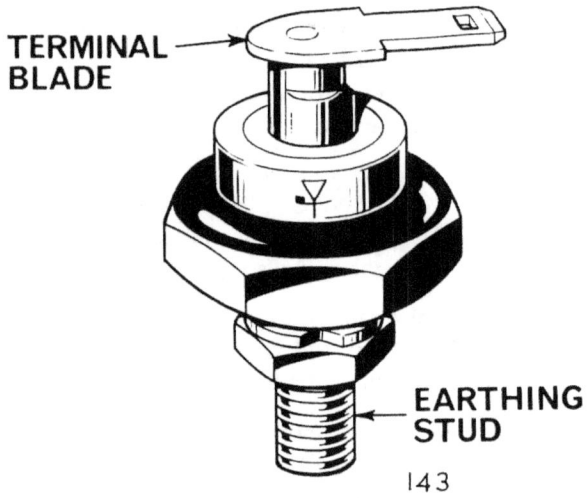

Fig. H11. Zener Diode

Assuming the battery is in a low state of charge its terminal voltage (the same voltage is across the Diode) will also be low, therefore the maximum charging current will flow into the battery from the alternator. At first none of the current is by-passed by the Diode because of it being non-conducting due to the low battery terminal volts. However, as the battery is quickly restored to a full state of charge, the system voltage rises until at 14 volts the Zener Diode becomes partially conducting, thereby providing an alternative path for a small part of the charging current. Small increases in battery voltage result in large increases in Zener conductivity until, at approximately 15 volts about 5 amperes of the alternator output is by-passing the battery. The battery will continue to receive only a portion of the alternator output as long as the system voltage is relatively high.

Depression of the system voltage, due to the use of headlamp or other lighting equipment, causes the Zener Diode current to decrease and the balance to be diverted and consumed by the component in use.

If the electrical loading is sufficient to cause the system voltage to fall to 14 volts, the Zener Diode will revert to a high resistance state of non-conductivity and the full generated output will go to meet the demands of the battery.

TESTING THE ZENER DIODE
Procedure for testing on the machine

The test procedure given below can be used when it is required to check the performance of the Zener Diode type ZD715 whilst it is in position on the machine.

Good quality moving coil meters should be used when testing. The voltmeter should have a scale 0–18, and the ammeter 0–5 amps min. The test procedure is as follows:—

(1) Disconnect the lead from the Zener Diode and connect ammeter (0–3 amps minimum) in series with the Zener (ammeter +ve to Zener).

(2) Connect voltmeter (0–18 or 20V) across Zener (+ve to earth).

(3) Start engine and gradually increase speed observing meters (m/cycle lights off).

Notes

(a) It is essential that the batteries used are in good condition and in reasonably good state of charge. If the battery condition is uncertain, it should be temporarily replaced by a good battery for this test.

(b) When the voltage across the Zener Diode reaches 12·75 volts, the Zener current ammeter must indicate zero.
Increase engine speed until a Zener current of 2 amps is indicated. A satisfactory Zener Diode should then show a voltage between 13·5 and 15·5 volts inclusive.

ELECTRICAL SYSTEM

LOCATION AND MAINTENANCE

The Zener Diode is mounted on an aluminium heat sink with an area of approximately 25 square inches. Providing the Diode and the heat sink are kept clean, and provided with an adequate airflow, to ensure maximum efficiency, no maintenance will be necessary.

The heat sink is fitted behind the left hand switch panel and to enable the Zener Diode to be removed from its heat sink, the left hand switch panel must first be removed as described in Section E2. Disconnect and remove the batteries so that the two bolts, nuts and washers securing the heat sink and breather pipe clip can be removed. The Zener securing nut and earthing strap should be carefully removed from the heat sink and the Zener lifted clear after disconnecting the Lucar connector securing the feed cable to the top of the Zener.

Note: When the Zener Diode is refitted to the heat sink it is essential that the earthing strap is refitted correctly i.e., between the heat sink and Zener securing nut. It must **NOT** be placed between the Zener body and heat sink as this could cause a heat build up, possibly resulting in a Zener Diode failure.

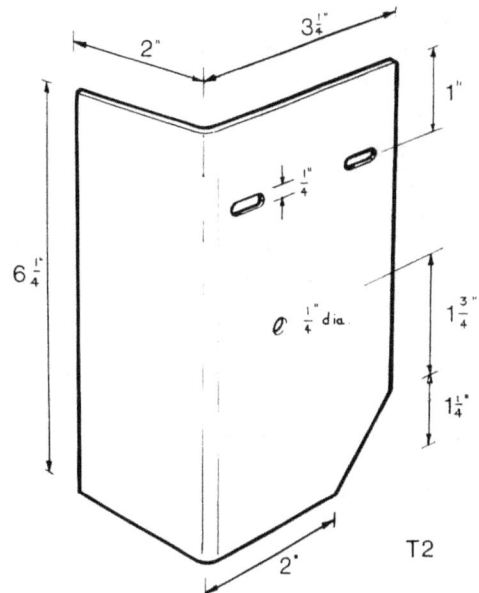

Fig. H12. Zener Diode heat sink

DO NOT overtighten the central fixing stud. Maximum torque 1·5 lb./ft.

SECTION H6
A.C. IGNITION (E.T.) AND A.C. LIGHTING SYSTEMS

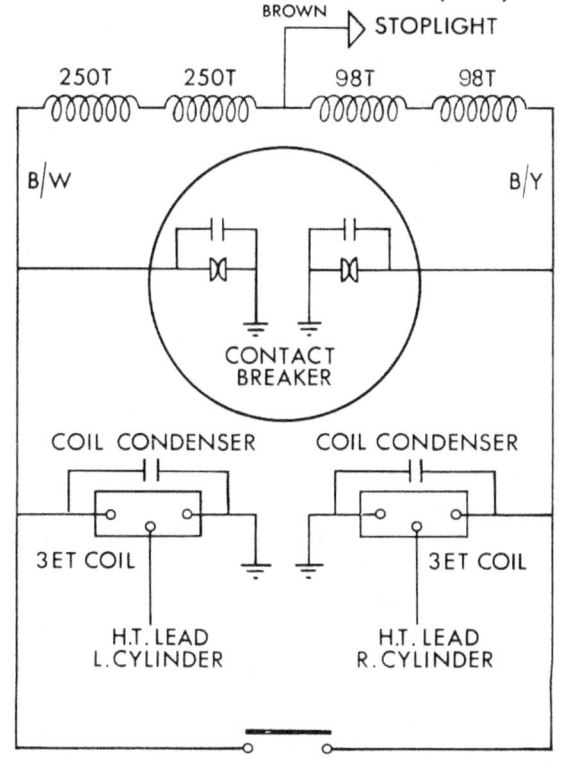

Fig. H13. Schematic illustration of A.C. ignition (E.T.) system

DESCRIPTION

The A.C. magneto (energy transfer) system consists of two 3 E.T. ignition coils, a contact breaker and an alternator specially wound for A.C. ignition and lighting. There are five leads from the alternator, two for ignition purposes and three for direct lighting purposes. The circuit diagram, Fig. H24 in Section H13 illustrates the stator oil connections.

The main features of the A.C. ignition system for twin cylinder machines is that the ignition coil and contact breaker points are connected in parallel. In practice this means that when the contacts are closed the current can flow directly to earth.

When one set of contacts open, the current has to pass through the ignition coil primary winding to earth through the second set of contacts which are arranged to be closed at the same instant. From this it can be seen that the availability of a spark at either cylinder is dependent upon both contacts being clean and adjusted correctly (see Fig. H13).

Another feature is that the E.T. system operates on a rising current in the ignition coil primary winding and not falling primary current as in the conventional coil ignition system.

H ELECTRICAL SYSTEM

H6 PART A. A.C. IGNITION

The accurate and efficient working of the A.C. ignition system is dependent not only upon the piston/spark relationship that is involved but also the rotor/stator relationship at the instant of ignition. The stator is fixed to the left crankcase and requires no maintenance other than to check that the leads are not rubbing on either of the chains. The rotor is located on the crankshaft by means of a dowel fitted to the engine sprocket. When the rotor is removed care should be taken to refit it in the appropriate position with the rotor hole located as shown in the table below, in accordance with ignition timing requirements.

Dowel Location	Ignition Timing Full-Advanced	Dowel Remarks
"S"	37° B.T.C.	Standard
"R"	41° B.T.C.	Racing
"M"	39° B.T.C.	"Mid" position

It is beyond the scope of this Manual to advise on a deviation from the standard setting, as so many factors are involved. If it is required to alter the settings from standard, then advice should be sought from a local Triumph Dealer.

The 3 E.T. coil, condensers (capacitors), and high tension leads must be kept clean and free from dirt or water. Also, it is important that the sparking plug is maintained at the correct gap setting and that the centre electrode is kept clean.

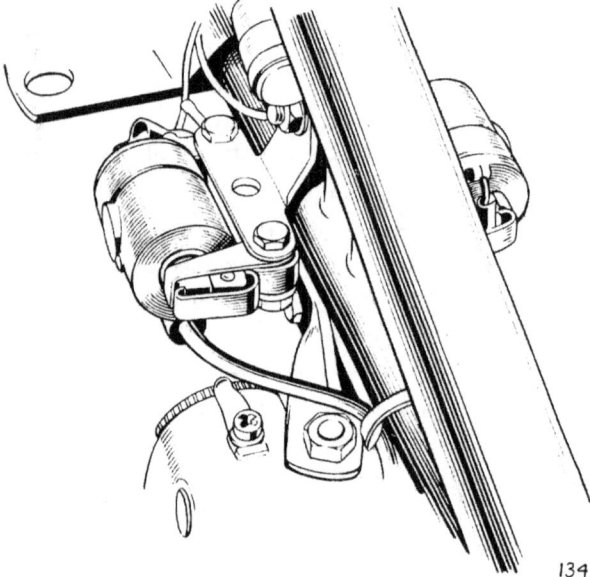

Fig. H14. A.C. ignition coils fitted on machine

Both sets of contact breaker contacts must be kept clean and adjusted correctly to the gap setting given in General Data. A fault at either set of contacts will adversely effect the ignition spark at BOTH cylinders.

H6 PART B. TESTING THE A.C. IGNITION SYSTEM

First, ensure that the timing, contact breaker and plug gaps are satisfactory, and then disconnect both H.T. leads and check that a spark is available by holding each of the cables about $\frac{3}{16}$ inches (4 mm.) from the cylinder head in turn and operate the kickstarter. A good spark should be produced. If it is not, then the 3 E.T. coil and alternator ignition supply are suspect.

As it is not possible to test the 3 E.T. coils accurately on the machine, the following test procedure should be adopted.

Two 6 volt external batteries are used for the next two tests, in conjunction with the A.C. ignition coils on the machine.

A.C. ignition coils are not designed to run under such conditions, overheating occurring in the primary windings.

Each test should be undertaken in as short a time as possible, and the batteries connected in circuit only when actually necessary to run the test.

(1) Disconnect the five alternator leads under the engine.

(2) Unplug the black/yellow lead from the condenser at the right hand side coil (under the petrol (gasolene) tank.

(3) Connect the black/yellow lead to the positive (+ve) terminal of a (6V) test battery.

(4) Connect the negative (−ve) battery lead to the condenser terminal.

(5) Unplug the black/white lead from the condenser at the left hand side coil (under the petrol (gasolene) tank).

(6) Connect the black/white lead to the positive (+ve) terminal of a second (6V) test battery.

(7) Connect the negative (−ve) terminal of the second test battery to the left hand condenser terminal.

(8) Remove the sparking plug wire from each plug in turn and with battery wires connected, open and close the contact breaker points. If the coils and condensers are satisfactory, a good spark will jump from the plug lead to earth (ground).

(9) If a poor spark (or no spark) is noted, check all wiring connections, and repeat (8) above. If the system still does not spark, instal new condensers and repeat (8). If still there is no spark, check the ignition coils by substitution.

ELECTRICAL SYSTEM

H6 PART C. CHECKING THE ALTERNATOR OUTPUT (A.C. Ignition Models)

To facilitate a check to be made on the alternator output, a separate ignition circuit must be used as given in Section H6 Part B above, so that the engine can be run at 3,000 r.p.m. (approximately 45 m.p.h. in top gear).

Pay careful regard to the warning given in the previous section (H6 part B) concerning the possible overheating of the A.C. ignition coil primary windings.

The preferred alternative method is to use two MA6 ignition coils, bolted together, with the machine's C.B. leads, BLACK/WHITE, BLACK/YELLOW connected to the appropriate C.B. terminals on the test ignition coils. The test coil S.W. terminals are linked together and fed to a test battery (−ve) negative terminal and the battery (+ve) positive connected to the ignition coils cases. A jumper lead is also required between battery (+ve) positive, and motorcycle frame earth (ground). The H.T. leads are connected to the (appropriate sparking plugs.

With all five alternator leads disconnected under the engine start up the engine and run at 3,000 r.p.m. (equivalent to approximately 45 m.p.h. in top gear). Connect an A.C. voltmeter (0–10V) with a 1 ohm resistor in parallel between the pairs of alternator leads given in table, Fig. H22 Section H12.

(i) If the readings are equal to or higher than the figures quoted for the particular model, then the alternator is satisfactory.

(ii) A low reading on any group of coils indicates either that the leads concerned are chafed through or damaged due to rubbing on the chains or that some of the coil turns are short circuited.

(iii) Low readings from all parts of the test indicates a partially demagnetized rotor. In this case the rotor must be renewed.

(iv) A zero reading for any group of coils indicates that a coil has become disconnected and is open circuit, in which case the stator should be replaced.

(v) A reading obtained between any one stator lead and earth (ground) indicates that some coil turns have become earthed (grounded) to the engine. In this case, brush the stator with paraffin (kerosene) or petrol (gasoline). DO NOT LEAVE TO SOAK. Retest on the machine. If still faulty, replace the stator.

If any fault does occur always check the stator leads for possible chain damage before attempting repair or renewing the stator. It is beyond the scope of this manual to give instruction for repair of faulty stator windings. However the winding specification is given in table Fig. H22 to provide the required information for local repair work, should a correct replacement stator not be immediately available.

H6 PART D. DIRECT LIGHTING SYSTEM

The electrical power for the direct lighting system is supplied by three of the five alternator leads, namely the red, brown and brown/blue. The leads are connected as shown in the wiring diagram (Fig. H20 in Section H11). In order that no one pair of coils is overloaded, the electrical loads are connected as shown and no deviation from the standard arrangement shown should be made.

An apparant loss or reduction of power at any of the lights may well be due to a high resistance caused by a loose or faulty connection. In the event of a fault occurring, always check the wiring connections, giving particular attention to the red earth (ground) lead from the alternator and headlamp. Note that a short circuit in the brown stop lamp lead will result in the ignition system failing, hence the stop lamp switch connections should be always kept clean and dry.

In the event of a fault occurring which cannot be traced to the circuit connections the alternator should be checked as described in Section H6, Part C above.

SECTION H7
ELECTRIC HORN

DESCRIPTION
The horn is of a high frequency single note type and is operated by direct current from the battery. (On A.C. models a similar horn specifically designed for A.C. current is fitted.) The method of operation is that of a magnetically operated armature, which impacts on the cone face, and causes the tone disc of the horn to vibrate. The magnetic circuit is made self interrupting by contacts which can be adjusted externally.

If the horn fails to work, check the mounting bolts etc., and horn connection wiring. Check the battery for state of charge. A low supply voltage at the horn will adversely effect horn performance. If the above checks are made and the fault is not remedied, then adjust the horn as follows.

HORN ADJUSTMENT
When adjusting and testing the horn, do not depress the horn push for more than a fraction of a second or the circuit wiring may be overloaded.

A small serrated adjustment screw situated near the terminals (see Fig. H15), is provided to take up wear in the internal moving parts of the horn. To adjust, turn this screw anticlockwise until the horn just fails to sound, and then turn it back (clockwise) about one quarter to half a turn.

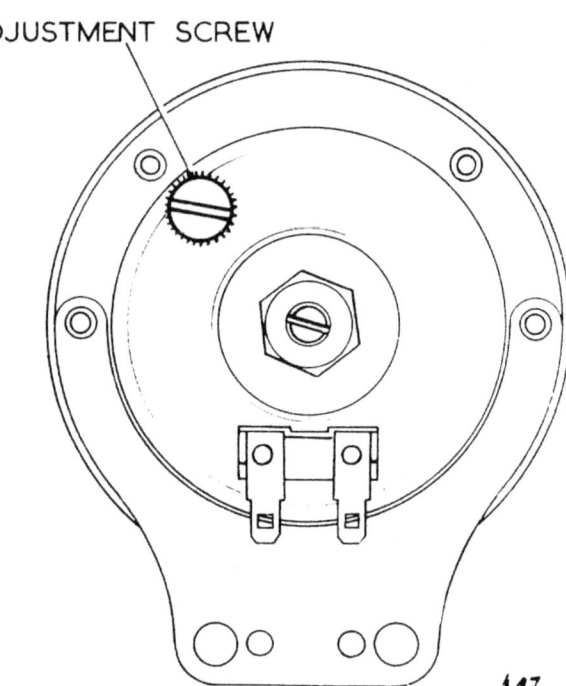

Fig. H15. Horn adjustment screw

SECTION H8
HEADLAMP

DESCRIPTION
The headlamp is of the sealed beam unit type and access is gained to the bulb and bulb holder by withdrawing the rim and beam unit assembly. To do this on 3TA and 5TA models, slacken the screw at the top of the nacelle cover adjacent to the speedometer and prise off the rim and beam unit assembly. Slacken the screw at the top of the headlamp on the T90 and T100 to remove the light unit. The bulb can be removed by first pressing the cylindrical cap inwards and turning it anticlockwise. The cap can then be withdrawn and the bulb is free to be removed.

When fitting a new bulb, note that it locates by means of a cutaway and projection arrangement. also note that the cap can only be replaced one way, the tabs being staggered to prevent incorrect reassembly. Check the replacement bulb voltage and wattage specification and type before fitting.

Focusing with this type of beam unit is unnecessary and there is no provision for such.

BEAM ADJUSTMENTS
The beam must in all cases be adjusted as specified by local lighting regulations. In the United Kingdom the Transport Lighting Regulations reads as follows:—

A lighting system must be arranged so that it can give a light which is incapable of dazzling any person standing on the same horizontal plane as the vehicle at a greater distance than twenty five feet from the lamp, whose eye level is not less than three feet—six inches above that plane.

The headlamp must therefore be set so that the main beam is directed straight ahead and parallel with the road when the motorcycle is fully loaded. To achieve this, place the machine on a level road pointing towards a wall at a distance of 25 feet away, with a rider and passenger on the machine, slacken the two small screws on the adaptor rim at either side and tilt the beam unit until the beam is focused at approximately two feet six inches from the base of the wall. Do not forget that the headlamp should be on "full beam" lighting during this operation.

ELECTRICAL SYSTEM   H

SECTION H9
TAIL AND STOP LAMP UNIT

Access to the bulbs in the tail and stop lamp unit is achieved by unscrewing the two slotted screws which secure the lens. The bulb is of the double-filament offset pin type and when a replacement is carried out, ensure that the bulb is fitted correctly. Check that the two supply leads are connected correctly and check the earth (ground) lead to the bulb holder is in satisfactory condition.

When refitting the lens, do not overtighten the fixing screws or the lens may fracture as a result.

See also Section H18 Tail and Stoplamp unit, and Fig. H34 Access to tail/stop light and direction indicator bulbs.

SECTION H10
FUSES

The fuse is to be found on the earth lead from the battery positive terminal on later models. It is housed in a quickly detachable shell and is of 35 amp fuse rating.

Before following any fault location procedure always check that the fuse is not the source of the fault. A new fuse-cartridge should be fitted if there is any doubt about the old one.

A fuse can be fitted to any Triumph coil ignition model and all that is required is a small proprietary fuse holder obtainable from most Triumph Dealers. In all cases the fuse rating must not under any circumstances be below 35 amp. rating and must be fitted on the earth lead between earth (ground) and the battery positive terminal.

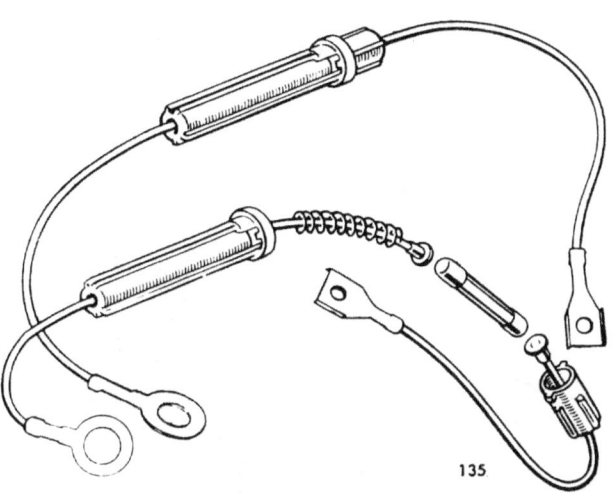

Fig. H16. Exploded view of fuseholder assembly

SECTION H11
IGNITION CUT-OUT ("KILL") BUTTON

An emergency cut-out (kill) button is provided. This is mounted on the handlebar and can be used to stop or "kill" the engine.

NOTE: Two types of cut-out buttons are in current use, one for coil ignition machines and one for A.C. magneto equipped machines. Although both cut-out buttons appear identical externally, the internal connections are arranged differently. They must not be interchanged and if a replacement is required, refer to the appropriate replacement parts list.

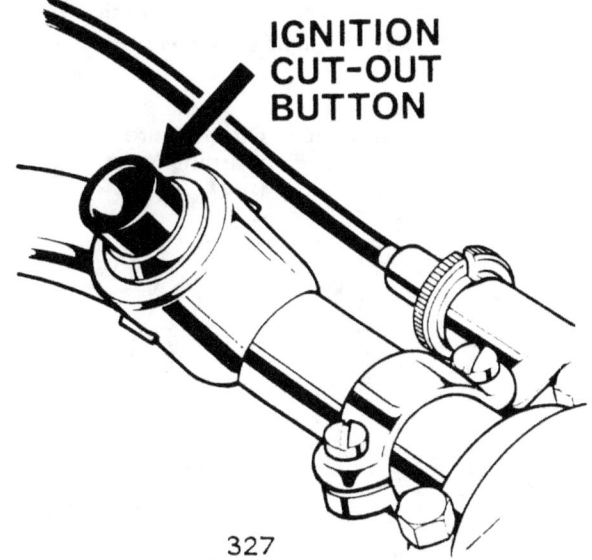

Fig. H17. Ignition cut-out button

SECTION H12
WARNING LAMPS

IGNITION WARNING LAMP

Two warning lamps are incorporated in the T90 and T100S electrical system. One is to warn the rider that he has omitted to switch off the ignition with the key provided. The lamp remains alight whilst the ignition is turned on whether or not the engine is running. It is not intended to act as a "no charge" lamp as in automobile practice.

NOTE: On earlier machines where an ignition warning lamp only is fitted, this is coloured red. On current machines fitted with both the ignition and main beam warning lamps, the ignition lamp is coloured green.

MAIN BEAM WARNING LAMP (where fitted)

The main beam indicator lamp is incorporated in the headlamp unit and is illuminated when the main beam is in use. The colour of the lamp is red, whether fitted by itself (A.C. Magneto models) or with the ignition warning lamp.

Warning lamps are fitted into the headlamp shell on all models.

Machines having the oil pressure switch have the red warning light connected to this switch. This means that the warning light shows as soon as the

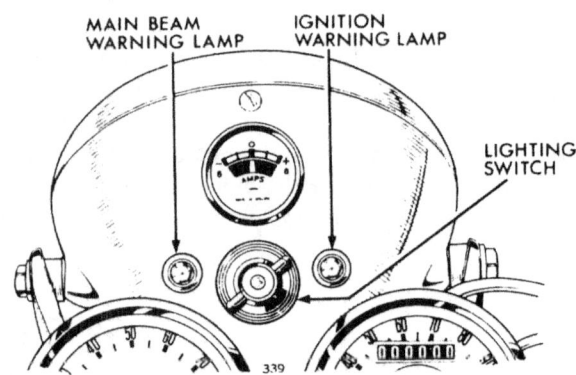

Fig. H18. Location of ignition and main beam warning lamps (T90 and T100SS)

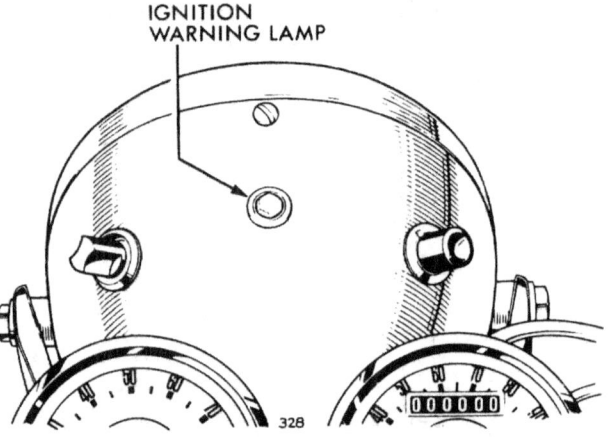

Fig. H19. Location of main beam warning lamp (A.C. magneto models only)

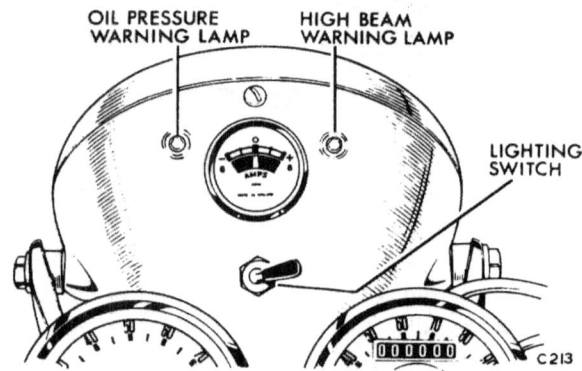

Fig. HH2. Headlamp T100S, T100T, T100R

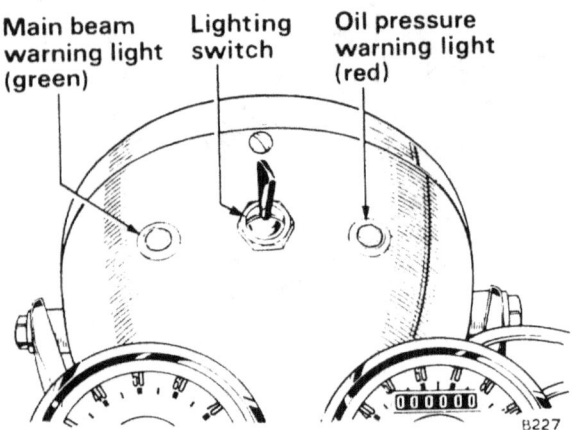

Fig. HH1. Headlamp. T100C

ignition is turned on with the engine stationary, but extinguishes as the oil pressure increases after the engine is started. The switch is pre-set to disconnect at 7–11 lb./sq. in.

The green warning light indicates the high beam. The bulb for each warning light is detachable from inside the headlamp shell.

ELECTRICAL SYSTEM

SECTION H13
WIRING DIAGRAM

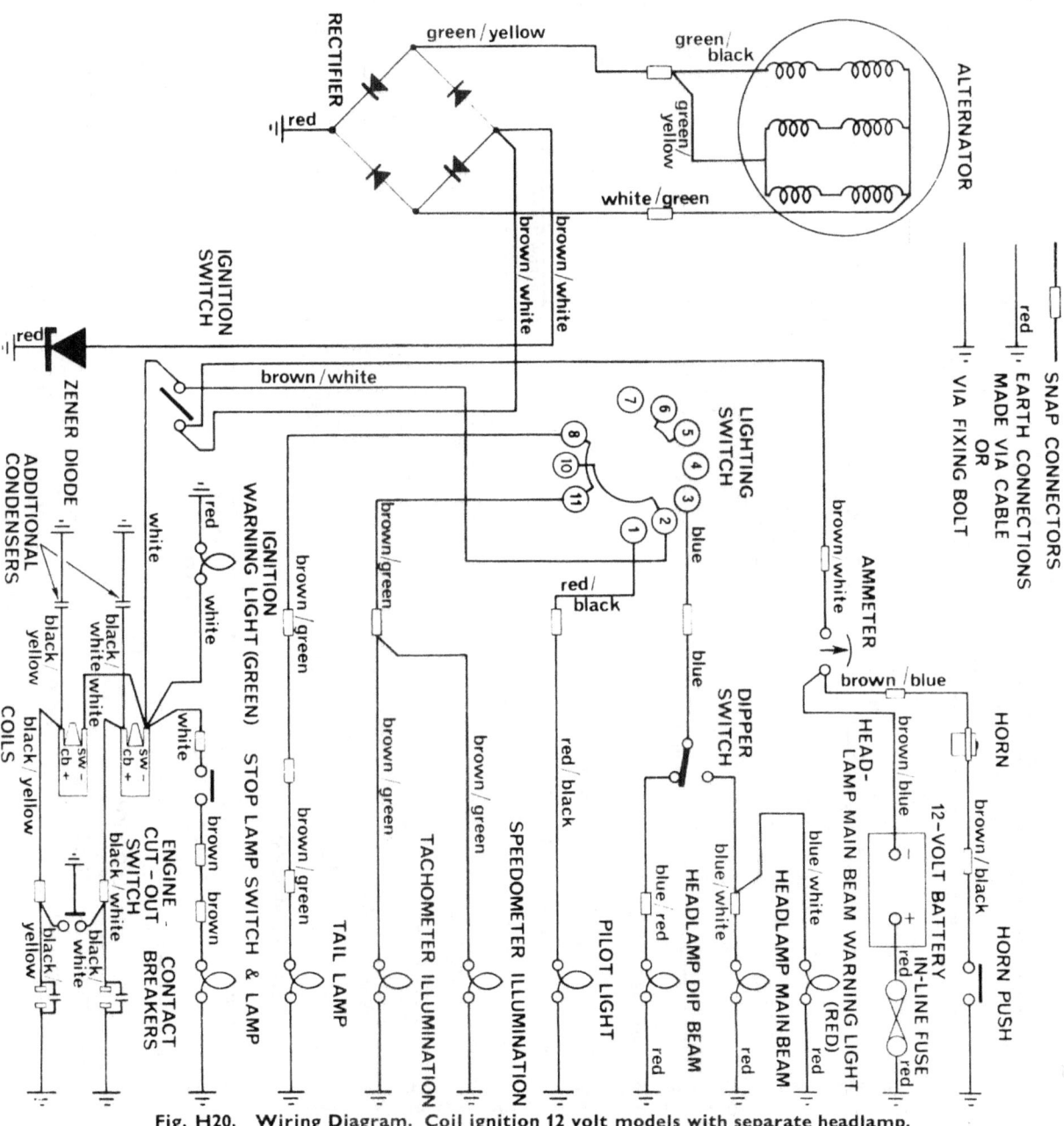

Fig. H20. Wiring Diagram. Coil ignition 12 volt models with separate headlamp. Engine number H.49833 onwards (U.S.A.)

Note. The main beam warning lamp (where fitted) is connected to the headlamp main beam wire (blue/white) by a double snap connector. The ignition warning lamp is connected to an ignition coil by a white wire incorporated in the wiring harness.

ELECTRICAL SYSTEM

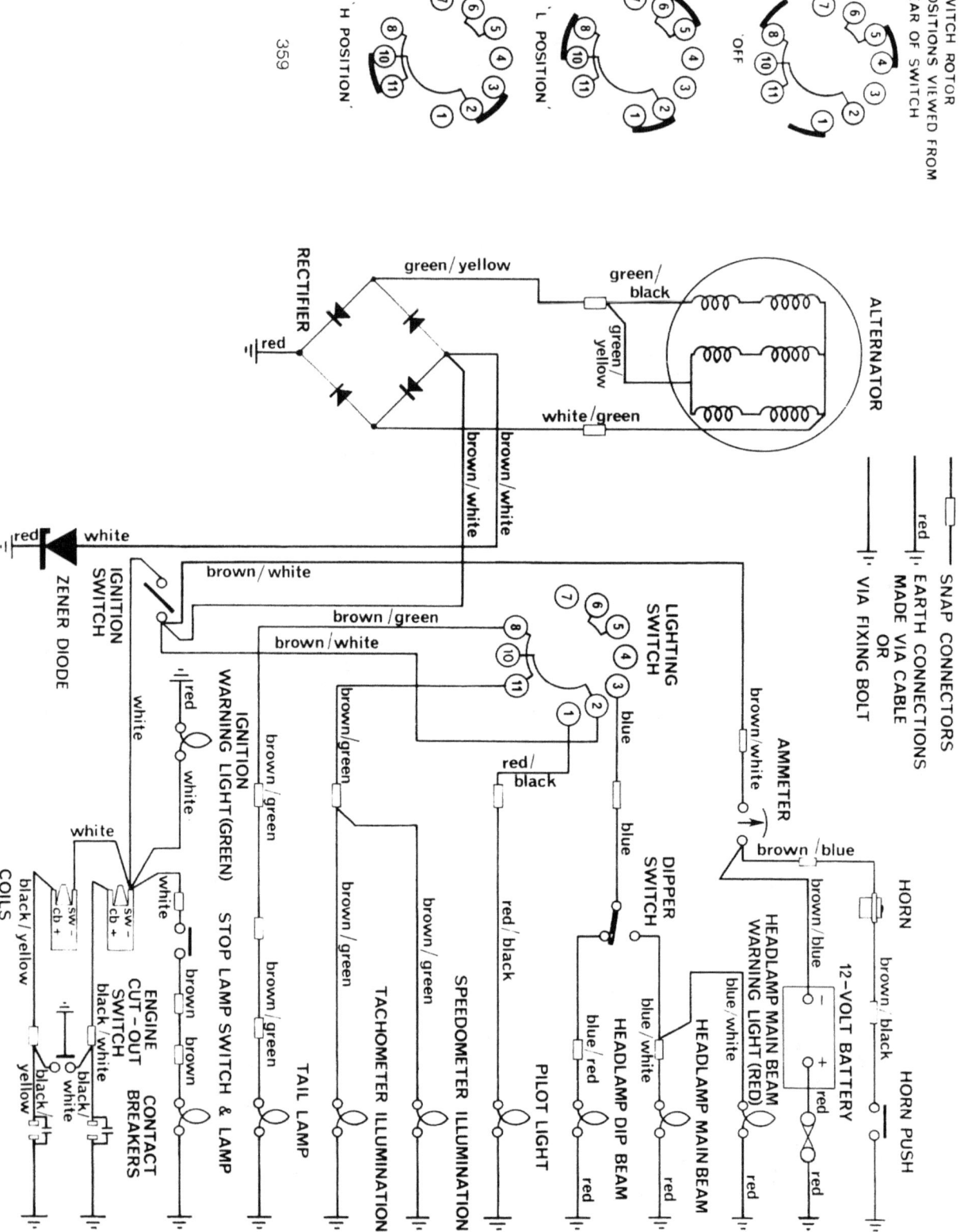

Fig. H21. Wiring diagram. Coil ignition 12 volt models with separate headlamp
Engine number H.49833 onwards (Home market)

Note. The main beam warning lamp (where fitted) is connected to the headlamp main beam wire (blue/white) by a double snap connector. The ignition warning lamp is connected to an ignition coil by a white wire incorporated in the wiring harness.

ELECTRICAL SYSTEM

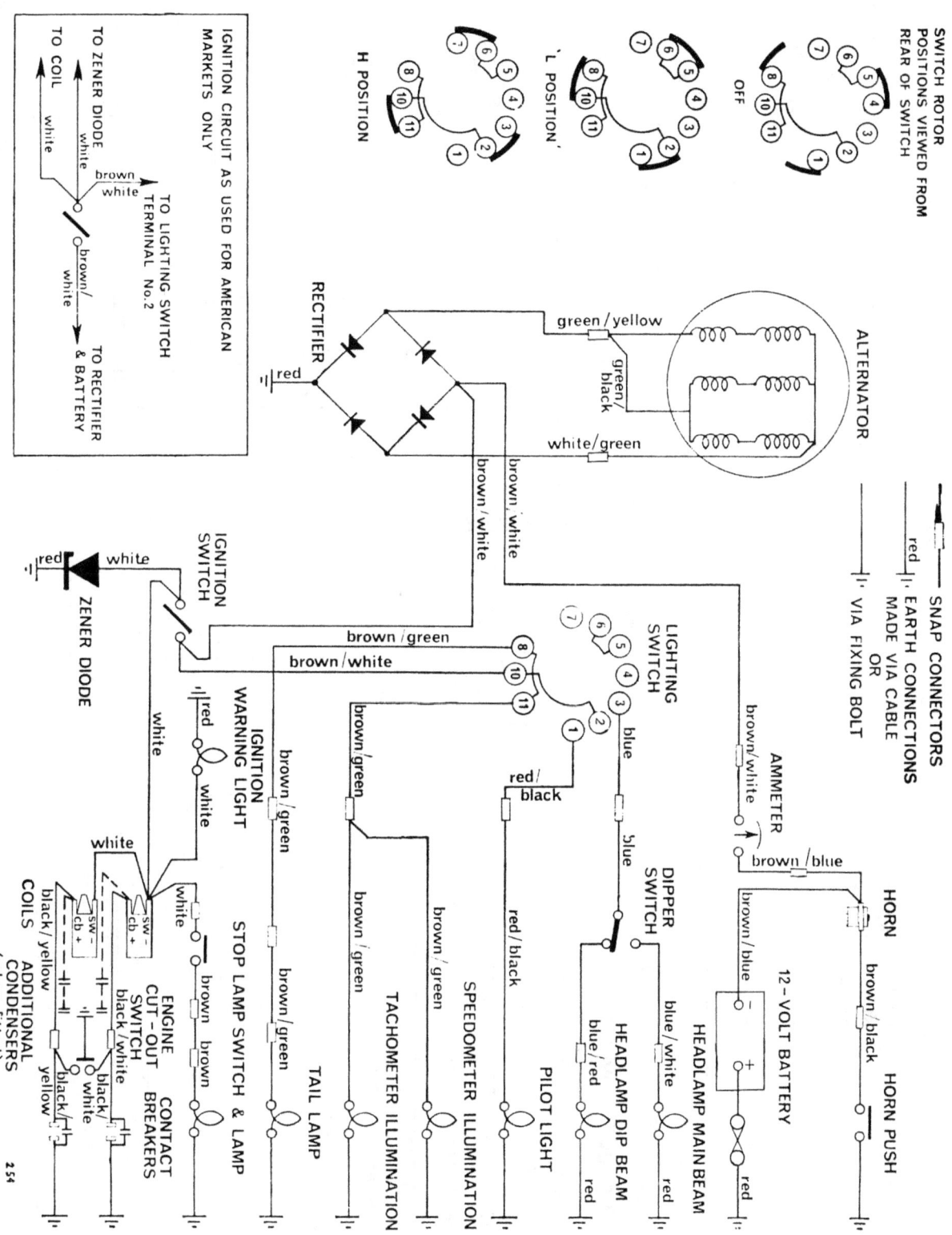

Fig. H22. Wiring diagram—Coil ignition 12 volt models without nacelle up to H.49832 (Home and Export)

Note. The main beam warning lamp (where fitted) is connected to the headlamp main beam wire (blue/white) by a double snap connector. The ignition warning lamp is connected to an ignition coil by a white wire incorporated in the wiring harness.

H ELECTRICAL SYSTEM

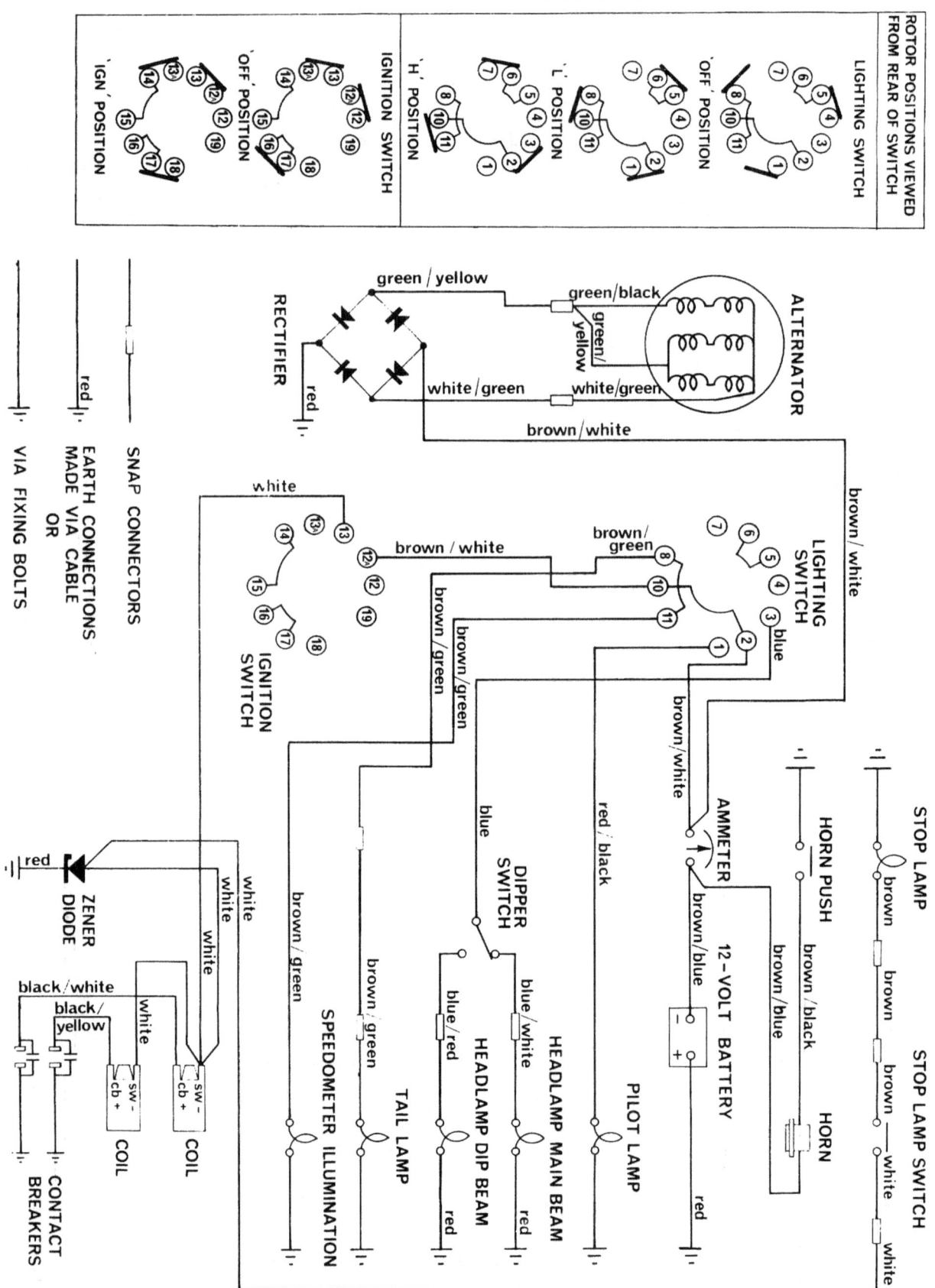

Fig. H19. Wiring diagram—Coil ignition 12volt models with nacelle

Note. The main beam warning lamp (where fitted) is connected to the headlamp main beam wire (blue/white) by a double snap connector. The ignition warning lamp is connected to an ignition coil by a white wire incorporated in the wiring harness.

ELECTRICAL SYSTEM

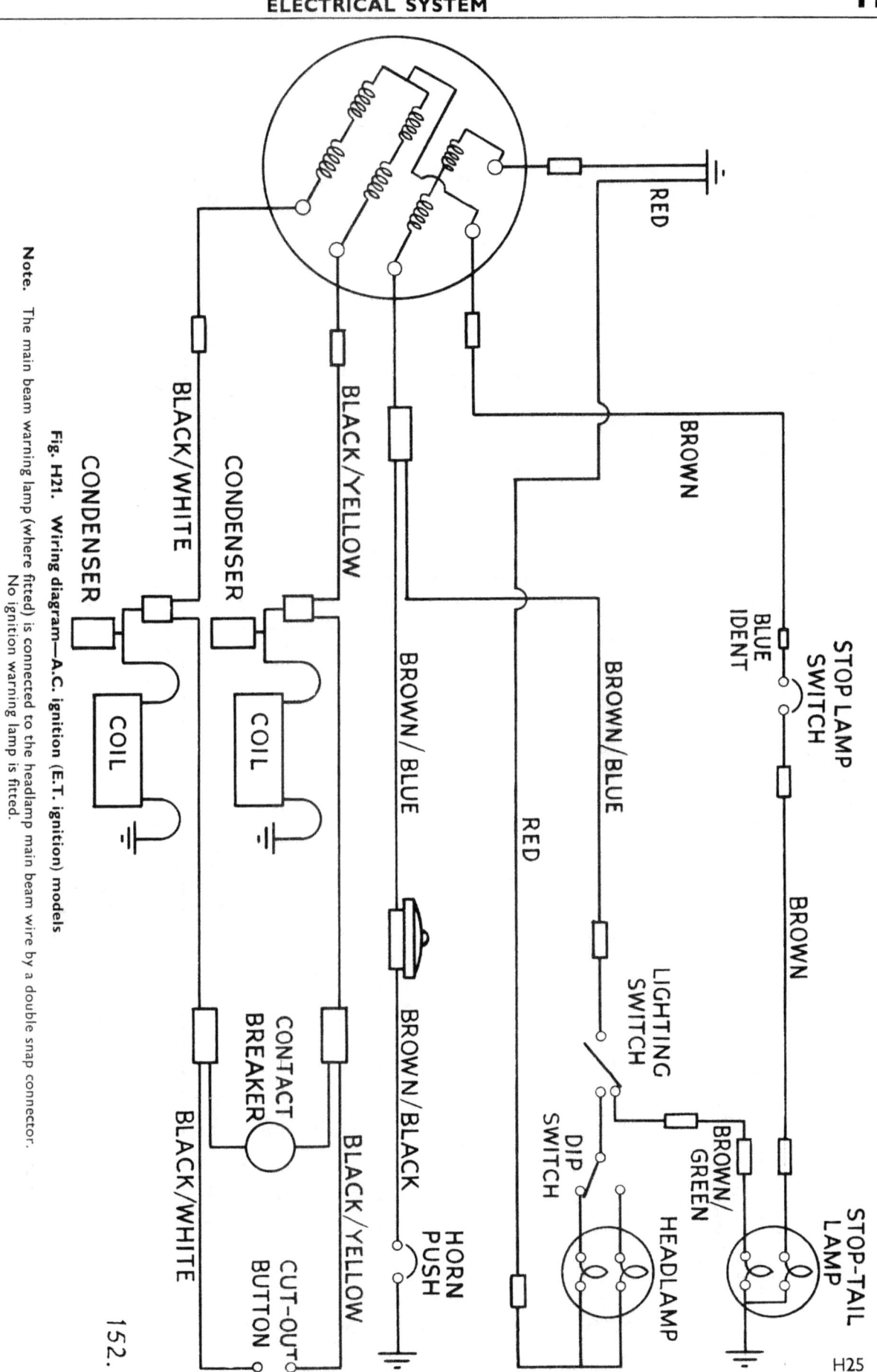

Fig. H21. Wiring diagram—A.C. ignition (E.T. ignition) models

Note. The main beam warning lamp (where fitted) is connected to the headlamp main beam wire by a double snap connector. No ignition warning lamp is fitted.

ELECTRICAL SYSTEM

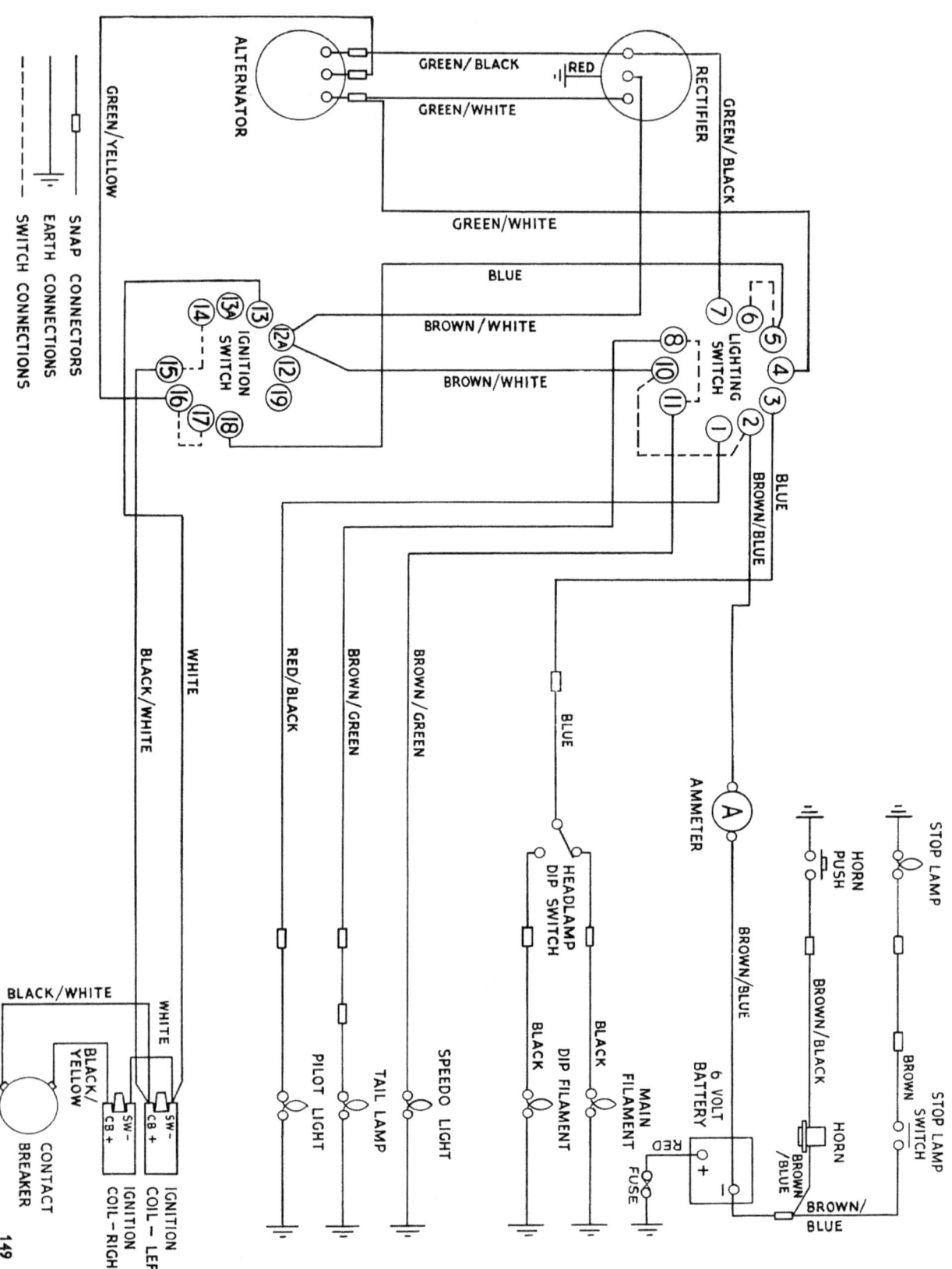

Fig. H25. Wiring diagram—Coil ignition 6V models

ELECTRICAL SYSTEM — H

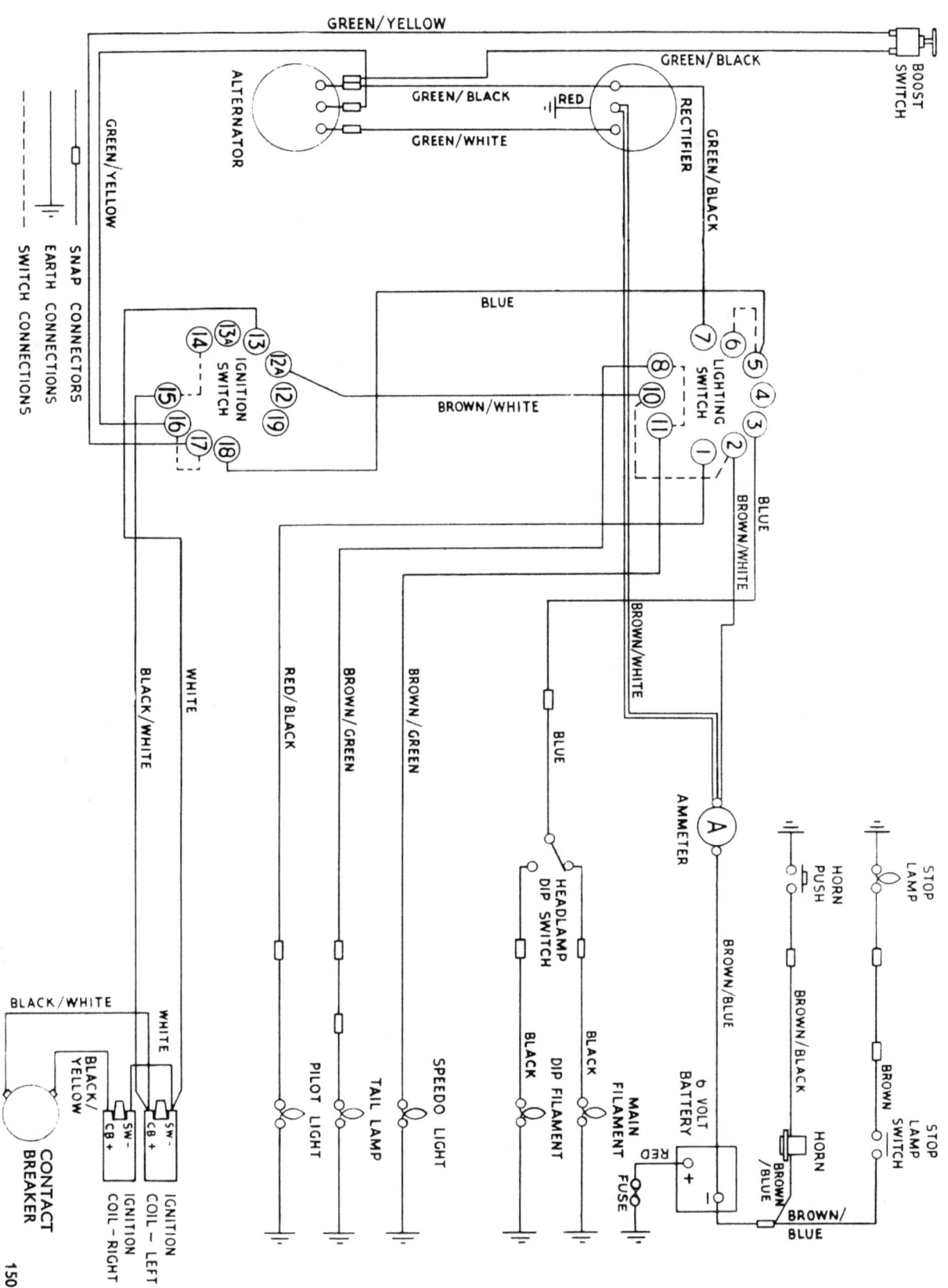

Fig. H26. Wiring diagram—Coil ignition 6V Police models with boost-switch

ELECTRICAL SYSTEM

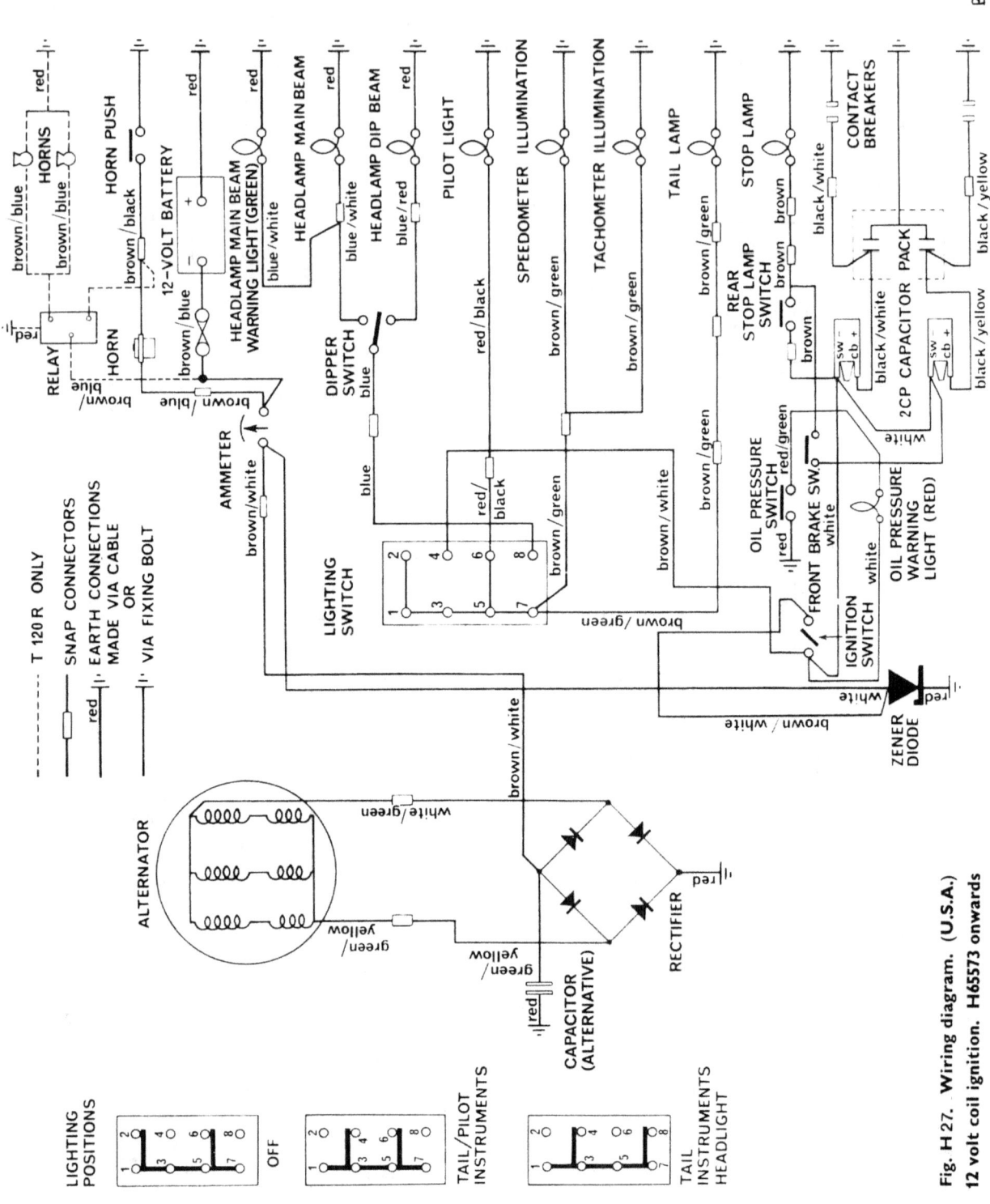

Fig. H 27. Wiring diagram. (U.S.A.)
12 volt coil ignition. H65573 onwards

ELECTRICAL SYSTEM

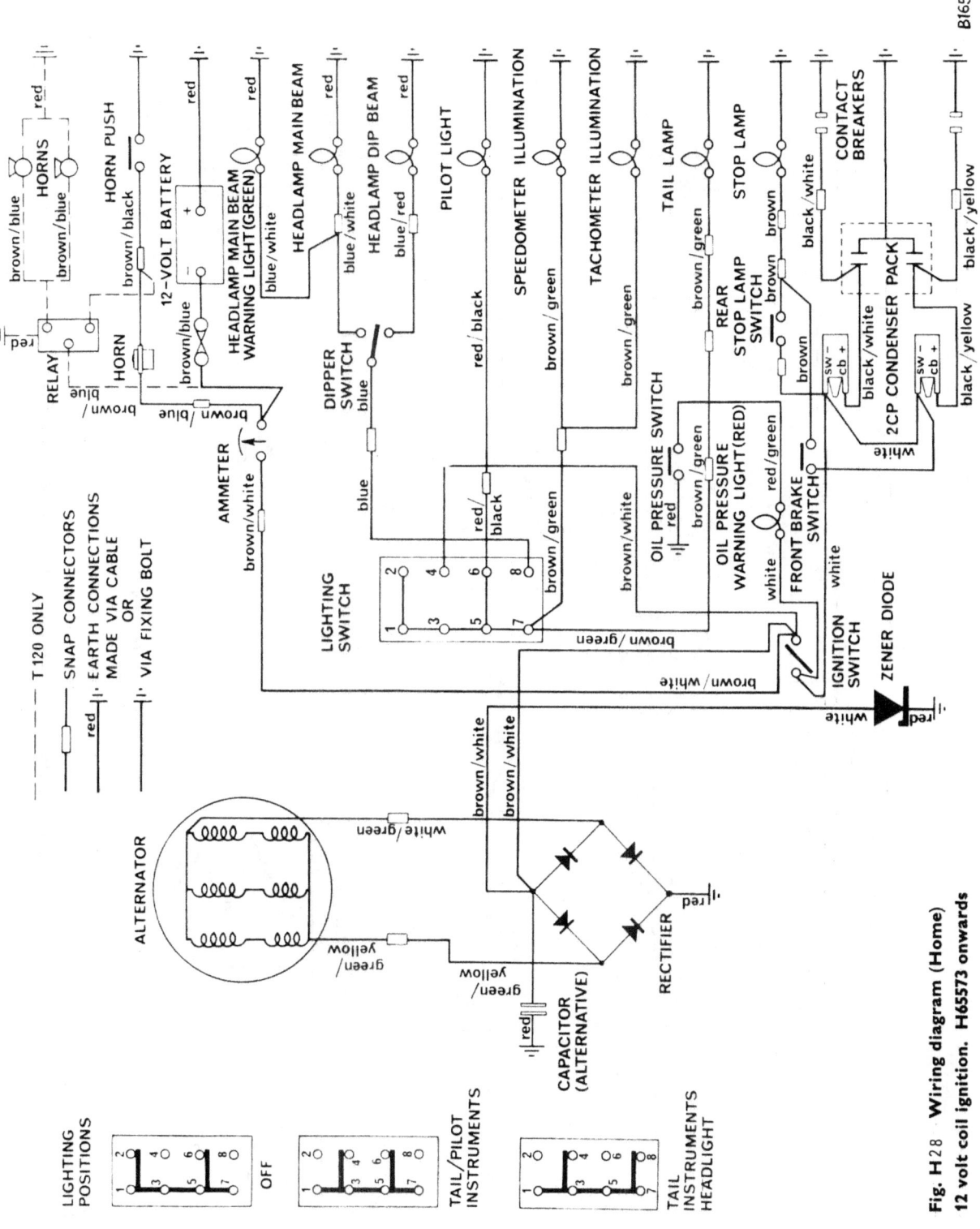

Fig. H28 Wiring diagram (Home)
12 volt coil ignition. H65573 onwards

H ELECTRICAL SYSTEM

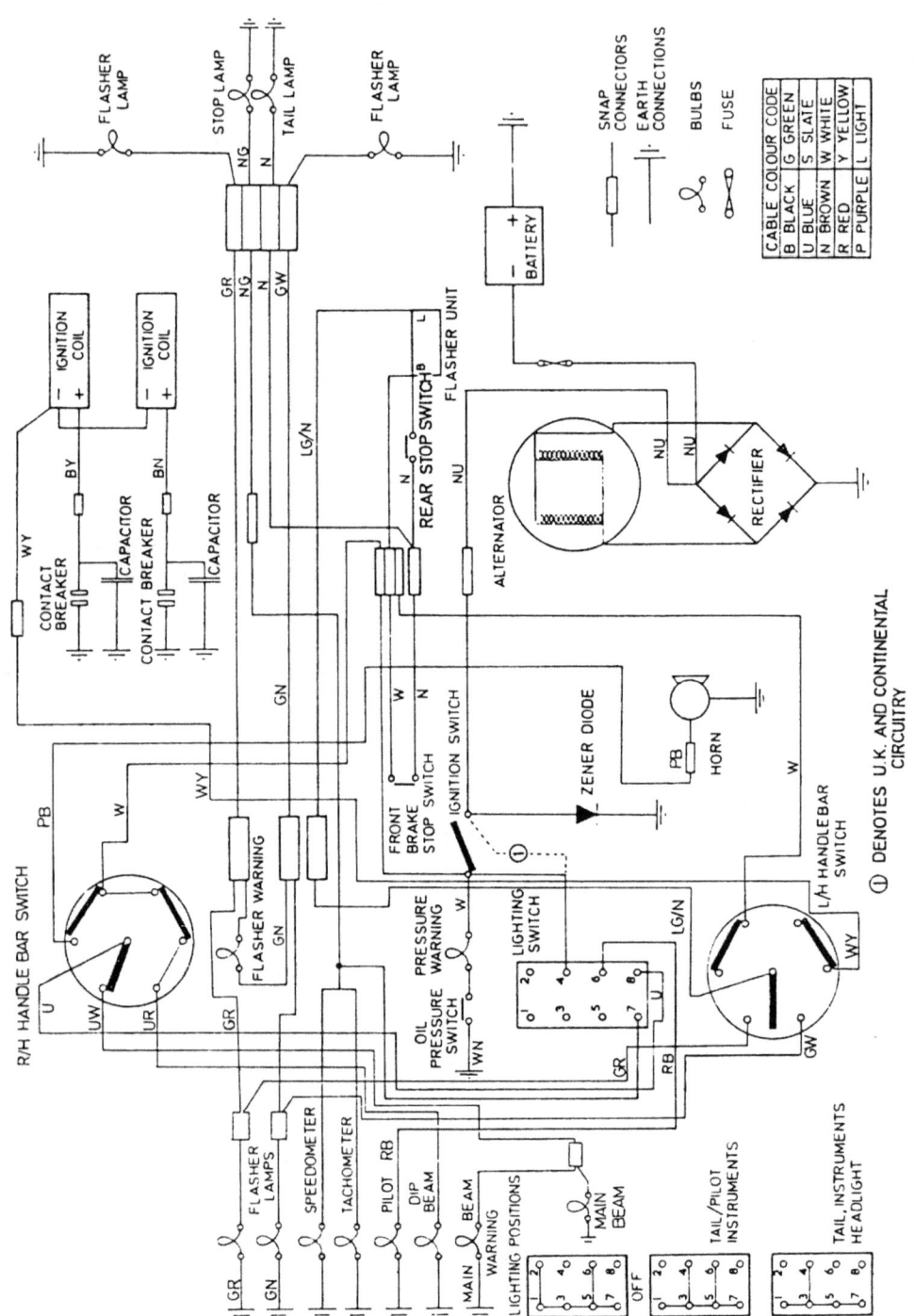

Fig. H29. Wiring diagram (12 volt-coil ignition) KE00001 onwards

ELECTRICAL SYSTEM

SECTION H14
ALTERNATOR AND STATOR DETAILS—
SPECIFICATIONS AND OUTPUT FIGURES

MODELS	System voltage	Ignition type	Alternator type	Stator No.
3TA, 5TA, T90, T100	12 V.	Coil	RM.19	47162
3TA, 5TA, T90, T100	6 V.	Coil	RM.19	47162
3TA, 5TA (POLICE)	6 V.	Coil	RM19/20	47167
T90, T100 (E.T.)	6 V.	A.C. IGN	RM.19	47188
T100C, T100R	12 V.	Coil	RM.21	47205

Stator number	System voltage	D.C. input to battery amp. @ 3,000 r.p.m.			Alternator Output minimum A.C. volts @ 3,000 r.p.m.			Stator coil details		
		Off	Pilot	Head	A	B	C	No of coils	Turns per coil	S.W.G.
47162	6 V.	2·75	2·0	2·0	4·0	6·5	8·5	6	140	22
	12 V.	2·0*	2·1*	1·5*						
		4·8†	3·8†	1·8†						
47164	6 V.	2·7	0·9	1·6	4·5	7·0	9·5	6	122	21
47167	6 V.	6·6‡	6·6‡	13·6‡	7·7	11·6	13·2	6	74	19
47188	6 V.	Not applicable			5·0	1·5	IGN. 3·5 LIGHTS	2	250	25
								2	98	20
								1	98	20
								1	98	21

Coil Ignition Machines
  A = Green/White and Green/Black
  B = Green/White and Green/Yellow
  C = Green/White and { Green/Black / Green/Yellow } connected

* Zener in Circuit
† Zener disconnected
‡ With Boost Switch in Circuit

A.C. Ignition Machines
  A = Red and Brown/Blue
  B = Black/Yellow and Black/White
  C = Black/Yellow and Brown

Fig. H30. Alternator – minimum output and stator details

NOTES

SECTION HH

ELECTRICAL SYSTEM

	Section
LEFT AND RIGHT HANDLEBAR CONTROLS	H15
IGNITION SWITCH	H16
STOP LAMP SWITCHES	H17
TAIL AND STOP LAMP UNIT	H18
FLASHER LAMPS	H19
OIL PRESSURE SWITCH	H20
ZENER DIODE LOCATION	H21
IGNITION COILS, LUCAS TYPE 17M12	H22
CONDENSER PACK 2 CP	H23

ELECTRICAL SYSTEM

SECTION H15

LEFT AND RIGHT HANDLE BAR CONTROLS

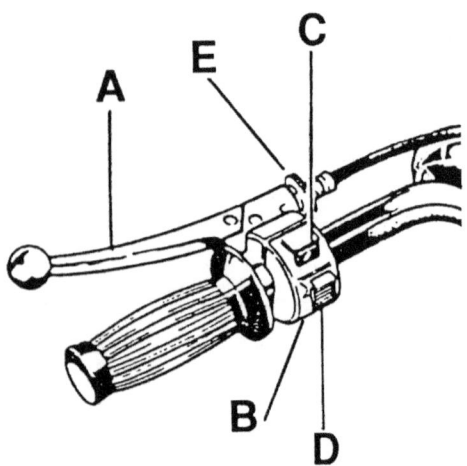

Fig. H31. The left handlebar controls

1971 Models

A Front brake lever
B Engine 'Kill' button
C Direction indicator switch
D Not used
E Twist grip
F Throttle stop screw
G Friction adjuster

1972/3/4 Models

A Front brake lever
B Headlamp flasher
C Dipswitch
D Horn push
E Twist grip
F Throttle stop screw
G Friction adjuster

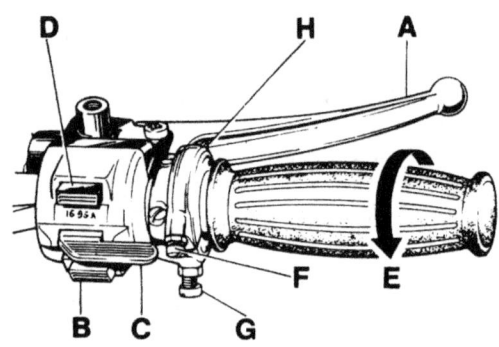

1971 Models

A Clutch lever
B Horn push
C Headlight flasher
D Dipswitch
E Clutch cable adjuster

1972/3/4 Models

A Clutch lever
B Not used
C Engine 'Kill' switch
D Direction indicator switch
E Clutch cable adjuster

Fig. H32. The right handlebar switch

SECTION H16
IGNITION SWITCH

All models are fitted with an ignition switch incorporating a "barrel" type lock. These locks use individual "Yale" type keys and render the ignition circuit inoperative when the switch is turned off and the key removed. It is advisable for the owner to note the number stamped on the key to ensure a correct replacement in the event of the key being lost.

Three Lucar connectors are incorporated in the switch and these should be checked from time to time to ensure good electrical contact. The switch body can be released from the headlamp bracket or switch panel by removing the large nut retaining the switch in the panel and the switch pushed out.

The battery leads should be removed before attempting to remove the switch to avoid a short circuit.

The lock is retained in the body of the switch by a spring loaded plunger. This can be depressed with a pointed instrument through a small hole in the

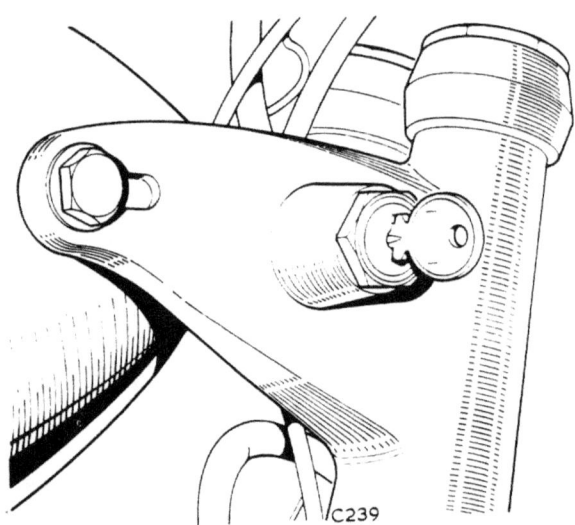

Fig. H33. Ignition switch in position

side of the switch body and the lock assembly withdrawn after the lock and switch together have been detached from the machine.

ELECTRICAL SYSTEM

SECTION H17
STOP LAMP SWITCHES

The front and rear stop lamp switches are both sealed units requiring no maintenance other than a routine check on security and cleanliness of the terminals. The front switch is fitted into the front brake cable below the headlamp unit. It cannot be removed without stripping the cable after removal of one nipple.

The rear stop switch is fitted to the rear chainguard, and any adjustment should be made with the clip on the rear brake rod to which is fixed the operating spring.

SECTION H18
TAIL AND STOP LAMP UNIT

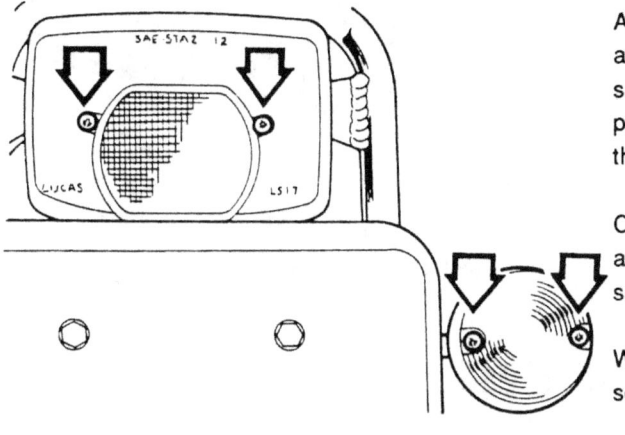

Access to the bulbs in the tail and stop lamp unit is achieved by unscrewing the two slotted screws which secure the lens. The bulb is of the double-filament offset pin type and when a replacement is carried out, ensure that the bulb is fitted correctly.

Check that the two supply leads are connected correctly and check the ground (earth) lead to the bulb holder is in satisfactory condition.

When refitting the lens, do not overtighten the fixing screws or the lens may fracture as a result.

Fig. H34. Access to tail/stop light and direction indicator bulbs

SECTION H19
FLASHER LAMPS

Access to the bulb in the flasher lamp can be obtained by unscrewing the two cross head screws. To remove the bulb, depress inwards and turn anticlockwise. When replacing the bulb make sure it is securely fitted.

REMOVING AND REFITTING FRONT FLASHER LAMPS

Remove headlamp rim and light unit (See Section H8). Disconnect the green/white wire from the snap connector. Remove the flasher lamp by slackening the locking nut and turning the lamp unit anticlockwise.

Finally pull the wire through the flasher lamp stalk. When refitting, check the general data for locking nut torque.

REMOVING AND REFITTING REAR FLASHER LAMPS

Disconnect the battery terminals, and remove the tail lamp support. Disconnect the green/white or green/red wires at the Snap Connectors and proceed as in the removal of the front flasher unit.

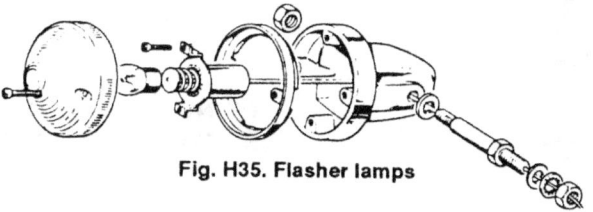

Fig. H35. Flasher lamps

SECTION H20

OIL PRESSURE SWITCH

The oil pressure switch is a sealed unit fitted into the front of the timing cover on all models.

The switch is designed to operate at 7-11 lb./sq. in. at which stage the warning light will be extinguished.

There is no simple method of checking the operation of the switch except by substitution.

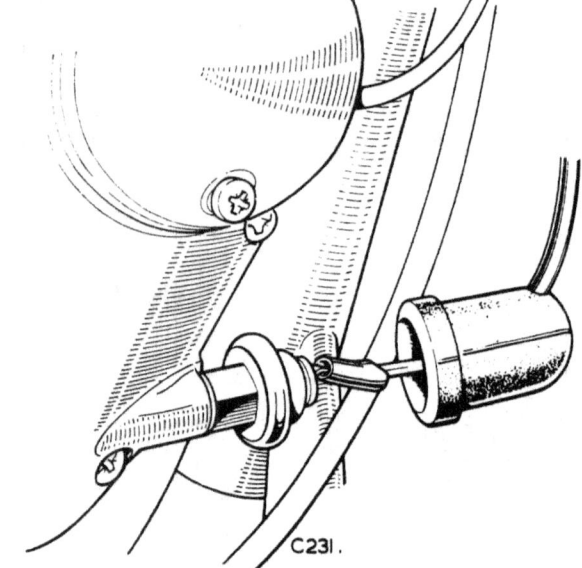

Fig. H36. Location of oil pressure switch

SECTION H21

ZENER DIODE LOCATION

The Zener Diode ("A" Fig. H37) is mounted on a bracket below the headlamp, and the aluminium heat-sink ("B" Fig. H37) is finned to assist cooling. The order of assembly is shown in Fig. H37.

To remove diode only, disconnect the brown/blue double "Lucar" connector from the diode. Remove the black plastic plug from the front of the heat sink (See Fig. H37.) and unscrew the "nyloc" nut which secures the Diode. When refitting, the Diode nut must be tightened with extreme care. (Maximum tightening torque 22/28 lb./in.)

Take off the finned heat sink, remove the front bolt from the retaining bracket. A double red (ground) earth wire is attached at this point.

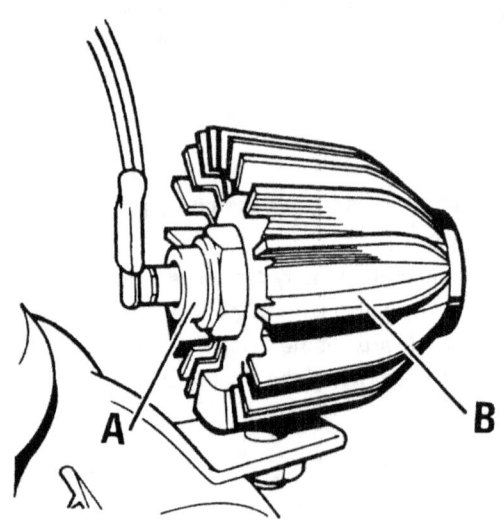

Fig. 37. Finned heatsink

DO NOT ATTACH THE (GROUND) EARTH LEADS BETWEEN THE DIODE BODY AND HEATSINK

ELECTRICAL SYSTEM

SECTION H22

Ignition coils, Lucas Type 17M12

The twin ignition coils are mounted to the frame beneath the gas tank. Keep the tops of the coils clean particularly beneath the electric terminals. Inspect the cables for frayed wires or damaged insulation. Any damaged section of cable must be replaced. The coils should be positioned so they cannot short circuit against the fuel tank.

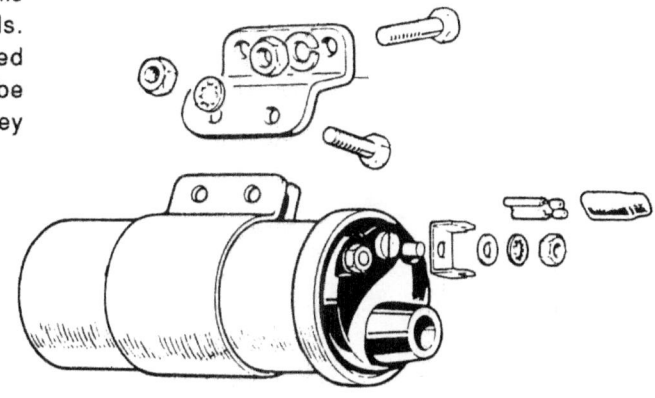

Fig. H38. Lucas Type 17M12 Ignition coil

SECTION H23

CONDENSER PACK 2 CP

The two condensers are mounted on a common plate with a rubber shroud. The condenser pack is located beneath the forward petrol tank mountings. Ensure that the connections, especially the earthing tag, are clean and tight.

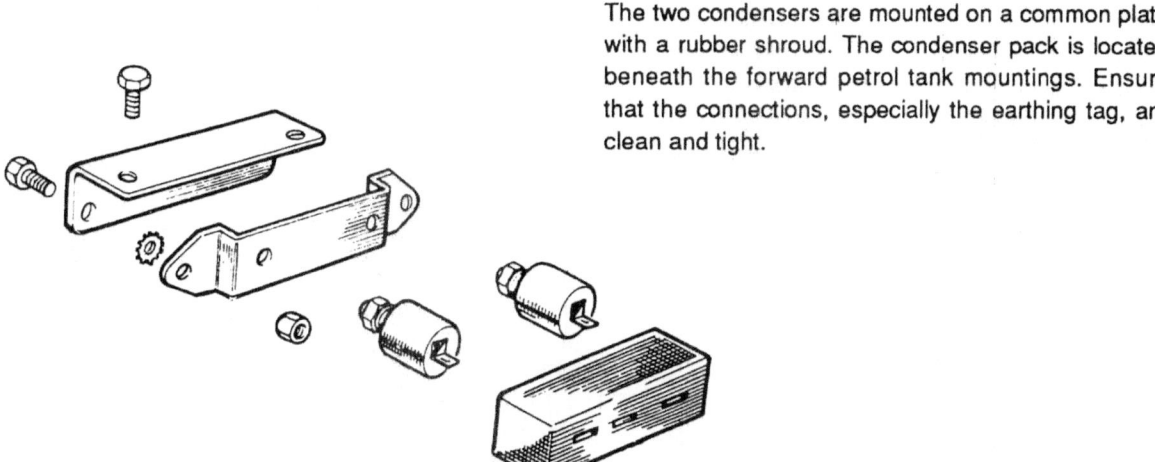

Fig. H39. Lucas Type 2 CP Condenser pack

NOTES

SECTION J

WORKSHOP SERVICE TOOLS

INTRODUCTION

This section of the Workshop Manual illustrates pictorially the workshop service tools that are available for carrying out the major dismantling and re-assembly operations on the UNIT CONSTRUCTION 350/500 c.c. Triumph Motorcycle.

The section is divided into sub-sections relating to the main section headings in this manual, illustrating those tools mentioned and used in the appropriate section text.

	Section
ENGINE	J1
TRANSMISSION	J2
WHEELS	J3
FRONT FORKS	J4
MOTORCYCLE TOOLKIT	J5

SECTION J1
ENGINE

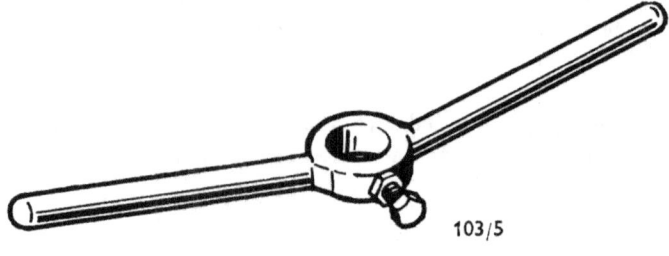

Z69. Die holder

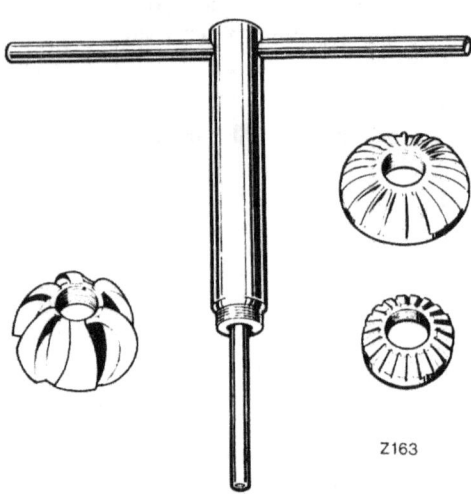

Z48 Spherical blending cutter 350 c.c. twins
Z49   ,,   ,,   ,,   500 c.c. twins
Z51 Valve seat cutting tool 350 c.c. twins
Z52   ,,   ,,   ,,   ,,   500 c.c. twins
Z54 Abor and Pilot for use with above
Z163 Blending cutter

Z144. Replacer adaptor
(Used with Z89)

Z145. Extractor adaptor
(Used with Z89)

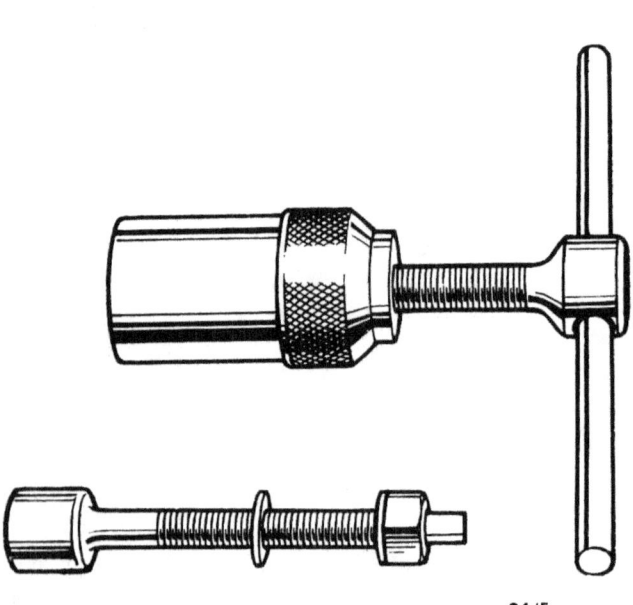

Z89. Camshaft pinion remover and replacer

SERVICE TOOLS

ENGINE (CONTINUED) J1

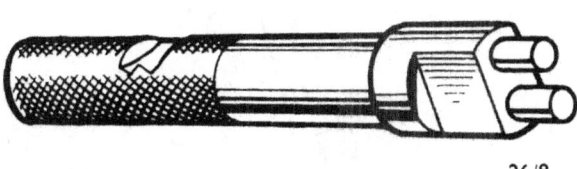

Z23. Tappet guide block punch

Z133 Drive shaft sleeve

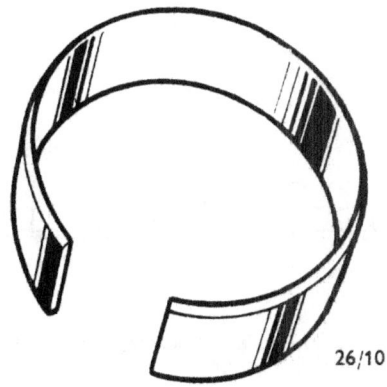

Z130 350 c.c. Piston ring collar
Z130 500 c.c. Piston ring collar

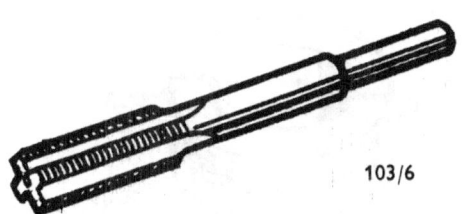

Z73. 14 mm. tap

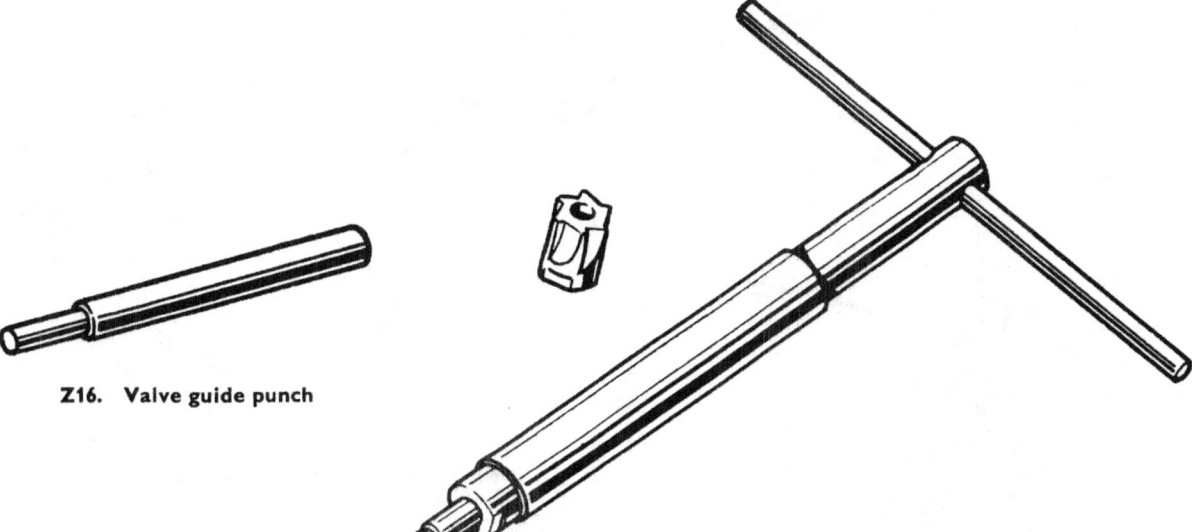

Z16. Valve guide punch

Z55. Left side reamer, camshaft bushes
Z56. Arbor for left side reamer, camshaft bushes

ENGINE (CONTINUED) J1

D484. Contact breaker cam extractor

D486. Pilot for contact breaker oil seal when replacing timing cover

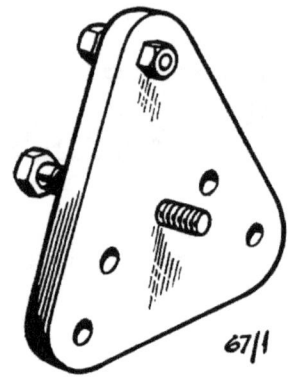

Z151. Crankcase parting tool and sprocket extractor

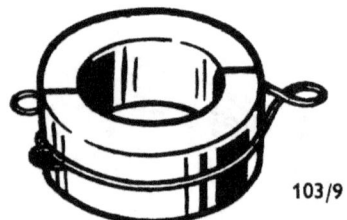

Z122. Crankshaft balance weight (490 gms.) with Z107 spring

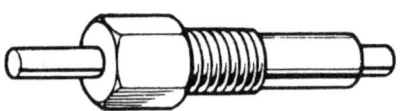

D571. T.D.C. Locating Tool body
D572. Plunger

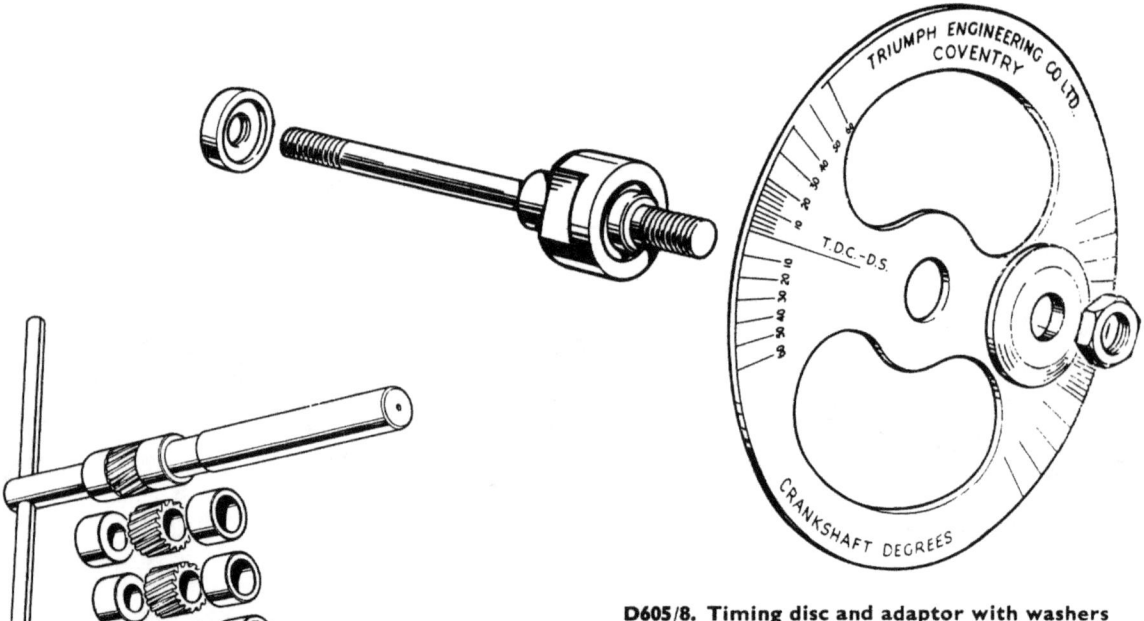

Z128. R/H main bearing line reamer

D605/8. Timing disc and adaptor with washers
S1—51 Nut

SERVICE TOOLS   J

ENGINE (CONTINUED) J1

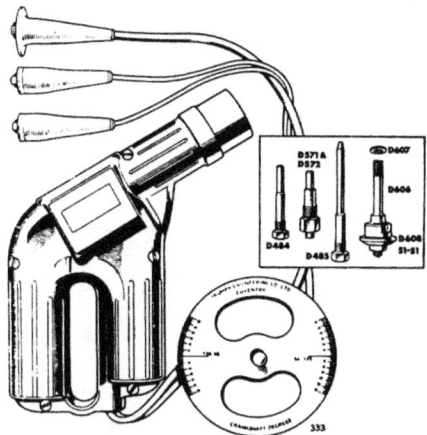

CP207. Stroboscope timing kit

SECTION J2
TRANSMISSION

D662/3. Clutch hub extractor

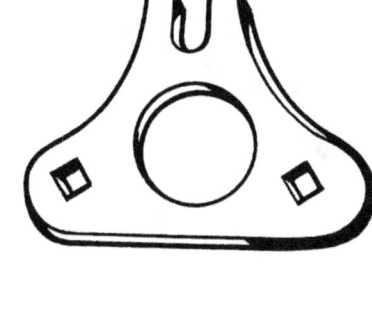

DA70. Clutch nut screwdriver

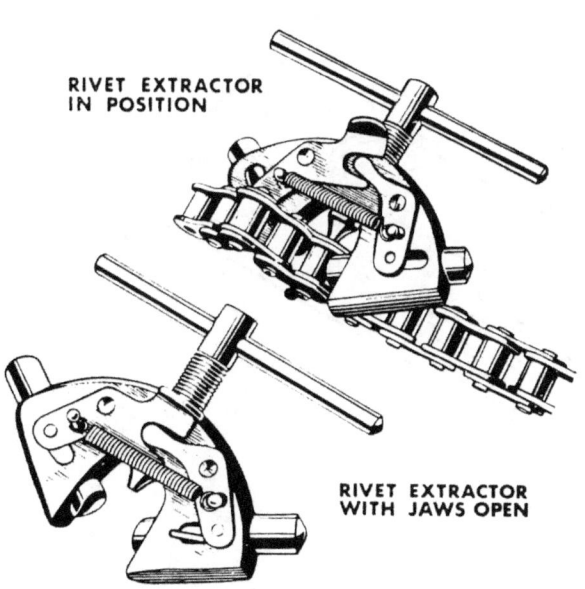

167 Rear chain rivet extractor

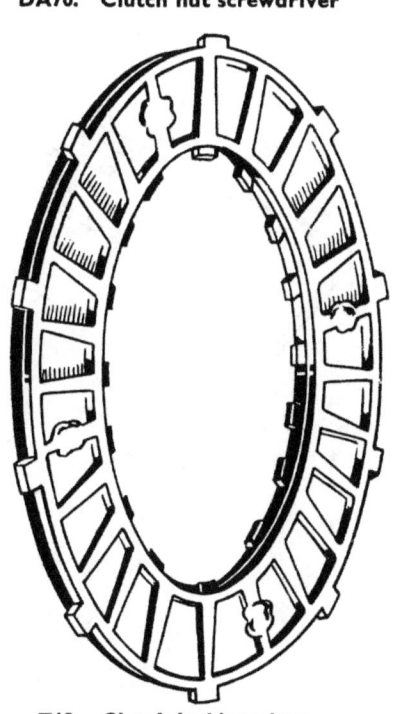

Z13. Clutch locking plate

J5

SECTION J3
WHEELS

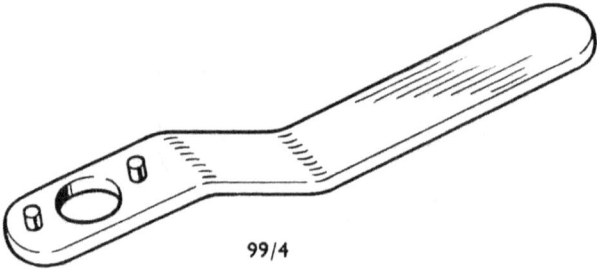

99/4

Z76. Wheel bearing locking ring spanner

SECTION J4
FRONT FORKS

99/2

Z19. Fork stanchion plug and drift

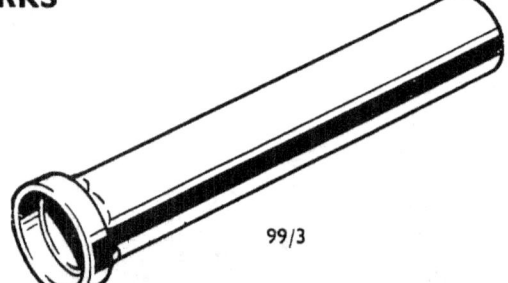

99/3

Z24. Drift for fork crown and stem bottom steering race

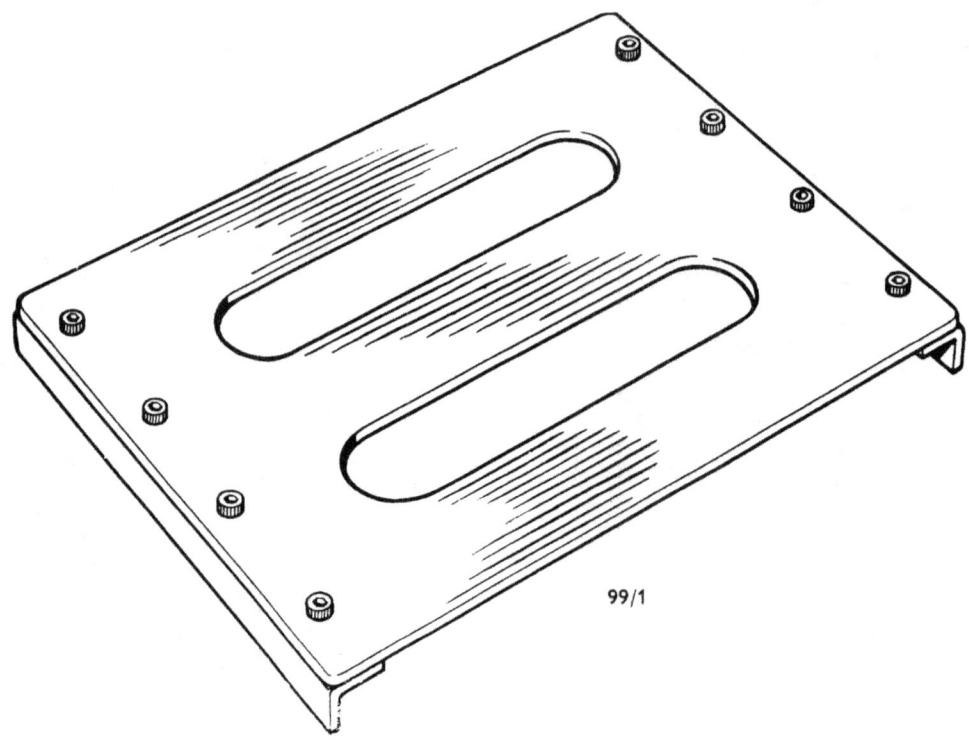

99/1

Z103. Front fork alignment gauge

SERVICE TOOLS   J

FRONT FORKS (CONTINUED) J4

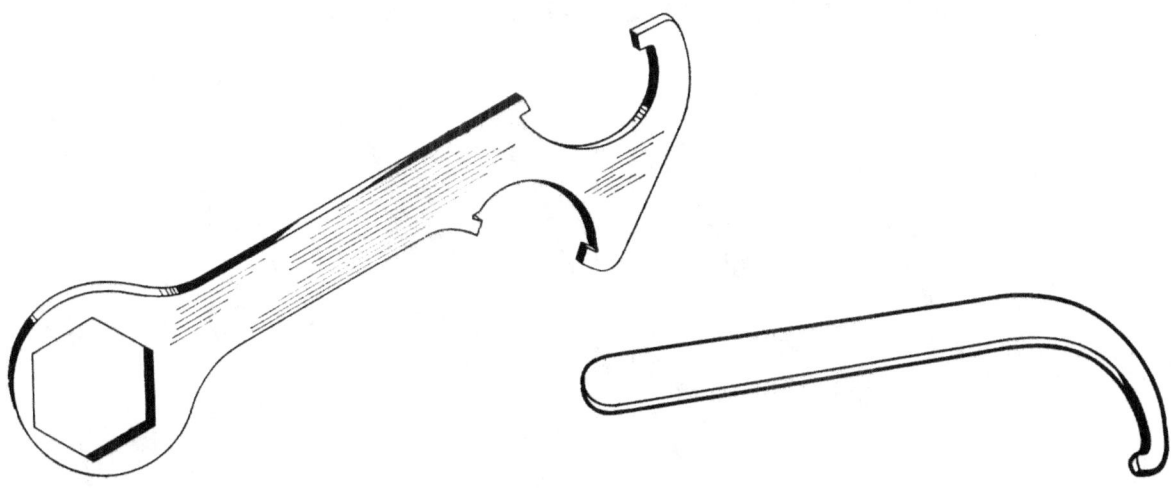

D220. Fork sleeve nut and stanchion cap nut spanner

D527. Fork sleeve nut spanner

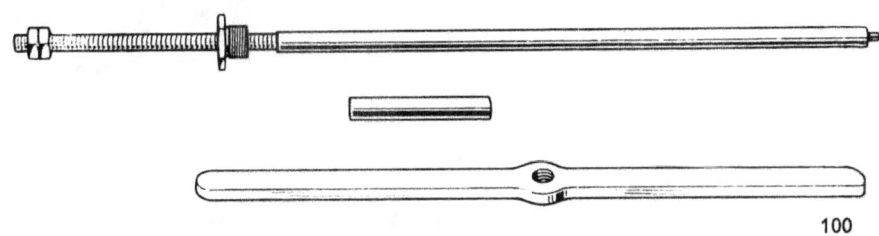

Z127. Tool for extracting fork stanchion from bottom member

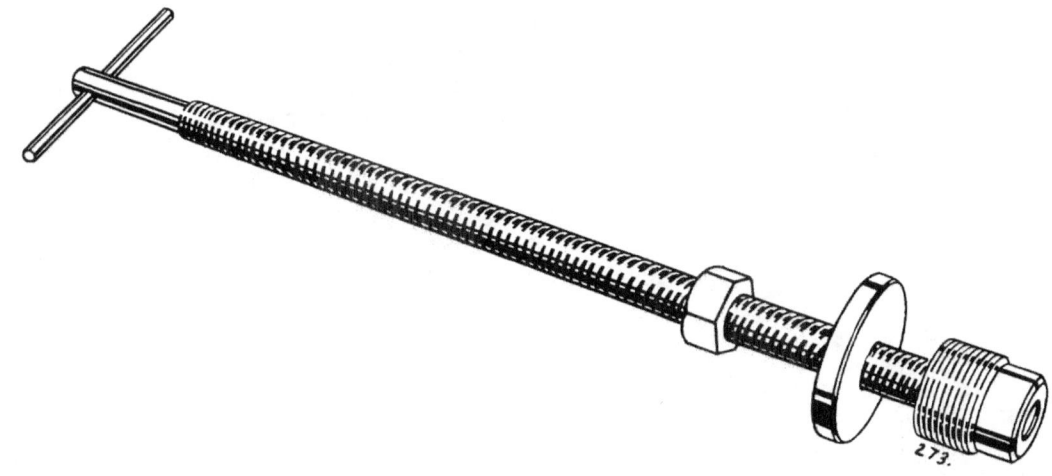

Z161. Tool for assembling front forks

SECTION J5
MOTORCYCLE TOOLKIT COMPLETE. D446

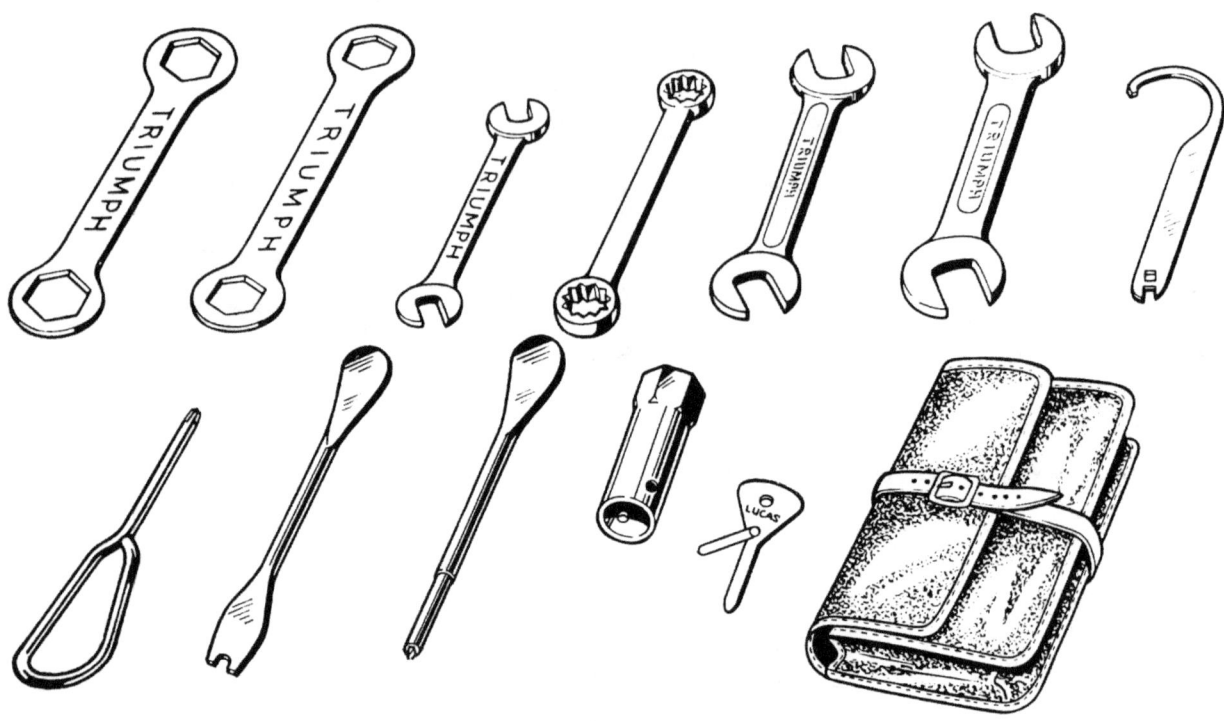

132

D446	TOOL KIT
D360	Open spanner, $\frac{1}{8}$ in. × $\frac{5}{32}$ in. whit.
NA55	Open spanner, $\frac{1}{4}$ in. × $\frac{5}{16}$ in. whit.
DA16	Open spanner, $\frac{3}{8}$ in. × $\frac{7}{16}$ in. whit.
D370	Ring spanner, $\frac{3}{16}$ in. × $\frac{1}{4}$ in. whit.
PA57	Ring spanner, $\frac{1}{2}$ in. × $\frac{9}{16}$ in. whit.
D311	Ring spanner, $\frac{5}{8}$ in. × $\frac{11}{16}$ in. whit.
D87	Box spanner, spark plug
D363	Tyre lever and tommy bar
D364	Tyre lever and clutch key
D362	"C" spanner and tappet key
D336	Phillips No. 3 screwdriver
400935	Ignition screwdriver and feeler gauge
D291	Tool roll

SECTION JJ

WORKSHOP SERVICE TOOLS

INTRODUCTION

This section of the supplement illustrates the additional workshop tools that are available for carrying out major dismantling and reassembly operations on 1969 season 500 c.c. machines.

The section is divided into sub-sections relating to the main section headings.

	Section
ENGINE	JJ1
WHEELS	JJ3
FRONT FORKS	JJ4

A number of workshop tools have been improved, and hence new part numbers have been allocated. When purchasing any of the tools mentioned in Section J, quote the amended part number as listed at the end of this Section.

SECTION JJ1
ENGINE

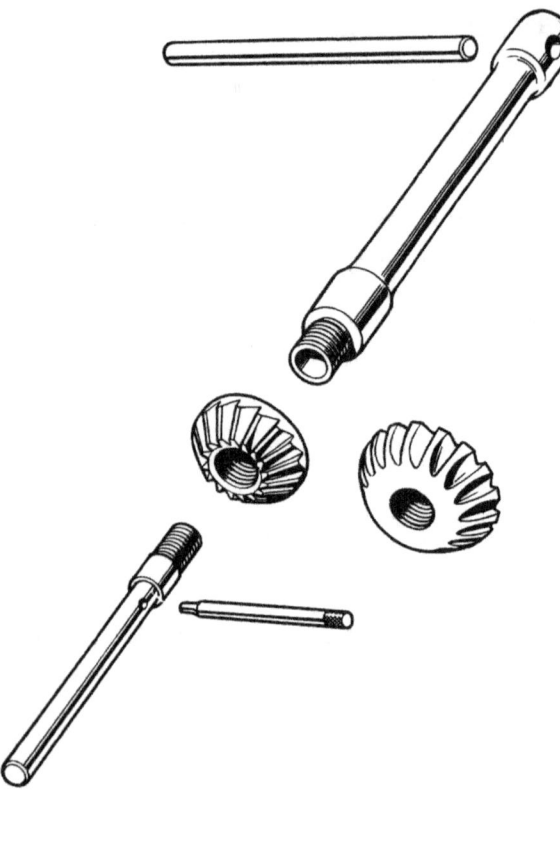

D1833. Valve seat cutter (inlet)
D1832. Valve seat cutter (exhaust)
D1836. Blending cutter (inlet)
D1835. Blending cutter (exhaust)
D1863. Arbor, pilot and tommy bars

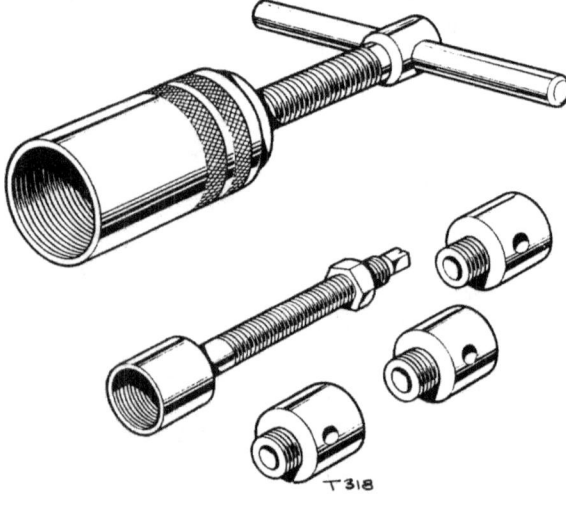

D2213. Camshaft pinion extractor and replacer with adaptors

61–6063. Valve guide removal and replacement tool

SERVICE TOOLS

ENGINE (CONTINUED)

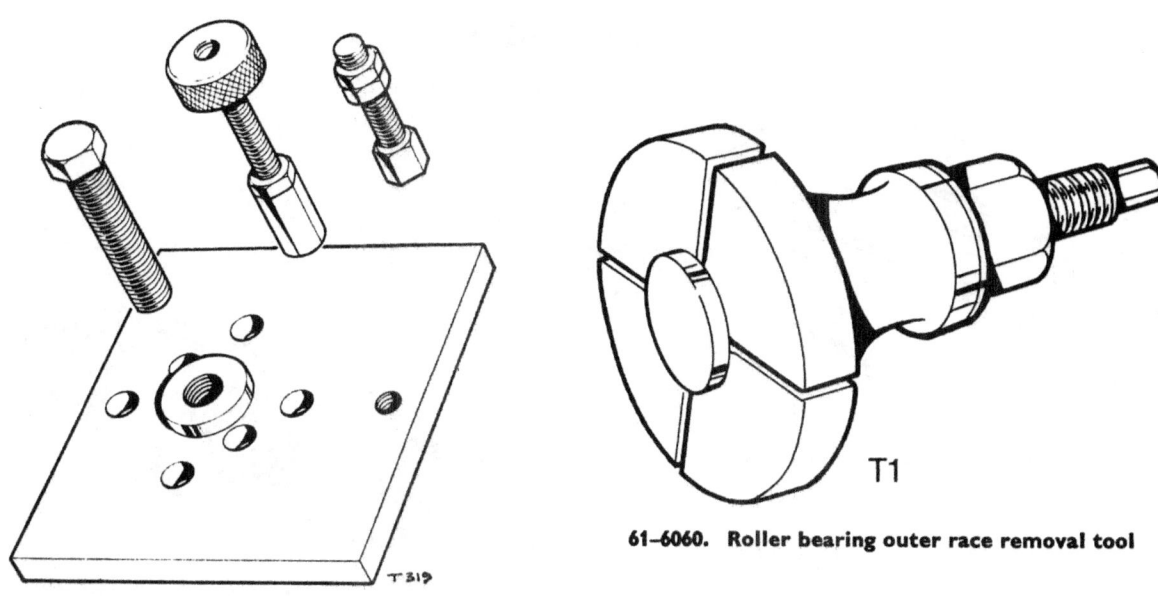

61-6046. Engine and gearbox sprocket extractor

61-6060. Roller bearing outer race removal tool

SECTION JJ3

WHEELS

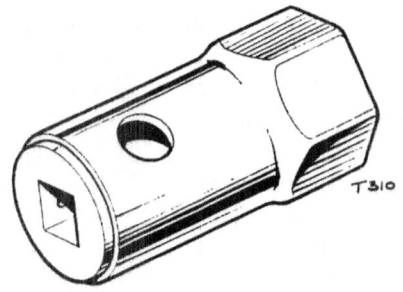

61-6062.   Front brake plate box spanner

SECTION JJ4
FRONT FORKS

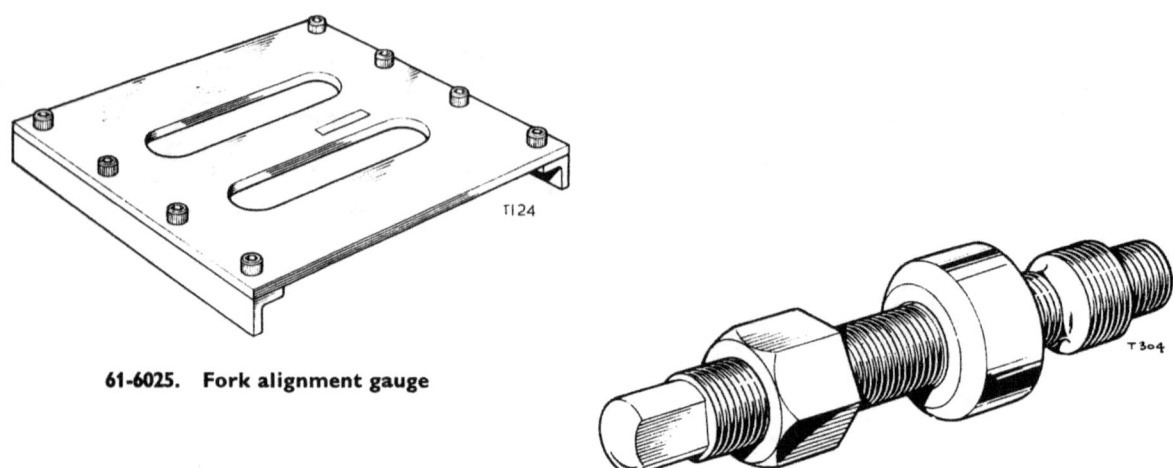

61-6025. Fork alignment gauge

61-3824. Fork leg extractor and replacer

ALTERATIONS TO PART NUMBERS

Part No.	Description	Amended Nos.
Z48	Seat cutter. Ex.	D1832
Z49	Seat cutter. In.	D1833
Z51	Valve seat cutters, blenders, arbor and pilot — Blending cutter 350 c.c.	D1834
Z52	Blending cutter 350/500 c.c.	D1835
Z54	Blending cutter 500 c.c.	D1836
Z163	Arbor, pilot and timing	D1863
Z89	Camshaft pinion remover and replacer	D2213
Z23	Tappet guide block punch	61-6008
Z130	Piston ring collar 500 c.c. (number error)	Z132
Z16	Valve guide removal and replacement tool	D2219
Z151	Engine and gearbox sprocket extractor	61-6046
Z76	Wheel bearing locking ring spanner	61-3694
Z169	Fork stanchion removal and replacement tool	61-3824
Z24	Fork crown bottom cone drift	D2218
Z103	Fork alignment gauge	61-6025
Z170	Fork assembly tool	61-3824
D2014	Chaincase timing plate	D1825

VELOCEPRESS MANUALS – MOTORCYCLE BY MAKE

AJS 1932-1948 SINGLES & TWINS 250cc THRU 1000cc (BOOK OF)
AJS 1945-1960 SINGLES 350cc & 500cc MODELS 16 & 18 (BOOK OF)
AJS 1955-1965 SINGLES 350cc & 500cc (BOOK OF)
AJS 1957-1966 FACTORY WSM - ALL SINGLES & TWINS
ARIEL UP TO 1932 (BOOK OF)
ARIEL 1932-1939 PREWAR MODELS (BOOK OF)
ARIEL 1933-1951 (WORKSHOP MANUAL)
ARIEL 1939-1960 4 STROKE SINGLES (BOOK OF)
ARIEL 1958-1964 LEADER & ARROW (BOOK OF)
BMW R26 R27 (1956-1967) FACTORY WORKSHOP MANUAL
BMW R50 R50S R60 R69S (1955-1969) FACTORY WORKSHOP MANUAL
BRIDGESTONE 90 SERIES FACTORY WSM & PARTS CATALOGUE
BRIDGESTONE 175 SERIES FACTORY WSM & PARTS CATALOGUE
BRIDGESTONE 350 SERIES FACTORY WSM & PARTS CATALOGUES
BSA SERVICE SHEETS MASTER CATALOGUE ALL MODELS 1945-1967
BSA BANTAM D1 TO D7 1948-1966 FACTORY SERVICE SHEETS MANUAL
BSA BANTAM ALL MODELS FROM 1948 ONWARDS (BOOK OF)
BSA DANDY FACTORY WORKSHOP MANUAL (COMPILATION)
BSA SINGLES & V-TWINS UP TO 1927 (BOOK OF)
BSA SINGLES & V-TWINS UP TO 1930 (BOOK OF)
BSA SINGLES & V-TWINS UP TO 1935 (BOOK OF)
BSA SINGLES & V-TWINS 1936-1939 (BOOK OF)
BSA C10, C11 & C12 1945-1958 FACTORY SERVICE SHEETS MANUAL
BSA OHV & SV SINGLES 250-600cc 1945-1959 (BOOK OF)
BSA C15 & B40 1958-1967 FACTORY SERVICE SHEETS MANUAL
BSA OHV & SV SINGLES 250cc (ONLY) 1954-1970 (BOOK OF)
BSA B31, B32, B33 & B34 1945-60 FACTORY SERVICE SHEETS MANUAL
BSA OHV SINGLES 350 & 500cc 1945-1967 (BOOK OF)
BSA M20, M21 & M33 1945-1963 FACTORY SERVICE SHEETS MANUAL
BSA TWINS A7 & A10 1948-1962 FACTORY SERVICE SHEETS MANUAL
BSA TWINS A7 & A10 1948-1962 (BOOK OF)
BSA TWINS A50 & A65 1962-1965 FACTORY WORKSHOP MANUAL
BSA TWINS A50 & A65 1962-1969 (SECOND BOOK OF)
DOUGLAS 1929-1939 PREWAR ALL MODELS (BOOK OF)
DOUGLAS 1948-1957 POSTWAR ALL MODELS FACTORY SHOP MANUAL
DUCATI 160cc, 250cc & 350cc OHC MODELS FACTORY WORKSHOP MANUAL
HONDA 50 ALL MODELS UP TO 1970 INC MONKEY & TRAIL (BOOK OF)
HONDA 90 ALL MODELS UP TO 1966 (BOOK OF)
HONDA 50-65-70-90cc OHC SINGLES 1959-1983 FACTORY WSM
HONDA 125-150cc TWINS C/CS/CB/CA FACTORY WORKSHOP MANUAL
HONDA 125-160-175-200cc TWINS 1964-1980 WORKSHOP MANUAL
HONDA 250-305 TWINS C/CS/CB 1959-1967 FACTORY WSM
HOHDA 250-350 TWINS CB/CL/SL 1968-1973 FACTORY WSM
HONDA 450 CB/CL 1965-1974 K0 TO K7 WORKSHOP MANUAL
HONDA C100 SUPER CUB FACTORY WORKSHOP MANUAL
HONDA C110 SPORT CUB 1962-1969 FACTORY WORKSHOP MANUAL
HONDA TWINS & SINGLES 50cc THRU 305cc 1960-1966 (BOOK OF)
HONDA TWINS ALL MODELS 125cc THRU 450cc UP TO 1968 (BOOK OF)
INDIAN PONYBIKE, BOY RACER & PAPOOSE ILL PARTS LIST & SALES LIT
J.A.P. ENGINES 1927-1952 & MOTORCYCLES 1934-1952 (BOOK OF)
MATCHLESS 1931-1939 ALL MODELS 250cc THRU 990cc (BOOK OF)
MATCHLESS 1945-1956 350 & 500cc SINGLES (BOOK OF)
MATCHLESS 1955-1966 350 & 500cc SINGLES (BOOK OF)
MATCHLESS 1957-1966 FACTORY WSM - ALL SINGLES & TWINS
NEW IMPERIAL ALL SV & OHV FROM 1935 ONWARDS (BOOK OF)
NORTON 1932-1939 PREWAR MODELS (BOOK OF)
NORTON 1932-1947 (BOOK OF)
NORTON 1938-1956 (BOOK OF)
NORTON 1955-1963 MODELS 19, 50 & ES2 (BOOK OF)
NORTON 1955-1965 DOMINATOR TWINS (BOOK OF)
NORTON 1960-1970 TWIN CYLINDER FACTORY WORKSHOP MANUAL
NORTON 1970-1975 COMMANDO 850 & 750cc FACTORY WSM
NORTON 1975-1978 MK 3 COMMANDO 850 cc FACTORY WSM
PANTHER 1932-1958 LIGHTWEIGHT MODELS 250 & 350cc (BOOK OF)
PANTHER 1938-1966 HEAVYWEIGHT MODELS 600 & 650cc (BOOK OF)
RALEIGH MOTORCYCLES 1919-1933 (BOOK OF)
ROYAL ENFIELD 1934-1946 SINGLES & V TWINS (BOOK OF)
ROYAL ENFIELD 1937-1953 SINGLES & V TWINS (BOOK OF)
ROYAL ENFIELD 1946-1962 SINGLES (BOOK OF)
ROYAL ENFIELD 1958-1966 250cc & 350cc SINGLES (SECOND BOOK OF)
ROYAL ENFIELD 736cc INTERCEPTOR FACTORY WORKSHOP MANUAL
RUDGE 1933-1939 (BOOK OF)
SUNBEAM 1928-1939 (BOOK OF)
SUNBEAM 1946-1957 S7 & S8 (BOOK OF)
SUZUKI 50cc & 80cc UP TO 1966 (BOOK OF)
SUZUKI T10 1963-1967 FACTORY WORKSHOP MANUAL
SUZUKI T20 & T200 1965-1969 FACTORY WORKSHOP MANUAL
SUZUKI TWINS 1962 ONWARDS 125-500cc WORKSHOP MANUAL
TRIUMPH 1935-1949 SINGLES & TWINS (BOOK OF)
TRIUMPH 1937-1951 (WORKSHOP MANUAL)
TRIUMPH 1945-1955 FACTORY WORKSHOP MANUAL
TRIUMPH 1945-1959 TWINS (BOOK OF)
TRIUMPH 1956-1969 TWINS (BOOK OF)
TRIUMPH 1963-1970 UNIT CONSTRUCTION 650cc FACTORY WSM
TRIUMPH 1963-1974 UNIT CONSTRUCTION 350 & 500cc FACTORY WSM
VELOCETTE 1925-1970 ALL SINGLES & TWINS (BOOK OF)
VILLIERS ENGINE UP TO 1959 INC. 3 WHEELERS (BOOK OF)
VILLIERS ENGINE UP TO 1969 (BOOK OF)
VINCENT 1935-1955 (WORKSHOP MANUAL)
YAMAHA 1961-1967 YA5 & YA6 (WORKSHOP MANUAL & ILL PARTS LIST)
YAMAHA 1971-1972 JT1& JT2 (WORKSHOP MANUAL & ILL PARTS LIST)

VELOCEPRESS TECHNICAL BOOKS – MOTORCYCLE

1930'S BRITISH MOTORCYCLE CARBS & ELEC COMPONENTS (BOOK OF)
1930'S BRITISH MOTORCYCLE ENGINES (OVERHAUL & MAINTENANCE)
1930'S BRITISH MOTORCYCLE GEARBOXES & CLUTCHES (BOOK OF)
CATALOG OF BRITISH MOTORCYCLES (1951 MODELS)
LUCAS ELECTRONICS BRITISH M/CYCLES REPAIR & PARTS (1950-1977)
MOTORCYCLE ENGINEERING (P.E. Irving)
MOTORCYCLE ROAD TESTS 1949-1953 (Motor Cycle Magazine UK)
SPEED AND HOW TO OBTAIN IT (Motor Cycle Magazine UK)
TUNING FOR SPEED (P.E. Irving)
WIPAC (COMBO) MANUAL NUMBER 3 + M/CYCLE & SCOOTER MANUAL

VELOCEPRESS MANUALS – SCOOTERS BY MAKE

BSA SUNBEAM SCOOTER WORKSHOP MANUAL 1959-1965
BSA SUNBEAM SCOOTER 1959-1965 (BOOK OF)
LAMBRETTA 1947-1957 ALL 125 & 150cc MODELS (BOOK OF)
LAMBRETTA 1957-1970 LI & TV MODELS (SECOND BOOK OF)
NSU PRIMA 1956-1964 ALL MODELS (BOOK OF)
TRIUMPH TIGRESS SCOOTER WORKSHOP MANUAL 1959-1965
TRIUMPH TIGRESS SCOOTER (BOOK OF)
VESPA 1951-1961 (BOOK OF)
VESPA 1955-1963 125 & 150cc & GS MODELS (SECOND BOOK OF)
VESPA 1955-1968 GS & SS (BOOK OF)
VESPA 1963-1972 90, 125 & 150cc (THIRD BOOK OF)

VELOCEPRESS MANUALS – MOPEDS & MOTORIZED BICYCLES

CYCLEMOTOR (BOOK OF)
NSU QUICKLY 1953-1963 ALL MODELS (BOOK OF)
PUCH MAXI N & S MAINTENANCE & REPAIR (3 MANUAL COMPILATION)
RALEIGH MOPEDS 1960-1969 (BOOK OF)

VELOCEPRESS MANUALS - THREE WHEELER'S

BOND MINICAR THREE WHEELER 1948-1967 (BOOK OF)
BMW ISETTA FACTORY WORKSHOP MANUAL
BSA THREE WHEELER (BOOK OF)
RELIANT REGAL THREE WHEELER 1952-1973 (BOOK OF)
VINTAGE MORGAN THREE WHEELER (BOOK OF)

VELOCEPRESS MANUALS – AUTOMOBILE BY MAKE

ALFA ROMEO GIULIA WORKSHOP MANUAL 1300 TO 2000cc 1962-1975
ALFA ROMEO GIULIA TECH MANUAL CARBURETED CARS FROM 1962
ALFA ROMEO GIULIA TECH MANUAL FUEL INJECTED CARS FROM 1969
ALFA ROMEO GIULIETTA & GIULIA 750 & 101 SERIES 1955-1965 WSM
AUSTIN-HEALEY SPRITE & MG MIDGET WORKSHOP MANUAL 1958-1971
BMW 600 LIMOUSINE FACTORY WORKSHOP MANUAL
BMW 600 LIMOUSINE OWNERS HAND BOOK & SERVICE MANUAL
BMW 2000 & 2002 1966-1976 WORKSHOP MANUAL
CORVAIR 1960-1969 WORKSHOP MANUAL
CORVETTE V8 1955-1962 WORKSHOP MANUAL
FIAT 500 FACTORY WORKSHOP MANUAL 1957-1973
FIAT 600, 600D & MULTIPLA FACTORY WORKSHOP MANUAL 1955-1969
JAGUAR E-TYPE 3.8 & 4.2 SERIES 1 & 2 WORKSHOP MANUAL
JAGUAR MK 7, 8, 9 & XK120, 140, 150 WORKSHOP MANUAL 1948-1961
METROPOLITAN FACTORY WORKSHOP MANUAL
MGA & MGB OWNERS HANDBOOK & WORKSHOP MANUAL
MG MIDGET TC, TD, TF & TF1500 WORKSHOP MANUAL
PORSCHE 356 1948-1965 WORKSHOP MANUAL
PORSCHE 911 2.0, 2.2, 2.4 LITRE 1964-1973 WORKSHOP MANUAL
PORSCHE 911 2.7, 3.0, 3.2 LITRE 1973-1989 WORKSHOP MANUAL
PORSCHE 912 WORKSHOP MANUAL
TRIUMPH TR2, TR3, TR4 1953-1965 WORKSHOP MANUAL
VOLKSWAGEN TRANSPORTER, TRUCKS & WAGONS 1950-1979 WSM
VOLVO 1944-1968 ALL MODELS WORKSHOP MANUAL

VELOCEPRESS TECHNICAL BOOKS - AUTOMOBILE

FERRARI OWNER'S HANDBOOK
HOW TO BUILD A FIBERGLASS CAR
HOW TO BUILD A RACING CAR
HOW TO RESTORE THE MODEL 'A' FORD
MASERATI OWNER'S HANDBOOK
PERFORMANCE TUNING THE SUNBEAM TIGER
SOUPING THE VOLKSWAGEN
SOLEX CARBURETORS (EMPHASIS ON UK & EU AUTOMOBILES)
SU CARBURETORS (EMPHASIS ON UK AUTOMOBILES)
WEBER CARBURETORS (EMPHASIS ON ALFA & FIAT)

VELOCEPRESS BOOKS & GUIDES - AUTOMOBILE

COMPLETE CATALOG OF JAPANESE MOTOR VEHICLES
FERRARI 308 SERIES BUYER'S AND OWNER'S GUIDE
FERRARI BROCHURES AND SALES LITERATURE 1968-1989
FERRARI SERIAL NUMBERS PART I - ODD NUMBERS TO 21399
FERRARI SERIAL NUMBERS PART II - EVEN NUMBERS TO 1050
HENRY'S FABULOUS MODEL "A" FORD
MASERATI BROCHURES AND SALES LITERATURE

VELOCEPRESS BOOKS – RACING

CARRERA PANAMERICANA - MEXICAN ROAD RACE (BOOK OF)
DIALED IN - THE JAN OPPERMAN STORY
VEDA ORR'S NEW REVISED HOT ROD PICTORIAL

AUTOBOOKS WORKSHOP MANUALS

FOR A COMPLETE LISTING OF THE AUTOBOOKS WORKSHOP MANUALS THAT WE CURRENTLY HAVE AVAILABLE, PLEASE VISIT OUR WEBSITE.

www.VelocePress.com

Please check our website:

www.VelocePress.com

for a complete
up-to-date list of
available titles